CLOWN SECRET

IRA SEIDENSTEIN

Clown Secret. Copyright © 2018 by Ira Seidenstein

All Rights Reserved. Except as permitted under current legislation no part of this work may be photocopied, stored in retrieval system, published, performed in public, adapted, broadcast, transmitted, recorded or reproduced in any form by any means, without the prior permission of the copyright owner, except for short quotes for the purpose of academic publications and reviews. For information, contact Ira Seidenstein, PhD at iraseid@gmail.com

ISBN: 978-0-6484216-0-3 (Paperback)
ISBN 978-0-6484216-1-0 (Ebook)

CONTENTS

ACKNOWLEDGEMENTS v

FOREWORD vii

PREFACE xiii

INTRODUCTION xv

Chapter 1   THE ERUPTION AND EVOLUTION OF THE METHOD: QUANTUM THEATRE: SLAPSTICK TO SHAKESPEARE 1

Chapter 2   THE FOUR ARTICULATIONS FOR PERFORMANCE 39

Chapter 3   SOME KEY PROJECTS 141

Chapter 4   SHENANIGANS AND CHAGRIN 237

Chapter 5   IN THE NAVY 257

Chapter 6   BEING AUSTRALIAN 300

Chapter 7   CLOWN VS GOD...NOTES ON THE CLOWN MOVEMENT 309

Chapter 8   SHAKESPEARE BITS 349

Chapter 9   CO-CREATING 401

Chapter 10   FRIENDS AND COLLEAGUES 424

Chapter 11   LAST BUT NOT LEAST 430

ACKNOWLEDGEMENTS

Thank You to a galore of participants in my classes, to my colleagues, to my friends, to people who I shared living with, to people I shared life with, to my family. Each person who I helped also helped me. It has been an international voyage so Thank You goes to people in an array of countries and cultures. There is something special in this book for each of you. You'll have to find it for yourself. This book from the beginning pages to the last pages is a risk.

FOREWORD

Caspar Schjelbred

A MASTER OF HIS ART

The first time I met Ira was in spring 2008 at La Fourmi, a café situated right on the edge of Montmartre and the more mainstream ninth arrondissement of Paris. We had e-mailed briefly the day before. I was curious about what he had suggested to us at the Improfessionals, the improvisational theatre company I was part of: a potpourri of workshops on physical acting, slapstick and clown.

I hardly knew anything about either of those things then. But there was something about the way Ira presented his work on his web site that intrigued me. It was very upfront. Not someone trying to sell himself. Here was real intellectual and thought provoking content clearly based on a long and varied career.

Within a minute from sitting down with Ira at the café I had a strong impression that I was in front of a man who really knew what he was talking about. Like for real. And those are two words that are worth emphasising when it comes to Ira and his work: *for real*.

I can not remember what we talked about. He most certainly asked me more questions than I asked of him. We must have talked about improvisation. I thought I knew something about it. Which I did. But a week or so later, after a first introductory workshop with Ira, I clearly understood that knowing about something is not at all the same as knowing it.

In that short three-hour session my mind reached down and touched base. It was like standing on solid ground after being at sea. I finally knew what improvisation was. Ira spelled it out: make a pause, and in that pause there is a binary choice. Either continue what you were doing or make an adjustment. It's one or the other.

That blew my mind. It was so incredibly simple and obvious. No one else had told me that before. None of the acting or improvisation teachers I had met. Nor was it written in any of the many books on improvisational theatre I had read. I surmised that either they did not know it or they did not care to explain it – and I did not know which was worse.

At any rate, I knew for sure that this Ira Seidenstein knew something fundamental. I felt certain that he was teaching us something he really knew. There was no pretending. No mystification. No paradoxical teaching. No bullshit. Here was someone who laid all the cards on the table right from the start. Someone who cared about what was true. Here was someone I could trust.

I followed my intuition that I needed to learn more from this man. And so I began organising workshops for him in Paris whenever the occasion arose. I still had no idea what I was in for or who I was working with. All I knew was: he knows more than I do and there is something very special about the way he works.

It was not until January 2010, at the end of the first Quantum Clown Residency in Brisbane, that I understood why I had invested myself in Ira's work and indeed gone all the way to Australia on the other side of the planet to attend a proper three-week workshop with him. It was to honour my own creativity. As simple as that. As difficult as that.

For what does it actually mean to honour one's own creativity? It is something that goes way beyond and deeper than simply being creative. Coming up with stuff is not enough. Resolving problems is not evolving. Not as a human being. What I have come to understand after ten years of investment in Ira's work is that honouring my own creativity means creating – or recreating – myself. It means becoming whole. Not *being* whole (holy), but *becoming* whole, and as such, being of a piece, being of the world, being wholly in the world as it is, being as one is becoming in the world.

I remember those summer mornings in West End, Brisbane, 2010. The early light, the exotic sounds, the warm and humid air, the unusual smells. But most of all the feeling that I did not want to get out of bed and go to the workshop. I was afraid. Each and every morning. Because I knew that once I stepped into that space there would be nothing to hide behind. Or at least there would be no point in trying to. Because Ira sees everything. Nothing in the workspace escapes him.

For those of us used to maintaining our façades it is very destabilising when someone sees right through them all. I was certainly not used to being truly seen. Well of course! When I had never actually shown myself except by chance or mistake. I had a very clear feeling of being at a threshold. I patently knew that there was only one way to go. Forward. I had to get up there and stand before the eyes of the world with nothing but myself. I had to face myself. I did not want to. But I did it anyway. Every day.

I returned to Brisbane in January the next four years and Ira would come to Paris once or twice per year. I had begun practising his exercises regularly and eventually created my own solo show to try it out in public. It was during that period he became my mentor. Today I am proud to be his main associate and happy to also call him my friend. My understanding of his work now is that if you really invest yourself fully in it, then it is not his any more, it is yours.

Over the years I have observed how not just what Ira does but what he is scares some people and makes others angry. As a teacher and director – and often even just as a person – he offers more than most of us are able or willing to deal with: an opportunity to deal with ourselves. To feel and to see the world we are in. And to see others in this world as feeling and seeing: seeing and feeling us.

Apart from being exceptionally curious and knowledgeable about both the practise and the traditions of theatre, clown, circus, and whether it be as teacher, mentor, associate, friend – or as here: author – Ira is a remarkable and very funny storyteller. Enjoy reading! You just might learn something.

Caspar Schjelbred

August 2018

WARNING: THIS BOOK MEANDERS THROUGH TIME AND PLACE AND PROJECTS AS A DREAM WOULD. TIME IS NOT JUST LINEAR BUT OVERLAPS WITH OUR PAST EXPERIENCES AND CURRENT PERCEPTIONS. GO WITH IT. IT WILL MAKE SENSE AS A LIVED EXPERIENCE AS YOU READ. THINGS WILL APPEAR AND DISAPPEAR AND REAPPEAR AS THEY DO IN LIFE

PREFACE

The secret held tight by the finest performers is that logic releases the power of the subconscious. This secret relies on universal principles. CLOWN SECRET will reveal those universal principles which are immediately useful and will place the secret within the reader's grasp.

When I fell into the theatre at the age of 21 I had no intention to formulate a method. Even now after more than 40 years of development I do not view it as a method to exclude other methods. This work/method is a tool which can and will enhance any other theatre, performance, acting, or clown method. This approach proposes no particular performance aesthetic and therefore it is a non-dogmatic.

Although one chapter gives explicit step-by-step instructions for each of the main exercises, the rest of the book is anything but dry. The exercises are about human creativity and the interaction between the body and the mind. The final exercise requires a listener, it is to "Tell the Story of a Clown". Clowns live not only on stage or in cinema, they live in the stories told about them.

I learned that when I went to purchase The Bulletin magazine with the 'clown' Barry Humphries on the cover. The shopkeeper told me how much he hated Humphries. I asked if he saw Humphries live. He said no and then as he told me of the horrible things Humphries did on television the shopkeeper laughed more and more.

It is through stories that we see the mythological reality of the clown. In this book I tell an abundance of stories, all true, that I have lived through.

And as I tell, many others lived through those with me. My family, friends, colleagues, teachers, and shipmates during my Navy years.

The secret from another perspective. This book started in 2015 with the next 4 paragraphs below:

Let's start at the beginning. No, let's not. My favourite line from Shakespeare is: "There are more things in heaven and earth, Horatio, than are dreamt of in your philosophy".

So far so good. Good though very difficult. Difficult but interesting. Interesting like the Chinese curse "May you live in interesting times". Our times, circa 2015, are unfortunately becoming too interesting. Because they are so interesting, or, because I find them so and find the times can be seen as cursed or as blessed, I am choosing now to sit and write about a secret life. The secret is the mystery of being a clown-man. Similar to the mythological faun that was half-man/half-goat. A faun is different than the satyr or the centaur which were also mythical beasts of half-men and half-beasts, or, like mermaids half-women and half-beasts.

Although science tries to explain what was previously unexplainable there are things that may very well be outside of the realm of pure science whose properties are inexplicable via scientific methodologies. Carl Sagan in his last interview spoke about science and the things that were outside of the realm of science. He explained that those areas outside were the realm of faith and religion. His criticism of religion is primarily towards those who inaccurately mix science and religion. That interview happened to be only a few weeks before his death. It was a very fine interview given by Charlie Rose. I saw it on youtube.

Some things in my faun-like life are outside of the realm of science. Some of those occurrences follow the norms of any individual's life's unfolding whereby one finds that life has more surprises further along than one assumes in the early stages.

INTRODUCTION

This Introduction is layered and complex. It is a stimulating chapter on its own. It is meant to jiggle the reader. To juggle the norm of dividing acting from clown. Instead here is a new way to understand how to honour the complex interaction between acting and clown.

A foundation of physical organic logic releases the subconscious creativity. Such a foundation makes play plausible, the imagination intimate, and one's creativity limitless.

The great actors, directors, clowns, and artists had practical secrets. Their private intimate personal secrets remain secret. However, their professional secrets follow patterns which I have observed, practiced, then analysed and formulated into an introductory template. That template is presented as the chronological series of exercises in Chapter 2. That template is called: "The Four Articulations for Performance". That template or any of its exercises or principles can be used immediately and continually as my associates have proven each in their own way and evolving circumstances. That template is a practical tool for the whole method "Quantum Theatre: Slapstick to Shakespeare".

Theatre, acting, and clown each have a continuum or a lineage. Many aspects of those lineages overlap. In this book I focus on the interacting relation of movement, acting, clown. The body/mind is the foundation of their continuum. The method, principles, exercises provided in this book have long proven just as useful for dance, circus, and creativity in general.

My method is an integrated unity of movement, acting, clown, creativity. Each exercise in Chapter 2 even if only described in physical and mechanical terms is directly applicable to all performing arts and creativity.

Central to my method, "Quantum Theatre: Slapstick to Shakespeare", is the key universal principle any excellent performer possesses and uses. The key universal principle is in two parts, one is physical and one is creative. The physical can lead to the creative and the creative can lead to the physical. Many physical techniques use logic that is at once mechanical, scientific, organic, AND a logic that is at once mechanical, scientific, organic is also used in acting, clown, and creativity.

CLOWN SECRET will explain several other universal principles which can lead you directly to excellence in performance and creativity. The explanation will be done in narrative form here in the Introduction and most chapters. Chapter 3, for example, is written in an anecdotal, freeform, storytelling narrative related to numerous projects of the author. Chapter 4 tells more anecdotes structured differently related to working with certain people and certain places. Within Chapter 3 and other narrative chapters are numerous secrets and principles placed for the reader to find. Perhaps you don't like the words 'secrets' or 'principles'. You are welcome to substitute whatever word works for you. Chapter 2 presents the template of practical exercises with step-by-step explanations and instructions.

SOURCE, RESOURCES, SORCERERS

In Australia the Indigenous culture and knowledge is based on a lineage from elders. In the continuum of time each culture has evolved and adapted. In the theatre the modern lineage is the result of a cross-cultural continuum mixing East and West both of which are rooted in indigenous practices that were often formalised into rituals. Even the most ancient rituals attributed to gods had to be constructed via human movement, intellect, imagination, and creative play with the elements, ideas, and ideals. Victor Turner is the scholar who conceptualised theatre as ritual.

BOOKS

Japanese director Tadashi Suzuki has stated that still today the best books on acting and theatre are those written by Stanislavsky. The most recent translations are by Jean Benedetti who was the first to incorporate Stanislavsky's final manuscripts. Benedetti's final translations are: An Actor's Work: A Student Diary (2008) and An Actor's Work on a Role (2009) which are both published by Routledge Press. I.S.A.A.C. Associate Heleen Van den Bosch, who studied in Russian those final manuscripts of Stanislavsky concluded "The more I get involved in Stanislavsky and the field of acting techniques in general, the more I see how unique the Seidenstein Method is. It starts where the others try to end, at the very essence of performance. It is truly liberating and fundamental to any kind of performance."

One of the most lyrical writings about the hidden dimensions of acting and theatre is the 43 page introduction that Viola Spolin wrote for her book "Improvisation for the Theatre". Her thoughts are completely inspiring for clown and creativity as well. The insight of the English drama for education teacher Dorothy Heathcote also provides immediately useful ideas and principles applicable for acting, theatre, clown. Naturally Spolin, Heathcote, and Stanislavsky are describing spontaneity, play, imagination, creativity.

A Dictionary of Theatre Anthropology by Barba/Savarese has a subtitle "The Secret Art of the Performer" which presents a key 'secret', a duality, that they call Pre-Expressivity and Expressivity. Two years later "There Are No Secrets" by Peter Brook was published.

They, Barba/Savarese, and Brook are both right. Opposing views in most fields are part of a whole. It took time before the quantum physicists agreed that there is simultaneously a wave and a particle.

As Barba/Savarese explain, actually, there is a secret art the observer may not notice starting with their naming of the duality of Pre-Expressivity and Expressivity; and, as Brook explains there are no secrets because we - some of us - performers know what those secrets are. My point is that not everyone knows those secrets even though they are obvious to some. and that now I present publicly in a simple, concise, useful chronology what the most important 'hidden' principles are. In one way or another those principles were codified in the ancient treatise of Indian theatre, Japanese theatre and are to varying degrees also in other theatre forms. My method makes the key principles achievable via concise exercises which can be used on a daily basis.

The clown secret within this book is the singular interaction between several dualities and principles.

The secret is real and occurs simultaneously, spontaneously and consciously.

In the arts the conscious releases the subconscious.

The sculptor must know the tools and the material. Some sculptors work towards a vision, but the traditional Maori sculptors claim that the rock or stone reveals its hidden sculpture. An actor must interpret a role. Thus the most famous role Hamlet can be interpreted in endless ways. I would suggest that rather than an actor being corralled into a director's vision of the play, perhaps a director needs to make room for the actor's interpretation of a role such as Hamlet. A clown character emerges from the passion, pursuit, interests, instincts, desires and obsessions of the individual actor. That is the clown as a performing and professional artist.

Real clowns are a fluke of nature. They do not emerge. They appear. They appear in most if not all families, classrooms, communities, work environments, even in politics there is always a Puck that is a nature spirit with a suit and a smirk.

In this book Clown Secret I will 'talk' with you about another duality, that of the clown in art and the clown in life. I live as both. The thoughts and ideas and stories and exercises may assist you to understand from a new viewpoint about the clown that emerges and the clown that appears.

We may not be able to replicate the circumstances of the most noteworthy artistes but we can practice and adapt their secrets. I made a choice to reveal what is normally hidden. By 'hidden' I mean what is very rarely discussed even in the highest professional circles though it has been written about in various ways by Spolin, Heathcote, Barba/Savarese, Brook as well as in the ancient practices in various Eastern cultures and in the performance practices in most Indigenous cultures. What I have done is to distill that information into what I call "Universal Principles" focusing on exercises which contain the essential Universal Principles for performance which will yield results today and over a long career. The exercises and principles can be readily shared with other people. The same principles and exercises can be used with any other performance method, and, importantly, the principles and exercises do not impose an aesthetic. So one of the secrets as to the way this method works is that it focuses on universals but not on any particular aesthetic or dogma.

MY METHOD

My method has created a concise pathway to practice finding and using one's instincts in a practical and philosophical way. This method is as useful for teachers, directors, choreographers as it is for performance artists as diverse as acrobats, actors, composers. In this book I will reveal the key secrets that the great actors and clowns rarely find the words to describe, as the process for those practitioners is so intimate to their own instincts.

DUALITIES

The method makes use of various dualities. These can assist the mind to accept and use paradoxes and seeming opposites. One key secret is the duality which every excellent performer has control of: inner and outer knowledge. We could say the inner is awareness and the outer is craft. Barba/Savarese's work is in part from the lineage that Stanislavsky presented on the inner and outer process of 'actor' and 'character' (I recommend the recent translations of Jean Benedetti 2008, 2009). I view my work and method as part of that lineage which had already begun to create an East/West integration. I also view my work as part of other lineages in clown, art, philosophy. Therefore my lineage is a braid composed of multiple strands.

In my approach the inner uses four elements which I call The Principle of Four and the outer uses four elements which I call The Four Articulations.

The Principle of Four and The Four Articulations are revealed within the exercises in Chapter 2. In creativity there is a constant duality which is at once mechanical and intuitive. There are cause and effect factors in life, art, science. In Chapter 2, I am explicit about the method via the exercises which are described step-by-step. In Chapter 2 I also name and explain many of the formal principles which can actually be practiced by your use of the method and the template of exercises at your own discretion. Once you are familiar with that template the same principles can be applied and adapted to any performing art as well as to creativity in general. In the other chapters I mix the implicit secrets within the true stories and anecdotes.

FRAMING

In addition to explicit principles there are aspects which may be of the mind or heart or spirit depending not on their reality but on the terminology we frame them in.

In a practical way the method teaches a principle I call "Framing". The performer learns to frame what they are feeling in an explicit way that their stage partners and the audience can read. The exercises in Chapter 2 provide a way to learn to frame.

Creative expression, like in a movie or a cartoon, occurs organically frame by frame. Put another way, in performance the story is told beat by beat, one feeling or emotion or thought at a time. It is fundamental that the nature of being human is to be creative organically day by day, moment by moment. One can be equally creative in business, philosophy and science as in the arts.

In this method the body, intuition, logic, imagination and intellect form one's creativity in a holistic and professional way. By the very nature of creative harmony the exercises are healing for the practitioner and create a healing energy for those around including stage partners and audience members.

Often when I have been a guest teacher or director in a professional institution, either a company or a professional level school, often, not always, the head of the program will inform me early on which actors to watch out for i.e. whom they claim is 'talented' or 'trouble'.

I developed a way to ignore such warnings. Like many theatre practitioners I was interested in finding ways of assisting any actor who participated in my process. One of the secrets is that the actor or clown must find their own individual practice. A method can help that, but a method can also hinder. Every actor knows that truth. It is not a secret, but it is treated like one.

HISTORIC LINEAGE

Many of the well known theatre practitioners sought ideas and principles from the Eastern or Asian countries. Artaud connected with Bali. Stanislavsky with yoga and Chinese opera as revealed to him by Mei Lanfang. From Stanislavsky emerged Meyerhold, Vahktangov, Michael Chekov, Strasberg, Adler, Grotowski. Grotowski was also inspired from yoga. From Grotowski emerged Schechner and Barba. Schechner was aligned with yoga and Indian theatre. Barba with a spectrum of influences. Copeau with Japanese Noh Theatre, and from Copeau's lineage emerged Decroux, Saint-Denis, Barrault, Marceau, Dullin, and Daste. Jean Daste, Marie-Helene Daste (daughter of Copeau) and Claude Martin taught Lecoq.

Lecoq in his last years became more fascinated by, perhaps even obsessed with, the Japanese Noh Theatre as it had the secrets he sought. The Noh Theatre, the theatre of India, the opera theatre of China were all formulated first through indigenous, shamanic cultural performance practices. In the 1500s and 1600s many indigenous theatre forms became professional as in England the Mystery Plays evolved into London's professional theatres which started in the late 1500s. Around this time in Italy the commedia dell'arte gelled. Its name commedia dell'arte implies and means professional actors. The rest of Europe followed similar patterns. In France Molière (Jean-Baptiste Poquelin) moved from being a traveling commedia player to becoming a national playwright whose legacy merged with others leading to the founding of the national theatre La Comédie Française. Later the Swedish national theatre Dramaten was founded and from that their modern theatre and cinema emerged via August Strindberg, Ingmar Bergman and others.

In the 1400s the man known as Zeami (Kanze Saburo Motokiyo) formulated the principles of the Japanese Noh Theatre. He used a key image of a flower going from seed to bloom to compost as the ideal image of acting and theatre. Zeami was taught Noh by his Father. The Noh had arisen organically through the Indigenous Japanese culture. Most regions had their own form of Noh and their troupes included women. By the 1600s this theatre form became professional and in the warrior class the Samurai groups each sponsored their own Noh troupe. "I saw something very basic in Noh, something that we of the West must have had in the past but have lost. Noh has the basic characteristics of drama in a strong simple form" (Noh The Classical Theatre by Yasuo Nakamura, p. 29). Other excellent books on Noh are by Kunio Komparu, and, by Eric C. Rath whose book discusses "how memory becomes tradition". The Noh by the way has a clown tradition connected to it called Kyogen. When Yoshi Oida and I taught at a tiny festival in 2008 and we met it was like "I meeting I" - clearly two clowns who are theatre practitioners. He is Kyogen trained and hopped out of that or transformed his training to work with Peter Brook. 20 years before we met I saw Yoshi perform in Peter Brook's production of The Mahabharata in a rock quarry in Adelaide. Akram Khan and Bruce Meyer were also in that production. My friend Kerry Dwyer and I made the pilgrimage to that show via roundtrip bus Sydney/Adelaide just to see the all-night version of the show which was performed 6pm to 6am.

The performing arts of theatre, acting, clown, as well as dance seek to conjure the past, the present, and the future. The French-Romanian playwright Eugene Ionesco said "Japan's Noh is the avant-garde theatre of the present. Its technique is of all ages".

My method in a new way distils the mysteries of theatre, acting, clown. The newness is in its use of universal principles and a succinct template of exercises to discover how those universal principles can open and anchor one's creative imagination in performance. The overall vision is complex as it views East, West, Indigenous, and post-modern practices as being from the same human instinct of storytelling. Storytelling in the indigenous sense for the purpose of understanding the interrelation between Human, Cosmos, Earth.

At the same time, like in Ikebana, the Japanese art of floral arrangement, one is to integrate Present (blooming), Future (budding) and Past (dormant). Storytelling is Past (what happened), Present (the communication between the actor and the audience, which Stanislavsky called prana and Copeau referred to as communion) and Future (the personal value as interpreted by the individual listener).

In the grand schemata of "Quantum Theatre: Slapstick to Shakespeare" I set up integer based principles. For example, The Principle of Three has several interpretations of which the main one is "Time-Timing-Timelessness". Time is the past agreed upon starting time of training and duration time; Timing is the adjustment in the present of starting later or earlier or working longer or shorter periods of time depending on the present needs of the participants and practitioners; Timelessness is the future result or goal of the performance work to be transformative with no time limit.

After distilling the mysteries of theatre, acting, clown and performance in any medium I framed the essence of those mysteries into a practical template which is enclosed in Chapter 2 "The Four Articulations for Performance". Those four articulations are: Articulation of the Body; Articulation of Space; Articulation of Time; and lastly the Articulation of Space-Time Continuum which includes the first three Articulations in an integrated and interpretive way.

My claim is that the great clowns were thinking in a way that attuned the mind with the space-time continuum and is similar to the way a shaman worked as well as great artists in any medium. Chapter 2 provides the concise exercises to experience and embody and release this ancient and primal wisdom from within yourself. That is the body-mind in relation to creative expression. At the same time the method assists you to align with the global lineage of theatre, acting, clown.

EMERGING LINEAGE TODAY

I found too often in performance training that the teachers subconsciously appeared to be trying to turn each student into a 'red rose', so to speak. There are a 'thousand' variations of roses and there are a 'thousand' variations of what a student or actor can take from a course. In fact, a student does not need to be a rose, they can be any other type of flower such as a tulip or gardenia. Or they can be a different type of plant than a flower, they can be a weed such as a dandelion which has enormous healing properties. Courses are not the solution to the individual's desire. It is the engagement with oneself and with the lineage. Read. Study. Practice (any performing idea or technique).

My sense of loyalty leans as much toward the students as to the staff. I view all humans as unlimited in their potential, that includes teachers and directors. Naturally some people have their talents more to the foreground and others have their talents more hidden, sometimes even from themselves. Most of the so-called 'talented' students do not excel, nor do they always succeed, whereas some of those with hidden talents will succeed sometimes more. This book is not straightforward because the solution to your creative desire is rich and complex and not straightforward. You have to engage with this text.

My practical method is primarily an interaction of movement/acting/clown/creativity.
Within that interaction the duality of actor/clown is primary.
That duality is intellectual/intuitive.
In my method the word "Shakespeare" is a symbol for the actor & intellect, whereas the word "Slapstick" is the symbol for the clown & intuition.
The majority of my generation of clowns came from a theatre or acting background. Along the way we tended to increase our focus on physical training for mobility, dexterity, health, expressiveness through body

language, and pure skills such as dance, mime, juggling, magic, acrobatics, music, slapstick. Each of us emphasised some of those more than others.

ANECDOTE

Rarely do Bill Irwin, the famous clown/actor, and I meet or write. We hardly know each other as we did briefly long ago when we each lived in San Francisco, but we recognise something connected. Our most recent conversation was in NYC where he has been based for many years. The end of our conversation was while walking from a hole-in-the-wall cafe in the Broadway district. Bill had just finished filming for a TV show as an actor. He grabbed a quick soup and sandwich where we were to meet. Soon we walked to his gig. He was carrying a large sports bag with his costume and props inside. He was performing for a Broadway benefit. We had a laugh about the absurdity of us at our age walking one or the other to a gig. We were discussing the teaching of clown. He understood that I had a passion for it but he had trepidation about teaching and near the end of our conversation he said "You trained as an actor didn't you"? I replied "Yes". He continued "I'm so glad I trained as an actor. That's the problem. The people who want to learn clown can't act." Ironically, a few years later he asked me to help him get a teaching gig (a few days) in Belfast where at the time I was mentoring Ponydance and others. He had been an exchange student in Belfast during high school and wanted an excuse to visit. I just told you this totally absurd story because Bill is perhaps the single most employable clown in the world, but that is what happened, he wanted a short gig teaching clown. Life is stranger than fiction.

ACTOR & CLOWN - SIMPLEX/COMPLEX

In several plays Shakespeare referred to the actor as a metaphor for the human. The actor was sometimes called a player or a shadow. In the same spirit I view a clown as a metaphor for being human. The clown can present some parts of humanity in a more clear light, whereas other aspects are hidden inside the clown. Actor and clown is like head and tail of a coin. They are a pair. This is shown to us in the Western theatre's oldest symbol which is the pair of masks - comedy-and-tragedy.

INTRODUCTION

A clown is not one way but not another. A clown is fluid and moves between seeming opposites. Paradoxically a clown is viewed as a single entity such as "Happy Daze" (Art Jennings, Sr) or a clown doctor, say, my imaginary name of Dr. Ajar (open).

My generation of clowns is mostly theatre clowns (who each also have some experience performing in circus) Slava Polunin, Jango Edwards, Bill Irwin, Avner Eisenberg, Joan Mankin, Diane Wasnak, Larry Pisoni, Geoff Hoyle, David Shiner, Gardi Hutter and numerous others. The generation after us is led by the actor/clown James Thiérrée. There are a number of great circus clowns who are also fine actors even though their career is almost solely in circus. Those include Gary Grant, Fumigalli, Totti, Bello Nock, David Larible, Matthew Ezekial Smith, Mathew de Goldi, Rafael Nino and others.

Before our present generations there were Lotte Goslar, Carol Burnett, and Lucille Ball. Before them came Josephine Baker, Fanny Brice, and Gracie Allen, and significantly - the film clowns Chaplin, Keaton, Laurel & Hardy, W.C.Fields, Harold Lloyd, and The Marx Brothers - as well as - the numerous comic actresses who played opposite each of those most famous clowns - including Mae West who played opposite W.C.Fields, and Lucille Ball who had numerous small parts in films including occasionally with The Marx Brothers (Room Service) and The Three Stooges (Three Little Pigskins).

The whole world of theatre, film, television including the writers of drama and tragedy were inspired by such clowns as those people mentioned above.

Additionally, in my world view acting and clown have a rich and valuable interaction. There are a huge number of performers who excelled in that crossover but who are normally excluded from the discussions and writings about clowns. Some of those were considered comedians and not actors, and not clowns. Such Cartesian divisions take away the truth about the crafts of acting and clown. There is an incredible pool of talent who crossover those areas of acting, clown, comedian. Here are just a few to consider: Jim Carey, Debbie Reynolds, Marjorie Maime, Irene Dunn,

Mandy Bishop, Diane Keaton, Eddie Murphy, Richard Pryor, Flip Wilson, Peter Sellers, Morecombe & Wise, The Two Ronnies, Mike Myers, and a range of actors from television shows such as "Kids in the Hall", "The Young Ones", "Little Britain", "The Golden Girls", "MAD TV" (note the character "Stuart"), "Absolutely Fabulous", "In Living Color", "2 Broke Girls", "Seinfeld", "Baskets", and others.

There is a lineage in clown and a heritage in acting within which are secrets and this book provides a practical and intellectual way to find and to use those secrets. The usefulness of the book is up to your own interests but I provide clear and concise exercises (which are provided with explanations in Chapter 2) which even today can help you to open your creativity and imagination. They can be beneficial for writing, thinking, creating, and creativity is beneficial for your health. The exercises can be used by choreographers to create new movement and by directors to create original stage action. They can be used solo or with colleagues, groups, or taught for performance schools or companies.

Artistes such as Ball, Burnett, Keaton, Chaplin were only occasionally seen solo. For example Burnett and Ball each had astonishing success with their television shows but each show was a quartet. In fact like Seinfeld and The Golden Girls and All in the Family it seems that a quartet is one of the hidden secrets of great clowning. Even Laurel & Hardy as a duet had a few key players with whom they worked numerous times. Another 'hidden' secret is that most of the great clowns of film and television had teams of writers, directors, cinematographers.

One of the single greatest comedy writing teams served the great clown Sid Caesar. Caesar however always had three partners: Imogen Coca, Carl Reiner, Howard Morris. Caesar worked with the writing team daily on the 56th floor of a New York City building. The team included Mel Brooks, Woody Allen, Selma Diamond Carl Reiner, Larry Gelbert, Neil Simon, Danny Simon and head writer Mel Tolkin. By all accounts the daily meetings were extremely funny, chaotic, physical, fiery and productive. There are interviews on youtube with Sid Caesar and others.

THIS BOOK

Within this book you will find:
- a) a warm-up series of physical and physically creative exercises which will stimulate your imagination, creative output and professional integrity on a daily basis
- b) a document of some of my own processes and thoughts - which can be replicated and developed in your own way - which combines books, practical experience in the studio and in performance, and cross-referencing eclectic influences
- c) the value and norm of juxtaposing the physical and the metaphysical to create a lifetime source of inspiration
- d) a practical way to step into the mind and spirit of the hidden dimensions of the most universally known clowns such as Chaplin, Keaton, Lucille Ball, Carol Burnett, as well as the legendary live performance clowns such as Grock, Lotte Goslar, Popov, Emmett Kelly and the large array of adept clowns of today.

A VIEWPOINT

Like any professional clown one performs in all types of environments, events, situations, and in a variety of unusual circumstances.

I am simply offering a different perspective with some extremely useful solutions, tools and practical principles which can bring about a fresh outlook on the nature of creativity for any person as well as for any performance professional.

I clowned at home, in school, on the sports field, in the military, and out socially. I also performed as a clown in many different shows and performed about 75 different clown or comic characters. I am a clown. I am also a teacher, director, and theatre artist or auteur. My work has been in over 140 live shows; including for companies such as Cirque du Soleil, Slava's Snowshow, Opera Australia, Bell Shakespeare Company, and numerous small independent projects; in more than twenty countries.

In a few decades the world population has nearly doubled. Most nations and societies have changed, some irreversibly. Clowning and theatre have changed. Certainly two positive changes are the formalising of clowns in hospitals and in areas under crisis. Yet, people continue to ask questions about clown, acting, theatre, circus, which do not necessarily bring about a greater enlightenment for those genres nor for the general public.

With my method each participant is encouraged to test a constant duality which is at once mechanical and intuitive. There are cause and effect factors in life, art, science. On the other hand there are aspects which may be of the mind or heart or spirit depending not on their reality but on the terminology we frame them in. The Indigenous and folk people around the world had a refined knowledge about nature and survival and how things really worked over time and generations. Part of the gap in the performing arts as they evolve is that the elders have often been left out of the equation. I am now older than all of my great mentors. I will share with you some things they gave to me and many things which I have uncovered.

INDIGENOUS, FOLK CULTURES, USE OF INTEGERS

The Indigenous and folk cultures also had an imaginative way to conceive the interaction of all dimensions of life which could not be proved in a single generation. The Chinese culture, which is comprised of numerous ethnic and indigenous people, is one out of many which had a clear knowledge about nature, the universe, and mankind. The Indigenous Australians like most Indigenous cultures has a primary trilogy to their whole understanding. That trilogy is often termed universe-human-earth or heaven-human-earth.

My method which is singular uses universalities such as duality and trilogy. The method is partially an intellectual and philosophical game that uses integers each representing a different dynamic.

Integers are used in Taoism which sees the Tao as one but comprised of the duality of yin/yang; the trilogy of Heaven-Man-Earth; and Chinese medicine and martial arts use the quintet of The Five Elements and the Eight Directions.

Physics gives us The Four Forces. Medicine gives us The Ten Systems of Physiology and the eleventh that keeps those in balance which is called Homeostasis. Western acting is usually taught via the trilogy of Movement-Voice-Acting. However, separating those three becomes Cartesian and leads towards an overemphasis either in vocal and verbal aspects, or, intellectual aspects.

CLOWN CULTURE

Many fine actors have always intuitively understood the need to be equally physical, verbal, intellectual, and intuitive. If the body is enlivened the intuitive part of acting and being occurs naturally as it is in all Indigenous cultures.

Yet, all Indigenous cultures also had the wise woman or wise man who somehow had a higher developed intuition. Some cultures also understood that one person's intuition is refined for specific areas of life and another adept person had an intuition for other aspects. Any business manager soon learns to interpret the various intuitions of their primary staff.

To close this introduction let me come back to the notion of Elders, a notion which I claim has somewhat been forgotten in its significance for modern theatre, acting, and clown. In clown for example it is possible we can view the Fathers of Modern Clown as Chaplin, Keaton, Laurel & Hardy, W.C.Fields and perhaps another dozen from that generation. Likewise it is possible to view the Mothers of Modern Clown as Lucille Ball, Carol Burnett, Lotte Goslar, Josephine Baker, Fanny Brice, Gracie Allen.

I propose that like wise women and wise men those clowns and others learned directly from knowledgable elders and were mentored by other more experienced professionals early in their career. For example for a few years Charles Chaplin and Stanley Laurel toured together in the vaudeville clown troupe of Fred Karno. Karno and his older clowns mentored

Chaplin and Laurel on the job, on tour, for several years. Such clowns were physically adept and skilled, and innately continually aware of where they were in space and time, and were thinking on a higher level which I call the space-time continuum.

To work on a higher level creatively, my method provides a clear, concise template "The Four Articulations for Performance". A higher level on your own terms and for your own purposes can be directly enhanced by your use of the exercises explained in Chapter 2, and, the universal principles are illuminated by practicing your choice of those exercises or by using the template simply in the recommended order as presented chronologically.

CHAPTER 1

THE ERUPTION AND EVOLUTION OF THE METHOD: QUANTUM THEATRE: SLAPSTICK TO SHAKESPEARE

When I fell into the theatre at the age of 21 I had no practical intention to formulate my own method. Even now after more than 40 years of the method's development I do not view it as a method to exclude other methods. This work and method is a tool which can and will enhance any other theatre, performance, acting, or clown method. My method proposes no particular performance aesthetic and therefore it is somewhat unique for being a rare non-dogmatic approach.

The use of the word 'quantum' in the method's title implies several ideas which I will explain later. However, in relation to a non-dogmatic approach which most methods would claim, 'quantum' refers to a notion from quantum physics that tells us that the observer affects the observed. Many or perhaps even most performance teachers have a strong aesthetic which subconsciously effects how they perceive what a performer presents even in the experimenting environment of a studio and class. The students all know this. The students are in survival mode and are like children seeking approval and good grades and future support. The students know that many performance teachers and directors say one thing in words but mean another thing with their body language and facial gestures.

As a teacher when I have gone into a professional institution, either a company or a professional level school, often, not always, the head of the program will inform me early on what actors to watch out for i.e. who they claim is 'talented' or 'trouble'. I developed a way to ignore such warnings. My sense of loyalty leans toward the students first and foremost. I view all humans as unlimited in their talents. Naturally some people have their talents more to the foreground and others have their talents more hidden. All of the so-called 'talented' students do not excel nor do they always succeed. Whereas some of those with hidden talents will succeed sometimes more.

My method is as useful for teachers, directors, choreographers as it is for performance artists as diverse as acrobats, actors, composers. It is about the fundamental nature of being human which is to be creative. One can be equally creative in business, philosophy and science as in the arts.

QUANTUM THEATRE: SLAPSTICK TO SHAKESPEARE taps into the creative nature of the mind in the body using both the intellect and intuitive aspects of the mind. There is method to the madness.

Early in my theatre career which came to include clown, I heard and read of many acting and theatre methods which contradicted one another.
I wanted to know what works; when, why, and under what conditions.
I noticed that I saw fine actors from a variety of methods.
I also saw that even if a said method was meant to be excellent I saw many performers from such 'excellent' methods who were not excellent.
I saw that any acting method is good but that no method works for most actors.
I saw that what works is "The Principle of Four". Chapter 2 is explicit as it describes the exercises all of which support "The Principle of Four".
The only method that works is the actor's own, being 100% committed and aware.
My method goes for those central issues of commitment with awareness, but, with a proviso that the actor is the one in charge and not the teacher and not the director.

The actor is in charge of themselves even though production decisions in many situations practically need to be diverted to the person responsible for the overall production which is normally the teacher or director.

I saw that training in clown like training in many theatre methods used too much time with games. Some actors are better at playing games than others. Many clown games are competitive and in many cases it is the most mean-spirited that emerges the 'winner'.

I saw that actors who were good at games were not necessarily the best actors. They may or may not be, but the games do not in the end make a good actor. Games have their own value and use. Games also often put the actors in a submissive psychology of playing by the rules i.e. the teacher's or director's rules.

I saw that a teacher or director can bring about or bring out the best of an actor. They can also repress the actors greatest asset which is the actor's own instincts. Their instincts are related to their body and their body's intuition. My method directly and immediately provides tools which help any actor at any level to refine or deepen their own potential by focusing on "The Principle of Four" which is an integration of four key elements for performance. Any teacher, director, or choreographer can also learn these exercises and facilitate the exercises for and with others.

Early in my career I was interested in folk dance as something that connected us with the past, tradition, community and culture. I watched some folk dances and thought that even though they are traditional and even sometimes ancient dances, some individuals or cluster of people actually invented or intuitively created the dances. This simple thought was pure and opened a door to the idea of authenticity. This is the seed of my related processes which I have named "Authentic Clown"; "Authentic Shakespeare"; "Authentic Commedia". The exercises offered and explained in Chapter 2 lead directly to authenticity and can be applied to clown, Shakespeare, Commedia and any form of theatre or performance, including dance.

TRAININGS

Stanislavsky and Copeau were the key figures who ignited and inflamed a revolution of research about the nature of performance. Stanislavsky directly inspired Meyerhold, Vahktangov, Chekov (Michael) as well as causing an artistic revolution in the theatres of England, USA, France and Eastern Europe. He even inspired Grotowski who inspired Eugenio Barba and Richard Schechner. Copeau inspired Michel Saint-Denis, Decroux, Dullin, Barrault. Stanislavsky was directly inspired by yoga, the Chinese actor Mei-Lei Fong and the dancer Isadora Duncan, whereas Copeau was inspired by the Japanese Noh Theatre. Michel Saint-Denis understood how two lineages Copeau/Stanislavsky informed each other. That combined lineage was the basis of Saint-Denis university level program already in the 1930s and is still the basis for one of the world's most successful actor training concepts. Even the great Japanese director Tadashi Suzuki has almost all of his actors coming from straight university level acting and theatre courses which include training in Stanislavsky based systems. Almost all of Suzuki's actors also trained in their youth either in martial arts, ballet, or competitive sports. So before they enter his most arduous technique for training actors, they are each previously educated in classical Western acting, theatre history, and highly trained physically.

When actors study with me I recommend two things. First that they also begin to study a physical technique which has a long lineage and incremental learning. Therefore I suggest generally that they start to train once or twice a week in either classical ballet for adults, or, a martial art, or, Iyengar Yoga. The reason I suggest those three is that the teachers will correct the practitioner and that those systems are scientifically based and anatomically correct. The teachers are also all subject to an international standard to sustain their certification. The second thing I recommend are to get books and study. Here are the books I generally suggest in the first place: "A Dictionary of Theatre Anthropology" by Barba/Savarese (ideally the newer 2nd Edition). Another main book is the newest translation of Stanislavsky's pair of books under the title "The Actors Work" translated by Jean Benedetti. I will advise actors which physical training might be best suited to the personality or current needs, and, I will loan or recommend to them any number of books according to their particular interests.

THE ILLUSION OF 'TRAININGS'

We live in an era when "certified" needs to be understood that it does not mean "qualified". Many performance schools seem to offer 'everything'. It is a business ploy to attract paying customers (previously known as students) and to attract funding from bureaucratic government bodies.

For example, during the period that I taught at Australia's national theatre school NIDA, one semester I was asked to teach half a term of acrobatics once or twice a week for one of their groups. After I taught that term the school could 'officially' say that their graduates trained in acrobatics. Even though the reality was only a total of a few hours of instruction in a 3-year course.

Although it was via my own practice and study of something observable - acrobatics - that I made some of my breakthroughs in breaking the illusion of 'trainings' in theatre and related performing arts such as acting, clown, and 'physical theatre'.

We have within us as actors the ability to attune directly with the most ancient, original, and authentic theatrical inventions. My method is a direct conduit to achieve authenticity and original creativity even within a standard play with conservative direction. However, with each person the unfolding of their authenticity takes time.

AN EXAMPLE OF ILLUSION IN ONE 'TRAINING'

Social theorist Pierre Bourdieu notes that all fields use illusion as a means of control.

Dario Fo wrote in his book "Tricks of the Trade" and in his chapter "A Master With Whom I Disagree" in which he explains that, even though he and Jacques Lecoq were lifetime friends, he disagreed with Lecoq's method. He saw that even though people come to the course from numerous countries, when they graduate from the course they all look alike. According to Fo, the majority of graduates lost their authentic qualities.

Fo and Lecoq, and you, are part of a continuum of modern Western practitioners seeking a way to be an artist and a way not to be a bank clerk.

One of the best things in the Lecoq school is "auto-cours" which is 'self-study' which was imposed on Lecoq in 1968 when the students in Paris revolted against universities and education. His students told Lecoq they need to teach themselves or they will quit en masse. They negotiated for "auto-cours" where once a week they make a presentation on a given theme. However, along with this came another problem long known from the Lecoq based teaching and its derivatives: the adamant teacher's final definitions as to what is good or bad, right or wrong, red or not, clown or not. It is because of the teacher's final definitions that the Lecoq approach, and that of most of its derivative teachers and schools, is authoritarian and autocratic rather than authentic. This is the actual reason that Dario Fo noted repeatedly a homogenous result in graduates rather than authenticity or individuality.

Another valuable technique that was brought into the school is its regular class in Feldenkrais Method created by Moshe Feldenkrais. This method was brought in by dancer Monika Pagneux. The moment she graduated from the Lecoq school and Lecoq congratulated her, Monika said 'Your school needs the Feldenkrais Method and you need me to teach it'. It was her background in dance, her input, her way of teaching the Feldenkrais Method that gave the school its only actual 'method'.

In the 1960s also, Lecoq solicited the mastery of visual artist and art philosopher Gerard Koch to bring in ways to explore colour, shape, and space via Koch's understanding of art and related philosophy.

Clown, as Lecoq acknowledged, was brought into the school by Pierre Byland and the insistence of the students to explore clown.

One of my most inspiring teachers was Carlo Mazzone-Clementi who was Lecoq's formative muse. Carlo, even when he was my teacher, knew that I questioned some aspects of Lecoq's approach and curriculum. I view the Lecoq method as a useful survey course of a selection of theatre subjects, but, it is not training in those subjects. It is exposure to them over only a few hours per subject. Here is the hidden truth that every student of that school and its derivative schools knows. Although it is said that they study a subject for about one month, in fact, during that month they will have approximately 8 hours per week on a subject or 32 hours in the month for that subject. During that time it may well be only a total of 6 hours per student in a month per subject to be active, on the floor training. This is true for the schools and teachers derived from Lecoq and its offshoots. There is an authoritarian structure to the school and its derivatives. The student does not actually learn the subject. They learn exercises and they learn to please the teacher. Often the teachers were not actually mimes, nor clowns, nor actors, nor acrobats, nor were they in an actual commedia troupe of a minimum of seven skilled actors.

The simplest, concrete, observable evidence of the fallacy of 'training' is in a subject that is taught over the two years once or possibly twice per week - acrobatics. After 'two years' of 'training' which is no more than 2-3 hours per week, it would be extremely rare if any graduate of a Lecoq based school could actually do even basics, such as a proper front handspring or a row of three connected, fast, straight cartwheels.

Other classes are done by rote and the whole class is working, but even those classes are only a few times for each subject.

AUTHENTICITY

Nearly 20 years after Carlo and I first met he confronted me about my ideas. During a semester we were teaching simultaneously, he invited me around to his apartment.

After Carlo and I chatted a few minutes about a variety of topics he said "Now, let's talk about Lecoq." I asked why. "Because you don't like him. Why?". I said it was not that I don't like him it is just that I do not agree with some of his method. Carlo then said "What about ...?" And he named three or four wonderful performers who had at some point studied with Lecoq. I knew of each of his examples. Of course Carlo, like others, neglected to mention that those people also studied at other places and with other teachers and other methods and other techniques. I countered his examples with numerous other fine performers who never studied with Lecoq nor in his method. I explained that it is not accurate history to deny other methods they studied and which equally influenced their careers. I also said, as mentioned above, that it is a survey course and extremely superficial training in any of its subjects. Carlo said he agreed and was aware of the fallacies. He said "I see your point. You don't need Lecoq because you are authentic".

BREAKTHROUGH

One of the early breakthroughs in my method was seeing the difference in how children of circus performers learn acrobatics versus how theatre people are taught acrobatics. The difference was visceral and observable. Let me explain.

Carlo was the Founder of the Dell'arte school in California, and deeply inspiring every day, but, before I studied with him and his staff, I had a few months apprenticeship with the circus clown and former trapeze flyer Danny Chapman. Danny had been Boss Clown of one of the Ringling three-ring circuses each of which had over 20 clowns. Danny's backyard had hanging trapezes, a tight wire, a trampoline, unicycles, and a revolving ladder. Although I trained mainly by myself on the equipment, Danny would come out each day and sit in a chair with a coffee and just before he would go back into his house he would give me one pointer, a tip, or an instruction. Danny sent me to evening acrobatic classes led by former circus acrobat Willie. Willie was the main teacher for the children of circus performers. So even though the students were young they were all accomplished tumblers. Even though I was a novice I got to see how a proper acrobatic class was run, as opposed to the theatre version as taught in most theatre schools in which most people never even accomplish being able to hold a free standing handstand.

A LESSON IN SELF STUDY

Early on at Dell'arte, as mentioned already a few times, which had a Lecoq based way of teaching acrobatics, which I could see would lead nowhere... unless a student were to train on their own. So I went to a library and found three different books of acrobatics. I started to teach myself from those books early in the morning. I also practiced some of the theatre exercises from our classes. I trained 7am to 9am and then had a quick breakfast, and school was 9.30am to about 5pm with one afternoon per week free after 1pm.

A VALUABLE LESSON WITH A RUSSIAN TEACHER

Early on at Dell'arte Carlo was contacted to host a Russian clown seeking work. This circus clown had recently escaped from the USSR. This was in 1976 so the Soviet Union was a very restricted place from which even great artists such as Rudolf Nureyev and Mikhail Baryshnikov had to plan a great escape while touring in the West. So too for this clown, Oleg Panov, not to be confused with the famous clown Oleg Popov, but of the same generation. We had one acrobatic class arranged with Panov. The only English he knew in terms of teaching was "good" and "no-good". Of course he was only going to teach us basics but this included the headspring. We tried, and I could do it well enough right away to land on my feet but in a squat. Panov showed us now that to do it properly, the legs had to be straight just before the flip or spring. He showed that straight was "good" and bent was "no good". I listened to him, and did as he instructed, and the next time of course I did a very good headspring. But... the other part of this great introductory lesson was that none of my classmates held their legs straight when they did the spring action.

My lesson was: if they did the technique ("good" version = keep your legs straight) they could possibly do the trick but if they didn't do the technique the trick was nearly impossible. As with any jump, before the spring the legs bend. The bend in ballet is called a plié and its literal translation means fold. In the air the legs are straight. In landing the legs must bend. Bend, straight, bend. So, in movement sometimes the legs need to be bent and sometimes straight.

THE BEGINNING OF MY METHOD

Thus I can now briefly introduce the first series I created - "Core Mechanics". This is a series I created to practice the ten mechanical movements I observed in all dance, martial arts, or human movement skills. Movement #2 involves bending and straightening the legs as well as pointing and flexing the feet. The movement, complete with counts, is repeated four times. The whole "Core Mechanics" series is described step-by-step in this book's Chapter 2.

One of my fellow students at Dell'arte school came up to me and asked "How come you're getting so good at acrobatics?". I said I borrowed three acrobatics books and was teaching myself. He asked if I would start teaching him. A few weeks later another student asked him why he was suddenly improving in acrobatics. He told him, and that student asked to join my private class. Carlo saw that I was improving, and, heard that I was teaching some fellow students. So, after six months at the school I was hired to teach acrobatics and to act in a summer theatre festival called Qual-a-wa-loo that Carlo and his wife Jane directed. Jane and Carlo also mentored and looked after me to boost me along in this crucial period of learning. The festival was classic American summer stock theatre consisting of two ensembles each performing two plays on a rotating schedule. Each morning I taught the whole group and this was our warm-up, then we went into rehearsals.

On the first day of my teaching Carlo 'happened' to walk through the class as I was teaching and said "I hope you are teaching as you were taught" I replied "Definitely not!!". And he retorted "Aha!!" and left me to get on with it.

Carlo also came in six months earlier to one of our first acrobatic classes at Dell'arte. He disagreed with the way the class was being taught and essentially took over to show a way he knew to get us up, off our butts to play and work and learn by doing. He looked at me and took the base position for someone to stand on his shoulders. He reached his arms to one side which indicated which side I should enter from, and his hands were open indicating for me to put my hands into his hands and to step up. I went right up. Immediately he bounced up and down to feel if I was stable while he held the back of my calf muscles. Then he started to walk around the room changing directions suddenly. He made a few slow runs leaning both of us slightly forward and by this time he had let go of holding my calves and had his arms out to the side like wings but with his palms upward. Suddenly he stopped and without saying anything shrugged his shoulders upward and knocked me off with me landing on my feet standing in front of him. There was a well-worn - thin - carpet on the wood floor. He said "There!" - or more accurately with his Italian accent "Dere!". And he left.

WEST MEETS EAST

Very early at Dell'arte Carlo knew of an Aikido teacher coming to our district and he arranged for our class to have a 3-hour session. That strange class was far from the norm in Aikido training. This was George Leonard's way and a large part of the class was moving with our eyes closed. I was in heaven. I could quickly sense anyone near and in 360 degrees around. Several years later in my first teaching position I transformed that idea into a creative movement class done with eyes closed. I called it "Individual Tai Chi". Another thing that had fed into that concept was a book on Tai Chi in which the author expressed a need for tai chi to transform away from set form for combat and into a free flowing way for self-expression. That book is "Embrace Tiger, Return to Mountain - The Essence of Tai Chi" by Al Chung-liang Huang. Two other things that I read years later connect philosophically to what Huang and myself support. One was that the most scientifically disciplined yoga teacher, B.K.S. Iyengar, said in essence that 'real yoga' is when you just start your daily practice and intuitively create your practice anew each day spontaneously. The other person I'm thinking about is Tony Montanaro, the mime and teacher. He said in an interview that he hoped people would someday come to his theatre and that he and other performers would simply improvise freely and that the public would be just as open to receive whatever occurred in that performance as they would be at any other show.

SEEING BY SENSING

Another influence on "Individual Tai Chi" was Carlo's story of teaching theatre and movement to a group of blind people. He explained how that made him understand how actors could develop their own dormant capacity to feel energy and develop spatial awareness like people without the ability to see. Carlo thus developed three exercises which he taught us. In one exercise Carlo gave each actor a geometric pattern to walk and a set part of the room to keep repeating that pattern. Then all actors walked their own geometry at the same time which meant one had to open their awareness and adjust the tempo so as not to interfere with another actor. The other exercise specific to spatial intuition was Carlo's penultimate exercise "The Amazing Maze".

"The Amazing Maze" was set up by filling the room with all of the props and loose items available including boxes, chairs and benches. The school had several benches with vertical backs like park benches. There were two aluminum garbage cans placed on opposite ends of the large studio. There were two pathways between the garbage cans. One pathway was a straight diagonal line between the two cans; the other pathway had a bend, i.e. it was two connecting diagonal lines. The actor would start at the can called "Mother" and the goal was to get to the opposite can called "Home".

However, add in that the actor was blindfolded so completely that no light could come in the eyes. Additionally, the actor was turned in a circle on the spot about 5 times by either Carlo or an assistant. The actor was then placed with their back to "Mother" and facing directly on the straight diagonal towards "Home".

If the actor touched any object, they had to find their own way back to "Mother". Psychologically the mind shifts away from the goal "Home" and one soon wants to go to Mama to catch the breath and try again. Perhaps we only did this exercise on one or two days since it was an elaborate setup that occupied the entire studio and it took time for each person to try, and try, and try, and try. It created frustration and ambition and aggression and a sense of defeat in anyone.

AN ANECDOTE

In my case, I apparently nearly got to "Home" several times. In fact the first time I nearly walked straight there. But it is only a matter of one inch difference and the hand accidentally hits an object so one has to return to "Mother". However, to return one has to turn around 180 degrees while blindfolded. Nearly invariably one will bump into quite a few objects on the way back to "Mother". Thus on each return to "Mother" the frustration naturally will accumulate. So, I was fine to try again and again. Except I had a bad case of being a very spontaneous person. Some would say "a loose canon" or "a jack-in-the-box" in other words one never knew what I might do in life. I didn't know either. I was just always living life "burning the candle at both ends". So, suddenly, instead of carefully walking up the straight diagonal towards "Home", with my back to "Mother", I chose to go up the pathway with the bend. Only I ran. I started so suddenly that no one could stop nor help me. Only, instead of getting to the bend, I had run on a slight angle and ran - blindfolded - directly into the park bench. But, as I was running at full speed, I hit the park bench with such force that I did a full front somersault over the bench and landed on my feet into a squat. Carlo was at my side immediately to see if I was okay. I said I was, as I stood up with him holding me. But there was blood on my shin. I was fine. By luck.

The third exercise which Carlo created for developing the actor's spatial intuition was "The Sock Exercise". It is the opposite of "The Amazing Maze". The only object is a single sock that is placed at the opposite end of the room from the actor. The actor glances to where the sock is placed, then closes their eyes and walks to place their hand on top of the sock or to pick up the sock. If you just place your hand you can open your eyes and see how near to the sock your hand was. There needs to be a safety factor here because if the sock is near the wall even if the actor bends to place their hand on the sock they may hit their head against the wall. Additionally, no one should run :). The teacher or facilitator needs to stay alert in case anyone is veering towards a table, chair, wall, or other actor.

So we can see how Carlo's three 'blind' exercises and George Leonard's eyes closed Aikido and Al Huang's "Embrace Tiger" book influenced one of my early exercises "Individual Tai Chi" which I now offer in an adjusted format called "Neo-Expressionistic Dance". This is not dissimilar to the method of Ohad Naharin's of the Batsheva dance method "Gaga" but "Neo-Expressionistic Dance" is more freeform and open to gesture, acting, and mime, spontaneously expressed or explored.

CENTRAL TO "QUANTUM THEATRE: SLAPSTICK TO SHAKESPEARE"

Central to "Quantum Theatre: Slapstick to Shakespeare" is the idea that any physical technique has a mechanical and scientific organic logic, but, so too does creativity and clown.

I have given some brief indication of early influences on the method. First I have mentioned early processes encountering various techniques and taking time to investigate on my own in the studio. I also experimented while I did exercises within class. Additionally I went out and performed every weekend in bars/taverns. My first solo act was with a single monologue from Shakespeare. I would perform when the band took a break. I would perform mainly improvising clown, movement and text (monologue plus improvisational) for 20 minutes i.e. the duration of the band break. The actual monologue would take only 2 or 3 minutes if done straight, but, I played with it freely. Above all it was always a very physical performance. After months of performing Friday and Saturday nights with that improvised act and passing the hat and earning my living that way, I decided I wanted to experiment further with my theories and things I was studying in class and on my own. I created a second act which was non-verbal and pure movement with physical clowning. It too was 20 minutes and I also earned my income from that. My experiments were combined with finding excellent books which were based on someone else's decades of knowledge in acrobatics, handstands, floor gymnastics. Additionally I read biographies of vaudeville comedians, clowns, and actors.

CONSCIOUSNESS AND OTHER REALITIES

Before I did my solo acts one of my close friends at Dell'arte was Peter Anderson. He had a degree related to literature and he was a writer and musician. He played guitar and harmonica and sang. He was a graduate of The University of Michigan in Ann Arbor. We would clown around normally with each other doing different accents. He had an idea that maybe we could create an act together and perform it in one of the bars in Blue Lake near the school. He wrote a song about coffee and we sang that. One of my acts was as "Oral Bob". In our youth there was a tele-preacher named

Oral Roberts from the South. I would say I learned acting from imitating Oral Roberts, Hitler, and Charlie Chaplin. I would see them on TV and immediately imitate them. Many years later my Hitler imitation was a favourite of my German sociology professor Peter Dittrich who would fall about laughing and with a flood of laughter tears. Of course the little Austrian had taken acting lessons to develop as an orator. Specifically he studied how body language and gesture work with giving a speech. A few years ago in our ISAAC collective show in Paris one character was "Uncle Adolf the Shithead" and I had him wanting to be a stand-up comedian in Paris and had him coached by "Sarah Bernhardt". He was tragic and dreadful as a comedian and a disappointment to his coach Ms Bernhardt. But back to Oral Bob. I had the idea for Oral Bob to take volunteers from the bar/tavern audience who wanted to come up on stage and receive a healing from the Lord via the outstretched hands of Bob. However, when I took volunteers something happened to me and it seems that I opened up to be able to heal. So something happened to the volunteers and the audience bore witness. Although I was clowning, things got quite serious as the volunteers were visible and positively moved. I quickly moved them off of the stage and back to their seats and Peter and I got on with the rest of our show.

When it came time for me to do the solo show with my Shakespeare act I grew very tired. I only wanted to sleep and could not imagine performing. I had no scheduled venue. I only had the vague idea that I could ask at one of the bars/taverns in the larger towns of Arcata (7 miles away) or Eureka (15 miles away) as I did not want to try the idea close to the school in Blue Lake. So I lay down to sleep and figured if I wake up in time I will perform. But also if I did wake up in time I still had to hitchhike to either Arcata or Eureka. And a third gate to be tested was if I awoke in time and got a ride, I still had to ask if I could perform during the band's break. Suddenly I awoke and was hot and ready to go. I quickly changed went out and nearly immediately got a ride. I asked and soon I was performing my first solo clown act. It went very well. Some nights I would perform in 2 or even 3 bars/taverns. Some nights only one. It just depended on what I felt like that night.

YOGA AND BEGINNING ADVENTURES OF A TOURING ACTOR

The great English clown and actor, Max Wall, was asked what his philosophy of life was and he replied "One thing leads to another".

In my writings I will meander. I will travel back and forth in time the way the mind actually works. Traveling through memories, thoughts. Back and forth. A book which had a wonderful effect on my imagination was the autobiography of Karl Gustav Jung "Memories, Dreams, Reflections". It helped to give my unconscious permission to take its rightful place in life. If you google you can see some beautiful photos of Jung with his mentor and friend Sigmund Freud when they were on tour together in the USA. One of the photos is of them playing billiards or pool in an American bar. Although they had a falling out over their theories both were adamant about the importance of the unconscious and subconscious and the need for self-reflection which could be aided by an outside qualified practitioner. I view those two thinkers as a pair viscerally linked by their shared histories. Recently I read one of Freud's earliest books "Taboo and Totem". It is phenomenal in its depth and wisdom about the need in all humans to create things or ideas which are either taboo or totem. I address that need at the end of this book in the essay "Clown vs God ... Notes on the History of the Clown Movement". The first three chapters in "Totem & Taboo" focus on the knowledge within the Indigenous Australians that creates the central definitions of human cultures.

Early on yoga was to have a big influence on my movement study. My teacher Joan Schirle taught us Alexander Technique at Dell'arte and that also informed my ability to learn yoga on my own. Joan was a great influence in so many ways. She was a dancer and actress and a very alternative lifestyle gal. She, like my classmate Michelle Chilensa, knew a lot about herbs and natural remedies which I began to study and experiment with. It was not until my late 30s when I visited my Mother around her 80th birthday that she informed me that her Mother used to walk around with two paper shopping bags filled with herbs and that she would heal people. Additionally my Mother explained that my Great-Grandmother was the healer in her Czech village and was referred to by everyone as "The Mother".

Yoga was a major influence on Stanislavsky and Grotowski and Schechner. Yoga however is very much about the mind, and the mind in the body, and awareness in sensation and concentration. The central book on yoga is said to have been written about 500 B.C.E. by Patanjali. That book is The Yoga Sutras of Patanjali and my preferred edition is translated and explained by B.K.S. Iyengar. I consider the book and that translation and explanation to be one of the most valuable books for acting. Sometimes I refer to my method as "The Yoga of Acting". This refers to the value of developing one's awareness in body, space, time, and space-time continuum which become the overall practical template "The Four Articulations for Performance" which is the practical template that is explained step-by-step in Chapter 2.

MY TEACHER OF CLOWN

I came to yoga, as many do, by coincidence. Likely I saw some housewives yoga show on television as a child. I certainly saw the Jack Lalaine Show!!! I could always do the full lotus and in that position I could always walk my knees. I could also always do the splits. But the first time I encountered a yoga teacher was in Sarasota, Florida, which is the circus capital of the USA. I moved there to become a clown. The day I moved there I met an old clown who was younger than I am now. He was Danny Chapman and as a youth he had been adopted by an acrobatic troupe and by the time he was about 20 years old he was one of the few people in the world at that time who could do a triple somersault from the flying trapeze to a catcher. At that time he was in the Tom Mix Circus. Also in that circus in the same period was George Carl who was the top-mounter to a four-man high in the teeterboard act. George of course became one of the greatest modern clowns known for his microphone and harmonica act.

Danny had a backyard with circus equipment which I was allowed to practice on daily. He had hanging trapezes, tight wire, trampoline, revolving ladder, unicycles, and juggling equipment all of which I trained on daily during my four months apprenticeship. Danny wanted me to get acrobatics lessons so I went twice a week to Willie the postman who taught the children of circus artists. I had met another fellow who was interested in clowning and we went together to acrobatics 'class' which was more training on one's own and getting coaching for particular tricks. The first evening there happened to be a woman who wanted to teach yoga in the public schools and she needed photographs so Willie suggested she take us so that the children who were actual acrobats could keep practicing. My friend had done yoga but as it turned out each of the basic poses the teacher required I could actually do.

After half an hour of photos we got back on our mat and started training. Willie came over and asked what we wanted to learn to start with. Danny had already told Willie that I "was pretty good". That meant I was fit and able to learn. But for Willie that meant I knew some acrobatics, which I did not except for being able to hold a handstand for about one minute and being able to do endless cartwheels. So I said I wanted "to learn what those kids were doing". They were doing flips (back handsprings) and saltos (back saltos). Flips go backwards feet to hands to feet. Saltos go backwards from feet to feet. So I had in mind feet to feet but Willie had in mind feet-hands-feet. So I would jump up as for a salto but Willie wanted me to jump backwards as one does for the back handspring. After a few minutes Willie gave up on me learning that trick. I then went on to the mini-tramp and did front somersaults straight away on to a big mat.

A Dutch buddy interested in clown was new to the USA and had no place to live. I had rented an apartment in a motel on the Sarasota beach called Siesta Key. There was a spare room that I offered him so for two months we shared that apartment and began training and study together. The first morning after my first acrobatic class we did the 4-minute Chinese exercise plan to stretch, then we ran barefoot on this flat Gulf of Mexico beach and when we got back I said I wanted to do the back salto and asked my buddy to put his hands on my back like Willie did. Only willie had about 50 years' experience and my buddy had one class. I saw what the kids were doing and it looked quite easy. I also did them night before, but, with my coach's able hands and timing. I could jump very high. I just didn't know yet how to rotate. So I jumped up and came straight down. Basically ... my buddy needed so-to-speak "a shovel to get my head out of the sand".

That was the end of that. Not the end of me, fortunately and only a matter of luck. We then went swimming and when we came out we started to practice handstands. A little old man also in a swimming suit came up and said hello and asked what we were doing and said he used to be able to do handstands and said "catch my legs". He went right up to a handstand and with us holding his legs he started to do pushups in the handstand position. His name was Victor Drilea, he was 79 and had been an engineer and was born in Romania. He was also a teacher of violin, music, and singing and voice development. So he took us into the water up to our chest and started to teach us singing and breath control in the Gulf of Mexico.

It was only a few months earlier that our Pittsburgh theatre director Trudy Scott wanted us to go to a large experimental theatre festival in Ann Arbor at the University of Michigan, to see it and be a part of it. She brought a huge plastic bubble that could have about 30 people inside. Her idea was to set it up and let people come and go and do whatever they wanted. When I went in no one else was inside so I just sat there. After a few minutes an older fellow who was 'strange' looking like an old hippie came in and sat next to me and started chatting. We talked for several minutes. Then we were silent briefly, and I left. When I walked out several people were waiting to talk with me and asked "What did he say to you?". I didn't know who he was but everyone else certainly did! He was, as they informed me, Julian Beck who was like the king of experimental theatre along with his wife Judith Malina and their company The Living Theatre.

"ONE THING LEADS TO ANOTHER" - Max Wall

In truth I did not intend to go the festival. A relationship I was in had recently split up and the woman was also an actress in Trudy's group so I thought I'd leave space. But suddenly on the Friday I thought, wait a minute I don't have to be with Trudy's group and I can at least see the festival for myself. Little did I know that this festival was to be one of the major turning points in my life. So of course this also affected what is now my method, in several ways.

First of all I decided to go on a theatre adventure due simply to my own curiosity.

Second, I was exposed to a range of ideas I had not imagined. One of those was eating with some of Trudy's group for my first time in a vegetarian restaurant. My friends, including my ex had to translate i.e. explain what the different meals were.

Third, although I didn't understand it at the time, I met people such as Julian Beck and Richard Schechner, people who I would later read about and whose writings I would cherish.

Fourth, I saw two clown troupes of people also in their 20s (23-28 years old) who toured often together and it was from seeing those two troupes that I decided there and then that "I should be a clown".

Another important point was that I was already experimenting with reality. In naive ways that I considered shamanic. I decided that I would drive to Ann Arbor, for that festival, in my VW Super Beetle. That would take about 5 hours from Pittsburgh. I would park in the town centre, go into the first bar (tavern) and I would ask the first person I met "Could I stay at your house tonight"? Drove. Parked. Entered. Went up the the bar and ordered a drink. Waited. A man stood next to me to order a drink. We said "hello". I asked him immediately "Could I stay at your house tonight". He replied "You haven't even asked me my name". We exchanged names and I asked him again and he asked me why and I explained why I was in Ann Arbor and he soon said "Look I've got a wife and kids. You can stay on the sofa. But you have to promise me that you will leave in the morning". What a fab fellow! The next nights I stayed in a hall where many festival participants stayed.

The first festival event I went to was called "Clothes" and it was directed by Richard Schechner in a gymnasium so I thought I would go watch that show. However, when I walked in a fellow with a microphone said "Hello. Come on in. Make yourself at home. We'll be starting in a few minutes." He then saw me look around at the 100 or so people in the room talking, or sitting, or stretching. He said "Make yourself comfortable. You can stretch out and take off your shoes."

So I took off my shoes and started to stretch out and look around. Schechner announced that a few of his assistants would be coming around and if you wanted to give them your coats, shoes and socks they would put them aside to make room. People also continued gradually to enter the gym. Schechner explained that a little later the scaffolding which was up would be moved into two rows.

One of his assistants came by and asked if I would like to give him my coat and shoes which were off. How about my socks. Ok. And I can take your belt too if you like. Ok. Whatever. Soon a young lady about my age 22 came over to me standing in her bra and underpants and said "Hi, could I stretch out with you?» We did and we talked. More assistants were taking more items i.e. clothes as per the name of this 'show'.

Soon Schechner explained that his assistants would move the scaffolding and that the clothes would be laid out on the floor in between the two rows. He further explained that everyone would be expected to remove any remaining clothes and to place them in the separate sections by coats, shoes, pants, dresses, underwear, etc, and there wasn't much et cetera remaining. This is decades before mobile phones and lap tops were items of 'clothes'. Wallets stayed with clothes i.e. pants or jackets.

More people were half naked. And for some half was not enough. I was now in my underpants and the young lady had removed the top half of her greeting outfit. A small group of people by the door were standing and fully clothed. Schechner then explained that there would be no observers, only participants, so the people by the door would either have to leave or remove their clothes. They refused to do either. So Schechner said this is a democracy, we'll vote. So the 200 or so nudists or nudists-to-be all voted against the few standers who then left. Voilà. We were then asked to all stand and Schechner explained the only things which were to occur now. When we all mounted the two rows of scaffolding we could look down at all of the clothes which lay on the floor between the two rows, and if anyone at any time anyone felt like leaving they could do so and gather their clothes and dress themselves but then they would have to leave. So the young lady and I being more than happy with each other's company were the first, immediately, to decide to leave together.

Welcome to the world of theatre.

The next day in the afternoon I saw the clown troupe "The Great Salt Lake Mime Troupe" and they were great. I thought that looks like something I should do. They said they would put their gear away and the other clown troupe would set up in a few minutes so wait and see their show. At the end of that second show it was firm, and I decided that was it, I should be a clown. This troupe was "The Friends Roadshow". I went to talk to the main actor who was Jango Edwards. I thanked him and asked if he knew of anywhere to learn to be a clown. He named one place, Ringling Brothers Clown College in Sarasota, Florida.

I phoned the Clown College and they posted me the application that included a detailed questionnaire that asked many personal and a few philosophical questions. Essentially, I was a bit too honest and there were over 3000 applicants. I showed up anyways just in case. I was one of the 100 finalists for 50 positions but I was not accepted in that round. I wrote to Jango and asked 'now what'. He sent a letter with a brief reply and said - start performing on the streets to learn about audiences, and, get the book The Fourth Way. So with my Dutch housemate we drove and I found a bookstore that had The Fourth Way. It mentioned learning together so we started reading small sections and discussing the concepts. In the same bookstore I also bought a book on self-hypnosis and started to follow its plan which included having a bedside notebook and writing one's dreams first thing in the morning. I also learned to program my dreams before I went to sleep.

"WITH BOOKS YOU CAN LEARN ANYTHING" - Jeannette Seidenstein

From the other book, The Fourth Way written by P.D. Ouspensky about the teachings of G.I. Gurdjieff, I learned the essence of this philosophy that a) humans are "asleep", i.e. not conscious and not aware, and, b) that "The Work" was to wake up, and, c) do something.

So these two books about personal responsibility to transform one's life by shifting one's thinking processes and getting into action is central to my method. "The Four Articulations" exercises in Chapter 2 provide a practical, physical, and creative way to encounter awareness and to shape-shift how one is actualising one's physical and mental actions. You have control, not the teacher, not the director. When it comes to the duets then you learn to stand your ground and merge with the action and awareness of the other performer. As in Aikido your opponent is your partner, your partner is your opponent. To practice and learn you are both doing the same exercise but in opposite ways. You dance and play, so to speak, while you are doing 'the work'. As the Disney song goes "Whistle while you work". Likewise I see a profound practical and spiritual message in the old song "Row, row, row your boat, gently down the stream. Merrily, merrily, merrily, merrily life is but a dream".

We can also see the message in the yogic and Vedic sign for "Om" which has an elegant end '3', and a crescent new moon, and a dot. The new moon crescent separates the 3 from the dot. The '3' represents waking/sleeping/dreaming; the crescent new moon is maya or illusion; and the dot is reality. All mystical traditions explain the same idea - you are asleep, so wake up and move through life's illusions and seek and experience reality.

EXPERIENCE REALITY

When you read you can experience sitting in your chair, your posture, your breathing, your own thoughts and realisations now. My method allows you to practice reality and consciousness while you are busy doing something practical. The exercises are each very simple but they have a few instructions that your conscious mind must control so that your subconscious creativity can be free yet grounded. Any one of the exercises practised each day will have a residual of new ideas that in the next minute you could start to make into a performance piece if you want to. If you want to you will have to work, shape, construct, hone, edit, and polish the new piece. Perhaps over days or weeks or months or years as all clowns have done. No clown teacher can do that for you. Most avoid the real work of the clown which is craftsmanship. In my method you have a daily practice that gets you used to craftsmanship. Only you can do that. But gradually with The Four Articulations you can do that gently in your own way and rhythm.

LINEAGES. INFLUENCES AND EXPERIENCE

Although when I trained as an Iyengar Yoga teacher, as taught from 4am to 8am daily by Martyn Jackson, we would do three long poses daily: headstand, forward bend, shoulder stand; each asana for 15 minutes. Other poses were much shorter. But time and integers are of the essence for proper training in the performing arts. Generally speaking I find that very short exercises by far have the most benefit. Once an actor gets the hang of the exercises any short exercise can become a very long experience, exploration, or improvisation. Ballet uses counts, integers constantly. But even a long choreography is divided into very short sections.

In Aikido, Yoshinkan Aikido is what I trained in, it is said that each defence form has four directions which confuse or disarm an opponent. There are only three basic forms but each has two versions one version is to respond to a push and one is to respond to a pull. Each of those has a single arm version and a two arm version. These then evolve to over 100 different defensive techniques. The practice of each technique takes only a few seconds. In those few seconds there will be dozens of sensations which the body and mind register to allow each partner to flow with the other's energy. In a normal class practice we may do the same technique with perhaps 3 or 4 partners for perhaps ten to twenty minutes so we may repeat the technique nearly 100 times in twenty minutes and each time it is the same mechanics but a totally different experience.

My "Core Mechanics" is only ten movements in ten minutes, but, there are hundreds of counts. So what the actor and clown are learning is to increase their powers of concentration and awareness for ten minutes non-stop. The Yoshinkan Aikido grading tests generally take only ten minutes. Each belt has about nine steps with a grading or practical test at each step. But even working towards higher degrees of Black Belts, taking the next step grading one will barely make it through the ten minutes. Whatever level you are at, you are challenged to be masterful every second for ten minutes. That is the same for the novice as for the adept.

Likewise in my exercises even when a veteran performer attends my workshop or trains with me, they are provided with simple mechanic exercises which allow them to challenge themselves right there, now, in the studio, on the floor in action. There's no judgement. There is observation, support, feedback, discussion, engagement and always a chance to try again and again to hone, to shape, to polish, to release, to discover.

Jacqui Carroll who along with her partner John Nobbs and their young company members were all my teachers in the Suzuki Actor Training Method and in Frank/Suzuki Performance Aesthetics. In my first annual intensive with them Jacqui led us in one of Suzuki's more simple basics of stomping on a diagonal across the room evenly spaced like a row of sitting ducks at a carnival shooting gallery. After a few rounds Jacqui stopped us and said isn't it remarkable that although you actually rest until it is your turn to cross the floor again she could see that it takes everything for each actor to concentrate 100% during the floor crossing. So she was curious how long did the crossing take. It was about 30 seconds. In reality for a normal person to give even 30 seconds of concentration takes every ounce of will power. Naturally each person imagines they have full concentration all of the time, but, as Ouspensky and Gurdjieff learned from various mystical trainings who all agree, actually most of the time we are waking/sleeping/dreaming. It is our normal comfort zone.

Tadashi Suzuki, the theatre director, said that his method came from seeing a Japanese Noh Theatre actor give a demonstration and performance at a festival in Europe. Suzuki had earlier noted in Japan that in the regular theatre no actor could give 100% concentration for the length of a single monologue. Naturally all actors think they can. Whereas the Noh Theatre actor could concentrate without wavering throughout his one hour performance. So when Suzuki returned to Japan his mission was to create a way for the modern actor to train to have complete concentration.

Suzuki also said - To this day still, the best books about acting and theatre are the ones that Stanislavsky wrote. Stanislavsky's key books are the pair: An Actor Prepares and Building A Character. As Jean Benedetti explains, they are a pair, and were not printed and newly translated together until 2008 by Benedetti. His pairing and translation is available from Routledge Press.

NOT JUST A JOB

In 2000 I took a 2-year fixed term contract to be a theatre lecturer at Charles Sturt University in Wagga Wagga, New South Wales. Part of my contract was that I would be enrolled and completed my Masters Degree in Visual & Performing Arts. My thesis was "The Body of the Actor in the Space of the Theatre". I wanted to initiate a search for a scientific way to validate Stanislavsky's final conclusion that the most important thing in the theatre is the communication between the actor and the audience. Copeau called that "communion".

Of course I am not at all a scientist, and in the research I had something else I was thinking about which was metaphysics, so the thesis combined science in layman terms and metaphysics. What I did find was that energy in the body is essentially created via the exchange of sodium and potassium switching sides between neighbouring cells. They transfer via the cell membrane. Also the body is itself also electro-chemical and the air is also electrically charged. So my imaginary theory is that the energy of the actor's body electrifies the air, and that electrically charged air energises the body of each audience member. It is a nice theory that makes perfect sense to those of us in the performing arts but I will leave it in hanging in the air and on the shelf for someone with a scientific background to prove. There are also more interesting ideas in the thesis related to the value of using integers for brain and mind stimulus, and, the idea of ten physiological systems of the body being balanced by the eleventh which is Homeostasis.

During my time as a lecturer I also got inspired by education theory and shortly after I completed my M.A. I enrolled to complete my PhD in Education at the University of Queensland. I wanted to develop my academic writing and to be able to write about my method in an academically validated format.

ANOTHER VERY IMPORTANT BOOK

In Chapter 3 I tell about finding a book in 1994 which helped me with creating an overview of my method. That book was also not scientific but combined a layman's view of quantum physics and its symbolic reflection in the classic kabbalistic template called The Tree of Life which was defined in the 1200s by mystics in Spain, France and what was then called Palestine, particularly in the town of Safed which had a mystical enclave. As in the past many great philosophers were also medical doctors, they had a scientific education and approach to life's mysteries.

The book I found was "The Quantum Gods" by Jeff Love (1976). So I created a template and structure and named my method "Quantum Theatre: Slapstick to Shakespeare". I taught my first Quantum Theatre workshop in Copenhagen. Then I was hired for the first time to teach my own method which finally had a durable name. That contract was in Gothenburg, Sweden, and led to a number of contracts, experiments testing my theories in practical contracts as a teacher and director. As well I continued to study various related subjects. In that process I found that the great Swedish playwright August Strindberg had a deep interest in art and metaphysics and also in kabbalah. Eventually I wrote, directed and toured a play about Strindberg. Again I tell you about some of those things in Chapter 3 dealing with some of my own creative projects. The Swedish process finished in 1999 when I went to study in a traditional and cultural context at a centre for kabbalah in the USA.

"THERE ARE MORE THINGS IN HEAVEN AND EARTH..." (Hamlet by W. Shakespeare)

One day I was walking in my city of residence in 1999, Princeton, New Jersey, and I got a sudden cramp in my stomach which felt as if someone had just punched me in the gut. Literally, physically I got a gut feeling. It was so sudden and forceful that I grabbed my stomach and stood still on the street. It was a pleasant early afternoon. A normal business street. People walking by. But inside my mind it was a Kafkaesque moment because I had something stirring inside which nobody could see. I asked myself what the meaning of this was. The answer that came was that I should go back to Australia. I had been working and studying and developing for six years and did not feel ready to go back. The next two days the exact same thing happened again in the pleasant afternoons. On the third day I accepted the answer but thought or realised oh, I don't want to go back to Sydney. It wasn't that I didn't want to go back to Australia. So I thought - say what I do want. I thought I would like to experience living inland in a small town, and I would like a job teaching theatre, and I would like to earn a Master's Degree to study and to have a better chance for work as a teacher at a university.

Then I remembered that I had heard people talk about being able to find work via the internet. Only recently a friend at the kabbalah centre, who understood I had traveled a lot, took me one day to get an email address. I had it but had never used it. I had also heard that libraries had free internet. So I went to the library and they beamed me up. I went to search for a job teaching theatre at universities in Australia. Within a few minutes I located a university based in a small inland town that was advertising a theatre teaching position. I wrote my first email. The deadline was more or less now and I couldn't remember the time difference. So my email said I just found the notice, I was in the USA and I was not sure of the time difference but could I be considered. I said only a few sentences about my work to give some indication of my experience. Within 2 minutes I got a reply!!!! The department head said he had heard of me and I was not too late and they were very interested and he already passed my first email on to the head of theatre and he would reply momentarily. I then got that email and they were very interested to hire me for that 2-year fixed term contract! All that within 10 minutes, a $90,000.00 contract. And so it was.

Within their structure I was able to teach my own method openly. By the weirdest fluke they had already set their plays for the next year, 2000. Four of those plays had a central Jewish theme! One double play was Tony Kushner's masterpiece double bill Angels in America and Perestroika; the other play was George Sobor's Ghetto; and I can't remember the fourth play. I was to be the cultural consulate for all of those plays, as well as choreographer and character coach. Additionally I would be able to direct my own project which could include creating a play. It was a great immersion in my method. I created two plays while I was there: A Girl's Guide to Hamlet, and, Howard and The Doctor. Additionally I asked a friend who was a playwright in Canada, Peter Anderson, if he had anything of his and

I took the larger play for 2001 which was his verse play "Creation" and we did that in a church in Wagga Wagga.

ONWARD

I then relocated to Brisbane, Queensland, to do my doctorate in education. There I met with Frank Theatre and was involved with them for six years. My doctorate took longer than expected. One submits chapter drafts to one's supervisor for comments and suggestions. Nearly two years into the process I submitted a few pages that had a section which included addressing actors' health. My supervisor got very aggressive about the idea of combining health and acting. She had been a drama teacher herself and health had nothing to do with drama, theatre, or acting as far as she was concerned. As usual when I got feedback on my writings I would immediately be inspired to work with the feedback and as always I went straight to my office and began to rewrite and incorporate the notes.

In this case I extended that version of the new 3 pages. My 10 page version was to provide validation for my ideas. That didn't go well with the supervisor. We were getting nowhere quickly. I decided to push ahead and one day I showed up and submitted my whole 100,000 words PhD thesis one year early. I was told immediately that I could not do that. I said there it is. I waited a few weeks and heard no response. I asked if my supervisor had read the thesis. The answer was no. I then applied for a new supervisor. That process took one year. Universities do not like people changing supervisors for graduate degrees. In the process, I found out that in Australia a large percentage of relationships between graduate students and supervisors are failures. But the system is rigged to inhibit the graduate students from taking action. There is an inbred paradox: the graduate student is to 'create' new knowledge, but, the supervisor is supposed to be the expert in that field. There is a similar problem with most clown teaching. The teacher is supposed to be the 'expert' (they almost never are) and the actor is supposed to create an new, individual and unique character. Therefore I continue to remind actors before and after many exercises "I am not the clown, you are". It is up to the student, but, the teachers need to get out of the way.

In the process of resisting the university's processes to have me give in and keep my supervisor, one professor called in to 'advise' me said "Sometimes it's better to do just like a dog and roll over and take it". I knew my rights to request and wait for the university to offer me a new supervisor. In this interim I started to get work again and thus the process of completing my doctorate took a few years extra. During that extended period I began to do several short tours with Frank Theatre; two short contracts with Cirque du Soleil; toured in an independent theatre troupe in the UK for 7 months; I also created a quintet show "Chaplin's Eye"; and began ISAAC - International School for Acting And Creativity - which has been going since 2005.

In 2008 I began teaching ISAAC workshops in Paris and Belfast. I began to mentor the Improfessionals, an improvisation company in Paris led by Caspar Schjelbred and colleagues, and, to mentor the dance company Ponydance in Belfast led by Leonie McDonagh. In 2009, in the Paris metro en route to teach a weekend workshop, I had an epiphany and quickly wrote down some notes and exercise ideas. I showed the paper to the class and explained that I would teach some of those exercises and ideas starting in that workshop. The overall idea was "The Four Articulations for Performance".

Since 1993 I had a format for "Quantum Theatre: Slapstick to Shakespeare" which would amount to a 3- or 4-year university degree. "Necessity is the mother of invention" and in my subconscious I suppose it was necessary to take a giant leap forward by stepping back a bit, by having - instead of a 3- or 4-year program, to have a 5-day program which gave people a very practical insight into my whole method.

ONE BREAKTHROUGH LEADS TO ANOTHER

"The Four Articulations" workshop template, since 2009, uses a number of exercises that I created starting in 1976. I have also developed connected workshops, exercises and principles which I have taught periodically: "Authentic Clown"; "Authentic Shakespeare"; "Authentic Commedia"; and "Shakespeare's Clown Workshop". Those workshops each are ideally a minimum of 2 weeks. Additionally I have developed another 2-week process of a workshop/project within which we collaboratively create a one-hour performance which is performed in a small theatre a few evenings.

Another aspect of my method has been long term mentorships each of which starts casually for a short period. That began accommodating requests from people whose schedules did not coordinate with my workshops or long term trainings. The initial formal process is "Creative Mentorship" which is set up for long distance mentoring.

The last concept I will present now briefly is the ISAAC long course. A former student Jai Luke Hastrich wanted to assist me to restart ISAAC as a long course. I nominated to trial it for 13 weeks, Monday thru Friday 9am to 1pm. There were two participants: John Latham and Jai. One of the first days they were doing "The Laurel & Hardy Exercise" which is the first duet in "The Four Articulations". As normal with improvisational exercises, if there is no structured ending as in some of my exercises, I will often say "thank you" to the actor. Then I will give some feedback or ask questions or engage in a discussion about what occurred during the exercise. This time with Jai and John after quite a few minutes I said "Thank you, just wait there a moment please". I put my head down into my hands and closed my eyes. Naturally when Jai and John saw me drop my head into my hands they told me later they thought they had either done something very wrong or were simply awful. In fact it was the diametric opposite. They were so stunning, funny, professional and such consummate actors and clowns that I was taking a private moment to literally thank my lucky stars for having two such wonderful people in my studio. I told them that after I gave myself about 3 minutes' reflection.

It has always been my philosophy with teaching that each person who comes into a class, workshop, course, or project brings a special gift which is simply themselves as they are. Warts and all. Virtue and vices. Strengths and weaknesses. Additionally, they come for one reason consciously but for other reasons unknown to themselves which are subconscious. Furthermore, above all it is the unique relationship between a teacher and each student or actor which is the central process, thus it is not that the teacher knows something that the student or actor doesn't, rather the heart of teaching is a unique unfolding relationship between the teacher and each student which is their mutual discovery and growth.

I also know from experience that even an 18-year old, usually the youngest age permitted for a tertiary program, brings life experiences which the teacher does not possess. Just two examples out of thousands I have taught: one 18-year old in a university course was a farmer's child and during semester breaks and holidays he would go home and work on the tractor in the fields and do all other jobs on his parents' farm. He was also one of the most naturally gifted mimes I have ever come across. The other example I'm thinking of in the same course and also 18 was the daughter of two university professors, so she was born into an academic, intellectual and creative family from birth. In either of those two cases among hundreds of other such examples is that at 18 they had enriching life experiences which I did not have even as an experienced theatre practitioner. Teachers must respect the intellect and talent and potential and life experience of each student.

One of my Mother's many favourite sayings was "Don't judge a book by its cover".

I think genius is in humanity generally rather than only individually. Genius doesn't happen in a vacuum; there are numerous social and interactive factors that form the pressure that emerges as genius. I have seen brilliant talented young theatre people from Kiruna in the far north of Sweden and people of equal theatrical talent from Cowra in a southern region of Australia.

There is a saying that "the present is a gift". I think if I have a genius for anything it is in assisting anyone who stands before me to increase their chance of finding, shaping, and harnessing their gifts and talents which can in time release their individual form of genius.

I think teachers and directors can develop also with these very same exercises and principles explained in this book. I share numerous anecdotal stories and use our basic human nature of storytelling to share some often hidden universal principles for acting, clown, performance, teaching, and directing.

As I now lead towards a conclusion of this chapter I will quickly note just a few things I didn't mention which are valuable along a trail of influences which led to my method. When I got out of the Navy and started tertiary education I felt my old poor learning habits from school took over. Whereas when I was in the Navy I excelled at learning my craft as a Radarman and Operations Specialist. I thought I needed to try something drastic so I would study. I looked in the phone book and found a hypnotist. I phoned and the woman said briefly that the old hypnotist had passed away but she was his long time colleague. I think the man's name was something like Dewey. She then told me a few things about myself, over the phone, after one minute of us speaking for the first time. She was a psychic. I was able to see her now. I got in the car and drove into the downtown center where this little clinic was in an old arcade similar to the one I went to as a child to buy stamps for my stamp collection or my first magic tricks when I was in 6th Grade at Wightman Elementary School. So she explained about hypnosis and self-hypnosis and taught me a very simple technique. Place the tips of your fingers of your right hand over the back of your left hand and gently draw a small circle with your fingers. Keep making that tiny circle over and over and repeat several times "Everyday in every way I get better and better". You can do that any time you feel stuck or blocked as well as just do it when you think of it. It works. The question is what is 'it'. It is the mind in the body. Using the conscious mind with anything physical can release the power of the subconscious. No acting method works for most actors. Most clown teaching methods are ineffective for most students. The courses for acting, theatre, clown, dance, are all businesses. What works? When? And under what circumstances does a method work? What works really is only one thing. What works is when an individual harnesses their own curiosity, passion, and desire. If you harness your curiosity, passion, and desire then any performance method will have the illusion of working. But your curiosity, passion, and desire must be focused into an actual discipline or practice. As my teacher Carlo said "That's the damned thing". Or as the clown movie "Ghostbusters" theme song says "Who you gonna call?» You have to conjure your subconscious. You have to create your own discipline. My method, particularly for the purpose of this book, the short template in Chapter 2 will help you immediately to "get better and better". It works by being a physical practice to use your mind consciously in concise exercises which will immediately release your subconscious and as a result you will be able to create better artistically and you will be better able to create practical solutions for your work and craft.

The first hypnotist I met though was in a bar in Spain when I was in the Navy. He was a professional magician and a normal part of that craft is to understand aspects of hypnosis. He was next to me at a bar and spontaneously told me something I needed to hear. "Your asset is your youthfulness". He explained that it was a quality that I had for life.

One of the most important discoveries I made which is central to my method was that with stillness in the body the mind can be freed. I applied for a job on campus during my first semester which paid $1 an hour more than my landscaping job which was coming to a close as Autumn turned towards Winter. The new possibility was as an art model for the art department led by a Mr. Bruno. He was an immediately endearing angelic person very similar to the children's TV presenter Mr. Rogers. The job was explained very simply and involved taking a pose of stillness either standing or leaning or sitting or reclining. First five poses at 1 minute each. Then a few 5-minute poses. Then a 45-minute pose which was to be held again after the class coffee break. I was hired to start the next day. I entered the office and Mr. Bruno said "There's your robe". I asked what do I need a robe for? He said it was cold in the art room. I said I've just walked through there, it's fine. He said "But when you have your clothes off it will be cold". What!!??? It was only then he understood that unlike most people, I had no idea that an art model worked naked. He said I could wear my clothes today. He said some male models actually wore a jock strap or a bathing suit. I had neither with me. So, off went my clothes. On went my robe. It was time to start. I was to take the timer with me and ask a student to operate the timer. Off went my robe.

I took a standing pose.

Immediately a sensation like being struck by lightning happened. I was struck with energy right through the top of my skull. Years later I learned that the top of the skull is also known as The Crown Chakra. In Sanskrit that is named "Sahasrara" and some say it is not a chakra per se but something higher. Every mystical, spiritual, religious path tells about a form of awakening. In fact what is named as 'heaven' is actually an awakening within oneself. Swami Satyananda Saraswati provides a clear explanation of such phenomena in the book "Kundalini Tantra". As the fable goes "The kingdom of heaven is within". It is an experience. This experience happened to me when I stood still naked in front of a room of art students. In the next moment, in a split second suddenly my mind was filled with a drama in my imagination of what this shape could be if activated into movement. It was as if I had caught myself in action. The totality of the lightning through my skull and the vitality of the imagination was wonderful. It was the first time I truly experienced myself as a creative person. Creativity occurs by uniting the mind and body in stillness but ready for action.

It is only today in writing this and going to that book on my shelf of Swami Satyananda Saraswati's explanation of the other chakra related more to the back of the skull, The Bindu Chakra, that I see he explains that 'bindu' implies to bind but also to split. My experience was first the shock at the top, but a 'split' second later came the burst of creative imagination. The Bindu is said to be located towards the back of the head where some yogis keep a shock of hair, a small knot of hair. "Bindu is considered to be the origin of creation or the point where oneness first divides itself to produce the world of multiple individual forms" (p. 184). He explains also that bindu "is beyond the realm of all conventional experience" (p. 180).

Two years later a very similar experience occurred in front of my clown and circus teacher Danny. The first day I was to be a clown. Danny had my costume hanging when I arrived and he offered me a coffee. It was one of his costumes. An orange baggy suit - pants and jacket. He told me to put on the white shirt and pants and then he would put on my makeup. Then he had me put on my jacket. Then stand still in front of him and his circus apprentice Curtis from Wyoming who was also seated next to

Danny. Danny gave me a clown nose on an elastic string and said "Here's your nose. Go over there and stand still in front of us and when I tell you, you put on the nose". I stood still for about a minute. He said "Okay. Put it on." The very moment I put the nose on, a 'lightning bolt' went through the top of my skull. Immediately, a slight split second after the shock, Danny and Curtis burst out laughing. They were laughing so hard and fast that they were both shuddering. I looked at Danny and he had a burst of laughter and twisted away slightly. I looked at Curtis he too burst and twisted away. I was standing still except for my eyes and a slight head movement towards the two people. Small movements happened in my face or torso and each small movement caused other bursts from those seated. But as I moved ever so slightly the two of them began to squirm and tears came from their eyes and they could hardly look at me but had to keep looking back at me at the same time. Finally waving his arms Danny said "Take it off. Take it off. Take off the nose". I did, and that was an amazing experience like being in heaven. We were to drive in our vehicles and to be in the Siesta Key Parade. Danny and his family and Curtis and myself were placed behind a jazz band that was in a flat bed truck. Suddenly as the truck and parade started the band began and I started to dance and clown and mime. I did that non-stop for the whole parade. At the end Danny and family were very excited by what I did and said I was a wonderful clown. I had to leave quickly and get straight to work as a short-order cook at the beachside Sheraton at the edge of Sarasota.

Most of my creative exercises involve the active use of stillness which I call "Pause". For in acting and clown and performance stillness is only a pause between actions. Years later I read Tadashi Suzuki's book "The Way of Acting" which in his method is the art of stillness. He said the purpose of an actor is to move their centre around the stage. So the stillness is also within and not always describing that the body is still. The awareness is still. Sometimes the body is still in performance. The purpose of stillness in martial arts is to take action.

The secret within the performing arts is that there are very practical factors and at the same time there is an experience available that is beyond the everyday conventional.

Thus one of my early solo shows was titled "Getting Into Struggle". But I encourage everyone to stick close to the pragmatic. That is why I suggest to every actor or clown whether novice or veteran to get a movement teacher of a technique that is useful for daily practice and which ideally has been taught over centuries, and is incrementally structured in a scientific way. The only forms which meet that criteria are: classical ballet; martial arts; Iyengar Yoga. I do not say that Iyengar is better than other forms of yoga except that it is taught in a clear, scientific, anatomically correct manner, and, there is in those forms an accredited registration for their teachers whom they insist maintain their own learning.

Additionally I know that via the performing arts, even while in a training program, even a mediocre training program, then other aspects will open such as the individual's creativity and emotional maturing. Therefore the scientific physical training of either classical ballet, martial arts, or Iyengar Yoga will help to keep the blossoming actor or clown grounded and safe psychologically from the dogma that so many acting and clown teachers seem to proselytise.

The student though can also be guilty of practiced naivety in believing that their teacher is 'the way, the truth and the light'. Once I was accused by a student that "it was my way or the highway" whereas in reality I am willing to step out and say there are problems in the teaching of performing arts with regards to dogma. The truth is that any method of experimenting with one's creativity is bound to open up new areas in the individual.

So it is simply a practical necessity to stay grounded, to be the one in charge of your unfolding destiny, and to seek a tried and true technical, physical and scientific and anatomically correct practice, ideally with a highly qualified teacher who is still fit and healthy and ready, willing, and able to accommodate a wide spectrum of needs and to adjust their teaching according to the needs and attributes of each student.

The next chapter is the introduction template to Quantum Theatre: Slapstick to Shakespeare. The template, The Four Articulations for

Performance, is a series of exercises described step-by-step. "Get up, stand up, stand up for your rights" as Bob Marley's song advises us. So get up, read while you are standing and try out the first exercise. Take your time. Take your time. Take your time.

CHAPTER 2

THE FOUR ARTICULATIONS FOR PERFORMANCE

Introductory Remarks

The introductory remarks below are from an academic conference in April 2018 - Imagineers in Circus and Science: Scientific Knowledge and Creative Imagination. This was hosted by The Humanities Research Centre of the Australian National University in Canberra. Prof. Richard Weihe recommended me to the conference designer and organiser Dr. Anna-Sophie Jürgens.

"My method asks when you take away all of the tricks and outward skills what is the clown that remains? What is clowning when you get rid of the tricks? Importantly, what is the awareness developed within the matriarchs of clown such as Lucille Ball and Carol Burnett and within the patriarchs of clown such as Chaplin and Keaton?

Here is what I propose: the major clowns and the adept clowns work with an Internal Unity and an Expressive Unity.

The Internal Unity consists of four elements:
body/mind/feeling/awareness.

The Expressive Unity consists of five dualities:
Duality #1 - Upper and Lower parts of the body working in harmony

Duality #2 - Inner feeling and outer expression
Duality #3 - Feminine and Masculine lineages in clown ... and the Feminine lineage can incorporate modern dancers and the masculine can incorporate painters (I reference Kandinsky, Klee, Miró, Chagall)
Duality #4 - The greater clowns combined a high level of accomplishment in one or more particular skills with having awareness while executing the skill
Duality #5 - Acting & Clowning comprise a single unity

How does one go about training such a rich and complicated ideal of having a unity of those five dualities and those four elements?

Simple. "You put your left hand in, you put your left hand out, you put your left hand in and you shake it all about. You do the hokey pokey and you turn yourself around. That's what it's all about."

Seriously, let's get back to clowning.

THE FOUR ARTICULATIONS FOR PERFORMANCE

One of the central ideas of my method has been to find what is universal, and, a hidden unifying concept inside all acting and theatre methods. I relate this, metaphorically, to the Four Forces in physics which show the universal or undeniable factors throughout the known physical and mathematical universe.

The Four Articulations for Performance starts as a creative physical warm-up. It is also the introduction template for The Seidenstein Method and Quantum Theatre: Slapstick to Shakespeare. The template is a specific series of exercises moving from physical movements with set counts to free-form improvisations which have clear and simple steps, but, with no set aesthetic. The solo section takes about 40 minutes.

The first 15 minutes are physical exercises which have a variety of counts. Then a 5-10 minutes very brief vocal warm-up. That is followed by the 7 creative solos which take 15 minutes. Next is a series of 5 partner improvisations which take an additional 15 minutes.

In the early stages I lead the solo warm-up taking time to explain, demonstrate and answer questions. After a few days I ask participants to lead some of the first section and rotate the leaders each day. When a participant leads I stand in the back and can observe each participant and I begin to clarify details afterwards.

Following the basic warm-up of the solo and partner exercises comes another series exercises known as The Path of Honour. Each exercise is named after some great clowns/performers of the past. The Path of Honour exercises are mainly duets and solo improvisations. Each has a simple premise or set of instructions which can be freely interpreted.

The structure of The Four Articulations is:
- a)   The Three Loosenings
- e)   The Core Mechanics
- f)   Quantum Vocal Warm-up - originally suggested by Dr. Flloyd Kennedy of Being-in-Voice
- g)   The Seven Solos
- h)   The Three Duets; Triangle Exercise; The Whisper Exercise
- i)   The Path of Honour

INSIGHT

Early on in my career I saw that an actor from a supposed inadequate acting or theatre method could be the most wonderful actor in a production. Whereas actors from supposed 'best' methods could be weak, unskilled, inadequate, and superficial actors. Between these two paradoxes I observed what the excellent actor was simply doing and what the weaker actor was not doing.

I read numerous old school actor and comedian's biographies. Biographies written between the 1940s to 1970s. It was sometimes a noted truism that 'the hardest thing for an actor is to know what to do with their hands'. The first exercise I created went direct to 'the hardest thing'.

During these same early years of my career I read numerous books of differing and antagonistic books on philosophy. In this period I read a little bit about Leonardo da Vinci's "Vitruvius Man" diagram and what it represented. That was the microcosm of the human body and the macrocosm of the universe. At this time I devised my two central exercises: The Twist Choreography, and, The Creative Twist, both of which are a physical and creative embodiment of the "Vitruvius (Wo)Man" and both exercises also practice that 'hardest thing for an actor' which is the use of the hands in an integrated way.

Additionally and most importantly, along with the integration of the hands to the rest of the body's action, is the hidden element that the finest actors have mastered which is, as Stanislavsky noted, that at the same time the actor reflects their own inner creative imagination and feeling.

Heleen van den Bosch studied in Russian the unpublished final manuscripts of Stanislavsky. That study overlapped with Heleen's participating in a few of my workshops and acting in a few projects. Here is her statement:

> *"I ended up in Ira's workshops in the first place because I was a "hopeless" acting student. There was no teacher who could help me to learn how to use my "counterproductive" body. It was counterproductive because it didn't do what the teachers wanted. All the acting classes I had taken up to that point only taught me tricks, and, as it seemed, they weren't very helpful. It left me frustrated. By that time I had already worked on Stanislavski for a year and a half, mostly historical, and I understood what Stanislavski wanted to say, but I couldn't really put it into practice. For some reason it wasn't working and I couldn't figure out why.*
>
> *After only one day of work with Ira I learned that I could take ownership over this "hopeless" body of mine. It turned out my body wasn't hopeless at all, but pretty creative. I just needed to listen more to it, instead of dictating it what to do. It was also a relief to know that for the first time I was taught something I could train, I could practice something at home, without being scared to be led astray. I felt I was being put*

on the right track and by working with Ira for more than a week, something else changed as well. It completely changed the way I looked at my own research on Stanislavski. By feeling what it meant "to take ownership over my body", I understood what Stanislavski really was talking about. Because I felt and experienced it, his words started making more and more sense.

At the moment I'm still digging and digging deeper into those last chapters of his life and work. The more I read, the more similarities I discover... and the more I think Stanislavski would have loved to have participated in a workshop with Ira. Even in the early days you can find traces of this "Method of Physical Action". Somewhere in 1920 he already wrote: "If my mind and body go dead on stage, I make any kind of movement to come back into the moment. I can't explain why, but it works."

The more I get involved in Stanislavski and the field of acting techniques in general, the more I see how unique the Seidenstein Method is. It starts where the others try to end, at the very essence of performance. It is truly liberating and fundamental to any kind of performance."

All acting methods are good, yet, no acting method works for most actors. When an actor or performer is excelling, what universal principles are they using? Consciously or unconsciously? Why is it that The Four Articulations can enhance any acting or performance method?

The reason is that in each of the exercises the actor must concentrate on what they are actually doing - physically - and in a chronological, and, organic logic. This is done without an overriding aesthetic from a teacher, director, or method. In other words, first things first - the actor needs to know what they are doing physically and in space and in their own timing or rhythm.

Additionally, the approach I suggest requires the actor to stay conscious the whole time, yet to continually make mental shifts as each exercise progresses and proceeds through the template.

NOTE: MOST OF THIS CHAPTER PROVIDES TECHNICAL INSTRUCTIONS. IT IS MEANT TO BE READ ONE STEP AT A TIME - AND THEN STAND UP AND TRY THAT STEP. IT IS PROCEDURAL STEP BY STEP. SO IF YOU ARE INTERESTED IN TESTING THIS METHOD OR ANY OF THE EXERCISES YOU MUST TAKE YOUR TIME. TAKE YOUR TIME. TAKE TIME. EACH EXERCISE CAN BE LEARNED IN 5 OR 10 MINUTES. THEN OVER TIME ONE LEARNS THE SUBTLETIES AND WHAT IS 'HIDDEN' WITHIN THE EXERCISE. PART OF WHAT IS HIDDEN IS YOUR OWN ENGAGEMENT WITH THE EXERCISE.

The Three Loosenings has 3 exercises; Core Mechanics has 10; Seven Solos 7; Duets, Trio, Quartet is 5 exercises; Path of Honour 9. You are welcome to learn them solo, with a partner, or in a group. Have fun. Take your time.

A BEGINNING PRACTICE - THE TWO VITRUVIAN EXERCISES

The two Vitruvian twisting exercises, simple and concise, are like a seed that grows into an oak tree which further produces seeds for an oak forest which extends to provide a canopy for many varieties of smaller trees and plants and bugs and creatures to flourish. The great oaks themselves can hundreds of years later be harvested to provide wood to create houses, ships, ship's masts as well as wood for sculptural art works.

If one looks at a seed one can not see the tree nor the forest nor the variety of life and things which can be produced from oak.

Here is the first seed of my method and which I propose holds a secret expressed in a much more complex way within any acting or theatre method. This exercise, The Twist Choreography, and its sibling exercise,

The Creative Twist, can assist any actor, teacher or director to get more out of any acting or theatre method.

THE TWIST CHOREOGRAPHY

Although it may take a few minutes, a few attempts, and a bit of practice, this exercise takes only one minute once you know it. It is invigorating and energising.

To start - stand with feet about one metre apart. Stand in a normal wide stance like you would to do star-jumps (jumping jacks) or in ballet's 2nd Position (à la seconde) or the width of martial arts' "Horse Stance".
Initiate the movement via your pelvis and twist left and right continuously.
As you twist forward to the left the right heel should lift gently so that the right knee is not strained.
Likewise as you twist forward to the right the left heel should lift gently so that the left knee is not strained.

Some would consider that such a twist done while standing is more subtly initiated in the sole of the foot pressing gently 'invisibly' into the ground. That is how a martial artist would view it and may thus call it 'torque'.

So you stand with your feet wide apart and twist left and right continuously. At the same time using enough energy in the pelvis so that the arms splay outward.
The arms should be passive and not lifted.
The arms should not be flung. The driving energy should be from the pelvis, not the arms.
The energy used should be just enough so that the arms splay outward and down, but not too much so as to lift the arms to horizontal. The ideal is that the arms are about 45 degrees.
Then, as the arms are passive, they will naturally wrap around one's waist front and back.
The arms splay then wrap, splay then wrap, splay then wrap…
Note that the back arm must be bent at the elbow.

At the same time as the arms are passive yet splayed at 45 degrees, then, when wrapped front and back, the back heel should lift upward and forward so that there is no strain on that leg's knee.

When twisting to the left, the eyes should look towards the left and behind, and the right heel lifts as the foot gently points. Twisting right, eyes right, left heel up, and left foot gently points.
In between left and right, without stopping the movement, the eyes should face front.

All yogic twists start in the pelvis and spiral through the three moving parts of the spine in this order: (pelvis first) lumbar, thoracic, cervical.
It is the same for this standing twist: pelvis, lumbar, thoracic, cervical and additionally the ocular nerve is stimulated by engaging the eyes as you look left, centre, right, centre, etc.

That is the basic standing twist movement which is called 'big'.

There is now a choreography of 4 big, 4 small, 3 big and spin around.

A) "4 Big" Start with the four big left, right, left, right as described above.

B) "4 Small" The four small use the momentum in the arms as the heels now remain on the ground with the pelvis and eyes facing forward, and in four counts the arm movements dwindle. The movement should be left, right, left, right.

C) "3 Big" At the end of the fourth small movement of the arms to the right, the pelvis enlivens again with a big twist to the left with the right heel lifted up. Three big twists left, right, left. But on the third twist you actually lift your arms to horizontal, and open and stretch the fingers of both hands and at the same time spin on the left foot. The right foot will lift slightly above the ground as if drawing a grand circle and finish where it started. If you have difficulty spinning then simply walk the right foot around in a 360 degree circle while rotating on the left foot.

We now call this pattern "4-4-3". With each section 4-4-3 starting to the left side.

D) The final section is "Drop-Centre-Heel-Slowly unwind".

After the '3' big you will have your arms horizontal with the shoulders down and fingers wide open and looking straight ahead.
Drop the arms.
From the centre/pelvis twist to the left. At the same time bend the front knee and as usual lift the back heel. As in the regular big twist the arms will splay out and downward at a 45 degree angle.
This time you 'catch' the movement at 45 degrees and lift the arms to horizontal. With the left arm straight, fingers open, and eyes looking over and beyond the left hand. At the same time bend the right arm so that the right hand is flat, horizontal, but in front of the chest or sternum.

Then as the back heel goes down - the pelvis is automatically pulled back - which also straightens the front knee. At the same time the right elbow draws backwards while the right arm at the same time straightens.

Then you drop the horizontal arms and do the same process to the right side, 4-4-3-Drop-Centre-Heel-Slowly unwind.

E) The whole choreography is Left-Right-Right-Left:
To the left side 4-4-3-Drop-Centre-Heel-Slowly unwind.
To the right side 4-4-3-Drop-Centre-Heel-Slowly unwind.
To the right side 4-4-3-Drop-Centre-Heel-Slowly unwind.
To the left side 4-4-3-Drop-Centre-Heel-Slowly unwind. On this fourth and final section of The Twist Choreography do not drop the horizontal arms. Instead you slowly draw the arms downward until your hands are touching the side of your legs. While lowering the arms draw the left foot to the right foot with the heels touching and the toes splayed out gently at about 45 degrees. That standing position is the start of Core Mechanics movement #7.

The spinal twists in yoga are said to stimulate the central nervous system. Use of the eyes in The Twist Choreography exercise may additionally stimulate the optic nerve. Stimulating the central nervous system and optic nerve also connects with and stimulates the brain. The use of left and right, and counts and an asymmetrical pattern (left right right left, rather than left right left right), the use of the fingers and feet would all help to stimulate the brain and the mind.

THE CREATIVE TWIST

The next exercise description is THE CREATIVE TWIST which is extracted from The Twist Choreography. They are both anchors for your creativity. The Twist Choreography is physical and challenges one's concentration while moving. The Creative Twist is also physical and challenges the concentration while moving but additionally it does the following: challenges the legs to move in new and creative ways; holds the arms still in front of the body; allows the voice out spontaneously. This is the beginning of acting and the beginning of creating via one's body and voice.

There are five steps to The Creative Twist.

A) Starting from the pelvis, twist left and right, then as you are about to twist to the left again drop your centre/pelvis downward by bending your knees. At the same time as dropping the centre and bending the knees, raise your arms in front of you. The heels should raise as in The Twist Choreography, i.e. as you twist left the right heel lifts and the foot points gently, then as you twist right the left heel lifts and the left foot points gently. When you drop the centre the heels are down, the arms are up in front and elbows are bent. Those are the first three steps: twist, twist, drop. Practice that several times. Twist, Twist, Drop. Note: There are only two twists here, whereas The Twist Choreography starts with four twists. When you practice twist, twist, drop start left. Next time start right. And alternate the starting side each time you start twist, twist, drop. Often some people will have their hands parallel in front every time. They are your arms so you can control where you place them. Generally try to avoid having them parallel, so that one arm is higher than the other, or in a different shape, or the hand of one arm may be up and the other hand or palm may be down or sideways. Make sure the arms are always in front. They can be high or low, but always in front. The arms are generally in front when training in ballet, in martial arts, in chi gong, in Tai Chi. The scapula of each shoulder should be flat and relaxed without raising the shoulders up. The shoulders should be flat, open, down. Those are the first three steps of The Creative Twist - twist, twist, drop centre lift arms

B) With the arms still held in front and bent, the spine vertical, you then move your legs in 8 steps. Do not just walk forward. Use your legs by lifting or kicking or wiggling or sliding or prancing etc 8 times the same way each time and in the same direction on a line or a curve. Sustain the same rhythm through the 8 steps.

C) Now do steps 1-4 three times. Twist, Twist, Drop centre lift arms bent, move your legs some new way and take 8 steps in any direction keeping the same rhythm. Do 1-4 three times.

D) Final step starts after moving the legs about 8 times or about 8 steps, then keep the rhythm of the movement steady and continuous but after the 8th step let your voice out. To let your voice out release the breath, and shape the sound that comes out. For example wawawawawa or oogamoogagoogaboo or lmppppppffffweeeeeo. If your vocal sound is about 5 seconds it should be followed by 5 seconds of silence, then repeat the same sound-silence a total of four rounds. At the same time keep the rhythm of your steps continuous. Note: You are not matching the sound to the step either mechanically nor creatively. 1-4 is physical movement and the voice is simply released and shaped coming from the body via the release of breath and exhalation.

E) Now do steps 1-5 three times. Twist, Twist, Drop centre lift arms bent, move the legs 8 times in any direction, any rhythm, then on or after 8 steps let the voice out and shape it for about 4 to 12 seconds approximately and have the silence be the same amount of time repeating sound-silence four times while sustaining a steady rhythm in the movement of the legs.

The Creative Twist is done three times steps 1-5. However, on the third time one goes further and begins to play. On the third time after you have done the sound-silence 4 times, continue and do it a few more times and gradually start to adjust the arms. Do not drop the arms. Adjust them. Adjust the sound. Adjust the legs. Adjust is different than change. Change means you stop what you were doing and start something else. Adjust means you honour what you are doing, sustain it, and let it evolve in some small ways. Note: you still do 1-5 the same way, all the way through four sound-silence, but, now you continue. So you will do your walking rhythm all the way through this extended form, but after you have done the sound-silence 6 or 7 or 8 times you will adjust the voice, the legs, the arms and perhaps the sound and silence in its progressed and adjusted form continues 10 or 15 times with various adjustments. This extended version of The Creative Twist should take at least 1 or 2 minutes. If you like what you are doing though, why not continue? It is your exercise, your creativity, your imagination. You might even get an idea that you would like to develop and may want to write it down.

The Creative Twist is my main creative exercise. It is the main exercise because of its simplicity and universal application to creativity for any performer. Its simplicity allows for 'hidden' elements in one's subconscious imagination inside to be revealed outside and into a conscious expression. Most importantly it is a trigger mechanism for your creativity and imagination yet involving a conscious awareness of your whole body, breathing, play. It is finding for yourself, at any given moment, what you are playing with in terms of your body, rhythm, energy, breath, feeling, imagination, creativity, intellect, artistic conceptualisation. If you are Ophelia what do you play with in your rhythm of your entrance with the herbs and flowers? How do you walk into the scene? How do you walk onto the stage? What makes you notice the other actors and characters? What do you play with in your voice when you speak your first lines of that scene? It is dependent not only on your execution of the text but also on your interpretation of the text, character, and situation. The Creative Twist is about knowing what you are doing mechanically with the legs, arms, hands, breathing, voice. In a way, the text in theatre or performance comes after or from the body and voice and imagination. The body, voice, imagination precede the spoken word. The text in a play is the input, but, the actor must transform the input via their body, voice, imagination to the resulting output of the spoken word. The Creative Twist helps the actor to stay physical, grounded, real, active.

END - INTRODUCTION OF THE FOUR ARTICULATIONS FOR PERFORMANCE

Cross-Cultural. East meets West.
Modern meets Indigenous.

The template, the method and the exercises are to name and practice the basic universal principles. These universal principles which are explained throughout this book were articulated in ancient complex actor systems. The principles are articulated in other layered ways in Zeami's treatise defining the No Theatre of Japan; or, in the Natya Shastra treatise of ancient India. Such treatises originated via indigenous and shamanic practices in cultures throughout history. They all acknowledged the physical artistic expression, where one was naturally located in space and time (place and seasons), as well as expression of the human mind and psyche.

The preliminary four universal principles use articulation and awareness of: body; space; time; time-space continuum. The time-space continuum uses the body, space, and time, but in freeform ways. Being conscious in this template of The Four Articulations is related to citta in yoga, that is, one's mental awareness while involved physically. One book I recommend that explains how the mind/body works in yoga is the translation and explanation by BKS Iyengar in his "Patanjali's Yoga Sutras". Awareness in action as a universal principle in yoga is also practiced in martial arts, ballet, and classical acting, including Method Acting and Stanislavsky Technique and all of their derivatives. In the book "The Lee Strasberg Notes", he says he simply added 'spontaneity' to Stanislavsky's system. Those systems of yoga, ballet, martial arts, classical acting, and most clown 'training' each and all impose specific aesthetics upon the actor. The Four Articulations for Performance is explained in step-by-step detail in this chapter. Yet, there is no aesthetic imposed nor implied.

The primary universal principle in acting regardless of style is the harmonious and unified use of four elements: body-voice-performance-creativity. This unity I have named "The Principle of Four". The practice is to continually integrate the arms and legs; the hands and feet; the knees and elbows;

eyes and back. One cannot think about all of those at the same time, but, one can feel all of those via awareness of how one is moving in space. This universal whole-body awareness while moving is central to ballet, dance, and martial arts. This is what Patanjali's sutras explain. Throughout any creative exercise one should be centred and grounded with an open sternum, relaxed shoulders, open scapula, and generally with vertical and aligned use of the spine, unless one is making a creative or character choice to distort or to emphasise aspects of the body.

Perhaps the most advanced system for training actors is that of the Chinese opera in which all actors are also acrobats, singers, dancers, mimes. Yet the whole system is based upon Five Principles and Four Techniques. The Five Principles are: eyes, hands, torso, gait, Fa (integration of the first four principles). The Four Techniques are: Acting, Speaking, Singing, Acrobatics.

The Four Articulations for Performance is like an opposite system. Whereas the Chinese, Russian, Indian systems are complex, my system is concise. The five principles and four techniques are used in essence, in a much more simplified way in The Four Articulations. In my method "Principle of Four" is a modern Western approach integrating what the Chinese term five principles and four techniques, but, with the extra idea of the individual's freeform creativity.

Other essential universal principles for performance are integrated within the exercises. Some of those principles are: tempo changes; pause; use of neutral integrated to creative action; positive/negative in space; fingers integrated creatively to the whole body; the six directions (forward, backward, left, right, up, down); those are some principles that can readily be imagined or seen in good performance. They exist in many other methods also, but they tend to be layered beneath aesthetics.

Other extremely useful principles which are practiced in the main template of exercises are explained with the instructions in this chapter.

The Seidenstein Method/Quantum Theatre: Slapstick to Shakespeare/The Four Articulations for Performance are intended to be 'ecumenical' (sic).

That means this approach can work well with any other acting or theatre method.

This approach and its exercises can also assist any acting or theatre method to work better for more people. Almost all acting or theatre or clown or performance methods drive a performer towards particular aesthetics. That very easily becomes dogmatic. The Seidenstein Method focuses on universal principles in acting and allows a performer to investigate and invest based on their own culture, history and performance preferences. Each exercise is clear, specific, simple and adaptable. Most creative exercises have no more than 6 steps. Ideally one does the steps and also does them one's own way. This is yin/yang in action – i.e. accomplishing the task the director has set and also practicing ownership over one's body and journey. Acknowledging and recognising one's own discoveries which includes discovering one's habits, defaults, loss of concentration. Again, referencing Carlo Mazzone-Clementi, he said he "teaches the art of discovery". My work has been to provide a clear way to practice the 'art of discovery'.

The Seidenstein Method is a practical approach to acting and theatre starting with the main warm-up of The Four Articulations. The structure of Quantum Theatre: Slapstick to Shakespeare (established 1993) is a theoretical overview for acting and theatre. There are three templates of ten principles each. The Outer template of ten relates Theatre, Opera, Ballet, Circus, Commedia, Vaudeville, Slapstick, Mime, Clown and One's Artistic Vision as a continuum in the performing arts. The Introduction to the Seidenstein Method and the structure Quantum Theatre: Slapstick to Shakespeare is The Four Articulations which can be taught in five full days of 5 hours per day. Then - like in yoga or martial arts - it is up to the individual to practice even a few minutes a day, even just one or a few exercises. Those who are so inclined will of course invest more time in their own practice. Some people practice the template as presented.

The structure of The Four Articulations is:
    a) The Three Loosenings
    b) The Core Mechanics

c) Quantum Vocal Warm-up - originally suggested by Dr. Flloyd Kennedy of Being-in-Voice
d) The Seven Solos
e) The Three Duets; Triangle Exercise; The Whisper Exercise
f) The Path of Honour

THE THREE LOOSENINGS

In physical training we have different terms such as: loosening up, warming up, training, cooling down, stretching out.

Loosening up is a section that would usually precede stretching, warm-up or training in its various aspects such as cardio, musculation, articulation, strengthening, or flexibility.

We can learn from the old Chinese people who train early in the morning in city parks. Their training in chi gong, tai chi or other martial arts will usually be preceded by a loosening up process of various techniques.

The Four Articulations starts with A) The Three Loosenings. Like in any loosening or preliminary phase of a warm-up or training, one selects movements as The Three Loosenings to assist the joints to open, to lightly move the tendons and ligaments and to get preliminary increase in blood flow through the muscles and to get one's breath to be active and engaged.

All Three Loosenings work with the weight dropping to activate the breath, joints, ligaments, tendons, muscles. All Three Loosenings use weight and wait or action and pause. Throughout the Loosenings one must be alert and active to maintain a good posture with no distortion of the spine, neck, or head. All Three Loosenings use counts.

1st LOOSENING - THE INDIAN CLUB SWING

NOTE: Throughout the Three Loosenings LOOK FORWARD ON THE HORIZON.

Stand with legs open wide and the feet moderately turned out.
Raise and extend the right arm up and outward sideways so that it is in a straight diagonal line from the finger tips of the right hand to the pointed foot of the left leg. The right palm is open and facing downward with the fingers stretched lightly and apart. The left heel is raised.

First action. Drop the arm. Let the weight guide the arm. The arm will naturally swing in front of the body - the elbow will bend - guide the momentum so that the palm crosses in front of the face - as the arm bends back towards the right side - guide the palm past the right side of the head - to the back of the skull - then it sweeps upward towards the right - pausing at the start position of the right arm and fingers in a diagonal line with the left leg and foot.

Note: When the weight of the extended arm drops the left heel should naturally return to the floor.
Note: After the palm passes from behind the skull and the arm begins to extend to return to the start position the left foot will point.

Do this the same way and let the weight drop from the diagonal line three times on the right. Then three on the left. Then two on right, two on left. Then one right, one left, one right, one left.
This count is called "3-3-2-2-1-1-1-1". Note: we will use this count "3-3-2-2-1-1-1-1" in the second action, and we will also use this count "3-3-2-2-1-1-1-1" for the Second Loosening as well.

The first action has a repetition of pauses each time the action returns to its peak diagonal starting position. With the palm facing down. Fingers extended and open. Opposite side's heel lifted and foot pointed. A straight diagonal line. The pause is less than one second, a split second.

The second action has a continual flow. It has two parts to it.
Part one is the basic swing from right to left, left to right, continuously.
The preliminary starting position for the second action:
Swing both your arms to the right side and hold them in what is the initial starting position for the second action - the right arm is straight and the left arm is bent.

THE FOUR ARTICULATIONS FOR PERFORMANCE

Both palms are facing downward, the palms are open, the fingers are gently extended.
Let both arms drop and swing towards the left.
In that action the right arm will bend and the left arm will straighten.
When the pendulum swings the other way the right arm will straighten and the left arm will bend.
Note: the bend of the arm is always moderate and organic. Do not force the bend of the elbow. If the arm is relaxed it will simply bend naturally.

The basic action is based on a pendulum-like swing as the arms drop from the right and swing to the left and vice versa. Try this in one set of three swings in a flow starting from the right. Each swing goes from right to left. You do this first in a set of three continuous, rhythmic, pendulum-like swings. When you start the left heel is raised. As the arms pass from right to left the left heel will go down and the right heel will raise as the arms raise to the left side.
Note: Do not force the arms to raise up high. The starting level is with the straight arm at horizontal or barely above horizontal.
Note: Do not force the arms upward. The Loosenings are to allow the weight to drop downward to increase one's awareness of organic movement.

The swing starts with the arms towards the right, with the right arm straight and the left arm bent.
There will be three preparation swings from the right side before commencing "3-3-2-2-1-1-1-1".
It is ON the third preparation swing that the right arm will commence "3-3-2-2-1-1-1-1".
Throughout the "3-3-2-2-1-1-1-1" the opposite arm will continue to swing, repeating the bend/straight continuously in rhythm with the other arm.

Note: in a sense, one arm is more 'active' as it follows the pattern around the head to the back of the skull to being extended up and outward - and - with the heel of the opposite foot rising or dropping accordingly.

Note: in the beginning phase the second action is slightly more difficult than the first action.

Note: the first action of "3-3-2-2-1-1-1-1" involves a very slight pause each time the arm is extended - whereas - the second action is a continuum with the "3-3-2-2-1-1-1-1" embedded within the continuum.

The third action is to be active with both arms alternating extending and bending. At the same time the heel of the opposite foot will raise and the foot will point as the opposite arm extends away on a diagonal from the opposite heel.

Note: The initiating action will always be to drop the extended arm; one simply sustains an easy swing rhythm dictated by the weight and flow of the arm dropping.

If the third action feels too difficult, simply practice the first and second actions with the "3-3-2-2-1-1-1-1".

2nd LOOSENING - THE SKIER

NOTE: Throughout the Three Loosenings LOOK FORWARD ON THE HORIZON

Stand with feet in a narrow parallel with the feet directly below the hip joints.
Raise both arms with the left arm forward and right arm backward.

Gently, slowly drop both arms - but be sure to guide both arms through the following path:
As the left, front arm drops down and backwards the right arm is dropping also down and forward.
At the same time the knees bend slightly and the torso gently and naturally will twist towards the left side.
Try that again and make sure both arms start to go upward slightly past horizontal.
Try the whole introduction a third time. Feel that the arms naturally go upward.

THE FOUR ARTICULATIONS FOR PERFORMANCE

Now on the fourth time guide both arms to follow up, up, up as the torso turns to face forward and the left arm returns to the front, extended, and the back returns to its starting position back and extended.

Now do the whole action twice from the left hand forward right hand back - but - after the second round drop the arms only half way while bending the knees slightly; this will bring the opposite arm forward, that is, the right arm forward and the left arm backward.

Repeat the whole practice - the mechanics - of THE SKIER but now start three times from the RIGHT arm forward and LEFT arm backward. Each time the torso will now slightly turn towards the RIGHT. On the fourth attempt slowly guide the arms along the path upward and around so you return to this side's starting position of the RIGHT arm forward and the LEFT arm backward.

Now you can do the formal mechanical practice which is:
2 times starting with the left arm forward - all the way UP and around, including the torso twisting naturally towards the left.
Then a half-drop so that the right arm will be forward and left arm backwards.
2 times starting with the RIGHT arm forward - all the way UP and around, including the torso twisting naturally towards the LEFT.
Then a half-drop so that the left arm will be forward and the right arm backwards.

This the formal mechanical practice for THE SKIER:
2
Half
2
Half

At the end of EACH 2 there is a very slight PAUSE.
At the end of each Half there is a very slight PAUSE.

This PAUSE trains your awareness and concentration. This is acting and clown training.

PAUSE IS IMPORTANT. PAUSE COMES BEFORE APPLAUSE.

If you do the mechanical practice for THE SKIER a few times each day, then the actual practice described below is very easy.

If you practice the mechanical practice for THE SKIER every day, then you will know the following and will not need much explanation. Once you really know the mechanical practice well you only need to do the following.

3-3-2-2-1-1-1-1.
3 times starting LEFT arm forward
Half drop
3 times starting RIGHT arm forward
Half drop
2 times starting LEFT arm forward
Half drop
1 times starting RIGHT arm forward
Half drop
1 time starting LEFT arm forward
1 time starting RIGHT arm forward
1 time starting LEFT arm forward
1 time starting RIGHT arm forward

NOTE: The Half drop is simply the organic way to change the side to restart on.
NOTE: When you do '1' time only, the arms meet to be GUIDED TO FOLLOW THROUGH to naturally 'change' with the opposite arm in front. We could say "1 and half drop" as the instruction.
NOTE: Each time the arms drop, the LEGS BEND SLIGHTLY
NOTE: Always GUIDE the arms to begin to go UPWARD after the Half drop. Then simply GUIDE the arms to follow the upward path, turn the torso, and REACH the arms upward with a SLIGHT PAUSE up at the peak and allow the TORSO TO RETURN TO THE FRONT WITH ONE ARM FORWARD AND ONE BACKWARD.

THE FOUR ARTICULATIONS FOR PERFORMANCE

If you have any confusion, keep it simple, go back to the mechanical practice for THE SKIER.

Repeat and practice that every day, then the actual practice will be very easy 3-3-2-2-1-1-1-1 (including Half drop in between each pair of counts: 3-half-3-half-2-half-2-half-1-half-1-half-1-half).

3rd LOOSENING - THE LEG SWING

NOTE: Throughout the Three Loosenings LOOK FORWARD ON THE HORIZON

Stand with feet in a narrow parallel with feet directly below hips.
Raise the right knee in front so the thigh and knee are horizontal but the foot is down.
Keep the left leg and knee straight but not locked.
Six times in a row DROP the knee/leg/foot so that the leg slightly swings backwards and automatically returns to the front. Do not rush but do not pause except after the 6th time when the leg swings forward. HOLD THE LEG STILL. IN FRONT. HORIZONTAL. PAUSE. To do that the muscles around the right hip, which support the hip, will contract slightly to hold/pause.
NOTE: While you do this swinging of the legs, keep the arms relaxed - they will naturally move and swing a little. Do not force the arms to swing. Do not hold the arms still. Let them move naturally from the force of the leg dropping and swinging.
NOTE: The hold/pause after the 6th swing should be about 3 seconds. Long enough to feel your balance and to feel that the posture is correct with the opposite leg straight and the back straight.

Do the same procedure six times starting with the left knee in front so the thigh and knee are horizontal but the foot is down.

Now you will start again on the first side with the right knee up. BUT this time start with the left arm extended gently in front and the right arm extended gently back. So as you now swing the right leg again, six times the arms will also extend and swing.

Starting with the right knee up, the left arm front, the right arm back - then when you drop and swing, the right leg is back and right arm will naturally come front and left arm back - then when the drop and swing reverses, the right knee will come forward and up to horizontal and the left arm will come to front horizontal and right arm back horizontal.

Now try that as one continuous set of six swings, and after the 6th the knee will come forward, left arm front horizontal and right arm back horizontal and hold/pause about 3 seconds.
NOTE: During this hold/pause the arms are guided to drop and hang.

Do the same starting with the left knee up and thigh horizontal, with right arm front horizontal and left arm back horizontal.

Now do the whole 3rd Loosening:
6 times each side with the arms hanging and swinging gently/naturally.
6 times each side with the arms extending and swinging fully each time.

NOTE: On each 6th time as the leg swings forward, knee up, hold/pause 3 seconds.
NOTE: WHEN YOU SWING THE LEG FORWARD, NEVER KICK THE FOOT FORWARD.
NOTE: WHEN YOU SWING THE LEG FORWARD, THE KNEE IS UP, THIGH HORIZONTAL, FOOT DOWN.
NOTE: Throughout the Three Loosenings LOOK FORWARD ON THE HORIZON.
NOTE: This 3rd Loosening is also the preliminary movement for learning the mime illusion for riding a bicycle, in which case as the knee swings forward, the opposite foot's heel raises and one rises onto a demi-pointe. But for the purposes of the Three Loosenings this 3rd Looseing is to release the hip on each swinging side and at the same time to hold one's balance on the opposite leg.

END - THREE LOOSENINGS

THE THREE LOOSENINGS are followed by:
B. CORE MECHANICS

C. QUANTUM VOICE WARM-UP
D. 7 SOLOS
E. THREE DUETS, ONE TRIO, ONE QUARTET
E. PATH OF HONOUR

CORE MECHANICS

Core Mechanics (B) teaches the actor to scan their body while in action. Inside Core Mechanics the most essential movement is #6 The Twist Choreography. The essence of that is further extracted to be The Creative Twist (also called The Vitruvian Exercise). This is the embodiment of The Principle of Four which is an active conscious control/expression of body-voice-performance-creativity. Vitruvian relates to Leonardo da Vinci's most famous mandala of the human with outstretched arms representing the microcosm (human) in the macrocosm (universe). I was inspired by da Vinci's drawing and thus by Vitruvius as well. Those two exercises are explained in the beginning of this chapter. Take your time reading one step at a time. Try one step at a time, as it is explained.

In all movement techniques one has to know: are the feet to be flexed or pointed? Are the knees bent or straight? Elbows bent or straight? Hands relaxed or engaged? Are you meant to roll down or to bend forward? Which of the five actions are you to be applying in any given movement? In backward bends are you to move the bottom of the spine first or the top? Are your feet meant to be parallel or turned out? All of these and their opposites are used sequentially in Core Mechanics.

Core Mechanics takes ten-minutes. The order, counts, changes of direction are valuable for mind-body co-ordination. The Core Mechanics of human movement are essential basics and therefore can have a direct positive impact on one's health, state-of-mind, and ability to learn or teach any advanced movement technique from yoga and tai chi to dance or acrobatics. Core Mechanics has direct application to acting and led to the discovery of the universal principles in The Four Articulations for Performance, in Quantum Theatre: Slapstick to Shakespeare, and in The Seidenstein Method. Core Mechanics is also a 'secret' way to teach clowning. Excellence in clowning. In the ten minutes each actor has hundreds of details to work with and pay attention to, and improve and feel each day. Ten minutes is a 'good' length of a single clown act, or a scene in a show. Importantly - the actor learns to scan their body as one does in work that excels. It is that awareness WHILE moving, having to be present, yet think ahead, that makes Core Mechanics a phenomenal tool for developing to excel as an actor or clown.

CORE MECHANICS

Ten basic mechanical movements found in dance, yoga, and martial arts.
Roll-down
Knees Bend
Undulations
Swings
Lateral Basket
The Twist Choreography
Stretch Handstand
Forward Bend
Backward Bend
Spiral Roll-up

#1. ROLL-DOWN

There are three sections: roll-down; roll-back; flat back forward to horizontal.
There are two versions: arms relaxed and passive through the three sections, and; arms active and fingers engaged through the three sections.
Roll-down Version A.
Stand with feet parallel, toes facing forward, the width of your hips.
Section 1 - Part A - round your neck by dropping your chin downward. As you roll down, let the head hang down. Without any force, without trying to go to your maximum, without reaching for your toes, without trying to go down as far as possible.
Part B - head hanging down, arms passive, fingers relaxed. Lift the stomach by engaging the lower abdomen. Roll up from the stomach with the head

hanging down, until the end, then bring the head up and to a normal straight posture.

Section 2 - Part A - gently, slowly, by lifting the chin, rotate the head backwards at the same time as bending the neck backwards. Do not crunch the head downwards. Backwards but not downwards.

Part B - rotate the chin in a returning direction forward until the chin is in a standard downwards position while standing straight and erect. With the top of the spine and nape of the neck open. Eyes looking straight ahead.

Section 3 - Part A - while keeping the spine and back straight, draw the hips back slightly, dropping the open chest forward and downward only to horizontal. Do not drop the head downward. Do not round the back.

Part B - keeping the back flat and spine straight, at the same time, draw the pelvis forward in a manner that lifts the back from horizontal to vertical, straight, erect.

The practice for Roll-down Version A is done Sections 1, then 2, then 3, and done in that order three times. Each Part (A & B) of each Section is done in six counts. There are thus six parts - A, B, A, B, A, B. The range of movement for Section 1 is a big range. Section 2 is the smallest range. Section 3 is the medium range of movement. The time is the same. Section 1 is 6 counts down (starting by rotating the chin down) and 6 up (starting from the stomach). Section 2 is 6 counts back (rotating the head and neck) and 6 returning. Section 3 is 6 counts forward (with a flat back) by drawing the hips back slightly and 6 up by moving the pelvis forward to bring the flat straight back upward to vertical.

Roll-down Version B (with the arms and fingers engaged).
Stand as in Version A with feet parallel.
Section 1 - Parts A & B - 6 counts down, 6 counts up.
This time hands and arms are not passive but engaged.
Bring the hands slightly forward just in front of the thighs. With the hands slightly cupped so that the fingers are gently curved. Elbows are slightly bent. Scapula is open.
As you bend your chin downward and roll down and back up again, keep your arms, hands, fingers engaged.

Read Section 2 a few times before doing.

Section 2 - 6 counts in Part A, 6 in part B

Lift the elbows upward, then the wrists. As if you were a puppet and strings were lifting the elbows and then the wrists. Positioning your arms raised above with the palms facing each other as before - with the hands slightly curved. Note that this time the elbows are straight.
Warning: This Section 2 Parts A & B need to move in an anatomically correct order.
To go backwards it is very important to move the head and neck back FIRST and to KEEP the head and neck moving back THROUGHOUT Part A.
WHEREAS in Part B it is very important so as not to strain your back that you MUST KEEP the head backwards as you roll up through the pelvis and spine.
Note: To go backwards, the head and neck must lead. To return, the head and neck must stay back until the very end.
In Part A you go down the spine from the rotation of the head to the bottom of the spine with the pelvis going slightly forward as a counter balance for bending backwards.
In Part B you go up the spine starting with a small movement bringing your pelvis and hips in a backwards direction. Keeping the head and neck backwards until the very last movement while moving up the spine.
Read through all of Version B Section 2 just above - again - before trying it.

There are three moving parts of the spine going backwards: cervical (neck), thorax (middle of the back), lumbar (lower back) - plus here in Section 1 - Part B then the pelvis and hips move slightly forward to counterbalance bending backwards.

With the arms raised above the head, elbows straight, hands curved.
Begin by rotating the head and neck backwards. Just after you start rotating the head and neck, add the arms and shoulders moving backwards. BUT - BE SURE to KEEP the head AND neck rotating backwards WHILE the arms are moving backwards.

THE FOUR ARTICULATIONS FOR PERFORMANCE

This movement is very similar to the beginning of yoga's surya namiskar (salutation to the sun).

To return: Leave the head and neck backwards. Do NOT lift the arms. The arms will come up automatically AS the spine aligns vertically. Work the pelvis/hips forward first!!!!! Then slowly moving up the spine until the spine is vertical, THEN align the head and neck with the arms.

Now, open the palms as you spread the fingers wide and active and flat. Moving the hands from the previous curved position to a flat and open position.

Section 3 - Parts A & B - 6 counts in Part A, 6 in part B

Read a few times before doing.

Keep the arms aligned with the head.
Draw the pelvis/hips backward slightly. This works as a counterbalance to bending forward to horizontal WITH the arms, NOT dropping arms down but keeping them aligned with the head and along the same line as your back.
If anything, as you bend forward to horizontal, activate the arms up and backwards so to ensure that your arms do not drop down and forward.
To return to vertical - start by moving the pelvis/hips forward which will bring the back upward to vertical with the arms over your head. Palms flat and facing each other.
After Section 3, your elbows and arms come down to the starting position with the hands just in front the the thighs, now again with the hands cupped lightly.

Note: In Version 2 there are two brief interlude movements. The first is after you do Section 1, you will raise your elbows then your wrists before Section 2. The second is after Section 3, your elbows and arms come down to the starting position with the hands just in front the thighs with the hands cupped lightly.

Now repeat Version 2 - A B elbows lift, A B hands open palms flat fingers spread, A B elbows, softly lower to the starting position with hands in front of the thighs and hands lightly curved. Repeat this three times in a row.

To practice: Do Version 1 with passive arms and hands three times, A B A B A B. Then do Version 2 with arms engaged as described above three times.

In the normal practice of Core Mechanics - Movement #1, Version 1 and 2, takes about one minute.
Each of the 10 movements of Core Mechanics takes approximately one minute so the whole of Core Mechanics - once you know the movements correctly - will only take ten minutes.

The physical movements in Core Mechanics are found in ballet, yoga, martial arts, and good sports training. Core Mechanics is filled with hundreds of counts. One must scan the body while in action, while moving. One has to concentrate every second for ten minutes or do 600 seconds of total concentration. Learning to scan the body for ten minutes in minute detail is the mental or mind's basic process of any great performer. Awareness while doing. At the same time gradually one should pay more attention to one's breathing, the skin on the face should be soft, the back of the tongue soft and wide, the teeth parted, the lips barely touching, the eyes soft and generally facing in a forward direction. In Aikido and martial arts this is called 'soft eyes'. One is not staring forward. One is rather gazing and aware. The shoulders should be soft. The scapula open. The posture vertical, aligned, relaxed but alert.

#2 KNEES BEND

The knees bend then straighten - Heels flat then raised.

There are four moving actions: knees, ankles, knees, ankles. Then the reverse order moving: ankles, knees, ankles, knees. Do not do the movements sudden and jerking but do them slow and fluid in a count of a-b-c-d-e for each moving action: Knees, ankles, knees, ankles reverse ankles, knees, ankles, knees.

Stand with feet parallel at the width of your shoulders or hips.
Bend the knees by allowing the knees to move gently forward.
Rather than doing that fast in one bold action - let the knees gradually bend a-b-c-d-e.
With 'a' initiating the bending action and 'e' being the fully bent position.
The same principle of a-b-c-d-e is for each of the leg's main moving joints; knees and ankles.

Part A:
1. Bend the knees.
2. With the knees bent, flex the feet to rise up on the balls of the feet.
3. With the heels raised up, keep them raised and straighten the knees.
4. With the knees straight, keep them straight as you lower your heels.

Part B:
1. Keeping the knees straight, using the ankles to rise up on to the balls of your feet.
2. Staying on the balls of your feet, bend your knees without lowering your heels
3. Keeping the knees bent, lower your heels without straightening your legs
4. With your heels remaining on the floor, SLOWLY a-b-c-d-e straighten your legs gradually.

Repeat A B four times - A B A B A B A B

Now try to do Movement #1 Versions 1 & 2 three times each, then Movement #2 Parts A & B four times (be sure to alternate A B A B A B A B).

#3 - UNDULATION

There are different ways to do undulations.
Core Mechanics focuses on mechanical movements, not aesthetics.
The undulation, Movement #3 in Core Mechanics, combines actions from Movement #1 and Movement #2.

Stand with feet parallel at the width of your hips or shoulders.

You must read the following instructions through several times before attempting.
If you have problems with your back perhaps you should not do this movement?
Proceed with caution and at your own risk.
If you need to you can adjust any part of the movement in a way that you know for yourself is safe for you.

As with all back movements, if done properly, that is - done in an anatomically correct, organic, chronological order - they will benefit and even strengthen your back. However, CAUTION is required because a back movement done incorrectly can injure you or weaken your back.

If you are not sure - don't do the movement. You can ask any dancer or acrobat or yoga teacher for help and ask them to read the directions and help you to understand and perform the actions safely and in a way that is suitable for your body.

Note: In Core Mechanics' undulation, although your back will bend, DO NOT think of the undulation as 'bending backwards'!!!!!!! In fact you need to think of this undulation as a primary FORWARD action of the pelvis/hips which works as a SAFETY counterbalance to opening the back.

1. Gently bend the knees a-b-c-d-e.
2. Tilt the pelvis forward.
3. Gently press the pelvis further forward at the same time gently bending the lumbar and also opening the thorax (middle of your back). Only then, with the pelvis 'anchored' forward supporting the lumbar and thorax - only then gently bring your neck, then, your head, backwards.

Leave the head back.
Leave the head back.
Leave the head back.

4. Straighten your legs and automatically, without trying, your back, of its own accord will come up with YOUR HEAD BACKWARDS.
5. Only when your legs are straight and most of your spine - except for your neck - most of your spine is straight - then - you can straighten your neck - then rotate the chin in a downward and forward direction so that your head and neck and spine are vertical and aligned.

Repeat 1, 2, 3, 4, 5 five times.
Note:
The legs bend on 1 and straighten on 4.
The neck then head go backwards at the END of 3. The neck and head come up AFTER 4.

Now try Core Mechanics Movements #1, #2, #3 in the prescribed order and number of repetitions above.

Note: #1 uses three actions: roll-down/up; roll neck and head back/up; flat back fwd/up thus it is performed three times for Version A (arms inactive) and Version B (arms & hands active).
#2 uses four actions: knees, ankles, knees, ankles (then the reverse) so it is performed four times including the reverse (ankles, knees, ankles, knees).
#3 uses five actions: knees, pelvis tilt, pelvis/hips forward ending with neck & head back, legs straighten, ending by bringing neck & head up. So it is performed five times.

#4 - SWINGS

Stand with feet parallel at the width of your hips.
Raise arms up and above your head. Elbows straight. Palms forward. Fingers open.
In one action - release the shoulders so that the straight arms swing down and back slightly; at the same time release in the waist so that you bend forward and downward; at the same time bending your knees enough that your bottom drops down to a half-squat. Continue this action into a rebound reversing those three actions so that your arms return to above your head with legs straight and spine vertical.

Now repeat that swing three times in a row.

At the end of the third time - slowly with an a-b-c-d-e softly bend the knees while keeping the arms active and above your head - at the same time as the knees bend, the arms turn in a-b-c-d-e and the palms turn with the arms to face each other. Then reverse. Straighten knees while palms turn forward again to a soft rhythm a-b-c-d-e.

Now do this swing, with the a-b-c-d-e at the end, in three sets of three swings.

To practice: Do Movements #1,2,3,4 as a unit each in its own prescribed details and numbers of repetitions.

Movements #1-4 are done with feet parallel at the width of your hips. #5 is with feet comfortably wide apart.

#5 - LATERAL BASKET

This starts with a transition movement. Transition from feet parallel in #4 with arms over the head, to a comfortable wide position with feet gently turned out with the arms down and palms touching the outside of your thighs.

At the end of #4, i.e. after the third set of three swings, and after the third a-b-c-d-e, you will have finished with your legs straight, arms over your head, palms facing forward.
Then you open your legs wide by moving the left foot outward to the side. At the same time turn both feet outward (this is a moderate turnout at about 45 degrees). At same time you turn your palms to face outward towards the side and lower the arms until your palms come flat against the outside of your thighs.

Then bring your right arm to the front of your right leg with the palm softly facing upward. At the same time raise your left arm slightly forward but above the head with the right palm softly facing downward. As you move both arms, also gently bend each arm slightly.

THE FOUR ARTICULATIONS FOR PERFORMANCE

This is the base default position alternating the left arm up palm down, and right arm just in front of the right leg palm up. Both arms bent. This will alternate to right arm up palm down, and left arm in front of left leg palm up.

From the base position of left arm up palm down & right arm in front of right leg palm up - then stretch gently to the right side with your left arm close to your head. Reverse by coming up. When you are up change the arms - left arm comes out to the side and into the front of left thigh while right arm extends outward to the side while coming up above your head. Do a gentle lateral stretch left. Reverse once more so that left arm is again up and right is down with palm up. Lateral stretch right. Only on this the third time (you've done lateral stretch right, left, now right). Follow the natural curve of the body by gently bringing your torso down to the right. At the bottom of this curve your left hand will link fingers with your right hand, forming your arms like a basket. Keep following the natural curving movement of the torso around to the left side with your arms moving together at the same tempo as you reach a peak on your left side and bring your torso and arms upward at the same time until your arms are over your head.

Practice. Lateral curved stretch right (with left arm up and right arm down). Reverse your arms and stretch on left side. Reverse again and stretch on right side but follow through with the natural curve, joining your hands at the bottom, fingers interlaced, arms gently bent forming a little basket, and swinging gently to the left side and coming up with the torso and arms at the same time.

Practice 1-2-3-around right swing coming up left. Try in order: once right come up left. Once left come up right. Once right come up left. Once left come up right.

That is the pattern for Movement #5 - Lateral Basket = Right. Left. Right. Left.

However, there is a transition movement each time after the basket comes up. When the basket comes up your arms will be above your head. Arms slightly bent in a gentle curve. With the fingers interlocked like a basket. Then you drop both arms - at the same time - outward - to the side but the momentum means that if the arms are relaxed they will swing and cross in front of you. Then you catch the arms in a way that takes you into 1-2-3-around in the opposite direction.

So if you start left arm up 1-2-3-basket, then when your arms drop sideward and swing in front they will also like a pendulum swing back outward at which point you take the right arm outward and up, and left arm down and begin 1-2-3-basket to the left side leading with your right arm over your head. Repeat two more times. 1-2-3-basket right. 1-2-3-basket left.

Practice.
Start with the end of Movement #4 - Swings. Feet parallel.
Do the last set of three swings, a-b-c-d-e finishing with arms above your head palms forward.
Transition movement. As your left foot opens wide to the side, as feet turn out, as arms come downward until the palms touch the outside of your thighs.
Go to the base default position of Movement #5 - Lateral Basket. Left arm over your head. Arm slightly bent in a gentle curve with the palm down. At same time right arm in front of right thigh with arm bent and palm up. Then do the four sets 1-2-3-basket. Alternating right side with left arm up to start. Left side right arm starting up. Right side left arm up. Left side right arm up.

#6 - THE TWIST CHOREOGRAPHY

This is the same as described earlier in this chapter.
Review for clarification. Then proceed with the practice.

Although it may take a few minutes, a few attempts, and a bit of practice, this exercise takes only one minute once you know it. It is invigorating and energising.

To start - stand with feet about one metre apart. Stand in a normal wide stance like you would to do star-jumps (jumping jacks) or in ballet's 2nd Position (à la seconde) or the width of martial arts' "Horse Stance".

Initiate the movement via your pelvis and twist left and right continuously. As you twist forward to the left the right heel should lift gently so that the right knee is not strained.

Likewise as you twist forward to the right the left heel should lift gently so that the left knee is not strained.

Some would consider that such a twist done while standing is more subtly initiated in the sole of the foot pressing gently 'invisibly' into the ground. That is how a martial artist would view it and may thus call it 'torque'.

So you stand with your feet wide apart and twist left and right continuously. At the same time using enough energy in the pelvis so that the arms splay outward.

The arms should be passive and not lifted.

The arms should not be flung. The driving energy should be from the pelvis, not the arms.

The energy used should be just enough so that the arms splay outward and down, but not too much so as to lift the arms to horizontal. The ideal is that the arms are about 45 degrees.

Then, as the arms are passive, they will naturally wrap around one's waist front and back.

The arms splay then wrap, splay then wrap, splay then wrap...

Note that the back arm must be bent at the elbow.

At the same time as the arms are passive yet splayed at 45 degrees, then, when wrapped front and back, the back heel should lift upward and forward so that there is no strain on that leg's knee.

When twisting to the left, the eyes should look towards the left and behind, and the right heel lifts as the foot gently points. Twisting right, eyes right, left heel up, and left foot gently points.

In between left and right, without stopping the movement, the eyes should face front.

All yogic twists start in the pelvis and spiral through the three moving parts of the spine in this order: (pelvis first) lumbar, thoracic, cervical.
It is the same for this standing twist: pelvis, lumbar, thoracic, cervical and additionally the ocular nerve is stimulated by engaging the eyes as you look left, centre, right, centre, etc.

That is the basic standing twist movement which is called 'big'.

There is now a choreography of 4 big, 4 small, 3 big and spin around.

A) "4 Big" Start with the four big left, right, left, right as described above.

B) "4 Small" The four small use the momentum in the arms as the heels now remain on the ground with the pelvis and eyes facing forward, and in four counts the arm movements dwindle. The movement should be left, right, left, right.

C) "3 Big" At the end of the fourth small movement of the arms to the right, the pelvis enlivens again with a big twist to the left with the right heel lifted up. Three big twists left, right, left. But on the third twist you actually lift your arms to horizontal, and open and stretch the fingers of both hands and at the same time spin on the left foot. The right foot will lift slightly above the ground as if drawing a grand circle and finish where it started. If you have difficulty spinning then simply walk the right foot around in a 360 degree circle while rotating on the left foot.

We now call this pattern "4-4-3". With each section 4-4-3 starting to the left side.

D) The final section is "Drop-Centre-Heel-Slowly unwind".

After the '3' big you will have your arms horizontal with the shoulders down and fingers wide open and looking straight ahead.
Drop the arms.
From the centre/pelvis twist to the left. At the same time bend the front knee and as usual lift the back heel. As in the regular big twist the arms will splay out and downward at a 45 degree angle.

This time you 'catch' the movement at 45 degrees and lift the arms to horizontal. With the left arm straight, fingers open, and eyes looking over and beyond the left hand. At the same time bend the right arm so that the right hand is flat, horizontal, but in front of the chest or sternum.

Then as the back heel goes down - the pelvis is automatically pulled back - which also straightens the front knee. At the same time the right elbow draws backwards while the right arm at the same time straightens.

Then you drop the horizontal arms and do the same process to the right side, 4-4-3-Drop-Centre-Heel-Slowly unwind.

E) The whole choreography is Left-Right-Right-Left:
To the left side 4-4-3-Drop-Centre-Heel-Slowly unwind.
To the right side 4-4-3-Drop-Centre-Heel-Slowly unwind.
To the right side 4-4-3-Drop-Centre-Heel-Slowly unwind.
To the left side 4-4-3-Drop-Centre-Heel-Slowly unwind. On this fourth and final section of The Twist Choreography do not drop the horizontal arms. Instead you slowly draw the arms downward until your hands are touching the side of your legs. While lowering the arms draw the left foot to the right foot with the heels touching and the toes splayed out gently at about 45 degrees. That standing position is the start of Core Mechanics movement #7.

The spinal twists in yoga are said to stimulate the central nervous system. Use of the eyes in The Twist Choreography exercise may additionally stimulate the optic nerve. Stimulating the central nervous system and optic nerve also connects with and stimulates the brain. The use of left and right, and counts and an asymmetrical pattern (left right right left, rather than left right left right), the use of the fingers and feet would all help to stimulate the brain and the mind.

#7 - STRETCH HANDSTAND

For acrobatics I use a trilogy of: stretch handstand; jump or tuck handstand; and press handstand. Then there are a variety of other tricks-of-the-trade to teach or learn handstands.

For Core Mechanics I do not ask anyone to ever hold a handstand. In Core Mechanics I do not even ask them to try to hold a handstand. The training to learn and hold and develop a handstand is a separate practice.

In Core Mechanics the idea is to learn the correct alignment to take some weight onto your hands with one or both feet off of the ground, but, only for a split second. Going up and down safely in a controlled way and moving like a pendulum, i.e. just passing the peak.

Stand with heels touching and front of feet slightly turned out. Palms of hands touching the outside of your thighs.

In the first action you will keep the right heel anchored to the ground as you step forward with the left foot into a moderate lunge position with the arms over your head. Palms facing forward. Fingers open.

To intimate the first action.
Ever so slightly let your chest and weight fall forward.
As you fall, let you left foot step lightly forward to a moderate lunge. With the right heel anchored on the ground.
As you fall, and at the same time as you gently step into a moderate lunge, you bring the arms up, aligned with your ears, and parallel, so that the hands are the same width as your shoulders.
That is count #1 - fall to lunge with arms over head but not backwards.

Count #2 is to return to the starting position with the heels touching, feet slightly turned out, palms touching the outside of the thighs.

The action is to push from the left foot which is the front foot. Keep the right leg STRAIGHT. Do not lean backwards. When you push from the left foot you straighten the left leg and bring the left leg straight backwards with the heels touching and toes of both feet turned outward slightly.

Repeat #1 fall then #2 push.
Now do the same action falling to the right foot, and lunge with the left heel anchored. Push from the right foot straightening the right leg. Closing with the heels touching and the feet turned out.

THE FOUR ARTICULATIONS FOR PERFORMANCE

Repeat #1 fall then #2 push.

It is important that the action of the arms going up and palms turning forward is coordinated with the foot stepping into a moderate lunge.

Practice.
Part A of Stretch Handstand
Two times on the left and two times on the right. 1-2, 1-2 and 1-2, 1-2.

Part B uses a count of 1-2-3-4, twice on the left, and twice on the right.

Part B kicking up safely and returning softly.

DO NOT TRY TO HOLD A HANDSTAND IN CORE MECHANICS.

Part B's count #1 is exactly the same as in Part A. However in Part B it is count #4 that is the exact same as Part A's count #2.

Part B's count #2 is to kick the back leg i.e. the straight leg up in the air as the hands lower to having the palms on the floor. Part B's count #3 will happen immediately on its own as your straight leg returns naturally and softly to the position it was in as in count #1.

BE CAREFUL. DO NOT TRY TO HOLD A HANDSTAND. DO NOT TRY TO HOLD A HANDSTAND.

Count #1 fall to moderate lunge on left leg with right heel anchored and arms over head and palms facing forward and arms parallel the width of your shoulders.

Count #2 at the same time as you lower your torso and arms forward and downward to the floor, you also gently kick your straight leg upward with the FOOT POINTED UP TOWARD THE CEILING. The foot is flexed while on the floor and POINTED as soon as you BEGIN to kick the leg up. Just a moment - a split second - after you initiate the kick of the straight leg, you push off from the lunged leg straightening the knee and at the same time pointing the foot and at the same time kicking the formerly bent leg up so that its pointed foot meets the other legs pointed foot.

BE CAREFUL. DO NOT KICK UP HARD. BE CAUTIOUS. DO NOT TRY TO HOLD A HANDSTAND.

DO NOT SWITCH THE LEGS. In other words, if the left leg is in the lunge when you start then when you come down it should also be in a lunge. #3 is the same fixed position as #1. Arms over head. Torso forward. Arms aligned with the ears. Arms parallel. Same width as shoulders. There should be a straight line from the arms through the back and through the back leg which is straight. A straight line fingers to heel.

Thus count #3 happens automatically. But stay in position 3 long enough to make sure your posture is in a straight line and that you are not leaning backwards but that the torso is leaning forward.

Count #4 is pushing from the front foot on the lunge side and at the same time lowering your arms so that the palms touch the outside of the thighs.

Repeat 1-2-3-4 on the left side (left leg to lunge; left leg bent; right leg straight).
Now repeat two times on the right side 1-2-3-4.

Note: The first leg to kick up is the back leg (straight leg) and it is the last to come down!
The second leg to kick up is the front leg (initially bent but it straightens as you push off) and is the first to come down!

Practice left 1-2, 1-2 and right 1-2, 1-2 then left 1-2-3-4, 1-2-3-4 and right 1-2-3-4, 1-2-3-4.

Practice the transition from the end of Movement #6 - Twist Choreography to and through Movement #7 - Stretch Handstand.

DO NOT TRY TO HOLD A HANDSTAND IN CORE MECHANICS. GO UP LIGHTLY, COME DOWN SOFTLY.

THE FOUR ARTICULATIONS FOR PERFORMANCE

Start with Twist Choreography's last set to the left: 4 big, 4 small, 3 big, arms open on the 3rd and you spin around to the left - drop the arms, move the centre to the left, softly bend the left leg, take the arms up with the left arm straight and right arm bent, and the back heel up. As the right (back) heel goes downward the pelvis will be pulled back at the same time as the left leg and the right arm will straighten. You will then be facing forward with the arms outstretched to the side. Palms open and facing down, fingers spread open. Leaning right at the same time as pushing from the left foot and lowering your arms at the same time, closing the left heel to the right heel and ending with the palms touching the outside of the thighs. Thus as you close Twist Choreography you have the correct beginning for Stretch Handstand. The end of Movement #6 is the beginning of Movement #7.

Note: Movements 1-7 are standing, Movements 8-10 are on the floor.

#8 - FORWARD BEND

#8 has five sections.

Section 1. Forward Bend with legs forward.
Sit on the floor (or mat). Legs extended forward. Feet together. Feet pointed. Arms above the head. Hands lightly cupped. Fingers gently open. The action is to move the front of the rib cage forward towards the thighs. The arms should not drop. The arms should stay the width of the shoulders. The arms do not move - the torso moves forward.
Keep the back straight and arms still and legs straight and feet pointed as you bring the torso up to vertical.

Practice. Bend forward, return three times. The action should be smooth and gradual.

Section 2. Forward Bend with lowering arms and head.
The first action is the same as Section 1. Simply bring the rib cage to the thighs.

Second action, while looking forward with rib cage near thigh, then lower the arms and hold on to the legs with your hands.

Third action, pull yourself downward with the arms and hands, and lower your neck and head.

To return:

The first action, the head comes up and you gently try to lengthen or straighten the back.

Second action, raise the arms so they feel like an extension of the back - one line.

Third action, slowly bring the torso to the starting position with arms above the head and the hands lightly cupped.

Practice forward actions and return actions three times.
Forward actions 1-2-3 and return actions 1-2-3. Repeat two more times.

Section 3. Lateral twist and stretch. Seated with legs forward and feet pointed and arms over the head. Open the legs wide. Keep feet pointed.

A. Make a small twist to the left. Then keeping your arms over your head - keep them parallel, the width of the shoulders - at the same time bring the outside of your right rib cage towards your right thigh. Return upward to centre.

B. Twist to right. Lower outside of left rib cage towards left thigh. Return to centre.

Practice. Three times A, B.

Section 4. Pancake. With arms still over the head. Now flex the feet so that the toes point up and backwards but the heels are extended forward.

Note: Depending on your hamstrings, and inner thigh (abductors) flexibility, you will be able to do one of the following while seated with your legs wide apart and feet flexed.

A) if you are already used to such a pancake position simply reach forward lying flat with you hands over your head
B) If you are not all the way flat then let your arms relax and let your head hang forward which allows the weight of the arms and head to naturally stretch you

THE FOUR ARTICULATIONS FOR PERFORMANCE

C) If your pelvis is rolled back and you can't comfortably lean forward without stress then you do the following: place your hands on the floor behind you with the fingers pointing away from you, then, gently press the palms of the hand down to the floor, and, at the same gently straighten your elbow. This will push the pelvis forward into the correct position for stretching.
D) If any of those are too stressful you can try yoga variations such as bringing the soles of the feet together and holding on to your ankles or place your hands on your bent knees and gently straighten the elbows to increase the stretch pressure

Section 5. Splits. With your legs straight and open wide. Point your feet.

Note: Depending on your flexibility, do any of the following:

A) If you are already able or nearly able to do the splits with BOTH legs straight, then place your left hand on the floor behind you and your right hand on the floor in front of you, and by supporting yourself up slightly by using the hands on the floor, then rotate the back hip and at the same time turn your torso to the left. While in the split position, work the front of the right hip towards the floor, have your back straight and chest open. This is only if you are able or nearly able to do the splits with BOTH legs straight. Then, keeping the feet pointed, come back to the centre facing front again, then place the right hand behind, and left hand in front, and rotate to the right.
B) If you are not able to do full splits you can try to have your left hand behind, and right hand in front, and lift your pelvis up and off of the ground but keep both legs straight and turn towards the left. Hold for 20 or 30 seconds, then come down and reverse in the other direction - right hand behind, left in front, lift and turn towards the right.
C) If you can not accomplish 'B' with the legs straight. Bend your left leg, and, turn to face left. Stay 20 or 30 seconds. Then do the same on the other side - right leg bent, face right side. When you have your leg bent, put your opposite hand on the bent knee and try to have you back straight/vertical and chest open. If you feel stable and secure in that position you can then add torque. Make a very slight, small twist

with your torso gently towards the side of the bent knee and work the straight leg's front thigh gently in a forward and downward direction.

Transition. After Splits - or your version of working towards a split - then with both legs straight, feet pointed, legs open wide, bring your straight legs and pointed feet together. Relax your elbows. Contract in the lower abdomen/stomach and roll backwards while keeping the legs straight and arms hanging and bent until you are laying on your back with your arms near your sides, and the palms facing up.

#9 - BACKWARD BEND

The Backward Bend consists of a half bridge and a full bridge. The full bridge works three main parts of the body in this order: first, pelvis and back; second, arms trying to straighten; third, if the arms are straight, trying to straighten the knees which pushes your chest in a forward position while you are upside down or inverted.

Part A - Half Bridge.
Bend your knees. Have your feet flat on the floor close to your buttocks.
Keep your feet flat and heels down in the half and full bridge.
Hold on to your ankles, or your heels, or have your hands on the floor palms down.
Tilt the pelvis up and towards your chin.
Then raise the lumbar or lower back.
Then raise the thorax or middle back.
Then raise the upper back and open the chest.
At this peak position there are two directions - the pelvis is upward in the direction of the ceiling, and, the chest is forward in the direction of the chin.
Without moving the neck, allow the neck to relax. As in yoga - relax the skin on the face, relax the eyes, relax the back of the tongue and allow the teeth to be parted and lips lightly touching. Release any tension in the mouth. As in yoga, those details allow your breathing to be free.
To return, lower the spine and back in this order: upper, middle, lower, pelvis.

Two more times go up and down in the same order. To go up, start at the pelvis and bottom of the spine. To come down, start at the upper spine and gradually come down the spine until the pelvis melts to the floor.

Transition movement. Raise your arms vertical - shoulders on the floor - elbows and hands straight - fingers open. Then - bend your elbows and place your palms near or under your shoulders with the fingers towards your shoulders.

Part B. Full Bridge.
You will do exactly what you did for the half bridge, up and down, and you will also activate the arms. As your pelvis tilts, your hands press into the floor. As your back goes upward, you try to straighten your elbows. Keep the feet flat and the heels on the ground. Then if your elbows are straight or almost straight - without moving your feet, gently try to straighten your knees. As your knees and legs begin to straighten they will press your chest in a forward direction.
To return to the floor: keep your pelvis up until the back is on the floor.
To return to the floor: with control in your arms, begin to bend the elbows and slowly lower your upper back to the floor. Then roll down your spine as you did in the half bridge but keep your hands under your shoulders.
Repeat two more times up and down. Pelvis-back-arms-knees. Elbows-back-pelvis.

Note: when going up, lift your pelvis upward towards the ceiling but try not to let your pelvis move towards your feet. Try not to slide towards your feet, rather move towards your chest. When you come down do not slide towards your feet. By using the arms to control your descent try to come straight downward.

Practice. 3 half bridges then 3 full bridges.
Then.
Counter Pose.
Bring your knees to your chest with feet together and feet pointed. Place your hands on your shins. Bring your head towards your knees. You are in a little ball.

Then extend your hands and arms forward 45 degrees with the elbows straight.

Keep your head up and forward towards your knees.

Then while keeping the head forward - extend your knees up and forward 45 degrees in a dynamic way so that your legs and feet pull your back forward so that you are sitting in a V-position with your arms strong, straight forward past your legs.

While holding the V-position. Turn your palms upward. Open your feet slightly.

Keep your head up and forward.

Keep your legs and arms strong, straight, active.

Then with straight arms and legs lower your body until all of the bones touch the floor at the same time.

Heels. Back of hands. Back of skull. All touch the floor at the same time.

Then melt. Let go of any tension. Take a relaxed full breath.

Practice. Repeat from the ball to the V to your back to full breath. Three times.

#10 - SPIRAL ROLL UP

Part A.

Laying on your back. Palms up. Feet apart. Arms near your sides but not touching.

In one movement you will simultaneously do these five actions:

Contract in the stomach.

Both knees bend together to the right side.

Your right arm slides on the floor from your side to above your head and lies still on the floor. Your right arm will finish in straight line with the line of your back.

Your left hand will come in front of your body. Both palms will be down, on the floor.

Your head will rotate so that it rests on your right bicep.

Practice.
From laying on your back with palms up. Do those five simultaneous actions finishing with your legs bent, both palms down, head resting on the straight arm's bicep.
Do this three times on the right and three times on the left. Always start flat on your back with palms up to start. Palms down at finish.

Part B.
Resting on right side. Knees together and bent to the right. Head resting on right bicep. Palms down.
Extend the upper leg (left leg) so that the left foot slides on the floor and in a straight line with your back.
Extend the pointed foot. Extend the left hip. Keep your head downward towards your right arm. If you need to, simply gently press your left palm into the floor which will help you to sit up.
The left leg and foot work like a rope. The leg pulls the hip. The hip pulls the torso. The torso pulls the head. This is all organic. Be gentle. As your left leg pulls you up, your left hand can push into the floor, but your right arm should be passive and slide on the floor until your right hand is palm down near your right hip.
Repeat three times on your right side and three times on your left side.

Note: when you are sitting up, one leg is bent and one is straight. The hand on the side of the bent leg should be palm down near your hip. Be sure to be seated on both sit-bones. Also, sometimes people's straight leg will be turned inward and making sitting awkward. Rotate your straight leg with the foot pointed. And turn out so that the thigh is either upward or slightly towards backward.

Part C.
In one movement you will do the following four actions:
Keeping the outside hand palm down on the floor, reach the other hand, parallel and the width of your shoulders, coming to a palm down position. Bend the knee of the straight leg, bringing it parallel to the other knee, with the knees apart at the width of your hips.
At the same time move your feet from pointed to flexed.

Finishing with the balls of the feet on the floor and the knee that moved about one or two inches off of the floor.

So you come almost to your "hands and knees with feet flexed" except the second knee (this was the leg that was straight a moment ago) is slightly off of the floor.

Practice this from the seated position with one leg straight and the opposite hand on the floor palm down. Three times on the right. Left leg straight, then moving towards the right to come to 'all fours'. Three times on the left. Right leg straight, then moving towards the left to come to 'all fours'. "All fours" is an English expression for resting on your hands and knees.

Part D.
From 'all fours' with one knee slightly off of the floor and both feet flexed. Push your hips backwards from your hands against the floor and at the same time walk your hands backwards a bit until your heels are flat on the floor and your legs are half bent. Your head hangs down.

Note: Do not squat. Do not straighten your legs. Draw the hips backwards on a horizontal line as your push backwards from your hands.

Part E.
Your heels and feet are parallel at the width of your hips. Your feet are flat on the floor. Your legs are half-bent. Your head is hanging down. Your arms and hands are hanging down passive.

Then. Lift your lower abdomen/stomach. As you roll up your spine, your head hangs, arms are hanging and passive. Legs straighten at the same time and tempo as you roll up the spine.

Note: Do not 'stand up' …. But do roll up.

Practice from 'all fours' one knee slightly off of the ground.
Press back to get your feet flat with the legs half bent, head hanging, arms passive.
Activate the stomach and gently, at the same time as you roll up, also gently straighten the legs.

THE FOUR ARTICULATIONS FOR PERFORMANCE

Repeat three times. #10 Spiral Roll Up is done only once at the end of Core Mechanics.

CORE MECHANICS OVERVIEW

In Core Mechanics Movements 1-7 are standing. 1-4 are standing with feet parallel at the width of the hips. In 5 and 6 one stands in ballet 2nd position with feet wide and turned out moderately. 7 starts with feet in ballet 1st position turned out moderately with heels touching, then one steps into a moderate lunge, alternately left and right sides. 8-10 are done whilst on the floor either sitting or laying back, with 10 spiralling back up to standing with feet parallel as in 1.

After each movement below (except for 6 Twist) the first number represents the basic parts of the body used in that movement, the second number represents the number of repetitions, and in movement 1 there is a third number which indicates that there are two versions of this exercise. For example, in movement 1, "3 x 3 x 2" stands for: 3 parts of the body - spine roll fwd, top of spine roll backwards, flat back lean forward to horizontal; 3 repetitions; 2 versions - first with hands and arms passive (hanging, not engaged), then with hands and arms engaged. In movement #6 Twist Choreography the numbers 4-4-3 represent the repetitions of twists as in 4 big - 4 small - 3 big.

The following list of the ten movements of Core Mechanics is for anyone who has already completed a five-days introduction. The list is not instructions. If however you have movement training, you can search on youtube for "The Four Articulations". In that video I present only the Three Loosenings and Core Mechanics. The video was filmed during Winter so I start with a vigorous 4 minutes Chinese exercise routine.

CORE MECHANICS - List of the 10 movements and their counts. Not instructions.

1) Roll Down – 3 x 3 x 2. Three movements of spine a. fwd roll down, b. neck backwards, c. flat back fwd to horizontal. Two sets, one without use of arms i.e. arms simply hang and the other active use of arms.

2) Legs Bend Straighten – 4 x 4. a-b-c-d-e concept, i.e. movement vs action.
3) Undulation – 5 x 5. 5 parts a. plié (as in #2), b. turn pelvis upward and fwd, c. push hips and pelvis fwd (think FORWARD) moving through spine to full arch with head and arms hanging, d. straighten legs, that will straight back (keep head back!!), e. roll up neck (as in #1).
4) Swings – 3 x 3. Reach arms above head, release armpits, hips, knees at once swinging down & back return like a pendulum to arms above head.
5) Lateral Basket – 4 x 3. Take wider position turn out feet.
6) Twist Choreography – 4-4-3-drop-twist-heel. Left-Right-Right-Left. Use eyes. 4 big - 4 small - 3 big. Arms drop - pelvis twist - back heel lowers to initiate slowly unwinding arms horizontal.
7) Stretch Handstand – 1-2 x 2 (left & right). 1-2-3-4 x 2 (left & right). Reach hands away from front foot and returning bring front foot in close to hands. Position 3 is the secret.
8) Seated Fwd Bend. a. 3 x straight, b. 3 x Torso-Arms-Head/Head-Arms-Torso, c. open legs wide with arms over head (as in Lateral Basket) 3 x left/right, d. rest fwd 30 seconds deep breaths, e. straight leg splits left & right. Secret is rib-cage to thigh.
9) Arch & Bridge – lay on back, bent legs. 3 Arches. 3 Bridges. Back-Arms-Legs.
10) Corpse Pose Spiral to Roll-Up.

Core Mechanics was created in 1976 by Ira Seidenstein.

END - CORE MECHANICS

CORE MECHANICS IS FOLLOWED BY
QUANTUM VOCAL WARM-UP
SEVEN SOLOS
THREE DUETS, ONE TRIO, ONE QUARTET
THE PATH OF HONOUR

QUANTUM VOCAL WARM-UP

My colleague Dr. Flloyd Kennedy had attended a number of my workshops and suggested that I precede the first creative solo, The Creative Twist, with a short vocal warm-up. Originally we used a selection of techniques from her work called Being-in-Voice. One can use many exercises, techniques and methods to draw from to do a vocal warm-up. You are welcome to select your own. I prefer to keep this section very brief, minimal.

A good voice warm-up should be preceded by a short physical warm-up. The Three Loosenings and Core Mechanics will be adequate for that purpose.

The main things I prefer to focus on are the concentration and relaxation for the purpose of vocal awareness which includes good posture.

There are two sections: 1) "Vocal Hello", and, 2) "Cultural Singing"

Section 1) The Vocal Hello

Step 1 - relax while taking conscious breaths
A) Relax your face, your jaw, your eyes, your shoulders. Relax your tongue, let it be soft and wide. Allow the back of the tongue to relax.
B) Place your hands on your belly.
As you breathe, keep the shoulders down and relaxed.
C) Take 2 conscious breaths in and out through your nose. Keep your mouth and tongue relaxed.
D) Take 2 more deep breaths - imitating the way a baby breathes: when you inhale, let your belly expand slightly, and when you exhale your belly may contract ever so slightly.
E) Take another 2 complete breaths, but, this time, let your rib cage expand sideways.

Step 2 - hum and maaa
A) Relax and be aware of the mouth as if it were a cave.
B) Inhale. On the exhale hum for about 6 to 8 counts. Repeat twice.
C) Same as B but at the end of 4 counts let your mouth open so the sound maaa or aah is released for another 4 counts. Try to have the sound of the hum be the same minimal intensity as the maa or aah. Repeat the hum/maaa or hum/aah three times.

Step 3 - deep aah

A) Inhale. On the exhale let a deep note aah out for 4 to 8 counts. Repeat three times. Try to relax enough so that the deep aah is smooth and soft. It does not need to be loud.

Step 4 - Using the first movement from Core Mechanics, the Roll Down. Only for this vocal work do not contract the stomach when you roll up. The Roll Down begins with the head rotating with the chin dropping towards your chest. For this vocal work use your lower voice register and let out a deep aah. Try to roll down and roll up in a single breath at the same time as letting the aah out. If you are short of breath, then top up your breath (inhale again) at the end of the roll down before the roll up. Repeat the deep aah Roll Down three times.

Step 5 - loud 'hey', a relaxed shout across the room. This is percussive. Repeat three times.

Once you are familiar with this warm-up, instead of repeating the exercises three times, only repeat them twice. Remember this is a minimal warm-up, a "Vocal Hello". Use any other exercises that you prefer, but use a minimal amount of time.

That warm-up can take 3 or 4 or 5 minutes.

When I do other work, particularly with classical acting and Shakespeare, which follows after the daily training in The Four Articulations, I will begin that class with a voice warm-up that includes more work focused on one's lower voice register, and then proceed to articulation and diction exercises, and then on to movement with any Shakespeare monologue or soliloquy.

Section 2) Cultural Singing
3 to 5 minutes

Each actor should face outward towards the wall or window or facing outdoors. Stand at least one metre from a wall or window.

Each actor sings the first childhood song that comes to mind. In any language. If you don't remember the words, you can use "la la la...." or "da da da ...." to the tune. If it is not a childhood song, simply sing whatever song comes to mind. As this is done often in a room with 16 people singing at the same time, the volume should be 'turned down' - minimal. You do not need to sing the whole song.

Then as this song fades or evolves, another tune or song will come up and you sing that.

You may sing one song. You may only remember the chorus and you can repeat that. You may only remember a few of the words so you can sing la la al or da da da etc for the missing words.

The objective is to sing whatever comes up. To release your subconscious. Often this exercise will release memories and thoughts about your past. In a group situation I will say "1 more minute" and then I might say "when you are ready bring your song to an end". Then I will sometimes ask the actors to join me in a circle, standing, and ask "Did anyone notice anything?". Of course people notice all kinds of things, but they may not want to share any of that. Some people will share something that they notice, or they will notice what comes up from their mind, memory, or subconscious.

END - QUANTUM VOCAL WARM-UP

QUANTUM VOCAL WARMUP IS FOLLOWED BY:
SEVEN SOLOS
THREE DUETS, ONE TRIO, ONE QUARTET
THE PATH OF HONOUR

After the Quantum Vocal Warm-up the actors begin The Seven Solos. In a group situation The Seven Solos are done simultaneously. But the timing is individual. The general goal is to do The Seven Solos in about 15 minutes. For one year I had mainly two full-time students. For several months their seven solos took about 45 minutes. Then one day I pointed that out to them and said «let's try this week to keep The Seven Solos to 15 minutes and see how that feels for you».

So even though I say 15 minutes, you may want to take 2 hours. That is up to you. However, doing The Seven Solos in 15 minutes is a different experience than doing them in 45 minutes or longer. Longer or shorter is not 'better'. They are two different experiences. Another actor who worked with me for five months full-time would become so creative during the 2nd Solo that he would just stay with whatever idea evolved and from that exercise was able to create many wonderful solo clown/mime acts which we would then work on and develop during the day. We would rehearse and edit and polish each of those over several weeks. During the weeks we may work on several pieces each day.

The Four Articulations for Performance is in fact something quite remarkable in its enabling individuals, teams, and groups to 'find themselves' progressively and methodically, yet with no overriding aesthetic imposed on one's self discovery. The purpose in part is to provide a practical warm-up that is pleasant and productive and creative for performers - on a daily or regular basis. However, isn't the overall goal to increase or to rediscover one's creativity? If so then The Four Articulations for Performance is a diving board for your own process, for your own creativity, which may be in writing or composition or visual art as well as the performing arts. Creativity is as much an experience and experiment in the mind and body as it is in a specific craft or art form.

THE SEVEN SOLOS

The Seven Solos is a succinct series of creative physical exercises which challenge and focus one's spatial and temporal awareness. The exercises also challenge one's left and right brain engagement by providing a very simple set of steps and restrictions for each exercise, a short open creative opportunity to tap into your subconscious, and, conscious creative imagination; as well as into your emotional range; and, the energetic feeling in your body at any given moment.

The first three Solos are creative walking exercises, the next two exercises are in a stationary location, and the last two exercises combine walking and stationary elements within a geometric form as well as using the six primary directions of: forward, backward, left, right, up, down.

Within The Seven Solos there are various instructions as to whether the arms or legs are to be straight or bent at various moments at the beginning of the Solos.

Importantly, replicating a secret of clowning and good acting is the varied use of a pause applied as yin to the yang of action. A pause is not a stop as in a finality but is an arrested action like a cat pausing in its creative, imaginative, playful chasing of a mouse or a fly. It is a pause to proceed further and perhaps faster, rather than a pause to quit the chase.

One other concept is factored into these very simple Solos and that is an introduction of a few key universal principles that the more refined clowns and actors actually use in performance. For example, one that was introduced in Core Mechanics, Movement #2 - Knees Bent Knees Straight, the "a-b-c-d-e". This principle is to learn to 'take your time'. The action is prescribed by the instructions, but you are the one doing the action. If we think - bend the knee - it is considered a single abrupt action, whereas in fact there is a transition and transformation in the process of going from straight legs to bent knees and vice versa. Take your time does not mean go slow. It means maintain and increase your awareness of whatever you are doing as a performer, whether it is in any of the clown's or actor's four areas of being professional: warm-up or training or rehearsal or performance. The physical performers such as dancers and acrobats also learn to cool down or stretch out after any of those four sessions.

Generally speaking, another valuable training and performance universal principle is to have your eyes on the horizon.

As in painting, the artist decides how big the painting will be and makes the frame and canvas according to that size. In other words, sometimes in art and performance we make a limitation before we start. Each of the Creative Solos starts with a formal, clear limitation.

The Seven Solos.
The 3 walking exercises.

Creative Solo #1 - THE CREATIVE TWIST

During this exercise one can move freely in any direction throughout the exercise. Ideally, you have already read this exercise at the beginning of this chapter, and have practiced it a few times? If you have not, please go to the beginning of this chapter and read and try The Creative Twist. It is one of two central exercises which provide a reference point for all of the following exercises.

Creative Solo #2 - THE NOTHING EXORCISE

Named so, because it is so simple - it looks like 'nothing'. However, its simplicity allows something deep to come spontaneously from the performer in such a way that it often surprises the performer. The surprise is often that some creative idea just happens in a way that they never would have thought up as an idea. Thus the 'exorcise' part implies the clearing out of something deep within the subconscious. That occurs not by intention but by the simplicity of the exercise which allows new and untested ideas to arise organically without effort.

In this exercise, although it starts with a normal pedestrian walk forward until you Pause, after the Pause you can stay on the spot or move anywhere in any way depending only on your own spontaneous creative exploration. Furthermore, even though there are clear instructions to start the exercise, after the Pause you can proceed as you wish and there is no aesthetic imposed.

The Nothing Exorcise begins ideally at the back of a room, and the performer walks towards the front. This replicates starting "upstage" at the back of a theatre and proceeding directly in a straight line "downstage" towards the front. If working in a studio one only needs to walk about 4 or 5 metres. Although you start at the back of the room, you walk in a forward direction but there is no need to go all the way to the front. If you are working at home take small steps forward.

As you walk forward you will move your arms (one arm, either arm, or both arms together) about 3 or 4 times. The movement of the arm or arms is to be in front of you in any form. Do not move the arms continuously, rather move them to any position and keep them there 1 or 2 seconds, then from there move the arm or arms to any second position and keep them still 1 or 2 seconds, then from that second position move them to a third position.

Do not make a formal or expressive gesture with the arms or hands. Simply move the arm or arms to any position and hold them still as you continue to walk forward.

The arms can be: bent or straight; up or down; one arm can be in one direction, the other arm in another direction.

Do not make the arms parallel generally. Do not try to reach forward. Simply move an arm or both arms to any position. When moving both arms at the same time the arms do not need to match.

While walking in a straight line forward, move your arms to 3 or 4 still positions and move the arms from one position to the next without dropping the arms.

Anticipate stopping your walk. Do not force yourself to stop abruptly. While you are stopping in the last 1, 2, or 3 steps, do not move your arms. Do not move your arms while you are stopping.

Part A. Walk straight forward about 4 or 5 metres if in a studio or outside, or, a few steps if working at home. While walking move your arms to 3 or 4 positions holding the arms still for a moment. Do not drop your arms. Move the arms from one position directly to any other position. Do not make creative formal expressive gestures - simply move the arms to a fresh position. Anticipate stopping but do not move your arms while you are stopping.

When you stop - your arms will be still and in front of you - up, down, sideways, straight, or bent, etc.

Pause in that shape with the legs straight, arms in front, feet parallel about the width of your hips.

Your eyes should remain relaxed and gazing on the horizon.

Part B. Pause about 4,5,6,7,8 seconds. After you Pause in one movement you will move your whole body including bending the knees and moving the arms. Do not drop the arms. Move the arms but do not drop them and in the same moment also bend the knees and go with whatever feeling in the body gets triggered or initiated. Go with your feeling and improvise with that for 30 or 40 seconds or a minute or so.

Then stop. Relax the body in one second. Drop your idea. Drop what you are doing. Relax the arms. Do all of that in one second.

Then return to the starting position "upstage" and repeat the exercise 2 more times.

When you start the exercise you are standing "upstage" with the arms and hands relaxed and hanging by your side, fingers relaxed.
When you get to the front your arms will be active, still, and held somehow in front of you - up, down, sideways, bent, straight etc.
After the Pause move your whole body at once including bending the knees and moving the arms but do not drop the arms. This triggers a feeling or image or idea or movement rhythm. Go with that feeling, image, idea, or rhythm improvising spontaneously. Do not just talk. Move. If your voice or speech activates spontaneously, do not let that override your movement or feeling. Trust your movement, body, feeling. Keep going for 30, 40 ... 60 seconds or so.

If you feel the energy dwindling or dying down, simply add a detail to what you are feeling. Make it more real. More specific in any way. Add a second detail and your energy will naturally pick up again. You can stop, drop, change or adjust whatever you are doing at any time .... But if you stop, drop, change, or adjust, do so only for a few seconds up to perhaps 10 seconds and then pick up the original feeling or idea. You can go back and forth from the original to something else as many times as you want but the important thing is to be able to return to the original.

After you improvise for about 30-60 seconds simply stop and relax everything in one second. Then return to "backstage" and do another Nothing Exorcise.

Some universal principles here are: learn to anticipate; add a detail; make what you are doing more real; there is no imposed aesthetic unless you chose one to explore; the objective is simply to trigger your own imagination, creativity and subconscious in one simple movement; add a second detail; do the opposite. The word 'opposite' can be interpreted in infinite ways. If you are moving fast, the opposite can be slow or smooth or with sudden stops. If you are imagining a situation, the opposite can be moving with no image or moving in a different way or suddenly laughing or crying, something that has nothing to do with the original situation.

Sometimes in a workshop I will explain that when I clap, the actors should do the opposite, when I clap a second time they return to the original. Then a clap to a new opposite, next clap return to original. Once more a new opposite, clap to original. Often the performer is literal to the opposite, but by doing another opposite their mind begins to open, and by the third opposite they realise an instruction by a teacher, director, choreographer or colleague can be interpreted. Opposite does not have to be literal and it can be interpreted many ways.

This is an incredibly useful universal principle - not only as a simple tool but also to understand that as an actor, clown or artist, you need to interpret your own choices and release your own self imposed limitations in order to research and to allow the subconscious and your spontaneity to assist your creativity.

The art of spontaneity was the major adjustment that Lee Strasberg made to Stanislavsky's great system for training actors. This is explained in the verbatim book "The Lee Strasberg Notes" that is taken from his oral teachings during the last seven years of him teaching at The Actors Studio.

The Nothing Exorcise thus can be seen as the essence of great acting - trust your body, trust your instincts, trust your spontaneity, trust your interpretation and additionally challenge and break your own limited definitions of a role, a character, a direction. Play however you want for one minute. Then drop it. Relax immediately in one second. Try a new way for one minute. And again and again. If you find something interesting, play with it, do the opposite, come back to the original.

Creative Solo #3 - THREE WALKS

There are three versions of The Three Walks.
I use the word 'walk' but that can be misleading as it is not a normal pedestrian walk but a rhythm. I keep the word 'walk' to honour one of my teachers Carlo Mazzone-Clementi who occasionally had one actor at a time try to create many different walks. But I saw that unless the actor made an interesting shape then the walks were very cliché and predictable with mundane results. So I analysed what I was doing that made my results different. It was that I made a shape before I stepped forward and also that I played and created rhythms and virtually danced across the room.

Version A. Shape-Pause-Rhythm. Make a shape with your whole body. Include bending or engaging the knees and legs. Include your arms and hands and fingers.
Pause means hold the shape for about 2 seconds or so. Then make a rhythm that takes you across the room.

This exercise moves from Stage Right to Stage Left then to Stage Right then once more to Stage Left. Stage Right is a classic theatre term meaning the actor's right side as the actor faces straight forward towards the audience and Stage Left means the actor's left side. So in classic theatre when rehearsing, if the Director says 'could everyone please move one step Stage Left' that means everyone moves to the left side at that point when facing straight forward towards the audience.

This exercise thus reminds the actor of basic traditional stage craft and terminology. Additionally, this exercise works the stage movement in a perpendicular direction to The Nothing Exorcise that goes from Upstage towards Downstage. Both of those walking exercises provide an alternative to the arbitrary directional movement of the first walking exercise The Creative Twist.

Practice. Shape-Pause-Rhythm from one side of the room to the other side in a direct line or in a repeated pattern for example: zig-zagging; or spiralling left, right, left, right; or moving in small circles as you proceed across the room from one side to the other.

Note: This is not an improvisation per se, but a shape moving in a rhythm across the room.
Note: This is my simplest exercise.
Note: Its usefulness is unlimited in its application and adaptability for acting, clowning, improvisation, rehearsal, finding a character, creating a stage entrance or exit.
Note: Additionally, the universal principle of shape-pause-rhythm is used within several other of my method's exercises: in the last two Creative Solos; in The Path of Honour, which is the latter section of The Four Articulations; and in Auxiliary Exercises such as The Cleopatra Exercise and The Clown Knows Exercise.

Version B. One shape - three different rhythms. Version A is three times making a different shape with a different rhythm each time.

Note: Ideally the shape does not dictate the rhythm. Your interpretation of the shape does not need to be literal. Therefore the purpose of Version B is to assist an actor to learn how to unlock their way of thinking so that they can work beyond literal interpretations and work in more abstract and conceptual art thereby taping into their subconscious.
Note: This is a simple exercise but if practiced regularly it can and will unlock your creative potential. Even though it is so simple, and perhaps because of its simplicity, it is fundamental to the performing arts.

Version C. Shape-pause-face-rhythm. Sometimes people are so focused on the physical aspects that they block their facial and eyes expression. In Version A and B, in The Nothing Exorcise and in any improvisation, your face, eyes and voice should be free and at liberty to respond spontaneously to the way your body and imagination are unfolding dramatically at any given moment.

Note: 'face' means make an active facial expression including the expressivity of your eyes and breathing.

Note: Version A, B, C should each take about one minute or so to do.

The Seven Solos - The 2 stationary exercises

Creative Solo #4 - THE MIME EXERCISE

This exercise is done start to finish on one location.

The full name of this exercise is: "The-all-inclusive-mime-exercise-the-only-mime-exercise-you'll-ever-need-for-the-rest-of-your-life". Even though it is a joke, it is the actual name of the exercise and in essence it does show the heart of mime within a single exercise. As the great mime researcher and teacher Etienne Decroux and his prodigy Marcel Marceau found - in mime if you stay in one spot, you will conjure the most important mime techniques to express anything in the world through mime. Further, if the mime stays focused on one location, the audience's imagination can open.

Note: This is not to say that a mime can not or should not move off of one location, rather it is to say don't move unless you have to, and also, if you do move, you need to know what you were doing so that in the story you are able to return to an exact location. For example, in a mime if you were cutting bread on a table and then have to go to the refrigerator to get the butter and to a drawer to get a butter knife, then you need to retain a body awareness of all three of those locations. So the first thing is to know and stay on one location.

<u>This particular mime exercise is to learn the universal principle of the immense creativity in the fingers. It is also to learn the universal principle that the fingers move in relation to the whole body</u>. That is part of the basic concept in ballet called port-des-bras or the carriage of the arms during which the hands and fingers are to always be engaged and expressive and moving in harmony with the arms, legs, torso as well as the eyes. This same universal principle of the fingers moving in relation to the whole body is integral to martial arts training at a basic level, but does not usually involve creative expression with the fingers.

To start, stand with your feet wide apart. The feet should be gently turned out. Then bring your straight arms to any position. Be sure that the fingers are spread apart, straight, and with the palms of the hands flat and open.

The feet remain planted flat on the floor throughout the exercise.

You will move your fingers at the same time as you move your arms, legs (but do not move the feet!!!), and sometimes the torso. You move in a single trajectory or single curve or single rhythm. The trajectory is like shooting an arrow. When you shoot an arrow to a direct target, the arrow goes more or less in a straight line. If you were shooting an arrow for a long distance you would aim upward and the arrow would travel in a wide arc towards its target.

To start, the arms can be in any position, but they must be straight to start. As you move, engage the arms by bending and/or twisting them in any way. At the end of the trajectory the whole body holds in a shape and in a pause for about 2 seconds - long enough to be still and to stay and to know the shape of your body, your arms, your hands, and your fingers.

The basic practice is: reach-move-shape/pause.

Move only slowly. To be aware of the fingers while moving, one can only move slowly. Not so slow as in slow-motion, but moving in one continuous slow rhythm. If one moves fast - a single action instead of a trajectory - then you will only move your arms and not your fingers. The arms are able to move via the shoulders without moving the fingers or hands. The hands can move by moving the wrist without moving the fingers. So the idea in The Mime Exercise is to move at the same time the arms/hands/fingers but slowly enough so that you can observe whether the fingers are actually moving. While the arms/hands/fingers are moving, so too are the legs (but not the feet!) and perhaps sometimes the torso.

When the fingers stop moving - the body stops.
Or.
When the body stops moving - the fingers stop.

The practice is three times - start with arms stretched in any direction, then moving fingers and body (feet remain in the same spot throughout the entire exercise) to a shape/pause. Only on the third shape/pause you will then improvise from the shape/pause (without moving the feet). You will improvise three times from the same shape/pause. Each improvisation is 30 or 40 seconds or so.

Again, you use the universal principle of interpretation. In this exercise you interpret only the third shape/pause, and you interpret it three times. To interpret, basically you will use either the form (shape) itself; or the feeling as you start to move the shape after the pause; or you interpret via an idea. Interpretation as a universal principle basically uses either: form/shape; movement/rhythm; feeling; or, idea.

To interpret or to improvise, you do not need to try to make a formal story with a beginning, a middle, and an end. Time is often used as the closure. A short and very limited time sequence of 30 or 40 or 60 or so seconds is all that is necessary to get in touch with your feeling, energy, idea, shape, rhythm.

The universal principle I am now referring to is: if you have a good beginning and sustain your awareness then improvising is very easy.

Creative Solo #5 - JO-HA-KYU

This is the second Creative Solo that is grounded in a fixed spot. Basically where you start you stay. The Mime Exercise stays in one spot for the entire exercise. Jo-Ha-Kyu starts in a first spot and moves to a second spot and the improvisation stays on that second spot.

Jo-Ha-Kyu refers to a central principle in the Japanese Noh Theatre. This was written about by Zeami in the 1400s when he wrote the definition of Noh Theatre. Jo-Ha-Kyu was described as a flower that has bud, the bud blooms, the blossom then dies and goes into the soil from where the next generation or flower seed grows, buds, blooms, dies, and rebirths.

In this exercise I make a free interpretation of Jo-Ha-Kyu to be opening-reaction-resolution.

The staring position is a basic '1st Position' as in ballet. The heels touch each other and the front of the feet are open and turned out moderately at about 45 degrees. Arms are relaxed and hanging by the side of the body.

The opening action is to fall to the right side so that the right leg is bent slightly in a moderate lunge. At the same time as falling into a moderate side lunge, your arms open outward in a dynamic and strong action. Fingers are open and stretched. Pause a few seconds with energy alive but the shape motionless.

This is 'jo' which I interpret as "Opening".

From this shape, which was a side lunge to the right, you then move your centre to the centre and at the same time the left leg will bend. At the same time your arms move in a swift dynamic action towards the centre. The fingers remain open and stretched. Pause a few seconds holding this new shape. Do not move your feet.

This second shape is 'ha" which I interpret as "Reaction". It is an energy reaction like in physics "equal and opposite reaction".

From this second shape and pause you will then let your fingers come alive and improvise on the spot, without moving your feet.

Improvisations can start from any shape, feeling, movement, or idea. If starting from an idea it is so important to keep the body fully engaged with feeling. If starting from shape, feeling, or movement it is important to keep alive mentally, conceptually, intellectually while still working with feeling.

The Seven Solos - The 2 geometric exercises which include walks and use of directions

Creative Solo #6 - SIX DIRECTIONS

Six Directions is done within a small rectangle imagined on the floor. The rectangle imagined is about 2 metres (6 feet) long. About one metre (3 feet) wide.

It is a very contained and limited space.

The 6 directions are: forward, backward, left, right, up, down.
6 directions are also used in various cultural practices and shamanic practices for getting in touch with "knowing where you stand". The seventh element would be 'centre' which is relative to where you stand. This exercise starts in the centre but when you walk forward you will relax (neutral) in the front and when you walk backwards you will pause at the back of the rectangle. Then you step into the centre again and the next four directions (left, right, up, down) are all done in the centre. All of the directions are done within the 2 metres x 1 metre rectangle.

In between each direction you will come to neutral.
You start the exercise in the centre of the rectangle.
The first direction will take you to the front of the rectangle. Neutral.
The second direction will take you to the back of the rectangle. Neutral.
From neutral at the back you will then simply step forward to the centre of the rectangle. Neutral.
The next four directions (left, right, up, down) - do not walk!
When you turn in each direction ... as you turn/move, use your whole body including legs and arms and hands and face and eyes.
Start standing in a relaxed 'neutral' in the middle of the 2 x 1 rectangle.
Forward. Make a shape and rhythm to move forward to the front of the 2 x 1 rectangle.
There's no reason your rectangle can't be a bit bigger, but the more limited the better.
The important point is to stay focused in a very limited space. And to know what single direction you are moving in.
When you get to the Front of the rectangle, release to a relaxed neutral instantly.
Take another shape including knees, arms, hands, face, eyes - then in a spontaneous rhythm move backwards.
When you get the the Back of the rectangle release to a relaxed neutral instantly.
Then simply walk into the Centre of the rectangle. Stand in a relaxed neutral for one second. A pause. Then as you turn your whole body to the Left, include your feet. Do not walk. Do not step cut of the rectangle. Simply make a shape and improvise for about 10,15, or 20 seconds using

THE FOUR ARTICULATIONS FOR PERFORMANCE

your whole body including the legs, arms, hands, face, eyes. Then return to facing Front neutral. Pause.

Repeat the process of taking a shape and letting it move, and follow your feeling and imagination briefly for 10 - 20 seconds - repeat to the Right, Up, Down.

These short shape and feeling based improvisations help to teach the principle: <u>Have a good beginning. Good means it is physical, using your legs, arms, hands, fingers, feeling, imagination.</u>

Creative Solo #7 - THE PONYDANCE CIRCLE

Whereas the Six Directions Exercise is performed within a small rectangle, The Ponydance Circle is along a circle of any size. When performed in a shared space the circles of the performers will overlap with each other. Pony Dance is a contemporary dance theatre company based in Belfast. The Director/Choreographer of the company, Leonie McDonagh, was in two of my workshops and then hired me to work three weeks just with her and the four other main dancers of her company. Dancers everywhere are determined, hard working and resilient, so they can do anything I ask within reason and are always willing to try their best. So they were successfully doing whatever I asked, but, they didn't seem to be 'feeling' anything. That is related to the arduous method of dance which involves a lot of repetition and honing/improving as you continue.

So I made The Ponydance Exercise to help them to focus on 'feeling' and to learn how to follow their creative feeling or their own creative spirit. At first the amount of time they spent was open and undetermined by me. Then I limited the time in the same way as in The Six Directions.

Stand in a relaxed neutral. Whichever way you are facing will be Forward. After completing the circle moving towards the left or counter-clockwise, you will finish the exercise standing where you started, facing in the same direction.

Within a single circle you will complete three creative walks and finish with a relaxed neutral walk.

Each creative walk will start with a shape and a rhythm traveling along the circle in a leftward moving direction. For each creative walk you will stop where you wish, and keeping the shape and energy with a slight pause you will turn in any one of the six directions, either: forward, backward, left, right, up, or down. When you move in any one of those directions you will improvise with your shape, feeling, imagination, but you will not walk. Stay on the circle. The 'hardest' is to move in a forward direction because you have just been walking in a forward direction along the leftward circle. As in The Six Directions exercise you improvise for 10-20 seconds then come to a relaxed neutral facing forward.

You repeat with a new shape and new rhythm and new direction and another pause.

Repeat with a third new creative walk.

After the pause of the third creative walk you will then walk in a relaxed neutral way along the circle and pause to finish where you started The Ponydance exercise.

END - SEVEN SOLOS

Duets, Trio, Quartet
The Path of Honour
Auxiliary Exercises

DUETS, TRIO, QUARTET

There are three duets, one trio, one quartet.

1st Duet - POSITIVE/NEGATIVE

The ideas of this exercise:
Positive implies the body.
Negative implies the area around the body.

Positive/Negative is a basic principle in visual art. If one were drawing in black ink onto a white paper, wherever the black ink is becomes 'positive', wherever the black ink is not becomes 'negative' or empty space.

Actor A will become a shape of any sort.
Actor B will move in the space anywhere that Actor A's body is not.

Generally speaking Actor B should not touch Actor A. Once actors are familiar with the whole exercise and the principle there are no rules, or one can interpret what seem to be 'rules'. The instructions below are not 'rules'. They are to provide a safe space for Actor A to learn to hold still no matter what Actor B is involved with artistically. Actor B is to learn to improvise freely around Actor A.

The instructions of this exercise:

At the same time that Actor A takes a stationary shape, Actor B takes a shape that moves.

Actor A takes a shape. It can be standing or sitting or lying on the floor. It should be in the open space so that Actor B is free to move 360 degrees around Actor B.

Ideally, Actor B takes their shape independent of Actor A's shape. This means it is better if Actor B does not look at Actor A until Actor B has had a few seconds to settle into whatever image, feeling, character arises from within Actor B's shape which is a moving shape.

Ideally, Actor B's creativity is not dictated by Actor A's shape. Even if Actor A takes a creative shape like a statue of a person shooting an arrow, this does not mean that Actor B needs to play with that obvious image. Actor A is simply "a shape in space" and Actor B is free to improvise and play around that "shape in space" in any way.

IMPORTANT! Respect the safety and modesty of the actor who is still. At the same time the moving actor is 100% free to interpret and play dramatically or with clowning in any way that they want, provided that they do not touch the actor standing still - that they respect the safety and modesty of the actor who is standing still.

NOTE: Actor B's moving shape can move and play in any way and is not restricted to holding on to the original shape, rhythm, image, feeling, or character.

NOTE: When Actor B looks at Actor A, do not let Actor A's shape dictate how Actor B improvises.

This improvisation should last about 1 minute and then Actor B simply stops by taking a shape at which point Actor A takes a moving shape and begins to play with their own shape, rhythm, image, feeling, or character.

In the flow of "The Four Articulations for Performance" each duet is done only once. POSITIVE/NEGATIVE repeats once so that each actor experiences being the still actor once and the moving actor once. Sometimes it is very valuable for the time to extend more than 1 minute each. But in the basic template this exercise is only a format for experiencing and interpreting what a partner does. Another principle is that the two actors are actually in the abstract, or, in an artistic sense, 'only' shapes moving or holding still in a studio.

2nd Duet - THE SLAPSTICK EXERCISE

This is a phenomenal acting, clown, improvisational exercise. It incorporates everything from the other exercises so far in The Four Articulations.

Like any practical exercise it makes sense after you have tried it several times and have taken the time to clear up any confusion. There are three parts to The Slapstick Exercise. This exercise is different because there are more counts. However, the actual pattern of the counting is very simple: 1-2-3. There is a repeated action that happens with the 1-2-3. The repeated action with 1-2-3 happens four times, then the actors move their own body, then there are two more sets of 1-2-3, then, a final two more sets of 1-2-3.

There are three parts to The Slapstick Exercise:
Part 1
Part 2
Part 3
As a whole it looks like this:
Part 1
1-2-3
1-2-3

1-2-3
1-2-3

Part 2
MOVE YOUR BODY
Part 3
1-2-3
1-2-slap (this time the '3' count is a 'slap')

1-2-3
1-2-slap (this time the '3' count is a 'slap')

PART 1 of The Slapstick Exercise

A) Actors A and B face each other. Actor A places their bent arms forward like a table with the palms UP. At the same time Actor B places their bent arms forward like a table but with the palms facing DOWN. Actor B's hands are slightly above Actor A's hands.

B) Actor B gently slaps Actor A's palms. The actors reverse the hands so that A taps B's palms from above. Then they reverse hands again and B taps A's palms.

This becomes a 3-count rhythm. B taps A, A taps B, B taps A.

This 3-count rhythm repeats as a set four times. That is four times the duet repeats the 3-count rhythm.
However, after each set of 3-counts the other actor will start. Start means that the actor 'above', the actor with palms facing down, initiates the rhythm of 3 counts or three taps.
B taps A - A taps B - B taps A.

NOTE: The hand taps should be gentle, more like a tap.

THEN it is a complete set of four times of the 3-counts set.
There is a pause in between each set of 3-counts.
In the pause the actors change who starts.

This could be described as:
A starts - pause (to change so B starts)
B starts - pause (to change so A starts)
A starts - pause (to change so B starts)
B starts - end, finish, do not do more unless you decide to do an extra complete round of four times of the 3-counts set.

NOTE: Although the hands on top tap downward it is MUCH better to avoid the bottom hands reaching or slapping upward.

NOTE: In the first count, A starts and taps down. A is active. In the second count, A's palms are facing up so they receive B's downward tap, thus A is passive. In the third count, A starts and taps down.

Another way to describe the whole round of four times of 3-counts is:

1-2-3 change
1-2-3 change
1-2-3 change
1-2-3 FINISH

<u>IT IS VERY IMPORTANT TO LEARN THIS BEGINNING PART OF THE SLAPSTICK EXERCISE FIRST AS A WHOLE ROUND OF FOUR SETS OF 3-COUNTS FOR EACH SET.</u>

PART 2 of The Slapstick Exercise

MOVE YOUR BODY.

Immediately after the FINISH of one round of four sets of 3-counts, MOVE YOUR BODY.
1-2-3 change
1-2-3 change
1-2-3 change
1-2-3 FINISH and immediately MOVE YOUR BODY.

THE FOUR ARTICULATIONS FOR PERFORMANCE

NOTE: When you move YOUR body - avoid watching your partner moving their body.
NOTE: Focus on moving YOUR body.

When you MOVE YOUR BODY you can move any way that you want. As you move, play with whatever feeling, image, or character impulse that arises. STICK WITH IT. Stick with your impulse, your movement, feeling, image, or character. Keep it going as you gradually get near the other actor and they near you.

After 10 or 20 or 30 seconds the two actors should gravitate close to each other.

Keep your imaginary shape or rhythm, sustain what you are doing. Add, don't subtract.
Add bringing your arms up bent, either with the palms UP or DOWN.

Then - either of the actors can give THE SIGNAL of either having their palms up or palms down.
If their PALMS are facing DOWN they will START. If their PALMS are UP they will RECEIVE.
START means the actor will SLAP down until touching the palms of the other actor.
RECEIVE means the actor will have their palms SLAPPED.

PART 3 of The Slapstick Exercise

EITHER PARTNER can 'start', that means have your hands above and palms face downward.

1-2-3
1-2-SLAP

Then the other partner starts:
1-2-3
1-2-SLAP

The 3rd Part starts the same ways as the 1st Part. But it gets interrupted.

In the 3rd Part this final slap is not a slap on the palm, it is a stage slap.
In the STAGE SLAP I prefer a super safe approach until the risks are clear for everyone.
The priority is to not hurt anyone, including yourself. Depending on the pair of participants, one can not risk much more than what I will describe here.
This is the super safe approach.

For the person who will 'slap':
Signal to your partner that you are going to do the stage slap which is a fake slap.
Bring your right arm backwards which telegraphs to your partner that you will now do the stage slap from your right side, which means they will be 'slapped' on their left side.
Bring your STRAIGHT arm in the direction of your partner's cheek. Keep your hand at least 6 inches away from your partner's cheek.
You can stop abruptly AWAY from your partner's cheek. OR you can swing your arm up and away and then release the arm. OR you can drop your arm immediately.
So the arm goes BACKWARDS to signal, the arm stays STRAIGHT, the palm always stays AWAY from the partner's cheek, RELEASE the arm immediately after the 'slap'.

For the person being 'slapped'.
WATCH for your partner's signal. Your partner is meant to bring their arm BACKWARDS and STRAIGHT.
When they bring their arm and palm towards your cheek you do three actions in this order:
CLAP your hands at about waist level.
BRING your hand on the side which has been 'slapped' up to your cheek.
TURN your head to the opposite side but KEEP your palm on your cheek.

Then the person who was hit will give the signal to start, i.e. with their palms facing downward.

THE FOUR ARTICULATIONS FOR PERFORMANCE

1-2-3
1-2-SLAP

NOTE: If A starts 1-2-3, then B responds by starting 1-2 .... but is then interrupted by the slap.
The next round of this section is started by B's 1-2-3 and then A responds by starting 1-2 but is interrupted by the slap

THE SECRET:
THE SLAP DOESN'T 'MATTER'.
THE REACTIONS ARE WHAT'S IMPORTANT.
WHEN YOU ARE SLAPPED - WHAT DO YOU PLAY WITH?
WHAT DO YOU IMAGINE, CREATE, IMPROVISE?
WHEN YOU SLAP - WHAT DO YOU PLAY WITH? WHAT DO YOU IMAGINE, CREATE, IMPROVISE?

NOTE: Once you know the counts, the mechanics, the structure, the safety; feel free to adjust it, play with it, improvise with it.
NOTE: For example, the 1-2-3 / 1-2-SLAP sections do not need to start with a formal both hands up or down as in the beginning of the whole exercise. In this section the '1' can start with one hand, or one finger, or with a nod, or a kick, or a bump, etc.

THE WHOLE STRUCTURE:
1-2-3 change
1-2-3 change
1-2-3 change
1-2-3 FINISH and immediately MOVE YOUR BODY.

Either partner can start the next section.
1-2-3
1-2-SLAP

Then the other partner starts:
1-2-3
1-2-SLAP

3rd DUET - THE GODOT EXERCISE

You will need to have a single A-4 printed paper of the script.
You can obtain the required section from the play via the online text. Simply google Waiting For Godot text Act 1 and scroll to the section that starts «Vladimir: I hadn't thought of that.» and goes until «Vladimir: I think so too. *Silence.*» Copy, paste, print.

You hold the text in one hand.
You do not need to memorise the text.
You are to read it while acting, while improvising, while playing, while creating, while interacting with your partner. It is all done while you are holding the paper and able to read your lines.

This exercise replicates what happens in the early stage of rehearsing a play and the actors have to work on the floor moving while holding the script in their hands.

However, in this work and method you are not rehearsing the play. You are not trying to be the characters in the play. You are not rehearsing for a production. You are doing a freeform exercise or open improvisation WITH a piece of paper with some text in your hand.
The exercise is also for you to move any way that you feel or want to at any moment.
NOTE: Don't worry about your partner, but, stay aware of them. You do not need to see everything or anything that they do. There are no rules. There is a simple structure: freeform improvisation WITH a paper in one hand WITH text on it WHICH you can read WHEN you need to.
NOTE: Give your partner space and time.
NOTE: Another aspect of the exercise is to help actors to stop doing specific actions to certain words. FOR EXAMPLE in the text there is a line "But am I heavier than you?". Very often actors will point to themselves on the word "I" and point to their partner on the word "you". Avoid doing that and you will find infinite ways to say and live the text. The text says the word such as 'I' and 'you' so you do not need to mimic the word nor act it out.

THE FOUR ARTICULATIONS FOR PERFORMANCE

NOTE: This particular script and section was chosen for the purposes of two actors playing, improvising and creating. The text can be said in almost any way and still make perfect sense.

NOTE: The challenge is to be totally free even though you have a piece of paper in your hand and at various times have to read the text while moving, acting, improvising, playing.

NOTE: Ultimately I encourage actors to play in the same way even when I am directing a play. Eventually they will make discoveries of things 'hidden' in the text; situations and relationships of the characters and the actors.

THE TRIO - THE TRIANGLE EXERCISE

Three people stand in a triangle about 2 metres from each other.

One person starts to move and the other two imitate the movements as best as they can, trying to move at the same time as the person they are following.

Try to maintain the triangle and the distances throughout the exercise.

The person in the front should move anyway they want and adjust it so that the people following might be able to move with them.

After about 1 minute, approximately, the leader will in their movement improvisation either turn to their left or right. If they turn left the person on the left will organically take over the leadership. If they turn right then the person on the right becomes the leader. After another minute, approximately, the new leader will choose to turn left or right and relinquishes the leadership at the same time when the new leader takes over. The leadership can change as many times as the actors choose. The whole improvisation should take about 3 to 6 minutes.

The movement can be dance or mime or body language or chaotic or flowing, etc.

When you follow you will be doing movements in new rhythms and aesthetics which you normally would not choose, but you could. So the idea of this exercise is that done regularly it will expand your vocabulary of movement and increase your creative choices.

NOTE: If there are 1 or 2 'extra' people then do the same exercise in a diamond to accommodate the extra people.

THE QUARTET - THE WHISPER EXERCISE

This exercise uses the principle of the 3rd Solo - the Three Walks, i.e. Shape-Pause-Rhythm.
This exercise transitions from the earlier training into clowning principles. Particularly learning to really listen, observe, delay, interpret, and respond to what a partner offers at any moment.

One actor, '1' is in the centre of the room facing towards the audience or other participants.
Three actors A, B, C, stand at the side of the stage area to the far left of the central actor '1'.
A, B, C stand in a line perpendicular to 1. 1 is facing forward, but, A, B, C are facing 1.

1 Stands relaxed neutral.
Either A, B or C can spontaneously go first simply by making a shape, pause, and making a rhythm that takes them directly to the left side of 1. Let us say that B went first. After the rhythm, when B is standing in their shape close to 1's left side, B raises one of his/her hands as if to whisper into the left ear of 1. B will then say anything to 1. Say it loud enough so that 1 can hear it and slow enough so that 1 can understand it. However, B (or whoever walks towards 1) can say whatever they want and however they want. The can say one word or a paragraph or make a sound or speak in gibberish or in any foreign language.
NOTE: Although A,B,C should speak clear enough so that 1 can understand, A, B, or C can also choose to 'tease' 1, for example by speaking a language that 1 can not understand. Generally though, the idea is to say anything that can be clearly understood.
After B speaks they adjust back to their original rhythm and move behind 1 in the same line/entrance that they began on the left side. B will finish on the far right side and they can then sit or stand where they finish and watch what 1 does with what they have been told/whispered.

THE FOUR ARTICULATIONS FOR PERFORMANCE

1 should delay responding to B's speech. Delay abut 4 to 8 seconds, like a "pause". Then 1 can interpret and improvise with whatever B said or how they said it or if the speech was not understood, i.e. if it was just a sound, or gibberish, or a foreign language which 1 can not understand, or simply unclear .... then 1 should still improvise after the delay based on the sound, or energy, or feeling with which B communicated.

1 should improvise about 40-60 seconds, approximately. Then 1 comes to a conclusion by standing relaxed neutral, ideally on the same spot where they first stood.

As soon as 1 comes to neutral then the next actor, C or A, spontaneously, goes by taking a shape, a pause, then making a rhythm that takes them close to the left side of 1. They repeat as B did: take hand to 1's left ear and whisper/tell 1 something clearly. Then resume the shape and rhythm and move in the same line of entry behind 1 and to the far right side of the room. Relax and watch what 1 does.

When 1 comes to neutral again the remaining actor will proceed: shape, rhythm, hand, whisper, rhythm, relax on the right side of the room, watch what 1 does.

When 1 is done with their interpretation of whatever the third actor said, 1 will come to relaxed neutral and hold still for a minimum of about 4 seconds.

THE WHISPER EXERCISE introduces the idea of INTERPRETING what your partner says or does.

INTERPRET does not mean imitate and it does not hold any obligation other than to listen and feel. Delay your response, then INTERPRET any way you want, then come back to neutral in order to signal to the remaining actors that you are ready for the next person, or signal at the end that you have control of yourself by holding still and being relaxed neutral for a minimum of 4 seconds.

One of the benefits of this exercise is that when A, B, and C observe 1's INTERPRETATION then A, B, and C should see that there are other ways to play, clown, improvise, INTERPRET than what is given, even if what is given is a clear 'direction', for example if C says "You must sit down". 1 does not need to sit down. Or 1 can sit down in 100s of different ways including for example going to sit in slow motion but never sitting. Or one can INTERPRET "You must sit down" with a feeling of being insulted for being told that, or, with a feeling of joy that you can now sit down which does not mean sit down, it means experiencing and improvising and playing on with that sense of 'joy' or sense of 'insult'. That's an example out of 100s of possibilities. A, B, C are 'clowning' while they move across the room in a clear physically creative way of a shape and rhythm.

Normally I never ask what was whispered. It is a private moment or joke between those two actors. This is a principle of clowns clowning for their own delight. Clowning can be nice, mean, tricky, funny, serious, poetic. There is no aesthetic imposed on the actor who whispers except to have enough control to repeat their shape and rhythm after they have paused to tell 1 actor something.

This exercise also places a demand on 1 to listen, to delay reacting, to interpret, and to have enough control to be able to estimate 40-60 seconds of improvising and to be able to cut the feeling and come to neutral to be able to give a professional signal to the next actor on the side.

NOTE: There is no obligation of 1, the actor in the middle, to tell a story nor is there any obligation to make what they do explicitly understood by the viewers. 1, the actor in the middle, only needs to stand in relaxed neutral, delay, interpret any way that they feel or want to, and to be able to come back to a relaxed neutral ideally on the same spot where they began. This takes total control and awareness, but, simultaneously the actor will go deep into their own trance/imagination.

The actors can rotate or have another group of 4 do the exercise. If there are many in a course then perhaps 3 actors per day can be in the middle position. The exercise can be adapted to 2 or 3 actors.

THE FOUR ARTICULATIONS FOR PERFORMANCE

END OF DUETS, TRIO, QUARTET
The Path of Honour
Auxiliary Exercises

THE PATH OF HONOUR

This is the official final section of THE FOUR ARTICULATIONS FOR PERFORMANCE.
There are a few auxiliary exercises.

Most of the exercises in THE PATH OF HONOUR are named after famous clowns. However, the exercises are not to imitate those clowns. Rather, the idea is to locate some special aspects of clowning that was highlighted by those particular clowns. Additionally the names are there to provide an impulse to do your own research about the history of clown, particularly by studying the work of the great clowns.

IDEALLY FOR THE PATH OF HONOUR AND THE AUXILIARY EXERCISES WEAR AT LEAST A HAT AND COAT TO CLOWN IN. PREFERABLY DO NOT USE A CLOWN NOSE AT LEAST UNTIL YOU HAVE TRIED THE EXERCISE MANY TIMES WITHOUT THE CLOWN NOSE. SOME OF THE AUXILIARY EXERCISES USE A CLOWN NOSE EVERY TIME.

In the classic theatre "stage left" means the actor's left side of stage as when the actor faces the audience. "Stage right" means the actor's right side of stage as when the actor faces the audience. "Upstage" means the back of the stage. "Downstage" means the front of the stage.

In clowning there is a principle for the clown's initial relationship to the audience:

A) The clown is surprised that there are people in the room. Or the clown is surprised that there is an audience in the theatre. As in The Buster Keaton Exercise.
B) The clown knows there is an audience and is coming out to entertain them. As in "Charlie Chaplin - The Entertainer Exercise.

C) The clown has something that has happened offstage and the clown brings that feeling with them. As in the case of Laurel & Hardy Exercise, and, in one of the auxiliary exercises such as The Clown Knows Exercise.

1. THE LAUREL & HARDY EXERCISE

Two chairs. Place them in the centre of the room facing the audience. The chairs face "downstage". Place the chairs close but not touching.

The two actors enter 'in character'. Use the principle "Shape-Pause-Rhythm". That principle is presented in the 3rd SOLO exercise.

The actors are independent. Their individual entrances are juxtaposed with each other.

Each actor sits in one chair with the attitude with which they entered. When each actor sits they start facing "downstage".

There are six steps or cues. Those six steps or cues are like the spring board for the improvisation. Those six steps are for the two actors and characters to subconsciously tune in to each other's energy.

DO NOT IMITATE EACH OTHER.
DO NOT GRAB THE OTHER'S HAT.

Actor A is the one sitting in the chair on stage left. This is considered the Oliver Hardy role.
Actor B is the one sitting in the chair on stage right. This is considered the Stan Laurel role.

NOTE: When speaking use your body language. Speaking is not just the words or sound but also the feeling and attitude being expressed, being shared.

Action 1 - Actor A is 'upset' and says "This is another fine mess you have gotten us in to this time". Then ...

Action 2 - Actor B says "But, but, but, but ...." continually until Actor A INTERRUPTS by ...
Action 3 - Actor A puts their hand and index finger up, vertically up, and says "Sszt"! Then ...
Action 4 - Actor B turns front, neutral face, THEN .... after a PAUSE of a few seconds .... cries .... until ....
Action 5 - Actor A says "Will you stop that" Then ...
Action 6 - Actor B stops that.

NOTE: The objective is for any two actors to create a spontaneous energy between them within these 6 actions. So that the 6 actions already generate a sense of play, of listening, of provoking, of feeling, of responding ..... which simply continues after Action 6.

NOTE: Let Action 6 be alive. In other words: What happens to you the actor/character when the other says "Will you stop that" and you stop that? What happens to you the actor/character when you say "Will you stop that" and the other actor stops that? So - you PLAY with stopping and PLAY with asking the other to stop.

The energy should be such that the actors continue for at least 2 minutes freeform.

There is a pattern of six steps which can be done in infinite ways. Maybe one or both actors do not actually sit. Not one of the SIX ACTIONS is NOT sitting. The instruction to sit in the chair is a formality which the actor may do for 90 improvisations but perhaps on the 91st they feel like 'trying something else'.

Each of the six actions can be done in infinite ways.

NOTE: The exercise is about the transference of energy in six beats; creating a lustre of energy in six beats in the six actions.

2. THE BUSTER KEATON EXERCISE

This has a geometric formula or structure. Recall or review that in the SEVEN SOLOS the 6th and 7th exercises are geometric.

There are two lines in this exercise.
The entrance line goes from stage right to stage left, but, it has two circles and a point.
The exit line goes from stage left to stage right.

A. Start upstage right. With back to the audience.
You will walk backwards creating a path of two circles.
The total of the two circles should get you all the way to the other side of the room. To stage left.
But not as far as the wall. All the way means as far as you can WITHOUT touching or going all the way to the wall.

B. From the start, you will raise your arms behind you as if you were reaching with both hands to grasp a loose thread on your back, or behind you. As you walk backwards you keep pulling at the imaginary thread, as if you had the thread and were pulling it out further and further, i.e. continually.

C. After you complete the second backward circle you will have YOUR BACK DIRECTLY TO THE AUDIENCE. Then you relax your arms by your side. Standing neutral. And simply turn towards your right. Turning on the spot. Turning neutral to face the audience.

THEN.
D. The idea here is that you see the audience seeing you set them.
In that split second you have a feeling.

E. Capture or "frame that feeling" into a whole body shape-pause-rhythm moving sideways while looking at the audience. "Take it out" by exiting on a straight line to stage right. When you have exited just to the far side of the hall or stage, simply turn to facing off stage and come to neutral.

You can do this (E) instantly without knowing what you're feeling by doing it mechanically, i.e. just take a shape-pause-rhythm moving sideways to exit stage right. Then simply turn to facing off stage and come to neutral.

NOTE: This is a short exercise that takes about 1 minute in total.

THE FOUR ARTICULATIONS FOR PERFORMANCE

NOTE: However, once the actor really is familiar with the whole exercise and has control in each action of A, B, C, D, E; then they can improvise/clown as they are exiting in 'E'.

3. CHARLIE CHAPLIN - THE ENTERTAINER

A) The actor begins upstage, stage right.
The geometric pattern for this exercise is an "L" shape entrance and a reverse "L" shape exit.
B) The "L" Entrance. The actor with their back to the wall (stage right) walks straight until the halfway distance and then turns to their right and walks straight towards the audience.
C) The actor stops about two metres directly in front of the audience (other participants) front row.
D) The actor will prepare to sing a song, and then sing a song, or part of a song, or will improvise a song.
E) Suddenly either the song finishes, or, for some reason the character stops singing, abruptly. Either something stopped the character from singing; for example somebody's mobile phone rings or somebody dropped something; in other words, something minor stops the clown. Or the clown/character stops.
F) In either case what happens is within that split second when the clown/character stops.
G) What happens the moment of stopping or the moment after? Similar to The Buster Keaton Exercise - capture that single feeling, that moment, and "frame it" and take it out.
H) Walk backwards until you get upstage. There the actor/character/clown turns to their right and exits walking forward towards the wall where they started stage right.

NOTE: Similarly to The Buster Keaton Exercise, the actor has to keep awareness of the geometry or the spatial aspect of the exercise. Also, like the previous exercise the actor will capture a single feeling and "frame it" and "take it out".

NOTE: In the Keaton and the Chaplin exercises the actor is practicing classic stage craft of how to make an entrance, how to make an exit, how to frame a feeling, how to take it out.

NOTE: The 'walk' in this exercise should not be a normal, pedestrian, walk. It should be a creative walk using a shape and rhythm.

NOTE: The 'walk' in the entrance does not have to be the same as the 'walk' in the exit. Something dramatic has happened to the character/clown. There is a reason that they stopped singing or after they stopped singing there is a feeling. A new feeling causes a change in the drama so it may be, maybe, possibly, that this changes something in the character and they exit according to that feeling.

NOTE: Although a character or clown may walk a certain way, if something dramatic happens like they drop a heavy weight on their foot they will then walk in a modified or different way.

NOTE: All exercises in The Four Articulations for Performance have mechanical and structured instructions. But the question is: What happens to you when you do the exercise with those instructions? Once you know the instructions very well and clearly, that means maybe after you have done an exercise ten or twenty times and are clear about fulfilling the instructions, then of course the hidden idea or the real idea is only: What happens to you? What do you choose to do with that, with whatever happens inside you?

NOTE: The "magic moment", the "quantum moment", is what happens in a split second when an actor or character or clown discovers something. How do they capture that moment? How do they "frame it"? How do they "take it out" or how do they "continue" with that feeling and how does that feeling "evolve" or "transform"?

I have demonstrated The Buster Keaton Exercise hundreds of times. The entrance is always similar but the feeling inside is always different. Then I come to neutral for 1 or 2 seconds, then I turn neutral still with my arms relaxed and hanging but alive inside. Then I pause 1 or 2 seconds and then -bam- the magic happens or I move into a shape and that becomes magical, i.e. a new feeling. Then my exit is always new to me and different physically and visually. Even though this exercise is extremely simple it is always different. So there is something profound in this exercise.

4. THE LUCILLE BALL/VIVIAN VANCE EXERCISE

We are not imitating the actresses nor their clown characters.
In their TV series, whenever they were left on their own together, Lucy would get Vivian to join in something dangerous, or sneaky. This is the moment they would clown. This is the moment of this exercise. Neither wants to do something called "that", whatever "that" is this time.

A) Immediately, even while entering the stage area something is happening inside the actor. Catch that feeling. "Frame it" into a shape or rhythm or body language.
B) The 'Lucy' figure is stage left and the Vivian figure is stage right. Do not worry about what the other actor/character/clown is doing. Pay attention to your own feeling and body language.
C) The 'Lucy' figure says "I would never do that".
D) The 'Vivian' figure says "Me neither".
E) The 'Lucy' figure says "Yes, I could never imagine doing that".
F) The 'Vivian' figure says "Oh, I could imagine you doing that".

NOTES: The objectives are: starting expressing whatever you feel as you begin to enter the stage area. You do not need a formal entrance like the Keaton or Chaplin exercises. The exercise starts when you move from your seat or chair. You can go with it or do the opposite. Or you can have an idea and try it. Whatever you do, though, has to involve your total body language and feeling. This feeling gets affected during those four simple lines of text. Don't change what you started with! Be affected, but, don't change. Change implies stopping what you are doing and starting again. Learn to accumulate rather than stop and then start again.

NOTE: Another objective is for the actors to work in just four lines to build a lustre, a positive energy so that they can improvise freely with that connection and see where it goes and how they manipulate or play with it, what they discover along the way, what it feels like to be spontaneous.

NOTE: Improvisers and actors will usually think after the fourth line of dialogue that 'Lucy' has to say something. There is no need to say anything after the fourth line. You are both welcome and free to say anything. But AMAZINGLY .... after the fourth line MANY improvisers and actors in the 'Lucy' role will then say "Really", and when that happens OFTEN the "Vivian" figure will say "Uh huh", or "Yep", or "Yes". When we have the 'really' and then the "Uh huh" OFTEN the 'Lucy' will say "naw" or "no" or "you're kidding" and then "Vivian" says again one of the "Uh huh" or "yes" etc. What I have just described to you is what I call "Improvitis". It is something that is tolerated in improvisation circles but which I do not tolerate more than twice in a group. I call it out. So, if like MANY improvisers and actors you have the impulse to say at those stages "really" or "uh huh" etc, just don't say those and you will begin to transform your ability to improvise not only in silence but also with text. The problem with things like the Really/uh huh Syndrome is that: a) it shows that the actors think they have to come up with text. They do not have to, and: b) if they avoid or avert that Syndrome they will begin to tap their subconscious. In creativity your subconscious is a phenomenal resource. The conscious and subconscious though are a dynamic duo!

By maintaining conscious control and "forcing" yourself not to say "really" nor "uh huh" if you are inclined to say those, by averting them you will signal to the subconscious to work its own magic. When that magic starts to happen, your conscious mind can also do its magic by guiding and working with the subconscious. This of course applies to all of one's habits or defaults or weaknesses. Learn to observe your habits, defaults, weaknesses. First, look out for them. 2nd, note when they happen. 3rd, when they happen, change or adjust them now on the spot. 4th, note the moment they are starting. 5th, when they start adjust them immediately to anything else. Noting your own habits, defaults, weaknesses is a sign of strength. As you start to work with them, to avert and adjust them, you will begin to become stronger and more versatile in your creativity.

NOTE: This exercise has no formal ending. The actors may find an ending but that is rare. This exercise is about learning to receive the journey that is uniquely unfolding right now, moment to moment, between two actors. Have fun. Try it many, many times.

NOTE: There is no 'that' in the first four lines. It is the FEELING and EXPRESSION that counts. How, in this moment, this character, this improvisation, do you EXPRESS the FEELING that you "would never do that"? Whatever 'that' is does not matter at this moment. Whatever it is, you 'would never do that'. It is the same for the next two lines. For the first three lines no matter what 'that' is, neither would, and nor could you even imagine doing 'that', no matter what 'that' might reveal itself to be later in the improvisation. It is a pure clown exercise. Pure improvisation. Pure play between two actors. It is never about the 'that' as the that could be a thousand different things. Drama is about feeling and emotion, what a human, or character is drawn towards or away from.

NOTE: THERE ARE NO RULES IN THIS METHOD. THERE ARE CLEAR INSTRUCTIONS, STRUCTURE, EXERCISES.

NOTE: BUT, DO NOT BREAK THE FURNITURE, THE COSTUMES, THE PROPS, THE CHAIRS, THE STUDIO, YOUR PARTNER, YOUR SELF. Kapish?

5. THE MARCEL MARCEAU EXERCISE - THE LION TAMER

In Marcel Marceau's solo show which he performed all over the world for 60 years, each show had about twenty short mime or clown acts. Each act might be only 3 to 6 minutes. The first half of the program was mime. Then after the interval he was in a slightly different costume which included a big top hat with a flower in it. This was his clown character "Bip" who was named after the Charles Dickens character "Pip" from the novel "Great Expectations".

In the whole show, Marceau had an assistant who was also a mime. The assistant would appear first, with an artist's easel with a sign. The sign had the name of the mime or clown sketch that Marceau was about to perform. The stage would be dark. In the dark the assistant would enter and stand still. The assistant and sign would then be lit and the assistant would do a 10 second mime or even just one movement or one gesture that illustrated what the sign said. For example, I'll invent something, for the sketch "The Painter" the assistant might put their hands up as if looking at a painting and then they might grab a paint brush and make one sweeping brush stroke and hold the end of the stroke frozen in mid air. There would be a sudden blackout. During the blackout the assistant would leave with the easel and sign, and also during this blackout Marceau would enter and take a pose to look like a painter. The lights would come up on Marceau standing like a statue. For some pieces the character was seated so in the darkness a box was placed and Marceau sat immediately, seated like a statue when the lights came up. When the lights were up and the music started, Marceau would begin that mime or clown sketch. When he finished he would hold. There would be a blackout during which time Marceau exited and the assistant entered with the easel and the next sign.

A) The actor holds a small hula hoop and takes a position/shape/statue.
B) The actor imagines the lights come up and after a few seconds of stillness the statue comes alive.
C) Whatever impulse the actor feels or wants to work with begins the mood of The Lion Tamer.
D) The actor/character/clown improvises from or with that feeling. Following their own impulses, imagination, humour, drama, story.

NOTE: Marceau was electric in the theatre. Youtube and videos are not the same as seeing this single human figure in the theatres. Marceau was one of the single most important influences on the whole modern clown movement. Even when he was 80 years old, the last time I saw him perform, the huge audience could be seen weeping during the emotional first half of the program. In the second half, when Marceau was the clown "Bip", the audience roared and roared with laughter. This live experience can not be witnessed adequately on film or video.

NOTE: We are not imitating Marceau. He did have a clown act for "Bip" named "The Lion Tamer". It can be seen on youtube with at least 20 years between him doing it as a young artist and later doing it after he edited and built the sketch over time.

There is no formal ending to this piece. It is rare that I have ever seen an ending in this. The objective is not to find or create an ending. The objective is to be real and true to your emotional improvisation.

NOTE: Once, in a circus in Bucharest, Romania I saw a very old lion tamer. But his lions were also very old. They were old friends. Family. There was no fear. No danger. The tamer and the lions were old and tired and both walked very slowly. Probably both tamer and lions had arthritis. So in this exercise the tamer can be any type of character. There may be one imaginary lion or several. But remember you are a lion tamer and maybe in the big circus cage or not. The lions too each have their own personality. One might be blind. One might be pregnant. One might be unruly. One might be affectionate.

NOTE: Again the conscious and subconscious can help each other. This is about your creativity. Have fun. Work hard.

6. THE JOSEPHINE BAKER EXERCISE

Josephine Baker was like a clown who was a dancer and singer and actress. She was a superstar in Paris, but, she was also a remarkable woman. Like Marceau she too worked during World War II in the French Resistance and both were activists/humanitarians.

This exercise uses music. Either iPod or any device with a wide selection of music. It requires someone other than the performer who can turn music on once and turn it off once. This person must first check the volume to be sure it is loud enough. Try it with a song that you are not going to play. The song you choose can be anything. But try not to let the actor hear it before. The actor will need to go with the music no matter what it is, so the music should be a surprise.

This exercise has an arc and teaches a performer to control and experience and enjoy a short creative arc over just a few minutes.

The steps are:
a) The actor sits on small bench at the far end of the hall or stage. They are meant to be viewed in 'the distance' like an image or a landscape or a sculpture. The image is a clown. The actor sits and then puts on the nose. The audience witnesses the actor, the person, becoming a clown. After they put their nose they put on their hat. The clown is waiting. Waiting generally. The actor is of course free to imagine who or what they are waiting for. The feeling can be 'just waiting' but it will arise and bloom into waiting with a particular feeling, a spontaneous feeling or a premeditated one. One can wait for a bus, or a ride, or a friend, or a boss, or a henchman, or for Godot. According to Beckett's play, we are all waiting. While waiting the clown/actor can not just sit still. They have to be physical although seated and also waiting. During the first 40 seconds or one minute approximately the actor/clown has to create a rhythm that can be seen by an audience. It can be small and subtle. Maybe it should be, because of 'waiting'. But this is not fixed. Perhaps it can be quite active. But this is only the first stage of the arc.
b) After about 40 seconds or a minute or when it is clear to the music person that the actor/clown has a rhythm .... let it go on a bit so that the actor should feel "Did they forget to put the music on?". This process is the norm of patience vs anxiety when we wait. The actor knows that the colleague will put music on. The clown does not know. But the clown and the actor should NOT respond to the music. The actor and clown need to sustain their own rhythm and after perhaps 10 seconds or so, very subtly, gradually the clown starts to move just a little bit with the music while still waiting. The music gradually affects the clown. So it happens that even though the music comes suddenly when the music person clicks the on button, the clown/actor must have control all during their preliminary waiting.
c) Gradually the music has more and more affect upon the waiting clown. But the artist, the actor has 100% control to interpret the music any way they want. The music does not dictate. It is simply an added element that is integrated.
d) Eventually as the movement continues to evolve and build, gradually the actor starts to take pressure on to their feet so that in time their legs have 5% of the weight, then 10, 15, 25, 50% and eventually via a

continual flow of increasing movement and weight the clown is finally on their feet and dancing in any way that has evolved.

e) On their feet there is a gradual increase in the intensity or joy or drama or trauma as the clown acts out their dance. This builds into a highly intense, energetic but controlled frenzy.

f) When the frenzy is finally sustained for 20 or 30 seconds the music person cuts the sound by hitting the OFF button. But the clown does NOT react to the sound disappearing. They carry on their frenzy for another 20 or 30 seconds and gradually, little by little, the frenzy begins to fade. Gradually the clown moves backwards towards the little bench. Gradually they begin a process of sitting themselves down, but still moving less and less until ...

g) Finally the clown is waiting just as they were in the beginning. Eventually the clown either takes a visible deep breath like a sigh and holds still. Or the clown just freezes alive and waiting but still.

The whole exercise should take about two and half to 4 minutes. Long enough to challenge one's peak energy and short enough that the concentration can be sustained and a perceivable arc is observed.

This exercise introduces the 'lost' clown art of pathos. It also is an exercise for the observers, the other participants to see with fresh eyes the pure image of the clown as a symbol of humanity waiting for .... ?????

7. JACKIE GLEASON - THE HONEYMOONERS EXERCISE

Jackie Gleason was a clown, actor, comedian who had a TV show and played several characters. Eventually he had another TV show, The Honeymooners, which was a domestic clown sitcom and a quartet of two working class couples. Jackie's character was a bus driver named Ralph Kramden and his wife Alice was played by Audrey Meadows. They had a lot of domestic tension as a couple, and life and work and money were constant issues. One of the interesting aspects of The Honeymooners was the portrayed difficulty of many domestic relationships. Ralph and Alice would argue. Alice would almost always win, but, Ralph would often have the final word which was often "One of these days Alice, to the moon", which meant he was about to blow his top.

1) The setup is the imagined apartment of the Kramdens. Only one chair is required and is placed in the centre of the playing space. Alice (which can be an actor who a is man or a woman or other) is doing something domestic at the edge of stage left. Alice can be cooking, cleaning, baking, washing dishes, etc - in mime. She is deeply upset because she has crashed the car and she has to tell Ralph. Again, note, they are lower working class and have very little money. Also Ralph, as a bus driver in NYC, always has a stressful day. Alice is trying to be domestic but is anxious for the moment Ralph comes home to see what kind of mood he is in and to find out how she should tell him the news.

The actor playing Ralph can be anyone, and stands at the side of the playing area as themselves and watches whatever the actor playing Alice is constructing in mime. Also the actor playing Ralph gives the other actor a chance to find their own rhythm. This first section should only take about 30 seconds. The actor playing Ralph should stand at the side of the stage, off stage so to speak, relaxed, neutral, watching.

2) Immediately after Alice has established the scene, then, remember Ralph has had a very rough day and is upset. Ralph enters through a mimed door. Keep it simple. Just open an imaginary door, walk through the opened doorway and slam the door. When you slam the mime door stomp your upstage foot. Your right foot. The noise of the door slamming jolts Alice in some way.

3) Ralph starts to pace the room stage right to stage left to stage right to stage left ... behind the chair. Alice should be in front of the chair by about one metre and on stage left. Alice in some way continues to be domestic, i.e. cooking or cleaning, but at the same time noticing that Ralph is pacing and upset. Alice then says "Have a seat honey". Ralph keeps pacing and says "I don't wanna sit down"!! After a beat or two (a few seconds), Alice, while still being domestic in her action, says "How was your day honey"? .... and Ralph goes to sit in the chair and starts saying something like "You

THE FOUR ARTICULATIONS FOR PERFORMANCE

wouldn't believe what happened today ......" or "You wanna know how my day was well wait til you hear this ....." or "Let me tell you how crazy this world is. Today for the first time I saw ....". There are unlimited ways to start, but the first sentences have to show that Ralph heard the question "How was your day Honey"? And is definitely answering that question from the beginning as soon as he goes to the chair or immediately when he sits.

Ralph then continues to improvise non-stop with details of what a terrible day he had. He speaks quickly, fervently and with energy. Seated in the chair but with body energy as well. Non-stop.

Alice is still trying to do her domestic chore but is effected as she knows she must tell Ralph that she crashed the car. Finally she has to speak and blurts out strongly "I crashed the car Honey".
Ralph keeps talking. It should look like he didn't hear Alice. Until after 10 or 20 seconds he gradually or suddenly stops talking and does a "slow burn" towards Alice. A slow burn is used in comedy to show that the actor slowly turning their head is upset and is likely going to explode even though they are trying to control themselves.

Then Ralph freezes for a moment, and then moves in some way. Maybe while seated or maybe by standing, and says "Alice. One of these days .... to the moon"!!!

Normally the 'scene' ends there. But if the actors find something interesting perhaps the scene goes on a little.

This exercise does have an ending. But it also depends on what the actors feel or find.

#8 - THE THREE STOOGES EXERCISE

This is open to experiment. It is good if the actors or the facilitator has seen some of The 3 Stooges films. They had several bits of slapstick that they used in most or many of their films.

The 3 Stooges were always Moe and Larry, but there were three different actors over time who played the third stooge. First was Shemp, then Curly, then Curly Joe.

Some of their schtick (comedy business, bits): for example Moe takes his right hand waves it up and down in front of Curly's face and then waves it sideways. Curly follows the right hand but suddenly Moe uses his left hand to slap Curly.

There is a false slap to the forehead by pointing the hand towards a partner's forehead, but as the hand goes forward, the palm of the hand bumps the actor's forehead.

There is a false nose slap. One actor GENTLY uses their forefinger and middle finger and GENTLY squeezes the other actor's nose and holds it. The actor holding the nose then uses their free hand to slap THEIR OWN HAND .... but as they do that, they release the hold on the nose. So this should not hurt the receiving actor. When the slap happens and the hand is released, the receiving actor grabs their own nose as if it had been hurt.

OBVIOUSLY EVERY ACTOR HAS TO BE OVERLY CAUTIOUS TO MAKE SURE NO ONE IS HURT.

I suggest that you watch The 3 Stooges to see what slapstick actions they repeat. It is all choreographed. There are sound effects. There are noises the actors make. The sounds cover the fact that there is little or no impact. However, professional slapstick performers can actually slap or punch or kick a partner in specific ways so that there is little or no pain at all. On the other hand, professional slapstick performers can take a hit and also know how to move WITH the hit or kick so that they make sure they are not stiff so they don't get hurt.

NOTE: THIS EXERCISE IS DANGEROUS AND RELIES ON ACTORS LEARNING IT IN THE MOST GENTLE, SAFEST, AND OVERLY CAUTIOUS WAY.

#9 TELL THE STORY OF A CLOWN

This is the last official exercise of THE FOUR ARTICULATIONS FOR PERFORMANCE. Each participant is to stand and tell the story of a clown they know or a clown they saw. It can be about a family member who was like a clown or someone in your neighbourhood or at work who was like a clown, or a story that you heard about a clown, or about yourself. You can tell it any way that you want. No matter how you tell it, be physical, use your body language. You can tell it standing, or seated. But be physical. Take the stage, have fun, tell the story.

END OF THE PATH OF HONOUR
END OF OFFICIAL EXERCISES OF THE FOUR ARTICULATIONS FOR PERFORMANCE

AUXILIARY EXERCISES

THE ADHD EXERCISE
THE CLOWN KNOWS EXERCISE
THE CLEOPATRA EXERCISE

THE ADHD EXERCISE

This is a freeform exercise for you to see how quick you can change your focus, yet give 100% focus where your attention is, but only for 1 or 2 or 3 seconds for each point of focus.

So you give something your total attention but only for 1 or 2 or 3 seconds. Your next point of focus is whatever your attention is drawn to.

You are meant to use one sense at a time. So if you look at this book and you widen your eyes and lean forward that is all one point of focus. As you do that you open to another impulse such as awareness of your head and you turn your neck to the left and as you do that you notice how bright the light is and you shrink away from the light and as you move your feet and stand up as you stand up in the action of standing you stop before you get all the way up and clap your hands and as you clap your hands you react to the sound .....

Each point of focus is 100%. It involves your imagination too. How you respond to what you notice and how you respond to what you do is part of your daily reality in life. We are sentient beings. All senses are always operating but we tune in and tune out continually.

This exercise should be done for at least 2 minutes.

THE CLOWN NOSE EXERCISE

This exercise uses a clown nose.
Ideally this exercise is done with at least a coat and hat, i.e. a bit of costuming.
This is a solo exercise.
There are two lines of text: "I should" and "Oh, I can't".
The actor works on a diagonal line starting upstage right and moving towards downstage left.
The actor faces the corner upstage right. They take off their hat, then, put on their clown nose, then put on their hat. Stand relaxed neutral for a moment.

Next, use the shape-pause-rhythm principle (see The Three Walks Exercise within The Four Articulations).

As your shape/rhythm/character/feeling moves in the diagonal towards the downstage left corner you say "I should". Keep physical when you speak. Let the voice, speech, words, come FROM the body. Let the body say what it feels. You should be affected by what you say and how you say it. If you say you should, then you should. But maybe you are reluctant or happy or scared etc.

Then you say -or something inside you changes- so you say "Oh, I can't".

I put a comma after "oh". Respect that small word. It is remarkable. Give it space.
Oh can be a realisation or a shock or a discovery.

THE FOUR ARTICULATIONS FOR PERFORMANCE

After you say you can't, you realise or feel or think or know that... you should, so you say "I should".

Thus you traverse between these two statements.
TAKE YOUR TIME.
There can be s-p-a-c-e between the two sentences. Space and time.
TAKE YOUR TIME.
HAVE FUN.
STAY ALERT EVEN IF THE CHARACTER IS SOFT OR SLOW OR LAZY.

NOTES: The objective is not the corner.
It is a story unfolding subconsciously of your feeling of «should» and «oh» and «can't».
Work along the diagonal to start with as it will help to give the improvisation shape in space.
Say each line only once, then the next line. In other words, at least until you have done this exercise ten or so times, don't fiddle with the text. Keep it simple.
Once you know the exercise and its simplicity, there are no rules.
Once you know the exercise, you can and should clown for and with the viewers, i.e. whoever is in the room watching the clown's dilemma of «I should» / «Oh I can't». This is like "The 'to be or not to be' of clowning".

There is a two-person version of The Clown Knows Exercise.
Clown A does the exercise as described for a solo participant.
Clown B stays behind, i.e. upstage of Clown A.
Ideally, i.e. at least until some actors have tried the duet version, Clown B stays behind, i.e. upstage, and Clown A does not look back towards Clown B.
An interesting aspect is that Clown B will get the laughs, but it is based on what Clown A is doing. So Clown B will know why the audience is laughing, but Clown A will not know.
In a way, Clown B is like the 'naughty' clown, the ratbag, the trickster.

This can also be done as a trio with two Clown B's both upstage of Clown A.

THE CLEOPATRA EXERCISE

An ordinary, simple chair is used for this exercise. Preferably a chair with no arms.

The mechanics of the exercise are to start on the left side and behind the chair, about one metre from the chair. Start standing with your back to the chair. As you turn to your right, you will make a shape as you are turning, then using the shape and a rhythm, move straight down the side of the chair on the left side, getting slightly (half a metre) in front of the chair on the left side, pause, then sit down, pause, then collapse or relax in the chair letting your hands and arms drop either on to your lap or to hang on the sides, pause, then get up relaxed neutral and repeat at least four times that whole process. Each time start with your back to the chair. As you turn you take a new shape and new rhythm. However each time that you sit in the chair, sit with the attitude and feeling of the shape and rhythm. Do not sit in the chair neutral. Sit with an attitude and feeling. About 30 seconds later you will do the collapse, to a relaxed neutral with your arms relaxed, and pause for at least 10 seconds.

The creative aspect integrated with those simple mechanical steps is that you imagine you are in a private space, such as your kitchen or living room or bedroom. You have a problem related to someone else. You have to tell them how you feel or what you think. You do not know what to say or you may know what to say, but you do not know how to say it.

You imagine that there is another chair facing your chair about two metres apart. In that chair is the imaginary person you must tell your problem to.

It may be that the person is not sitting but arrives when you do. They may sit first, then you watch them, or you may sit first, or you may both sit at the same time.

THE FOUR ARTICULATIONS FOR PERFORMANCE

This exercise allows for the part of us as humans which continually lives in a drama: it is too hot, or too cold; or it is really nice, or it is nice but will it stay this way; or it is nice but now I have to go to work; or I am happy to leave work but the traffic is terrible, etc. The human mind is always active and living a drama even if that drama is - I must stay calm, oops now I'm too calm, or now I'm not calm enough, etc.

When I do this exercise I work in the abstract. I never know who is seated in the imaginary chair nor do I know what the problem is. However, the example I give is: if you were living in a share house and you were in your bedroom in the morning and you were thinking about how you will tell your housemate that they need to put the dishes away after they wash them. Or it may be a much more serious or even much more joyous thing that is the problem. For example if you won the lottery and decide to move out but you know your housemates need your part of the rent every week.

The whole exercise should take at least 3 minutes. Take your time in each of the moments called as 'pause' above in the mechanical description.

I call this THE CLEOPATRA EXERCISE because in Shakespeare's play with Cleopatra in it, she is constantly living out her drama and no one knows what she will do next. So live out the problem and have fun with it and push the limits. Make it physical, funny, dramatic, inventive, experimental or whatever way works or is interesting for you.

CHAPTER 3

SOME KEY PROJECTS

In Chapter 2 - The Four Articulations for Performance, the final section Space-Time Continuum, the last exercise is "Tell the Story of a Clown". In this chapter telling clown stories is the beginning. I will tell some stories about a number of my projects. Like life, some stories overlap. Like in cultural mythology stories have repeated themes. The central theme here is how life and art interact and are interwoven.

This chapter is freeform. I tell anecdotal stories of some of my projects, some projects that I've been a part of, and some tales of how things unfolded. Some of the stories can be told from an angle of the ideas and some stories from the flow of time and sometimes like a good story, moving along in time, we know that time bends and shifts (note Arthur Miller's autobiography "Timebends"). Sometimes I go on a related tangent. I usually return to the main thread. Later. Within these stories I've woven in discoveries and philosophy and principles that have guided me. Like any story, the tale is one thing but what you the reader experience by being touched or moved from the tale or the way it is told, well it is your journey as much as it is me sharing my journey.

To date I have been involved in more than 140 live performance projects. Those projects include being in Cirque du Soleil and Slava's Snowshow as well as numerous small performance projects. Those projects have been in theatre, dance, opera, circus, performance art, as well as commissioned projects to create a show inspired by specific artists.

My own creations varied greatly but there were often the themes of: the actor and clown as a symbol for human nature; the inner world of a clown; the reality and crossover between men and women or masculine and feminine energies regardless of the actual gender; additionally many of the projects would be considered cross-cultural or multi-ethnic or intercultural. Often for my creative partners I would first write a scenario or outline. It was a natural instinct to create characters appropriate for my fellow performers in our projects, or for actors in projects which I was to direct.

Some projects I was involved with were related to visual artists and some related to authors and playwrights. Included within the 140+ live projects were 10 of Shakespeare's plays and another 10 projects inspired by his plays. Two such projects were "A Girl's Guide to Hamlet" and "The Madness of King Lear".

WARNING: THIS CHAPTER MEANDERS THROUGH TIME AND PLACE AND PROJECTS AS A DREAM WOULD. TIME IS NOT JUST LINEAR BUT OVERLAPS WITH OUR PAST EXPERIENCES AND CURRENT PERCEPTIONS. GO WITH IT. IT WILL MAKE SENSE AS A LIVED EXPERIENCE AS YOU READ. THINGS WILL APPEAR AND DISAPPEAR AND REAPPEAR AS THEY DO IN LIFE.

A FEW THOUGHTS ABOUT ACTORS, CHARACTER ACTORS, DIRECTORS

I do not believe in the myth of the all-knowing director or teacher. Actors doing a particular role on stage know that role more intimately than the director. Yet the director can view, from the outside, some of the interaction between characters that the actors may not be aware of in the same way as the director is. To an extreme one of the most experienced theatre directors was Sir Peter Hall. His knowledge was phenomenal, yet, if he were to direct a play in the same season as ten other directors they each would emphasise different aspects of the same play.

I saw many plays which had gone through all of the professional steps which include the director studying the play in detail before the first reading. That is part of what Peter Brook warned leads to "deadly theatre" as in dead theatre. The example he gives is a director of Shakespeare who knows every word in the play to such a degree that the director is mouthing the words during rehearsal as each actors speaks. Which means that the director is more focused on the words and very likely is not actually hearing or listening to the actors speech and voice. If the director has memorised the text and is unconscious that they are mouthing the text then they are not actually seeing what the actor is doing. Thus the director is unconscious and the directions they give create a deadly or dead theatre. To avoid this I usually read a play exactly one time all the way through and make no attempt to memorise any of it. Naturally as we rehearse I become more and more familiar with the text, but, as an observer and listener. As we work I will when necessary go back to a sentence or phrase or section of the text and interrogate that particular section. I work 100% collaboratively with each actor, but, we have different roles and theirs is to memorise and live the text, mine as director is to experience the text as a listener and observer of life and art. Two truly great directors give little or no direction to an actor - they are Ken Russell and Woody Allen. Whereas an equally great director gives extremely detailed directions, that is Ingmar Bergman. Whatever works.

In the professional norm, the first reading when all of the actors join for the first time with the director, what is done traditionally is reading the play as an ensemble for the first time, either sitting in a circle or sitting around a table. To avoid the problems of that protocol I lead a physical, vocal, creative warmup which on the first day takes one hour and the following days the warmup is 30 minutes. Additionally, I have the actors up on the floor the first day immediately after the warmup starting with the first scene with their scripts in their hands. In the first day I will make sure that each actor works on the floor so if necessary I will skip scenes to insure each actor has the chance to be on the floor working each day.

Some actors read well at the first reading and some don't. But in performance, in the end, a poor reader may discover much more than the good reader. The actor who really knows their part in the beginning, as all directors know, may tend to be a rigid actor to pry from their interpretation which has not yet had a chance to evolve through collaboration with the director and ones fellow actors/artists. To avoid such problems, some directors ask the actors not to memorise their lines before the rehearsals begin as many directors know if the actor had memorised they tend to be locked in. Other directors ask for the actors to have all of their lines memorised before the rehearsal period starts. Generally I say neither. Though in one case when I had a very short rehearsal period for the whole, uncut, Antony & Cleopatra in which case I asked the actors to be sure to have the text well memorised (at least a head start!!) before we began the rehearsal period.

In acting it is a myth that the more you know the better your acting is. I have seen fantastic actors who do little or no research. I have seen horrible actors who do extensive research. During my 8 years living in Sydney I began to see as many plays as possible each week. Often the actors were much better in the second half of the show. I guessed the obvious, that the actors even though professional still had not adequately warmed up for the start of the play.

I often didn't find the story clear yet sometimes if it was explicitly clear it wasn't rich or complex enough. I saw that production after production was inadequate. I grew suspicious about the professional protocol. I do not particularly enjoy reading plays. I read them not for enjoyment but to understand what the writer is offering both in text and implied stage craft. I read to understand the minimal number of props required. One of the finest books on directing was written by a notoriously boring director. Another book on directing which was simply filled with anecdotal parables was from a highly experienced director and one thing he said was if he could get a production to be 30% of what he hoped then he felt it was a huge success.

As an actor, often in a production on the first day the director would say 'we're going to do this, this, and this' i.e. wonderful altruistic hopes which rarely manifest. Additionally, as an actor, I heard a number of directors say they want us to really experiment and push the limits. That vision normally ends by the third day of rehearsal by which point the actors understand here is another director who says one thing but does another.

On the other hand I worked with over 100 directors some for just one day as in a commercial and some for several projects. I think each one had fine attributes. Some had big weaknesses but even they also had fine attributes. I also got to assist many of those directors many of whom were the ones who saw me resolve problems or make fresh creative solutions very quickly and it was they, the directors, who insisted I should be a director. In the beginning of my career process I worked with fellow actors in a collaborative way which included me as one of the actors and in those cases it was my colleagues who always said "You should direct us". Many of the directors I worked with when I was younger each had at least 20 or 30 years directing experience. They were all good.

I watched productions of Shakespeare, productions which were following the so-called vision of the director yet seemed to take Shakespeare's poetry and drama into obscure interpretations. I found that when I was directing if I sat still in rehearsal and authentically listened to an actor I could provoke them to become more and more clear and therefore more truthful as every word had meaning.

I would often go with the grammar more than the meaning. Grammar mechanically connects and separates and this helps with rhythm. Rhythm communicates the meaning of the words.

Some other acting premises which I work with are: the character who is speaking wants something even if they are helping the other character. I think life is a bit like that. We each have self interest, even if we are helping someone. We want our friends to be happy so they are more pleasant to be with. So in a play character A feels a need and an urge to tell character B to 'watch out'! It is this simple device which makes acting seem more real. Another premise is that character B (and the actor playing B) must show that they are listening and in the process of being affected by A while A is talking. Of course B's movement has to be quite minimal. Contrary to the truism "don't move while another actor is speaking". I insist that the listening actors move, subtly to show that they are listening and considering what is being said. This reminds me of "background action" in stage and screen productions in the USA which can be wonderfully rich. Can be.

SOME KEY PROJECTS

There were legendary directors with this great knowledge: Frank Capra, Hal Roach, Agnes de Mille, George Abbott, Bob Fosse, Hal Prince were amongst the 'legends' who mastered their craft.

In Shakespeare plays, with their complex language, I insist that before character/actor A responds to B, A must make a small movement of any part of their body..... BEFORE they start to speak. In that split second the movement pulls the audience members visual attention to the new speaker A and the audience will hear better. If the audience is given this helping hand the positive effect on the whole performance is palpable. I worked with one play director who worked in the most conservative, old fashioned way. He was brilliant. The effect was excellent. Owen Weingott told us it would take him three days to set the play. He had all of the stage action and character movements set before we started rehearsals. After three days we would work together to enrich and personalise the mechanics. This was very important as this was a farce i.e. a play with a lot of comic entrances and exits. The play was old too, "Come Blow Your Horn". When I studied my part I was shocked to see that Neil Simon's writing is grammatically perfect. There is no extra nor arbitrary comma. He is a master of comic writing. 30 years later I read his autobiography "Rewrites". Of course he worked with the greatest TV comedians during his formative years and was on the TV comedy writing team that included Mel Brooks, Woody Allen, Carl Reiner! But, it was Owen Weingott who taught me about acting in a comedy. He mentored me. I played the younger brother. The older brother was an actor steeped in method acting and it was remarkable to watch and learn from his process. The father was played by Harry Weiss who as a young boy escaped with his parents from Europe the day after the Kristallnacht tragedy. Harry had a photographic memory. He played the father 100% stern. Did no background research. He was hilarious and impeccable in timing. Valery Newstead had a simple way of working. Almost stoic. She used method acting craft. In the 1970s she brought Stella Adler to teach in Sydney for one month. As Val told me, Stella spoke only Yiddish with Val's husband during the month. Stella grew up in the Yiddish Theatre of her father Jacob Adler. The oldest actor in our Simon/Weingott production was 79. She had a solo singing act long ago in England. In our play she had one line. The last line of the play. She sat and watched every rehearsal. When she saw how I worked she asked me each day to look at her entrance and line.

I had an artist crisis in that play. Maybe in every production each artist should have a crisis? It means you are challenging yourself. A good thing for every artist. The stage manager from day one was very proficient. Too proficient for me. She sat as normal with the script open. She read each stage direction, followed each line of text, she did what she was supposed to do. However, I have my own process in the first days or week of rehearsal. I don't mind suffering for my art. I don't mind the anxiety that comes with not immediately knowing a line. It is that anxiety that drives the line from the back of my brain where it is stored. It is that anxiety that makes me study harder, better, more, and makes me seek the connection of any line to the whole of the play. But I like to work organically in layers. So I will often have a slight delay before the line 'appears'. In part this is because I actually like to hear and really listen and really watch the character who is speaking. I don't like to be thinking of my next line while I am meant to be 'really' listening and watching. However, in this case, during my slight pause which literally is usually only a lag of one second, the stage manager would jump in and say my next line. This is very very very frustrating. So after a few days of that it looked like I gave up. I did give up trying to out jump her which I could not do because of my process. At the end of that day Owen said he was very disappointed with my work and that I needed to practice hours at home. It certainly seemed that way. But, I also know that if you read a play once, the way that the brain works, that the whole play is already stored in your brain and mind. The issue is not memory it is recall. My split second delay was to develop my recall at each moment of dialogue. Val said too 'disappointing'. Everyone gave it to me. Even the little old lady shook her head. I got home. Went for a quick swim in the sea. Was so disappointed with myself and with everyone telling me how disappointed they were. So disappointed that the last thing I felt like doing was working with the thing that was 'causing' the suffering. So got a take away pizza and a bottle of vino and morosely ate and drank two glasses of wine. Then had an early night's sleep. I didn't pick up my script. I didn't look at the play. I knew that I knew the play. I knew the lines were in there.

SOME KEY PROJECTS

Some of our company greeted me with trepidation and some even added a bit of 'well, I certainly hope you worked last night'.

I was word perfect. Every line. Stage Manager never got the jump on me once. I knew all of Owen's and Neil Simon's wonderful stage action. After the run through everyone including Owen came up and congratulated me on my performance and for 'working so hard'. Except for the stage manager who was now 'out of job' of jumping on my lines.

AGENT, MANAGER, TOUR PRODUCER

My new agent Kevin Palmer came to see the play. He was particularly impressed that as a 36 year old I was convincing as the 21 year old kid brother. He had seen me only in An Imaginary Life which was a diametrically opposite production artistically speaking!!! Though in that as a 34 year old I played "The Child". It was on the opening night of An Imaginary Life that Kevin introduced himself, congratulated me, and asked me if I needed an agent? I said I had one. He said "Well if things ever changed contact me. By the way who is your current agent"? It was actually more a manager, Anthony Steele. As it turned out, Anthony and Kevin were best friends! They went lap swimming each morning and likely had a coffee after. I think they went swimming at 6am. Kevin would get to his office about 7am and have several morning papers and read the reviews and get ready for the day. Anthony had been a great director of the Adelaide Festival. Now he was to be director of a six months intensive international performing arts program for World Expo-88. He and his long time amazing assistant Margaret Pepper were going to have six months inundation prepping and six months on location in Brisbane. So for a year I was not going to have any management. So I contacted Kevin and he said "But I thought you had an agent" "I did" "What happened"? "Okay come on in and we'll have a chat". We made the deal and it was then he informed me that he and Anthony were daily swimming buddies!

I believe I was actually Margaret's first client as a manager. Anthony bequeathed me to her. She is incredible. But, I think I was a bit of a test case. She took her natural intelligence and formidable years with Anthony at the Adelaide Festivals and after tour of my duet *Soldier Boys*, and after World

Expo - On Stage in 1988 she built up the careers of numerous experimental performance artists. With them, it was she who built up the international touring for Australia's physical theatre performers. She managed, as an experiment or test case, the project I wrote for myself and a Dutch friend who wanted to work with me. However the majority, almost all of the actual touring for that duet that I wrote, "Soldier Boys" was arranged by professional schools touring managers in New South Wales and in Victoria. Norah was the NSW's person who master minded efficient schools touring in Australia. As Musica Viva had forged ways to tour a variety of classical and contemporary music in Australia.

I first heard about Norah at a meeting of independent artists of my age and ilk many of whom were either clowns, mimes, or puppeteers. In the meeting several people complained about somebody named Norah who was ripping off the artists and dominating the touring. They were also specifically complaining that she took 30%. Agents in acting take 10%. Several of them decided to set up their own touring businesses and within 2 years they discovered that Norah was completely accurate that in order for the manager of schools tours to cover costs and make their own marginal profit per touring show, they must charge at least .... 30%. When I met Norah on a recommendation I did not know anything about her story. She told me she was actually born in China and her family had escaped Russia and the Soviets. I was shocked when I arrived at her office. There in the large room were about 10 women each at a small desk with a vertical computer (1987) and a telephone on the desk (1987) and they were busy! They were making schools bookings for numerous independent performing artists. But, much more than 'just' making bookings they were in fact constructing very successful tours for each artist. As Norah explained to me her objective was for each performer to have enough money to buy a house, to have stability, to have a family. Her office was tiny with a glass wall so she was a part of the bigger room. The women, as I recall seemed happy. In the arts sector this was one of the greatest sites I have ever seen. It was bringing quality performing arts into nearly every school. It was providing a real income for artists. The performers were able to do about ten performances every week, and to have their weekends free. They were able to tour and see their own state. When I toured with her company, I was given a computer sheet (1987) which had each address, contact name and phone number and time of performance. Amazingly when our duet *Soldier Boys* toured in my used yellow Renault station wagon, we did not backtrack one kilometre! Norah and her office team knew what they were doing and they earned their portion of the required 30%! Norah had a wonderful friend and colleague Sue Russell who ran the tours in Victoria and we had an excellent tour through that state.

Back to the subject of directing. I would also sometimes have the actor make any physical choice even doing the opposite of what the text seemed to say and via that method suddenly the actor was totally truthful. Organically if allowed freedom an actor will dovetail their instinctual way of speaking and acting a text and this will soon meet with the playwright's intentions.

VALENTINO MUSICO

I directed the four plays of Valentino Musico in Sydney between 2004 to 2016. He is an unusual artist. It is hard to make sense of what he offers by just reading the plays. We met via our mutual friend Liz Hovey who as a young medical doctor performed in a project I had for 29 Jewish actors. Then several years later in a theatre foyer she introduced me to Valentino. He was a research lawyer(solicitor) for a State barrister. He had a play but could not get it read by any theatre companies. He told me what it was about and I said I'd at least be happy to read it (even though I do not like reading plays) and we could talk about it after I read it. I liked it very much. We did it as a co-op. Valentino produced it. The central character was based in part on Valentino's father. The character was only named "Braccio di Fero" (fist of steel). I had asked each of three close friends, three Italian-Australian actors to play the role. Each said for different reasons, no. One was dear friend Fred who didn't feel comfortable playing an 'Italian' at the moment. So I asked Fred to assist me with the production's auditions for roles not yet cast. As time for rehearsals to begin neared and I told Valentino "I have the feeling that I am meant to play this role". He is not a theatre person and could not understand how I could direct and play. By this time I 15 years experience doing just that, successfully. More significantly he could not understand how I could play his Italian father.

Valentino's nickname for me was "Americano" from the title of a popular Italian songs of the 1950s. He is an expert on pop, and rock n roll music. He has a photographic memory that is filled with obscure data about songs, artists, people, history, literature, politics and everyone's phone number and email address etc. Through his efforts as producer our production was sold out and each actor in the co-op made about one thousand dollars.

One Saturday was a matinee before the evening performance. Valentino's father rented a full size bus and brought all of the relatives who lived in a Western Sydney suburb about one hour's drive to the centre where our tiny theatre was located. In one of the later scene's Braccio di Fero acted by me stood and delivered a few lines only one metre in front of the real Braccio aka Valentino's father. After the show he came to me with a relative who could translate his thank you for the show. Soon the bus load left and Valentino and I went a block away to Little Italy for a meal. Valentino thanked me especially because it was the first time he ever saw his father cry. The father and mother were from a village in Calabria, but the father actually lived outside the village because as a youth he was a shepherd in the hills. When he came to Australia he got work in a factory and worked there 40 years. They had a 5 acre tract of land where Valentino and his brothers were born. I visited there once and the vegetable and fruit tree section was huge. There were about 100 chickens, and in the shed (garage) were several vintage cars. That first play was "Meat Pies & Mortadella" and was about the clash of cultures where Valentino grew up. The cultures being the Anglo-Australians vs the ethnic Australians. In parts of the play I had to speak in Braccio's village dialect of Calabrese so Valentino coached me for that. None of Valentino's Calabrese relatives or friends questioned my authenticity. They never asked Valentino if I was American or Australian. They never asked him if I was Italian. In fact he was shocked that they never asked if I was Calabrese, they only asked what village I was from.

BACK TO MY METHODS

I was able to create the foundation exercises of my method which allow actors and directors an efficient methodology to get truthful acting. Chapter 2's exercises each support that vision.

Likewise when I direct a play I am insistent that every action had to have meaning and truth even if the actor was working spontaneously. Yet, their spontaneity needed to be repeated and crafted by the actors and myself as director. It was teamwork. I chose to work counter intuitive to the normal protocol of the 'know-it-all Director'. I thought what would happened if the actors knew the text better than I did. It worked. Each time. I was simply all ears and eyes and responded honestly and I engaged with each actor as a colleague. I would do things that were forbidden in the norm. If I felt like it I would even demonstrate an action or even worse a way of speaking an occasional particular line. But if I did those things it was as much to provoke the actor's spirit as it was to get them to do what I did. As a choreographer I was used to standing in and feeling something, feeling how it works. Trying something out myself. Mostly though like any director I was primarily seated. But at any moment I might jump up to act out an idea and then just as suddenly I was seated again. I emulated working like colleagues and in a troupe not as the myth and fantasy of the 'all-knowing-director'. Sometimes it seems the more a director knows the less they see the magic that each actor brings even with the actors weaknesses and habits which no actor thinks they have. But all actors have habits. In recent years I have seen three exceptional actors each in three different productions and I hope to see each of those actors many times more. But after three performances each, I can see that each has a particular cadence to their speech no matter what character they are playing.

DECONSTRUCTION OF CODIFIED MOVEMENTS

In movement I try to assist trained dancers or physical performers to deconstruct their codified movements. In acting I try to do the same, that is, to get actors to deconstruct codified acting gestures and movements. Most actors act like actors and not like people. Even the most gifted actor needs to struggle to deconstruct their codified stage actions and gestures. Every actor has either habits or tendencies.

ACTORS DEFAULTS

One professional I worked with in several productions and that actor used 5 gestures in every play, in every scene. Some actors like to rub their thighs, or their hands, or their hair. Some actors like to 'prepare' in different ways before they say their lines, they rock back and forth or they like to open their mouth for a moment before speaking, or they take a false small step backwards before rocking forward and speaking. Some of these are 'tricks of the trade' to pull attention.

I remember reading in some autobiographies of actors and vaudevillians from long ago who wrote about professionals who "upstaged". Upstage is the back of the stage and downstage is towards the audience. The upstaging actors will gradually move a few inches behind i.e. upstage of their partners. That causes the partner to slightly turn their back towards the audience which will then be able to see the full face of the upstaging actor. It is a horrible, horrible, selfish habit and some very good actors have that habit. It was in a duet clown show that I realised 'wow, this is that thing I read about years before, my partner is upstaging me'. So when I returned for my next entrance a moment later and my partner upstaged, I simply then moved equally upstage so that we were well balanced. But he moved again, and so did I. That is how you deal with an upstager, it is very very simple just move equal to them. If they move 6 inches move 6. If they move 12 inches move 12 inches. It will be enough and they will stop upstaging you. Another upstager in a major show would always put his hand upon another actors shoulder and then move ever so slightly upstage only an inch or two but the partner had no way to counter act. Until I found the way which was to look dead straight dead centre to the audience and never turn even a fraction towards my upstaging partner. In that show when we two were first asked by the director to first take some time with the scene on our own and come back to him later. I had already clocked (noted) that this actor upstaged everyone in every scene. When we were alone we discussed an approach and tried it once. Then I said "Let's try the section again. Only this time lets nor worry about the other actor so much. So I won't worry if you upstage me and you don't worry if I upstage you." He replied "Do you think I'd actually upstage you"? And I replied with my dark Romanian eyes and staring straight through him "I don't have any doubt about that"! Game on. I always followed the director's directions, but, I did add my method which worked each performance. And was required each performance.

Other than that project I have never mentioned upstaging to the actors who upstage. In fact it is an unconscious action usually. A minor non harmful bit of baby megalomania. As director though I would coach the actor or actors who were far too generous to even imagine that someone in the modern age would upstage another actor. They would then suddenly be able to see the upstaging actor make their move and knew how to simply counter it.

Other actors like to stage a pause before they speak. These and hundreds of other habits or tendencies does not mean the actor is weak. It seems the nature of the beast is that habits and tendencies give actors a necessary thing to hold on to like the way an infant holds their soft blanket or teddy bear.

Ironically, it is we, the character actors who may traditionally be overlooked as highly versatile actors who can actually create a believable and total character on stage not via actors norm of analysis but via intuition, instinct, craftsmanship. One of the greatest actors I have ever seen is John Bell. He is unique because he is like a character actor and certainly knows how to time a laugh like an old vaudevillian. Yet he is a masterful classical actor and deeply steeped theatre expert. I have seen him create a number of totally immersed characters. However, his cadence is not that of the different playwrights, his cadence of speech is particular to his own emphasis of what it takes to be a good, clear, professional actor. In his case, as with three other such top classical actors in England, having an individual cadence to ensure clarity of text is an asset. Yet the rest of what he does physically is totally immersed with each character a new artistic creation as well as a unique character interpretation. Sir Antony Sher also is of the highest calibre mix as both a character actor and classical actor. He also is certainly daring and with his partner director Greg Doran they lift 'standard' plays to the highest standard.

ART COMMISSIONS
HUNDERTWASSER
One of the first commissions related to a visual artist was in Oslo, Norway when I was there to teach for the national ballet school and in a contemporary dance studio. The brief timeframe coincided with a Hundertwasser

art exhibition at the Sonja Heine museum/gallery. My partner and I were excellent at improvising with a minimal amount of discussion or preparation. We would move much more than speak and often our work had no verbal expression and sometimes no music or a minimal amount of music. Even when there was music we could also improvise freely interpreting the music. Memorable in that exhibition was that Hundertwasser insisted that live trees had to be in pots. However, the trees did not thrive well in the indoors and certainly by the end of the exhibition most would have been dead. Ironic given that Hundertwasser moved to New Zealand in part due to his environmental interests.

LEN LYE

One major commission was for the Len Lye retrospective at the Auckland City Art Gallery. That show was for daytimes and included a movement piece with one of Lye's most famous works of a room length wire that was electronically played as an instrument.

ANDERS ZORN

In Goteborg, Sweden my producers got a commission for an Anders Zorn retrospective and they gave me artistic freedom for that. I went to Stockholm to see the exhibition of Zorn's works. Then with the actors we had about 2 months of part time development and research. When we started it turned out that none of the actors identified nor liked Zorn's work which one can guess seemed dated. None the less as they researched and found that in his day he was actually a rebel and risk taker in his art. Additionally, his region of Sweden Dalarna had a more liberal view than some of Sweden at the time. Stockholm as the capital and royal city viewed itself to some degree as the keeper of morals. So when some of his nudes in nature paintings first appeared there was controversy. Eventually he came to be seen as one of or perhaps the national painter something like how Turner is viewed in England. A few years later I saw a large exhibition of another great Swedish painter - August Strindberg whose wonderful works are on another dimension.

ARTHUR BOYD

Certainly one of my favourite commissions came a few years later and when I was a more mature director or creator. That was for an Arthur Boyd retrospective in 2000. Boyd died in 1999 and had a long history with the Riverina district of New South Wales. The exhibition was to be at the regional gallery. I had just started a 2-years fixed term position as a Lecturer at Charles Sturt University - Riverina Campus at Wagga Wagga, New South Wales. So I made the project with one class of students, those in their first year. As usual I start with some casual research and reading. I do not obsess and try to know everything about a subject. Instead I read and let whatever hits my interest take its own creative journey. However I do shape, sculpt and edit the images as they begin to take shape. Like an actor or when directing one needs to identify intimately with the character or subject. Even if an actor is playing a despicable character they must find a positive way of identifying with the characters motivations and needs. It is a creative game just as when children like to play being scared by someone else acting out a monster.

In the case of Arthur Boyd, I loved each piece I encountered and found various aspects of his life intriguing. Then one early morning when I was sound asleep about 3am I awoke suddenly and a poem came to me about Boyd so I wrote it out and as I wrote more text came out. At next rehearsal I read the poem out to the actors and they liked it. The next night the same thing happened but with a new poem. After I read it out, one 18 year old from regional NSW said "Fuck, Ira, how do you come up with that shit"?. That by the way was certainly meant as a compliment. This was Ashley and he was and is a very fine fellow. He and the oldest in the class Tim were chalk and cheese from me or so it seemed at first. We had to go through experiences together to align. Certainly they were two people who would risk their life for a friend. Tim was about 40 and had a daughter whom he raised and Ashley now has about three or four children and is a happy chappy. Ashley and I had one more clash of cultures briefly during a rehearsal. We were working in a large group of about 20 actors and I asked him to come over to give him a directorial clarification. After a few minutes of explaining the new direction, I said "Ashley, I'm going to ask you to leave rehearsal for today. But don't worry you are very welcome to be back in tomorrow." His reply was "Fuck, Ira, what did I do now"?. My clarification was "Ashley, we've been talking for several minutes and the whole time you've been playing with your cock. So the lesson is you can't play with your dick while you are talking with a director."

The Boyd show was scheduled to be once only. As Boyd was deeply connected with the mix of Indigenous and non-Indigenous people of Australia, I wanted to see if we could have one or two local Indigenous musicians to accompany and integrate with the movement and poetry of the whole piece. The performance was to be in the room with the paintings and the choreography was to take place in front of specific paintings and naturally we were going to take images from the paintings and have them come alive.

I went to the university's Indigenous centre and explained the project. The woman in charge suggested two musicians one young and one older. I met with the young man and he came to specific rehearsals. Somehow his teacher of Indigenous music was busy every single time. So it was very much like Waiting For Godot. They had the specific Indigenous tunes selected from the local Wiradjuri Peoples. One song was the Wagga. Wagga in their Wiradjuri language means 'crow'. In Indigenous Australian languages repeating a word implies 'many'. So Wagga Wagga means 'the place of many crows'. And by the river there were many crows. Another song was for their Kangaroo dance. We did not do the Indigenous dances we only had those and other selected songs/tunes to accompany our choreographed pieces and the poetry.

Finally it was set with the gallery that we had only one rehearsal time in the space. That was a little more than an hour before the gallery opened on the day of the performance.

Meantime, I still had never met 'Godot'. On the day however, he was there with the young man and with the liaison woman from the university. I was introduced. We had to start. I did not know until after the run through, that the 'Godot' man was an Elder and that the run through from the perspective of the three Indigenous people was for him to approve or not their participation in the event. He approved. He also explained that it was

fine for the young man to be in traditional costume and body paint but that it was not appropriate for him. That had been my hope even when I originally spoke with the liaison person i.e. that one musician would be in traditional outfit and the other in modern. After the performance I was told that the Elder had been a friend of and had been mentored by Arthur Boyd. Also after the performance one of the professors from the university, Fred Goldsworthy, who was an expert in Australian film and literature asked me where I got the poems and I asked him where he thought they were from and he stated that they were wonderful and must be from Arthur Boyd's eulogy at his funeral. Maybe so, but, they came through my sleeping subconscious a la Edgar Cayce. Cayce was an American psychic with an abundance of archived records of his predictions and wisdom. He was called the sleeping prophet as he would go to sleep and then his predictions and wisdom were recorded while he spoke in his sleep.
The Boyd poems are in this book's chapter CO-CREATING.

INDIGENOUS THEATRE, OTHERS, RESOLUTIONS?

The Indigenous streams in Australia are in a long process of reconciliation in many fields including in the performing arts. There is a rich modern history of Indigenous theatre in Australia which started in the 1960s. There have been various projects and companies in several cities. There were people such as Beth Dean who pushed ahead with research and creative projects even though they were not Indigenous. I did so too as part of my show "Harlequin Dreams".

There are three main companies which have a reconciliation process at the forefront of their projects include Bangarra Dance Company and Big hArt theatre company. The third company that for several years has emerged is Moogahlin Performing Arts Inc which has hosted an Indigenous playwrights festival.

Moogahlin has been led by a team of three people: Lily Shearer, Liza-Mare Syron, Fred Copperwaite. Independent directors Wayne Blair and Wesley Enoch have a long rich successful track record as excellent directors of Indigenous themed projects. There are also several successful Indigenous women directors including Leah Purcell who are also actresses. There have been numerous projects which offer new insights into the Indigenous cultures as well as their relation to the unfolding story of Australian culture. Jack Davis was one of the early key playwrights and Andrew Ross was the director who assisted Davis' work to get produced. Ross also is the person who spotted Jimmy Chi's script "Bran Nue Dae" and Ross directed the great national touring spectacle of that play. Twenty years later an adaptation, a film version of Bran Nue Dae has been produced.

In 1986 via a series of coincidences I was cast to play "The Child" in the theatre adaptation of "An Imaginary Life". The original novel by the same title was written by David Malouf. The stage production producer was Wendy Blacklock and the Director and Designer was Kim Carpenter. The venue was the famous Belvoir St Theatre in Sydney. I thought perhaps my role should go to an Indigenous actor. In 1986 there were very few Indigenous actors readily available and trained for standard theatre work. I emphasise that there were some but they were in different parts of the country. The two famous actors were David Gulpilil and Ernie Dingo. The role and story though were actually not written as in Australia per se but meant to have been in Ancient Rome/Italy. None the less, I thought that I would prepare myself in a mimic Indigenous way. As I had done in a few other countries I found different creative ways to attune myself to the land. In the case of The Child I trained myself just around the corner from the coastal house I was living in at Clovelly beach. Behind the house was Gordon's Bay which was a rough rocky inlet. So each day I would swim in the sea. The entry was always dangerous as the sea crashed onto the rocks. Additionally though for the role I trained myself to run and jump amongst the huge rocks. It was a natural parkour route. I ran barefoot and was gradually able to run at a fast pace over the unpredictable rocks and gaps.

A year later I was contacted for a project that was to launch Australia's Bicentennial celebration. The producer came to my home at Clovelly. He wanted me to be the first image to disembark from the reenactment ship. They wanted a 'neutral' image which was to be me costumed as a dolphin. I was also told that I could name my fee as there was substantial financial support. I said that I thought it would be good to first contact the Indigenous community. He said he would be glad to do that. I never heard from him again.

I suppose it is normal that any artist in Australia has encounters dealing with the evolving issues around reconciliation between the Indigenous people of the land and those who are from elsewhere. I have had several encounters of these cultures as well as numerous other cultures.
That multi-cultural experience needs to be written about on its own.

AUSTRALIAN BITS

Several times I have made projects related to authors of literature and playwrights. "An Imaginary Life" as mentioned above was by David Malouf and the adaptation for stage was created by Kim Carpenter. My participation in this project has an unusual background. In the theatre projects come about through a higgley-piggley layered pathway. How I met the director Kim Carpenter was odd.

Two obscure events happened. Before I lived in Australia I lived for four years in Auckland, New Zealand - Aotearoa. One day in Auckland for no reason I decided to go into a newsagent and buy an Australian paper. I had never bought an Australian newspaper. Obviously I was thinking about Australia. There was The Australian paper in the newsagent Inside this issue was one theatre review and that was not a positive review. As it turned out, unbeknownst to me, my friend Stephen Champion was in that show. Even though the reviewer was very critical about the outcome I thought the director Kim Carpenter sounded interesting. I thought that is a director I should work with. Around this time I saw a movie and I rarely went to the cinema. This was "A Man of Flowers" an Australian art movie. For some reason I thought I should work with the lead actor Norman Kaye. Later, Norman was the main actor in Kim's production of An Imaginary Life.

After touring in Australia a few times, four people suggested that I move to Sydney. One was my friend Stephen Champion. He had been a member of the original Circus Oz when it became an actual touring ensemble, essentially in its second incarnation. He wanted out of Circus Oz and wanted to form a duet partnership with me. He said he could arrange theatres for us to perform in if we made a show. I wrote a clear scenario for us which I titled "A Regular Couple of Guys". I wanted to make a show about two men who were close friends and who lived together and who had a plutonic friendship. I wanted to explore the intimacy that men or people can have through plutonic friendship/love. Stephen wanted to change the title to an iconic Australian term "Two Up". Two Up is an archaic Australian gambling game which is permitted only once a year on Australia Day. Also 'two up' would hint to our partner acrobatic skills which we were likely to incorporate into the play. As part of our agreement I was to be hosted by Stephen and his girlfriend in the apartment they lived in seafront at Coogee. For one month. Long enough to make the show and get going into those theatres Stephen had contact with.

When arrived I had about $100 and no return ticket to anywhere. The first night at dinner as we discussed ideas about the show Stephen's girlfriend Antoinette said "Tell him"! As it turned out we had no theatres booked thus no work. I was a bit shocked and Stephen said don't worry. I worried. As it turned out, another Australian friend Terry Price of the great comic acrobatic duet Price & McCoy had a duet acro job offered at the Sydney Opera House but he got a much longer and full time contract offer for the new casino Jupiters far north of Sydney so he would move there. He asked if Stephen and I could take the Opera House contract but they said if Price & McCoy i.e. an established team could not do it they would hold an audition and we were welcome to audition.

AUDITION

The audition was for the opera Romeo et Juliette.
The audition was in 10 days. I needed that job. I was worried. I wanted a job and soon. I went into "Ira mode" and decided and said that I could choreograph three short acrobatic sequences. The audition was not in the glorious and famous Sydney Opera House. It was in the very old Australian Opera's costume loft in a downtown old business building and its up three flights of wooden stairs. It was literally in the costume loft with around 1000 costumes hanging neatly and many huge old wicker costume cases. The wooden floor was in bad shape from having the huge wicker cases rolled along its floor for many decades. The ceiling was too low for partner

acrobatics. In we went with about 6 other duets. There was a high back chair like a throne placed near one wall. Seated in the throne was an old man in a tidy denim suit. He had several rings on each hand. Standing next to him was a big woman in nice floral dress and her purse on her arm. What is going on here I thought? The woman was all business and simply said hello, welcome, who would like to go first. I was desperate for work. I piped up with no hesitation and said "We will". Off we went and did our longest short routine including a variety of tossing each other. We were very different builds but we were both smallish, strong, and flexible. The audition woman was the spokesperson even though that old man was the boss as one seated like a king and treated like one. Next. A couple went and the big fellow always tossed the little fellow except for one trick and as we could see it was actually the bigger fellow who was the better acrobat. Then each couple went. Most of them only had one or two or three tricks and their tricks were not connected let alone choreographed. After we all showed the woman and the king conferred and I could hear them say something about costumes. For God's sake I thought we're auditioning for this old man who must be the costume mister mistress. The woman then asked if anyone had anything else. I piped up and off we went to our 2nd choreography. She then asked anyone else? The same big and little couple followed us with only two more tricks. Some of the others had one or two more tricks. Then the woman and the mister mistress conferred again and again I heard them say something about costumes. So I piped up without being asked and the woman did not like that but the mister mistress of costumes nodded to me to show our next routine. The same couple could only repeat two tricks they had already shown. And speaking of showing …. the woman then said to the little fellow of that team, the one with the moustache "You're slipping love" and as the woman said that to the little moustached man she also looked and nodded towards his crouch. Oh wow!!! The woman had spotted that the little moustached man was a woman and she had stuffed her pants to look like a man but the stuffing was stuffed.

I had already been suspicious of this couple but for another reason. The little moustached man spoke with the big man in 'Hungarian'. But I knew it was gibberish and the big man had a permanent look of shock.

As it happened a few years later I was ordering a take away pizza and I saw a woman at a nearby table and thought I recognised her and said hello and apologised for not knowing her name nor where we met but I felt certain I knew her. We tried to figure how we could have met and soon found we were both acrobats. Bang. I knew who she was and of course she was the moustached man with slippage. She was lovely and funny and we had a good laugh and I left with my pizza.

All the acrobats were told to wait in the hall. The decision was made and the woman in the floral dress came out to tell us, we got the job in the opera Romeo et Juliette. As Stephen and I began to walk down the stairs I asked "Who was that old costume mistress in the denim suit"? He replied "That was Sir Robbie". I asked "Who's that"? "Sir Robert Helpmann". That was still no help as Stephen could see by my face. So he simply said "The movie The Red Shoes"! "Oh" got it.

A NEW BEGINNING. SYDNEY.

We were the first to rehearse in the Opera Australia rehearsal building in Surrey Hills. The huge room had tape on the floor marking out the size of the actual stage area. Sir Robbie's throne was in place. His assistant this time was a male dancer about our age 33. Helpmann spoke to the assistant who spoke to us. Very odd to me as there only the four of us in the room. First we were asked to do our three short routines which we presented for the audition. We, mainly Helpmann and myself, started to cobble together a long routine out of the three short ones. The most peculiar thing was that when Bobbie as Helpmann was known before becoming Knighted ... well when he had a comment he would slightly incline his head and the dancer would bend down and give Bobbie his ear. The dancer would then walk along the outside perimeter of the tape on the floor then would from Stage Left enter direct to us and give us Bobbie's notes or comments. When I heard the comments which were sometimes just complements I did not know if I should thank the speaker who was the messenger or look to Bobbie the Benevolent. So I would give a bit to both but to Bobbie I would also smile and lo and behold he would always smile back and nod to me, ever so slightly. None the less he was wonderful to work with and I cherish the fact that he used my choreography and together with all the

SOME KEY PROJECTS

nodding and cheeky smiles exchanged in the few days we cobbled together a fab acro duet.

Naturally with any big company time is money. So except for the first day we would only work together about an hour. A few days in we showed up and part of the set was there for us. This was a ramp so we could practice part of our entrance. The low part of the ramp was at ground level at the back of the venue and we were to run up the ramp and jump from the front which was perhaps a metre or metre and a half high. From the run we would jump on an angle away from each other to jump into a straddle split in the air. That is a lot of force on landing but we were young and fit at 33. However, when we finally got into the opera theatre in the Opera House which seats about 2000 people, the main set was up. Now time is even more limited. Much more limited. We had a few minutes to try the real entrance. The set was the forum balcony. We were to enter from opposite ends by walking up the hidden stairways which at the top were about 15 feet high we would face each other on the balcony which in the middle had a staircase of about 10-15 steps.

From our opposite sides we would walk swiftly towards each other and turn to face towards the audience and then we ran down the wide steps building the momentum so that we hit the ramp at top speed and our leap would take us well up in the air and far forward. Upon landing we took a quick cheeky bow. We went to opposite sides of the stage and began our routine in earnest. That included our signature move that I called "The Terrible Sixes". One of us ran a few steps to the other and was pitched up into a back saulto high in the air and backwards and the one who pitched prepared to run as soon as the saulto landed etc so we did alternating pitched saultos six times (three times each). A threw B and immediately after landing B threw A, AB BA AB BA then we went into the rest of the routine. We did a fabulous fake near fall right to the edge of the Orchestra Pit with me the top-mounter. If we made a slight error we would have landed well and truly into the orchestra. There were about 50 musicians. At a few moments in our act, when we looked out at the audience I could still a glance to the Conductor (I think his last name was Kaminsky) whose eyes were on fire and he always seemed to be enjoying our performance and we would have a moment's glance at each other.

I was living at Stephen and Antoinette's for my first six weeks of living in Sydney. Had we gone on the road as scheduled it would have been 4 weeks. The extra 2 weeks allowed for us to start in the opera and then quickly we found me somewhere else to live. I'm sure for them it felt like months. As quick as possible with Stephen's help I found a share house at the next beach, the house was on the seafront! Located in Clovelly on Walker Avenue and with a tiny park in front of the house so I could practice acrobatics.

But, while I was still living in Coogee one day the phone rang and Stephen was cooking and asked me to answer it. I said there was a woman on the phone. He asked her name and I said Kim. When he finished his phone conversation he explained that the high pitched voice belonged to a man named Kim Carpenter and he wanted an acrobat for his next theatre show and wanted to see if Stephen would be interested as they had worked together before. Stephen recommended another fellow we knew who was a fine acrobat but was hired to juggle in the same opera we were in. Sid Haylen, Jr. I asked why he didn't recommend me? He said "You would hate working with that director". That was the director I read a bad review about but thought I should work with him.

Very soon after this call it seemed that word got out about me as a talented or at least a skilled physical performer. One day a call came and Stephen answered and said it was for me. I spoke to the person who wanted to hire me for a day to coach him for a stunt in a play. We made a deal and a date and time. When I got off of the phone I asked Stephen "Do you know some guy named John Bell"? Stephen looked quite surprised and asked "Was that John Bell phoning for you"? At that time the living greats were: Sir Robert Helpmann, Dame Joan Sutherland, John Bell. But I didn't know that. On the appointed day I did the deed.

SOME KEY PROJECTS

AN OPPORTUNITY

Just after I moved to Clovelly somehow the Director/Choreographer Kai Tai Chan had also 'heard' about me so phoned and hired me to teach acrobatics one evening per week at his company One Extra's dance studio. I had about 20 people the first night and at least that for many every class. For the next run of classes I was offered to teach any other class. One of the people in my class was a wonderful modern dancer (with Classical Ballet training) named Rosalind Crisp who I thought was special and had yet to find her niche. I have never told her this, but, I created the next course for her. I thought she's too good to worry about not getting work. I thought if she can make a shift something good will come for her and particularly from her. So I created "Audience Communication Skills". It was shortly after that her own great quest began to emerge. It began to flourish when she merged with Andrew Morish and she founded Omeo Dance and likely has hardly been without work ever since.

Dancers can be amongst the most severely critical people I have ever met in the performing arts. That is only because of the detailed excellence required in ballet and many other forms, and, the extremity of competitive numbers of people vying for very limited opportunities. Additionally, in the traditional sense the majority of dancers finish their main career by the age of 30.

So I made the course based on my creative method to combine the physical with the imaginative. What was particular in that course was my secret that the people seated had to give feedback to the person doing an exercise. In that process I taught by osmosis. The people watching could hear how frequently I give clear supportive feedback, but, additionally if negative feedback or negative wording in feedback was given by anyone I would find a way to counter those words and support the performer and give the viewer a lesson that anything has potential and thus generally speaking every attempt is good. As I always joke that "You are already good. The question is how do you get gooder"? I am positive that the short course was an early turning point as intended for that wonderful modern dancer.

There are many such things, just as many teachers and colleagues have helped me, I have done many things to help many actors including close friends and associates, but, some of those are personal secrets. The professional secret is that sometimes a person in their career needs private unspoken intervention from their teacher, director, colleague, or friend. I am quite certain that a wide selection of my teachers, directors, colleagues and friends and certainly even numerous students have made important interventions on my behalf unbeknownst to me and other interventions made on my behalf I witnessed. I am sure each of my teachers and a number of my friends at Dell'arte School had to make interventions on my behalf. I was too loose, too unfamiliar with the territory, too burning with passion and curiosity, and too naive.

THE FOOL STEPS INTO THE ABYSS

I was very much exactly like The Fool card in the Tarot pack. That image is the fool with a small bag that contains all his worldly possessions held on a stick over his shoulder as he is about to step off of the precipice into the abyss - to step from the grounded know world into the future and unknown world.

I have stepped into the abyss countless times. I still do.

Moving to Australia was a risk that went wrong from day one and turned out right, right away. It is an imaginary life. As the childhood song says "Row, row, row your boat gently down the stream. Merrily, merrily, merrily, merrily life is but a dream" (possibly composed by Eliphalet Oram Lyte). That message is as mystical a message as I have ever heard. The actor and clown has to take life a day at a time. Even if we do not succeed every day, we can try every day to row gently down the stream. If we try we will achieve being merry. As another song says "You can get it if you really want, but, you must try, try and try, try and try. You'll succeed at last" (by Jimmy Cliff). One of the finest Australian actresses is Queenslander, Libby Munro. I had never heard of her until my friend Todd was in a 2-hander play with her and suggested that I see her work. He got me tickets to see the show and was humble enough to say that Libby was great and that he thought I would really like what she was doing. Libby Munro is a truly

SOME KEY PROJECTS

great actress. Todd was absolutely wonderful too but his role was the character who could never catch up with the female character as written into the play.

Naturally a few days later when Todd and I met I wanted to also ask about Libby's background. It was no surprise that she grew up in the countryside and with horses. Of course not everyone with such a background becomes an actress!!! She though does not take 'no' for an answer. She went to and graduated from THREE acting academies. That took 8 years full time. Finally she landed the role 'made for her' in a paying theatre company. Now it is a matter of luck to see and hope that more great roles find her. But she is not waiting for that. She has written a feature film and played the lead role and it will be released in 2018 "The Hunted". The play I saw her in was "Venus in Fur". But more than the play, the clips I've seen of the NYC production show that the Brisbane production was much greater, and that Todd and the director rode with the "no-holds barred" former Queensland cattle station woman Libby Munro.

Timebend ..... I'll get back to Australia later but this is the path that led me there ....

SCANDINAVIA

When I left the USA in August 1979 it was a vague plan, with no return ticket, to stay for three weeks to see the European one ring circuses, particularly their traditional clown routines. The clowns in the USA had a different tradition. I thought perhaps some of the old European clowns were still alive and doing the traditional clown acts and I wanted to see them live in circuses. I managed to see Popov live in Holland with the Moscow Circus; and the Rastellis family of clowns; and, "Papette" Alfred Pauwell; the Knie brothers; and others. Charlie Cairoli was unwell when I went to Blackpool so he wasn't performing.

I managed to stay longer than the three weeks. Then, one day in Paris I went to a large park to practice my acrobatics on the grass and a gendarme (policeman) came and told me to get off of the grass. I was a hippy clown from 4 years of living in California. I decided I need to get out of Paris.

A few months before, in California my Dell'arte classmate and friend Ole passed through one day with his Swedish wife Maria. We chatted for quite a while but they were traveling and had to move on. As they walked up the road from The White House home to many Dell'artians past and present I called to them "Hey Ole!! Do you need an acrobatic teacher at your school". He yelled back "YES"! I saw Maria say something to him. When we three next met in Stockholm she told me what she said to Ole "Well, we're going to see him again"!

I sent Ole a telegram from Paris and said I was available for work. He sent a telegram back "You're hired". We spoke on the phone and he informed me that if someone applies for a work visa Sweden allowed them at the time to work until the application was approved or not. Even if it wasn't true, I believed what he told me and went to the consulate and applied. A few days later I was on the train to Hamburg station and change to Copenhagen station to Helsingor to Stockholm. At that time the train cars to Sweden were transported via ferry from Helsingor, Denmark (referred to as Elsinore in Shakespeare's play Hamlet) across the narrow sea strait to Helsingborg, Sweden. When the train started to travel in Sweden I went to the back of the train to look. A small old ticket conductor came to me and spoke in Swedish. I had been in Sweden a few minutes so my Swedish was not so good :) I tried to explain in English and gestures that my ticket was in my compartment. At first he would not let me pass. Then he started yelling (yes, Swedish people do yell, sometimes) and kept using his metal ticket puncher towards me as if it were his weapon. Soon he let me past and followed and I gave him my ticket. A few minutes later while I was standing in the hall looking out the window to my new homeland, two young men, Swedes I assumed came up to me and made Italian hand gestures to me, laughing, and saying "Hey! Luigi! Luigi!!" With a fake Italian accent. Many years later I found out that the Swedes (not the nice ones) had an expression for people like me with dark curly hair - "svartskulla" which means 'blackhead'. Every country has a derogatory word for a foreigner. 'Gaijin' in Japan; 'wog' in Australia; 'wetback' and 'greenhorn' were the old USA expressions for people "fresh off of the boat". Nothing new under the Sun. Nations per se started little more than 200 years ago. Previously borders were fluid and changed with history. Every nation has

SOME KEY PROJECTS

been reliant upon foreigners for its own development. The Germans' investment into developing rural Ireland boosted the economy. The Turkish migration into Germany boosted the standard of living for the Germans (and the Turkish). The English invested and developed collapsing ancient estates in France. The Polish influx to England renovated en masse houses and small businesses which had seen better days, but are now revived by Polish workers. The educated from poorer countries continue to boost first world nations collapse.

I arrived in Stockholm with approximately $3.50. Maria and Ole's housemate Shashti (her yogic name) met me at the train station and escorted me on the bus to home. The agreement made with the household and I was that I could stay in the house about two weeks until I settled and found an apartment. The house was set up around their yoga group so they wanted to maintain that particular integrity. As it turned out I fit in well with everyone and everyone was kind and tolerant and generous enough to accept me, so I lived there for more than a year.

As I will explain a few pages further in this chapter, while I lived in San Francisco for two years (plus two years in Northern California). In San Francisco I only spent part of my time in theatre pursuits. Most of my days and hours were training in a form of meditation and healing that works with energy in a similar way to traditional or Indigenous healing that occurs or occurred in most cultures around the world. Ole had told the other few people in the house that I did energy healings which I did do. But, I wanted to leave that and stay with the theatre life and physical training.

We had a dinner guest one night, an American fellow who was some type of physiotherapist and worked at a healing centre named "Galleri Medmera" that was central near the Slussen train and bus centre. He offered to show me the centre. There the organiser asked me if I would do a public demonstration of the healing method I knew and they would put a small ad in the newspaper. Perhaps a dozen people came and one of those was a theatre student I was teaching at Clownskolan. Ulrika or Ulla was her name. After the demonstration she asked me to set up a course so she could learn this method. I saw that she sincerely wanted to learn so I spoke to the organiser and we set up a once a week 8-weeks healing meditation course in the method I was taught. The first class Ulrika/Ulla showed up with an interested friend. The second class they brought others and by the third class I had 8 students and I said no more but that I would set up another class when our 8-weeks finished. The original 8 students wanted more so I also set up a course to learn how to heal others. And things took off a bit. Within 6 months I had more than 40 students studying with me regularly. I also had a successful private practice within the centre in which I would do one-hour aura readings. On Sundays I had a free open healing clinic and I would do healings non stop for about 5 hours. Usually there were so many people though that I would set up a healing circle for an hour or two and after that I would see anyone individually.

There were 'orange people' working in the centre as well. Those were people who dressed in orange or red clothing and were part of the Rajneesh organisation which years later changed its name to Osho. They were very into 'rebirthing' at that time as their main healing practice. Many of them attended my courses and had private readings. Several times though in those private readings a problem arose while I was doing healings and to be quite blunt it was not as extreme, but, in fact I was having to do spontaneous exorcisms. No crucifixes and no heads spinning or spiting etc but it was still quite a scene. After several I saw a repeated pattern and even with the first such incident I explained that there was a problem I was picking up on with the 'rebirthing' technique. Very simply, that technique really 'opens' people up but it does not or did not at that time take care of people who were too open. So the method I was taught, I taught to their rebirthers and things started to improve enough that the main Rajneesh teacher of rebirthing made an appointment and flew from Europe to get a private reading and to get a lesson on my findings and the technique. The result was that she intended thus to change their method by incorporating this technique. I was starting to get invitations then to other towns in Sweden and that is when I understood I could not run this business by myself so I shut up shop. However, one person who had a reading with me and whom I taught some of the basic techniques to was very keen to develop further and she went to Berkeley as I did and graduated after a year and opened her own healing centre a few years later in Stockholm and she ran that for at least 15 years. She was also a mime and had graduated from the wonderful Mime Skolan in Stockholm that was long run by a Polish man who had been in the great mime ensemble of Tomaschevski. It was an excellent physical theatre school!!! My friends known as Reich/Szyber are graduates of that school.

MY FIRST WEEK IN SWEDEN

I went to the Clownskolan the day after I arrived in Stockholm with Ole. He asked me to be in the first class which was acrobatics so I could see what level the actors were up to and so they could be around me and see what level I was at then I would start to teach acro class the following week as well as other classes. Nice folks, but, when I was in the line waiting to do a round of tricks on the mat a young lady from Canada gently grabbed my ass and squeezed and said "Nice ass". Welcome to Sweden, Canada style. After class I went in to see the center of Stockholm. Ole had given me 20kr which was plenty for the day at that time.

It was already the autumn but that first afternoon I decided to try busking to earn a little extra money even though I was going to start teaching the next day. I had my green bag with my five orange lacrosse balls that I used for juggling and my hat. I found a big plaza which is the main plaza Sergel's Torg. It is huge. It borders the main walking street Drottningatan (Queen Street) which August Strindberg used to live on. On the plaza was the grand Kultur Huset. I went into the centre of the plaza. I put the bag down and started to mime and clown a little bit on the spot. The edges of the square are about 50 meters from the center in all directions. Little by little more and more people stopped to watch, but only at the outer edges which is not functional for busking when it comes time to pass the hat for donations. Shortly there were a lot of people. So I started to juggle. It was very cold. My fingers were very cold and not really good for juggling. But I tried.

Suddenly I noticed two policemen appear at the edge with the long steps. They stood still for a few minutes. I did not know what to do. I didn't want to get in trouble if I wasn't allowed to busk in that location. I did not have my official visa yet. I had no money to go anywhere in the world. I couldn't just pack up and leave without the police then coming to check my passport once they found I did not speak Swedish. I thought maybe they will see I am harmless and they will leave. They did the opposite and slowly started to walk directly towards me, down the steps. However, the people closed in. As the police came closer so too did many dozens of people. I did not know what they were doing. I kept juggling and playing until the police were on the plaza itself and walking to me. The people surrounded me. I stopped juggling. The police could not get close enough to talk to me. The people chased them away Swedish style which means they politely but forcefully told them to leave me alone. They did and many of the people gave me money.

I learned what I really needed to know about Sweden and the Swedish people right there day one.
So I am deeply indebted to Sweden, the Swedes, my friends Ole and Maria and their household, and Michael "River" Lynch who started the Clownskolan. It gave me, a wayward American with some values that made me want to see the world. And to see a world with some values different than in the USA. As the old Navy slogan said "Join the Navy and see the world", but the parody goes "I joined the Navy to see the world. And what did I see? I saw the sea." As it turns out River like myself had been in the US Navy before he became a mime/clown. Ole had been a graduate of the merchant naval academy and had been an officer on a cargo ship. We all three had been in service during the Vietnam War. I was stationed though in the Atlantic Fleet so far away from combat.

As Winter was nearing, it was already quite cold. I went to a second hand clothing store and found a wonderful long winter coat. It did not really fit as it was for someone much taller than I was. It was only 50kr which I now had earned so I bought it. At home I was given an extra down vest and a spare pair of the classic indigenous Lapp boots. A few days later I had a little more money and went again to a second hand shop and there was the dream hat of all clowns, a real Top Hat! So I bought it. That is how I looked all through my time in Sweden for 7 months of cold - Top Hat, huge too long overcoat, Lapp boots. There is a famous photo of August Strindberg walking on Drottingatan with his Top Hat and long overcoat.

SOME KEY PROJECTS

In the first week in the newspaper I saw a tiny ad for a clown show. I took the ferry from Slussen to Djurgarden and went to Gronalund's tiny Comedie Teater. There I saw "Clownen Manne". He had an extraordinary direct communication with the little children. Although I didn't understand the language I understood the communication. He really listened to them and twisted and misunderstood what the children said or asked. Some of this was guided or 'set up'. After 100s of performances every clown knows the most common replies from an audience. None the less clearly Manne listened, heard, and spoke directly to specific children who spoke up. He also was very skilled and there was a whole sculpturing of his entire show. The costume was unique and beautiful. Handmade by his wife Karin. The show was a 100% delight. I cried because his communication was so honest with the children. He stayed around as many clowns do so that people have the chance to talk with the artist and this included a lot of little children rushing for the chance to meet this creature known as a real clown. I waited my turn so after the children Manne and I met for the first time. We had a quick chat in English and he invited me to make a meeting at his home which was nearby I think in Ostermalm.

The next day that I was to teach I told the students about seeing this wonderful clown Manne and his show, but, the actors told me more. I didn't know but Manne even then was essentially the national clown so all of the students at Clownskolan were already in love with clown as children thanks to Manne. Many of them had seen him perform live. The show I saw was his signature show which I think he has performed more than 10,000 times - Min Bror, Min Bror (my brother, my brother). For many years Manne has performed a trio show with his daughter also a clown and actress, and his son who is a master of the Swedish folk music on violin/fiddle. I believe his wife Karin still makes the incredible costumes!!!

This is still all within my first week in Sweden. One late afternoon after teaching I went home to Tyresso and decided to have a walk into the forrest and to look at the lake from a cliff. There was no one else. It was still. I was in my Top Hat, too big overcoat, and Lapp boots. At the highest cliff over the lake I decided to lay down in my coat upon the earth which was moss covered rocks. I fell into a deep sleep. When I awoke it was if I had woken up a thousand years ago when the Vikings were here. It was at that stage I finally, just a week later, felt I had a new home which was not only Sweden but also not the USA. I had worked for this new beginning by taking a series of risks. I had to also trust my own vision and intuition and trust in what the universe had in store for me. I have faith. I had to trust turning down those three offers from Circus Vargas one of the USA's then thriving classic 3-rings circus; and turn down the offer from Ringling's circus Clown College, and turn down 'an offer you can't refuse' to be Bill Irwin's stage partner for his first show in NYC. It's been a great adventure so far, but, I can not overemphasis the opportunity I was given to help Ole to establish his school which this year celebrated it's 40th year. I did my job very well. I also am ever thankful to Ole, Maria, Manne, Sweden.

When I would go around in Stockholm that first year and I'd meet people and chat and they'd find out I was a clown they would always say "Do you know Charlie Rivel"? Then they would light up and tell me about the time they saw him. Really it was like they had seen Santa Claus. Soon I bought a copy of his book Poor Clown in English.

Then I was at the Festival of Fools in Copenhagen but a few of us clowns were not in the actual Festival so we rented a small theatre and had our own festival or fringe. I think Viveka Oloffson and Lis Helstrom were in our collective each doing our own show but supporting the others. Ole let me know he had just seen Charlie Rivel on the outdoor stage at Gronalund in Stockholm. My shows were done in Copenhagen so I took the train to Stockholm to see Rivel live!!! I was able to see his last performances the last four days of his contract. He was 86 and performed with his son and daughter who were each either 60 or 62. His daughter was his assistant and dressed in a beautiful dress and high heels and was stunning. The son was the pianist. On the last day I went back to meet Charlie by the stage door. His car and driver were waiting, he came out and I said hello and thank you and we chatted briefly and shook hands and he was tiny, about 5 feet tall but his grip was like a vice so the old acrobat and trapeze flyer was still strong. He then took me to meet his Fiancé who he told me was young, just 70. She too was stunning and close to 6 feet tall. I don't know

SOME KEY PROJECTS

if Charlie performed after that. Maybe he went next to Helsinki's tivoli? But he died at 87 years old.

Each of the four days in the show there was a point when Charlie momentarily sings like a bird. Suddenly several birds, seagulls perhaps flew across the stage. Each day. Same time. I told Clownen Manne and he said "Oh that's been happening for ten years" i.e. whenever Charlie performed there each summer.

EVERYDAY NON-REALITY

I awoke one Sunday with an idea to make a clown show in a theatre. I said I would do it in ten days time. The next day I found a theatre, Teater 9 and ten days later I opened my new show "Getting Into Struggle". I played it 3 nights. From that I evolved some of the ideas into a new more complete scenario called "A Clown's House". That show I toured. It was non-verbal and had no music. It was very physical and very funny. That show led directly to me performing in Australia and New Zealand.

I then lived in New Zealand for four years of teaching and performing. During that time I started to train in classical ballet. I did Limbs Dance Company's company classes three mornings per week. Then when a new contemporary dance teacher came from New York teaching Cunningham Technique I also attended that the other two days per week. Eventually with my performance partner we were Guest Artists with Limbs for their Sydney Festival season in 1984. We performed two duets which we created together but which I directed. We also had our duet show "Lilla Cirkus" and performed that on a fantastic new outdoor stage set up for the Festival in Hyde Park. We also performed and taught for Moomba Festival and I taught a physical theatre workshop for West Theatre in Melbourne. Then for the Adelaide Fringe Festival we had to throw together a new show because the venue was changed from a small theatre to a large cabaret stage named Little Sisters Cabaret. Unfortunately our advertised show had acrobatics but our new show did not and the advertising naturally built an expectation that was not fulfilled in the acrobatic department. We also had daytime shows - 2 shows per day - of Lilla Cirkus (which did include acrobatics, juggling, slapstick, mime, dance) touring in the schools of Adelaide and suburbs for three weeks.

Returning to Auckland I was hired again at nightclub called Retro. The owner started a male strip show and wanted me to join and to make clown pieces. I said no. But he asked me to at least come see the show. It was for women only and called For Your Eyes Only. I watched in the technicians booth and I saw how one very shy lady with glasses who looked like a classic librarian or pre-school teacher transformed during the show. She opened up and laughed and became bright and jumping with enthusiasm. So I said the show works and I started the next week. Soon it was on 2 nights a week and then such a success it went to 4 nights per week sold out. Then a touring ensemble was set up that did a nationwide tour for six months. I called myself "The Comic Strip" and did three numbers and counter to the macho strippers I made each of my characters fail. For example in one where I was to strip I could never get my clothes off nor undo my suspenders. Each piece was choreographed to one or two songs. I did that for one year. I enjoyed it because the audience was the best, vocal, shouting, laughing, open and having fun. I pretended I was in the olde classic American Burlesque that featured not only women dancers who did strip tease but also featured the Baggy Pants comedians such as Pinky Lee, and Phil Silvers. It was having a chance to live a bygone era.

SWEDEN SECOND PERIOD

I lived in Sweden in two periods. The first was late 1979 to late 1981. I was hired to help my friend Ole start his school known as "Clownskolan" which five years later he renamed "The Commedia School when he relocated to Copenhagen, Denmark. Clownskolan was begun in the mid01970s by the mime/clown Michael "River" Lynch. "River" relocated to New Zealand in 1978 which is when Ole arrived in Sweden and was able to take over "Clownskolan" and to begin a longer program. 1979 was the beginning of the new 2-years program. The first year it was only Ole and I who were the teachers. The second year I was getting work performing and touring my show "A Clown's House". So I taught part time when I was in Stockholm. A years later the school moved to Copenhagen and was renamed The Comedia School.

SOME KEY PROJECTS

The second period in Sweden was 1995 to end of 1998. However immediately preceding being in Sweden for that second period, first - from October 1993 to November 1994 I was teaching in Copenhagen at The Commedia School.

My own first project in this second period in Sweden was produced by three women who owned a juggling, magic, and children's toys store in Goteborg. That was called Commedia Butik. They also were producers of workshops and outdoor entertainment such as street performances and fire events.

I came to that in a roundabout way. A friend in Copenhagen suggested taking a day trip to Sweden. At the time there was a short ferry from Elsinore to Malmo. There we walked into a small used bookstore. There was one shelf with books in other languages. I saw a book "The Quantum Gods" by Jeff Love published in 1976. I opened the book and read about two sentences and said "This is what I should call my method. Quantum Theatre". Coincidently, there is a "Quantum Theatre" that started about that same time in my birth city of Pittsburgh. I found out about that several years later via internet. There is also now a book called "Quantum Gods" that is recently published and is not by Jeff Love but appears to be inspired by Love's book.

A few months later a gig was arranged for me to perform improvising as Harlequin in Eskilstuna, Sweden. I decided to visit Stockholm so I could meet with friends. I met with Carina Reich and Bogdan Szyber and they hired me for a one week project they were soon going to create in Goteborg. That involved more than 20 performers including myself and I was to be the physical trainer during the week of creation and rehearsal. We did one elaborate performance on scaffolding integrated with a large fountain and sculpture of Poseidon. The performance piece was named Poseidon's Drom (dream). The actors had a water system of hoses which ran along the arms and head. So as we moved the arms and heads the water spouted coordinated choreographically and with composed music.

During the week I walked past the window display of Comedia Butik. I went in to have a look and I heard a fellow behind me speaking in English with an American accent. I said hello and we introduced ourselves he was James who was a juggler. It happened that via a friend, James knew my name and knew I was teaching at The Comedia School in Copenhagen. He said that the shop owners sometimes organise workshops and he took me straight away to meet them. One was Aleka and two were Eva. We chatted for a few minutes and I told them about my "Quantum Theatre" method and idea and they bought it for a 2 months period. I returned in January 1995 and the first project went well so we extended several months. I trained 26 performers who had a variety of skills and backgrounds. In this period I thought since I am in Sweden now was the time to read about that national playwright August Strindberg. I got a book in English by the great Strindberg scholar Meyers. Strindberg fascinated me. Whereas with Shakespeare we know very little about him personally, with Strindberg we know everything. I began to write some ideas for a show about Strindberg. Eventually that show became "Artiste i Exile .... Requiem for Strindberg" which toured in the far north in five small cities, with 15 actors.

After my year or so with Aleka, Eva and Edda I was hired to teach and direct for a multicultural theatre project in an ethnic suburb of Goteborg. After a year there three other jobs eventuated in the north of Sweden. Those were in Lulea, Kiruna, Gavle. Then I got a final job teaching and directing in Goteborg at a private acting school. I directed Strindberg's play Himmlerikets Nycklar eller Sankte Per vandrar på jorden. (The Keys to Heaven ... or the Travels of St. Peter Around the Earth). That went well so with the same group of actors I directed "The Tempest" in a Swedish translation. In Strindberg's play I cast three women as the main trio of characters: the locksmith, the doctor of philosophy, and St. Peter.

The central role was essentially Strindberg as he wrote this play when through divorce he lost access to his children, and, in the play the locksmith looses his whole family in a fire. The doctor suggests that he travel around the world to find himself and the doctor offered to travel along. The first person they meet is St Peter who had lost the key to heaven and heard about this great Swedish locksmith but the locksmith asked where

SOME KEY PROJECTS

is the lock. But it was still in heaven and once St Peter came down to Earth he forgot how to get back to heaven so he joined the locksmith and doctor on their trip around the world. I cast one of the class's women as the locksmith, she was adopted as an infant from Ethiopia and spoke eloquent Swedish. That may have been only the third time the play had been performed in Sweden. It was considered a failure as a play. But I simply treated it the way I do Shakespeare's plays. I give each scene its own focus as if it were a complete play, and, organically we discover many aspects and threads to the plays which are usually skipped over. After that production I was coming in to begin the process for the next play, but, I had not selected the play yet. I saw one of our team in the hall looking at a poster of "Stormen" (The Tempest). I asked if he had seen that production and he informed me that he had not and that he hated that play. I asked why? In a few minutes I met with the whole group and said thank you and some thoughts about their fine work in the previous play. Then I said I was meant to announce the new play that we would produce. I asked if anyone had any guesses. There were a few guesses based on things I had spoken about in the past. Finally I said "Any more guesses? How about you"? And I looked directly towards the actor who hated The Tempest. His eyes widened and he shook his head and smiled and said "Stormen". Correct. I asked him which role do you think I've selected him to play. A bigger smile. After a few days of him working into playing "Prospero" he came in excited that he had a sudden flash that maybe Prospero could be blind. I said let's try it. The actor playing Caliban had been an actual foundling as Caliban is said to have been. This actor was found as an infant left in a doorway in South Korea. He was totally adept at Judo. I had already choreographed a fight between Prospero and Caliban. Now we had to try it with Prospero blind. So we did it like the famous fight in the dark from Chinese Opera's "Monkey Creates Havoc in Heaven". Prospero stayed blind.

ONE YEAR EXPERIMENT - STUDIO AND PROJECTS

In Australia an actor Tim McGarry who had worked with me before warned a new actor "You have to be careful what you suggest to Ira because he'll do it". That was said when I was directing "The Suicide" by Nikolai

Erdman. Our production was produced by dear friend and colleague Fred. There were three central actors who had worked with me recently in other productions before: Fred, Tim, Eva. We had continual trouble filling one role. The actors each playing that role would get paid work or quit. Finally 10 days before our season was going to open and another actor in that role left, I said to Fred, Tim, Eva that I have the feeling I'm meant to play that role. I said that in most of the scenes I would be in one of the three of the three actors was always not acting in. Thus they each could direct me if necessary or could at least see if my scenes worked. I already had nearly 15 years experience directing myself particularly in my own and ensemble clown theatre work. I also did this when I was in the Bell Shakespeare Company particularly in Richard the Third. Another colleague in "The Suicide" was a fantastic intellectual actor, Ellen Osborne. She was intellectually brilliant, but was also a black belt in Tae Kwan Do.

Ellen had been in my experimental studio/school for several months and had also been in that studio workshop production of Henry the Fifth. As I tell in my youtube show "Harlequin Dreams" I had a dream and interpreted the dream as telling me I should direct Henry the Fifth with 12 women. The dream came on the night after a daytime three hour meeting with only myself and director of the Bell Shakespeare Company, John Bell. We were discussing the coming year and he was offering me another year contract. But I was asking questions about the casting, about the direction of the ensemble and about the title of my position. For the first year John didn't know what I would do as we hadn't worked together and he was trying to create something 'new' so he suggested my contract title be "Resident Teacher and Choreographer". That was fine. However, I acted in all four productions and did most of the on-the-floor direction for Richard III. That production was John's vision about doing something Kurosawa-like and the incredible young designer went with that, but, I did the majority of on the floor direction. Additionally I was specifically hired to assist John to establish the company as an ensemble by using my method of training. I had taught nearly half of our company at NIDA, WAAPA, Nepean.

SOME KEY PROJECTS

Now, a year later, after seeing what I actually did, I suggested in our meeting that my title should be changed to either: Assistant Director; Director's Assistant; or Assistant to the Director as those terms were more accurate to what I had actually done the first year (besides teaching, choreographing, acting). John suggested first that he already had three volunteers (non-paid) to be his assistant on each of the three main productions. He then suggested that I'm still called Choreographer for Richard III. There was no acknowledgment that I actually did the majority of the on-the-floor direction of his vision which means it was co-directed. He then suggested that for Romeo & Juliet for which he said was to do "like you did with Richard III" but "to create a whole mime choreography" for the whole play, for which I was to be called "Movement Designer". The 'movement' in Richard III was completely integrated to the play/story/acting. We were doing Shakespeare plays not 'movement' theatre. And for the third play again he wanted to use the word 'movement' but not the words 'assistant' nor 'director' in any way.

Soon I neared another appointment so having 3 hours discussion about the company's evolution it was a Groucho sang "Hello, I must be going". I said I need to go in a minute as I was about to open a new piece that evening for Krissie Koltai's "Dance Collection" at the Performance Space. That was a piece "Harlequin Suits Me ... or, Can A Wog Be a Larrikin?" and was my purging of being in a dream job which had its own surreal qualities. That piece can be seen on youtube as the beginning of the show listed "Harlequin Dreams". That youtube show is in 5 parts. Parts 1 to 4 plus "Final Part".

HENRY THE FIFTH WITH 12 WOMEN

So, the night I had that end meeting with John and the same night I opened "Harlequin Suits Me" which includes a creative play on words using Hamlet's "To be" speech - I dreamt that night of Sir John Gielgud acting in Henry V at Bondi Pavilion.

When I awoke I remembered that vivid dream. I interpreted it that I should direct "Henry V" with an all women cast. That afternoon when I was going to the theatre to perform "Harlequin Suits Me" again I ran into an actress I had taught at NIDA - Maryanne. She was a brilliant, highly intelligent and physical actress. We barely said hello and I mentioned only "that I have this project" and she said "I'll do it". After that I informed her and suggested that she would play the title role. I ran into someone else and the same thing happened though of course I cast the next actress in a different role. Then I got to the theatre and separately two actresses each commented on my performance from the night before and they expressed their interest in my work and .... in an instant I cast each of them. The next few days I would run into different actresses I knew and the same thing happened they immediately wanted to be part of whatever I was doing. It was a most unusual group of 12 people. They were all experienced in performance but very different areas such as acting, dance, martial arts, singing. Dahlia Dior I knew as a singer in 12 languages who spoke 9 languages. What I didn't know until we ran into each other and she said yes to Henry V and as she was the oldest actress of the group so far, I cast her as The Boy. She then told me she had done a little bit of Shakespeare. She said in the 1960s she was in RADA (London's Royal Academy of Dramatic Arts) and her teacher for Shakespeare was sometimes Sir Laurence Olivier. But after one year she got a lot of work as a singer and she had no money so she just went with the work. She then suggested her daughter could be in our production, Lily. So she was. One of the dancers was Sam Chester who was as young and wonderful and fresh as could be. She was a contemporary dancer and cast with a fireball ballet dancer Jo who was to play Katherine with Sam as Alice. Their scene with the hairbrush was phenomenal due to their chemistry and stature. Jo would come in late every single rehearsal. Always only by a few minutes or even only a minute. I was very disciplined in those days and I always started a class or rehearsal exactly on time. Jo would always burst through the door like a bomb and bombshell. She was tall, statuesque, a volcano on heels and loved fashion. So each day she looked like a completely different person. When she was about 16 she won an international ballet competition in Russia but she never had much of a career. She was an outstanding actress. One day though she was marginally later than usual. Bam the doors flew open and as she stormed towards us she yelled "Well I did it!! I fucking did it". So we stopped and someone asked "What did you do Jo"? "I fucking threw my boyfriend over the hood of his car. Fuck 'im'!" She happened to have caught him that morning canoodling with another girl by his car. "Right! What are we working on"? And thus she entered rehearsal.

One day the three 'professional' actresses i.e. those who graduated from the main acting institutions in Australia as opposed to singers, dancers, martial artists, intellectuals as were their fellow cast mates …. so the three 'professional actresses' said they need to talk with me. They wanted to go to a pub after rehearsal. At that time I did not go to pubs. I'd meet at a cafe, a restaurant, a home, a beach, a park. We went to a near pub. They ordered us a beer. That means its serious. They said they really are fascinated by the other women, but, they're not really actors.
Really? Hmmmm. Really? Well they said our show shouldn't be for a season it should be once only. Okay. Whatever, three against one and the one is not paying anybody nor is the one earning any income either. So, fine, decision made let's enjoy the beer and chat.

The next rehearsal was a run through of one or two acts. Really, the non-actresses were rich generous enlivened actresses. And they knew their lines. And they knew what they were saying. And they knew what was happening in each scene. And they were very embodied.

We were using my technique(s) with Shakespeare. My theory is: Does it work or doesn't it; and, does it make sense to a viewer or doesn't it. If it doesn't then what do we have to adjust so it does.

I also let actors repeat small sections numerous times so that the text settles accumulatively and chronologically as the script unfolds.

I also say "What did you say"? "Excuse me, what"?. Speak up. Look here. Try this. What would you like to try here etc.

In our first meeting some of the actresses, not the non-actresses, were concerned as to whether they were going to be playing men or going to be women playing men. I said "I don't know. Let's work and find out". We did. They were actresses acting out a play. The actor actresses by the way were excellent and Maryann was a deeply honest and earnest theatre person. Wow! Her daytime job for years as an actress was in a full body costume as a banana for the famous TV show "Bananas in Pajamas". It's a job and good job for an actor. But ... what an outstanding stage actress and classical actress she was! And she loved researching the play and context and language. But.....

It was coming close to our big day. We still had two weeks. And it was great work I was seeing from each person every day and the progress was like a steady flow of lava. Nothing could stop this unique team of women who were more than actresses, they were amazing people. I contacted two people I knew who were highly knowledgable about music and performance. One was Mara Kiek of "Mara's Band" and "Martenitsa Choir" of Bulgarian womens singing. The other was Philip Griffins who was an 'all-round' musician who had also worked with Shakespeare productions in London. Dahlia the singer had a song from the time of the play ie the 1500s. A French drinking song about the knights which all school children in France knew. Knights of the round table. So that was a daily part of our training with Dahlia in charge. The song was simply to be the pre-show or pre-play song. The costumes were only to be beige carpenter overalls. With one exception for Katherine i.e. Jo the fashionista insisted her hairbrush scene she would wear a dress. Fine. How'd that go down with the other actresses non and otherwise? "Smile though your heart is breaking" sang Chaplin .... even if the smile is very small and only out of one side of your face.

So with ten days to go this group was 100% ready to do a full-dress (overalls and one dress) run-through. We had three props. A hairbrush, a leek, a chair. Mara and Phil sat still for the three and half hours of an uncut Henry V by William Shakespeare. It was crystal clear. Both music experts said there's no need for music because the text and voices are so clear. It was magical.
Then there's the proverbial - Next Day.

The three actresses told me "We have to have a meeting". You mean at the pub? No. A company meeting. We sat in the proverbial theatre circle on the floor. We waited for Jo to enter the circle. Directors do not like such spontaneous meetings.

SOME KEY PROJECTS

The actresses announced to the non-actresses and myself that they quit.
They don't have anything against the others who they deeply came to respect but they felt that the play would not be ready in ten days.
The nine non-actresses knew the play was already excellent and would gel and fire and even the clowning could expand within the direction and within the script as is. They knew we could and would also increase the physicalisation.
Jo wanted to beat the fuck out of all three on the spot.
I think all nine of the non-actresses who were deeply profoundly gifted actors were each deeply hurt. They were wounded deep inside. They were at a loss as to what to say though they tried.
We were willing to have a non public event just once for friends and family.
The axe had fallen.
I said to the triumvirate: "I stopped you from this once before. I'm not going to stop you this time. You decide"
The head rolled into the bucket. It was over. My dream came and went.
It was decided collectively that we should have a wake as they termed it.
So on the night this event - Henry V, uncut, with 12 incredible women each of whom was an exciting and unique actor was to be escorted from reality by a dinner across the street from our venue.
Fine.
Whatever.
The next day a coincidence happened.
My friend and colleague Fred contacted me and said he wanted to produce "The Suicide" (by Nikolai Erdman) and play the main role and wanted to see if I wanted to direct it. He had gone to his friends to see if they wanted to act in it and he was going to direct. As I recall it, each of those actors suggested he would be great as the lead role and why not get me (Ira) to direct it as we had already done a few projects together. Fred already had the venue sorted. A famous tiny theatre that had not been used in years for theatre. The Wayside Chapel in Kings Cross.

At the wake of Henry V almost all of the actors were there. Fred and I had most of The Suicide cast which like our Henry V was to have 12 actors. But I had one idea for the final role of Father Elpedi the Orthodox priest in The Suicide. I wanted Ellen to play him, but, on one condition. Ellen is

Greek heritage from both of her Greek parents. She had the most extraordinary thick black long hair. The condition was that she mould her hair into Father Elpidi's Orthodox beard. Deal made.

Shall I now tell you more about The Suicide? Later. Next book. In the meantime let's do the time warp again.

The Kiruna (Sweden) job was first a short stint teaching and then I came back and directed my project *Artiste i Exile ... Requiem for Strindberg*. One of the original 26 actors in Goteborg, Niclas, was a songwriter and musician and was excellent with English so he helped me translate the working draft of *Artiste i Exile*. I had developed a way to collaborate in which I would write a scenario and some text then with the actors via improvisation and collaboration we would co-create. The first show I created that way was in 1979 at the Eureka Theater of San Francisco. That show was *Zealous Zanies* and had about 15 actors including a few teams who were responsible for their own material. I was director, producer, and the Emcee as a clown. I interacted with the other performers and also as the space had many unusual entrance spots I would always appear from a different location. My first solo theatre show was *A Clown's Show* at the Eureka. In 1980 in Stockholm I created two solo theatre clown shows; *Getting Into Struggle*, and *A Clown's House* which became a touring show. It had performances in Sweden, Finland, Germany, Holland, USA, New Zealand and evolved into other solo shows in Australia.

TOSCANO, ITALIA

Via an associate Danica Hilton I was able to make a small workshop project in Tuscany, Italy. Danica and I met when the Australian Institute of Sport where she trained in elite gymnastics had finally acknowledged that she was going to be too tall to compete in the Olympics, so she returned home and decided to try the local youth circus. She was in my acrobatics class the day I started a 6 weeks contract teaching for the circus. After a few rounds of basics I said to her "What's your name?" And then "Did you train in gymnastics"? She was an exceptionally shy young lady and simply blushed and nodded 'yes'. A few years later her Mother phoned and asked if I remembered them and would I coach Danica once a week in performance to prepare her for the Cirque du Soleil audition for the program "Athlete to Artist" which was to assist elite athletes to transition into CDS acrobats. It was a six-months program at the end Danica was offered a full contract for 9 months creation of CDS Macau show which she went on to perform in for 4 years. Danica in her teens was national champion in tumbling, and, trampoline. She had a Russian coach for those but also had the wonderful South African coach Rodleigh Stevens to coach her in handstands and aerials. After her years with CDS she was with a boyfriend whose family were artists and wanted to make an arts festival in the tiny village where they lived - Bagni di Lucca, Toscano.

The project was called "Commedia Toto" and I wanted to combine imagery from the great film clown Toto and the Italian absurdist playwright Luigi Pirandello. I had two assistants who also acted in the show: Caspar Schjelbred and Elena Micheline. Elena was to be the head of research and was to play the central character which I called "La Atrice" (The Actress). As it was Elena found that Elenora Duse wanted Pirandello to write a play for her. He did so, but he called her character .... "La Atrice". Duse did not like that idea and did not act in the play. Also Elena found that Toto had acted in a screenplay by Pirandello. I wanted to use the image of Toto when he played Pinocchio as a vaudeville turn in a movie. I was contacted by a young mime from Holland who was interested in training with me. Kevin Gorczynski was an autodidact mime and by the age of 18 had already performed several seasons in a theme park in Holland. As it turned out for one season he had played Pinocchio. So I assigned him to imitate Toto's choreography and then he and I put together a group choreography for the end of the show.

Most of the actors had done workshops with me in Paris. This project was to be two weeks. I had always wanted to do a Mediterranean style project with a proper lunch, vino, siesta. Through my career I would not drink before sunset and normally only drank wine and that was with a meal and after I had performed. I arranged to have morning training at 9am until noon. Then a three hours lunch and siesta and we rehearsed from 3pm to 6pm. Bagni di Lucca and its connected villages have wonderful family run restaurants. A full meal was 10 or 11 euros. The vegetables and meats were mostly from the grandfather's garden or local. The pasta was homemade. The salads were all fresh local produce. The vino too was only local if not from the family then it was from their friends. I am not a workaholic and like to mix work with pleasure in the way that artists can if they choose to. Each day we would walk a few kilometres each way to and from a new lunch place. Some of us would also have a dip in the shallow fast moving cold river.

Kevin as the youngest was completely embraced by our group and several of them invited him to come to Paris and they looked after him there from start to finish. One of the people who had not trained with me before was a tall Parisian who worked in publicity and marketing for films. As our theatre was a classic with loges (private seating in the balcony) I had Olivier Pasquier play a well dressed drunk like Chaplin did when he was in the Fred Karno troupe. Elena La Atrice, Kevin Toto/Pinocchio; Danica Pierrot. In several shows of mine I have interjected Pierrot which is a theatre image I never get to see often enough. It is also a way for me to interject a bit of clown history and in this case more than referencing the French version of comedia dell'arte which gave us Pierrot, I also reference the landmark film that features Pierrot which is "Les Enfants du Paradise".

Heleen van den Bosch of Belgium played "Il Carabinieri" a Keystone Kops style policeman. Caspar played an intellectual in shorts and pipe. Bagni di Lucca had a local who was an opera singer and who ran the theatre lighting. I often like to use false endings in my own shows. "Comedia Toto" had three endings. First was a poem that Toto had actually written about a cemetery. That was a whole ensemble piece which was when La Atrice finally got to do her famous act. That was followed by a celebratory jig of the ensemble doing Toto's Pinocchio dance but adjusted for an ensemble by Kevin and myself. Finally in the bows the 'lighting man' is brought onto stage for a bow and thank you and he 'suddenly' began to sing to La Atrice. The song had been written by Toto and is titled "Femina".

The second year the Bagni di Lucca festival shrunk necessarily by 80%. Most of the same actors returned and this project was to create clown duets preferably each act was comical, physical, and involving various forms of slapstick. The third year the festival shrunk even more and that was not resolved until it was too late for us to organise our participation. Then the main family who started the festival moved to southern France and Danica and her husband moved to Berlin.

Part of my agreement for the festival was that they would provide accomodation for myself and my two assistants. There was an ambiguity about exactly where we were going to stay. So when our trio of Elena, Caspar, myself arrived it was still not 100% sure where we would stay. Jacqueline the festival organiser offered us two options for the first week. Her husband Jake looked at me and said quietly "I really think you will like the place up the hill". In no uncertain terms he was indicating with his eyes and face "take it!". But Elena and Caspar did not see his direct 'hint'. So we traipsed up, up, up the hill in a car. I was concerned about transportation in the evening. I was then assured 'don't worry it will work out'. Downhill in the morning was fine for us to walk perhaps 30 minutes. Uphill was a steep climb so late at night a ride would be helpful. Mind you this was just for the first week. After that we were to be in an apartment in the village.

The owner of the house had an assistant who also drove up in a car and met us at the front. I would not give Elena or Caspar any space to say no nor maybe as I had already been given the secret men's business look 'take it!'. So when we got out of the car I insisted we take our bags out as well and put them by the door. The key to the door was the long old fashioned steel ones. The door and lock were likely 200 years old. Also at that point we were asked if we wanted to see inside first or the pool in the upper part of the garden. We went in. At the entry was a small banquet table also likely more than 200 years old. It would seat 12 people. From there we could look into the kitchen in which one could have a cocktail party for about 30 people. That's the kitchen. You getting the picture. Speaking of pictures as we were toured through the house it was filled tastefully with oil paintings and exotic African wood sculptures. The real banquet table overlooking the valley would seat about 30 people. The other chairs and sofas and rugs were all beautiful and if not antiques they were from another era. We were taken through the sitting room filled with books. We went downstairs to the sleeping quarters I was shown my room which had about 200 of its own books and beautiful furnishings. Then we went to see Elena's room then Caspar's room and the downstairs living room with about 1000 books. When asked then if I wanted to see the pool I said no thanks .... we'll take it even if a pool is forced upon us. In our tour I did everything to shorten the time before I had the key in my hand and made sure the cars left. I still would not look at Elena nor Caspar who certainly are two of my dearest friends in the world. They had been studying with me by this point over a period of workshops during five years and they knew me well, but, this was different. They had never been on a theatre tour. This was all new to them. They were respectful and mindful of me. I just wanted us to have this unique situation.

Without a word I opened the door for them to go in I then closed the door and locked it with the ancient key .... and then turned and smiled and jumped and yelled and we all jumped and yelled and ran around like refugees who had their first indoor toilet in years. Elena said shouldn't we go see the pool? I said no lets get into our swim suits and go up with towels. The pool was one of the most beautiful private pools I have ever seen. Lodged firmly in the hills of Toscana below the owner's vineyard. It was about 20 metres long and wonderful. We swam and yelled and sang and played and then we went home. I said we had to dress up for dinner and after I changed I would fetch them in our downstairs living room. Unbeknownst to them I had two bottles of wine one can of tuna and a few apples. I set the table so that when they arrived the table was set. We then found candles and it was a night and a week and a festival and a show and a journey together to remember forever. A few days later I looked on the internet to see who the owner was. He worked for philanthropists and was an expert in helping them to invest in art. This was his own house. On its website it rents, depending on the season for 8000 Euros per week in the off season. The owner was the sponsor or patron of the short lived festival. Part of his patronage was housing us for a week before wealthy tenants who inadvertently subsidised this little arts festival.

PARIS

In Paris we have an informal ISAAC collective. Thank you to each and all who have been in my Paris workshops! When I come to teach a workshop some of these people come. Some have moved on. Some return later. Others are asking when is the next workshop. Several years ago we made a workshop project. The two-weeks though had no siesta as the hours were 10am to 4pm and after that Paris bistro style we have a tradition after each day to go to the nearest bar or bistro depending where the studio is located. We call this "Vin du Table" which means the cheapest wine. Many people have a juice or a mineral water and others get the drink of their choice. Most importantly we all have a chance to sit and chat about anything under the Sun. I also get a chance to listen and learn from anybody's different perspective or different interests from my own.

One workshop project had a fine collection of clown pieces we co-created. One of the newer participants was a fireball from Quebec, Michelle. She asked to have a coffee chat with me the next day. She said she and others from the project want to continue and she asked what do I suggest. First of all I said the show was yours/theirs so they are welcome to take it and book a venue and play it some more. That began their own process which has been going four years in different formats. Their first project was called "Requiem ... celebration for the death of a clown". So the collective is called "Requiem". Michelle is the artistic director but she manages it as a cooperative. Unfortunately (not) she got hired recently by a French theatre company that wanted to create a solo show for children. Michelle is the solo performer on stage but there is a team of 12 creatives - directors, writer, composer, designers etc. In between tours Michelle returns to Paris and leads the collective and also teaches in Montreal once a year. This year she led a Shakespeare project in Montreal.

The ISAAC collective has had several workshop/projects in recent years, each with a different theme. The themes have been "Beckett's Bits"; Shakespeare's Clowns and Comedia; and one which I'll describe "Cubist Clown Cavalcade".

"Cubist Clown Cavalcade" had a theme of pre-Occupation Paris. The national socialists occupied Paris by military force from 1941 to 1944. One person I know was a performer in Paris throughout the Occupation. He was a dancer, mime, acrobat and in that period he had a speciality of tap dance. He began his professional career in the Moulin Rouge at the age of 19. He had a Paris style cabaret in NYC for three years, then he was in Japan for several years and finally settled in Sydney, Australia. He is on screen a few seconds in Baz Luhrmann's film "Moulin Rouge" simply as a waiter albeit a comical one serving a few customers in a booth. One of the customers is a cameo appearance by Luhrmann's choreographer John O'Connell. The waiter is Aurel Verne a Jewish survivor of the Occupation who was not Deported to the death camps but survived performing nightly in front of the Paris public which at the time would have included numerous German soldiers in uniform. His career took him to NYC, Japan, Sydney where he stayed.

Cubist Clown Cavalcade was our story as a single evening. This represented the actual early 1900s Saturday evening soirees hosted by the Jewish-American-Gay-Secular couple Gertrude Stein and Alice B. Tolkas. They managed to stay in France during the Occupation but relocated to the the south. Their soirees regularly included Picasso, Hemingway, Apollinaire and many others. Our version was not historically factually accurate. I took poetic licence and used the inspiration from Stein/Tolkas' soirees. Elena Odessa Ray was Stein and Casey Douglas was Tolkas. Elena and Casey both hail from the USA and are long committed Francophiles resident in or near Paris. Elena is a linguist, equestrian sometimes playing "Annie Oakley" at Disney-Paris, she is also a burlesque performer and teacher, and a clown. Casey has long trained in ballet, mime, theatre. Elena, as I found out during rehearsal has mild narcolepsy so she will doze off during rehearsal. Casey has a unique vision limitation that allows her to see only in 2-dimensions so she has to be ever cautious around people and objects. Elena and she were a divine couple as Stein/Tolkas. Caspar played Apollinaire. Pauline Calme was Simone du Beauvoir and Jean-Paul Sartre. Emily Burton was The American Tourist and Michelle was la Jeune Fille Quebecoise - combined they were a reference to the ballet "Parade" of Cocteau which had a character "The Young American Girl". Thibault played a clochard a person living on the street who wants to be a clown to earn better money when begging. Paris has many clochards many of whom are like mascots or village fools each in a particular section of Paris. Jonny played "Uncle Adolf the Shithead" who really liked Paris and said he would "Like to spend a lot more time here". He wanted to become a comedian. So he had coaching from Sarah Bernhardt who was acted by Tamara Guenon. Heleen played the Italian policeman "Caribinneri" and Park Sanghyun played a mime/clown. Marion Lallor and Claire Amoureux played a pair of Pierrots who were intertwined into many scenes.

Our ISAAC collective in Paris also did other workshop/projects and with a number of other wonderful participants. I came to Paris in 2007 to visit my friend Isabelle and her family. I am the Godfather of her oldest daughter. At that time I had just finished a tour in the UK with an independent group Company Collisions directed on a project basis by Tanushka Marah. She and I met during the Frank Theatre workshop in London in 2006. Tanushka was a participant in our week long intensive led by our directors Jacqui and John. It was at Central School of Speech & Drama. As Frank Theatre we performed our show "Hamlet Stooged".

THE GRAND HOSTESS

When we heard about going to London on of the Frank members, Leah, asked me if I had suggestions for her to find work overseas. I said that one never knows when a director may see a show, but, specifically she was an outstanding actress but for straight acting work she should develop her voice and speech in ways in addition to our Frank voice aesthetic which is peculiar to the method they use. That method is from Tadashi Suzuki which involves a particular high volume and disassociation from diction and articulation as normally viewed in acting. Immediately after the London workshop we needed to have a dress run-through in the studio before we relocated for that performance at the Hoxton Hall. Tanushka said she couldn't see the performances and I suggested that she tell our directors Jacqui and John and ask if she could see the run-through. At that time I did not know Tanushka was a director but rather thought she was an actress. We finished the run through and she was talking with John and they waved for me to come over. They informed me that Tanushka wanted to offer me a paid contract as an actor in her coming production. John was 100% supportive and suggested that I could also teach their method for the project. We created the show in four weeks in Brighton and toured numerous places in the UK including Wales, Scotland and finished in Ireland. We also performed in the London Mime Festival in January 2007.

Before heading to England for the Frank Theatre project "Hamlet Stooged" and connected workshops in London, Aberystwyth, and Aarau I said to a friend in Frank who was from the UK, Jane Barber-Lacey, that I was going with the company but I would like to stay in a seperate place because I wanted to pretend that I was an English actor touring England. That was one of several of my theatre fantasies i.e. to be in an English touring theatre company whose most rich tradition I hold in high esteem. So I asked Jane if she might know someone in London who might have a spare room for our ten days. A week later she had a reply from a friend whom she had toured in the UK with. Annie Firbank said I was welcome to stay at her home in Stoke-Newington. What happened as a result was a match made in Heaven. Annie was a fair few years older than me and had been an actress her whole life and indeed had toured numerous times with a very large variety of companies and projects. Of course the notable companies stand out which included the RSC and Complicite. But she also toured globally and even in recent years projects have been at the Trafalgar, Old Vic, and a film project in Bulgaria. Annie's early years were in India as her Father was part of the British and Indian armies. She's an absolute pearl of a lady, well more of a rough diamond with a posh voice. She is a deeply dear friend whom I can never give enough to but who spiritually looked after me more than once. And much more than 10 days. When I came home with the good news that Tanushka had hired me Annie being a veteran actor asked the quick list of logical questions. I was excited that the project was to be based in Brighton the famous seaside haunt of generations of actors. Annie though cuts to the chase .... "Well where the fuck are you going to stay until then"? ... with her posh accent, ever sparkling eyes, and endless charm earthy and otherwise. She can get away with murder. As in many 'in-between' times in my life I came up with a lame idea of going to Brighton early. Like two months early. Annie said no. Most of my life and 'career' has been 'in-between' jobs. As per the Jerry Lewis movie about the clown Jerico that is titled "Hardly Working". I've been hardly working my whole career. So like many friends Annie knew I didn't have "a pot to piss in". So she insisted that I will absolutely not stay anywhere except her house. Thank you Annie a thousand times over. I already had a beautiful room filled with the newest theatre books and poetry and the bed below a exhibition poster of August Strindberg's paintings. The poster was given to Annie by her friend and past touring colleague Sir Ian McKellan. Sheesh. Pardon the name dropping. C'est la vie.

Here are a few quotes from a few friends who witnessed my version of an unusual life: clown and singer Jane Birmingham "If you fell into a bucket of shit you'd come up smelling like roses"; ballet mistress Elaine Haggren "You live on a wing and a prayer"; comedian Bruno Lucia "You live like someone who earns $200,000.00 a year".

To be sure, I have an extremely naive outlook on life. There are so many simple things I just don't understand. Those who have known me though throughout my life also see that I live not only by luck but by faith. What do I have faith in? I have faith in friendship, kindness of strangers, the miracle of the universe and how it flows in its own ways, in Shakespeare's line from Hamlet "There are more things in heaven and earth Horatio than are dreamed in your philosophy" and if you put all of those bits together then some would say that I have faith in God. If you amassed those things just mentioned and see that God is simply another word for Universe then you understand me a little bit more.

Annie did much more than host me. She looked after me. She made sure I ate well and she made sure I got to see London and a lot of great theatre. She would pick and choose what I saw. She would cajole me and insist and kick me out of the house to go and explore London. She'd be ever waiting for me to come home from a show at 11pm or midnight and she'd have food and drinks for me and interrogate my inadequate reports. She later hosted me numerous times when I began to visit London on my own theatre passages in search of reality after being in Cirque du Soleil.

For the first several years of visits Annie would never tell me anything about herself. I knew though that she had graduated from R.A.D.A. about the age of 21 and was taken immediately into the very renown last actor-manager touring Shakespeare company run by Sir Donald Wolfit.

He is the person that the play and film "The Dresser" is biographically about. Annie was his Ophelia to 'Sir's Hamlet! A portrait of her in that role is in the National Portrait Gallery. But Annie is a jobbing actor who hates the use of the word "actress" and her central interest in theatre is what's new and what's her current or her coming job. She also has a huge range of friends and interests. She's long been an advocate of daily exercise such as swimming in the frigid Hampstead lakes as well as doing regular yoga and Pilates. Her single kitchen mouse is well looked after and seems as ageless as she.

As mentioned I had a very hard time getting her anything as a gift. My first attempts I was scolded for as she needed nothing and knew I had nothing to my name. Honestly, I do not know how I survived most of my life. Except by "a wing and a prayer". Finally after getting to know her as a friend I started to find small things I could bring to her. If I chose flowers I had to be quite cunning in exactly which flowers would not get me a verbal backhander but rather an igniting of her twinkling eyes and girlish joy and smile. Annie was absolutely insistent that a touring actor must have a fold up umbrella. How right she is! And a scarf!

As I write this, it is 12 years since we first met. I am looking forward to see her in just 2 months. I always ask "if there is room at the inn" as she and I term the annual question.

So the first real gift I could give to her was the miraculous finding on my last day after I had told a fantastic tale which I shall now tell you. A small private story of being a troubadour or mountebank ie touring performer.

DOWN THE GURGLER

It was 1994 and I had been living in Copenhagen for nearly one year. Teaching only a few classes per week. I got so desperate to earn money that I started busking. Buskers have long been hardcore professionals with high skill and high interest in making money. I knew I was a lousy busker. I was a wonderful street performer at events when I was hired and paid a normal fee but was free to improvise and rove about. So I started busking and earning a small amount of money as Harlequin on the main walking street. I only felt right at the fountain near my favorite Cafe Europa. I would always make a little bit to tuck away and enough for a cake and coffee as a personal reward. The Autumn was settling in. It was getting colder. This week was rain each day so I could not perform but I got my reward anyways. On Friday I was really hoping that Saturday would be dry and warm and sunny Autumn style. Saturday was horrible. I was determined but also had no money for my 'reward'. Rain was pouring down. Every single person on the walking street had their umbrella up. I stood in a doorway. What should I do. What can I do. All I could do in this full rain was to take my hat off put it on the ground and stay in a handstand. I had my head up and could see my hat. Empty. I could see my hands totally covered in water. Not wet but covered in water as it flowed all along the pavement and flowed over the back of my hands and around my hands and hat. Some few small coins had been dropped in my hat. I then stood up and rested my hands and wrists. Still the rain is pouring down. Back up to a handstand. I stayed. After a few minutes I had enough for my reward. My bag as usual I had placed by the cafe's bar. I came into the cafe soaked. I took my bag. Went into the bathroom and wrung out my Harlequin one-piece Lycra costume and and dried myself with an abundance of paper towels. Perhaps one of the all-time most delicious coffee and cake rewards. Doing those handstands was one of the all time low points of my 'career'. I think when the three women in Goteborg hired me .... they had to advance me some cash. There were only a few times when I had to be advanced cash in that way. Several times though such contracts were in fact turning points in my life. I have experienced the idea that "behind every cloud is a silver lining" ... or perhaps behind every clown is a golden story.

Annie loved that story. The gift I happened to see in a small shop was small, about the size of a hand, and made of wood. A child's toy of a clown in a handstand. His joints had elastic threads so when you pushed the bottom of the toy i.e. the base, then the clown's joints would collapse and move and when you released your finger from the bottom, the clown was whole again and in a handstand. When I arrive now at Annie's the clown is placed on the central spot in her house which is the small kitchen table where all conversations occur.

BRIGHTON AND BEYOND

In the UK there is a "Digs LIst" for each town. 'Digs" is the British touring actors term for where you are staying in each town on tour. Where you dig in the same way a soldier digs a trench. As in the USA and elsewhere some people have bed and breakfast available in their home for a fee. In Brighton, Tanushka took me to one place which she had organised that had a good location near rehearsals. It was a flophouse run by a woman from Eastern Europe who was very quick to sort out anybody's personality, particularly if they were of any use to her. The very first minute I could speak privately to Tanushka I said I will stay this week but this will not work out. We found another place run by a former English actress. She was so wonderful and welcoming. I stayed there for the whole of rehearsals and touring. The hostess still occasionally acted. She played one of the mother's in television series "Little Britain". Not the mother of David Walliams 'bitty' character but, rather the mother of his "bitty" character's fiancé's mother. She also had been a young actor in the theatre company where Keith Johnstone devised his series of theatre exercises and improvisations. All of those actors were graduates of the best acting schools in London and were newly experienced young professional actors.

I loved touring with Tanushka and company. We were seven actors including she and I. There was a brilliant production manager who toured with us. Geoff. He had been a classical violinist and at a young age had a touring group of ten musicians. After a few years he realised he did not really like classical musicians as people. He had a love for Appalachian fiddle which they could not relate to. Thus he became a lighting and sound technician for theatre and a production manager. For the last several years he has worked at London's Arcola Theatre. Over the touring seasons some actors changed. Bron Lim decided she didn't want to take the follow up contract as she wanted to settle and have a family. She was an outstanding actress and colleague and so too was Denise Evans who took over the 'granny' role. I was the 'grampy' role 'Rio'. With us also as an apprentice for a period was Bronagh Mary Lagan who is now an experienced and wonderful director based in London.

SOME KEY PROJECTS

Our small team was eclectic and eccentric. I was really thrilled to share our time together with each and all of them. There are now about 13 children from that small group. Of course one of the unusual aspects of our group was that Tanushka is English/Palestinian and I am not :). As with almost any ethnic duet ..... when everyone else in the group is not 'ethnic' but is Anglo/Celt you should realise rather immediately that the only cultural difference is the dominant Anglo/Celt versus anyone else. Of course no one in that group was a 'versus' person. They could not have been more kind, generous, and welcoming. However, on a rare occasion or two after our performance Tanushka and I would be out talking with the public post-show. Sometimes one would ask one of us the usual question every ethic person has sometimes several times a day "Where are you from"? So one of us was Palestinian and one of us wasn't, but, of course even more than wasn't .... one of us was Jewish which to some seems the opposite of Palestinian but to my world view ..... perhaps no ethnic group is closer to being Jewish than are the Palestinians. Certainly the few times I was with Tanushka's family it was very much a celebration of our closeness. For those who don't know, Palestine was the name the Romans gave to the Jewish regions known at various times as Canaan, Samaria, Judea, Galilee, Israel. The Romans conquered all of those areas and in the process to suppress and control the Jews, they gave a new name Palestine. Some people have estimated that 25% of the Palestinian people living in Samaria or the West Bank are of recent Jewish heritage. Along with the ancient Jews there were also Bedouin's as there are along much of the Southern Mediterranean along with Berbers. The Berbers and Bedouin's and Druze do not view themselves as Arabs. Arabs are from Arabia. Originally.

Our story created by Tanushka was called "Nothing Left to Lose" which is a term imposed upon and from within some groups of young Arabs, or Palestinians, or countless other periodically repressed peoples particularly many of their youth. Nothing left to lose though is psychological and depends on details and circumstances. Nothing left to lose can mean a suicidal approach or it can mean the exact opposite as there is nothing left to lose, let's find the way to prosperity, joy, happiness, sharing. The recovery in the town of Jenin is a remarkable extremely successful story of total recovery and flourishing through collaboration between Israelis and Palestinians. It used a normal, practical, business model. That model could work internationally and within any country to succeed where there is nothing left to lose but success. The Untouchables in India could claim nothing left to lose but success as there are more and more programs providing them with ways out of poverty and into advanced education and opportunities which did not exist even just a few decades ago. Most of the people of Ramallah for example are highly educated, successful and numerous are even wealthy through good business practices. But our story was that a village of clowns was repressed and was about to be attacked by an advanced military but they chose to fight with their fists and shovels. At the climax of our story the sound of the military's helicopters came in for the final assault and all of the clowns die. The moral of that production's story in retrospect now a decade later is that in fact that story was nihilistic and suicidal. That is fine for a play, for theatre because theatre is not reality. The better show would be about the lack of hope in Jenin which collaboratively between Jews and Arabs showed that there is always room for hope.

To be sure, I refer to the Middle East as the Muddle East. It is a quagmire of the world. Both remarkable and problematic not only in cross cultural issues but within each culture. The West is hardly better, except that the West took whatever they could when they could and often left problems in their wake. But if we examine the world further we see that it is a muddled world with still wonderful people and events and developments.

That newer show could be called "There is Always Room for Hope". Or maybe "We Must Always Make Room for Hope".

Our show was non-verbal but we had a devised gibberish language with a few terms agreed upon and which through the show the audience could come to recognise.

One town we toured to in southern England was the venue which was the very first arts centre created after World War II. We met someone there who invited us to visit his artistic home well outside the town. So one of our company drivers was the actor Sarah. So we three she, Tanushka, myself went to lunch at the arty fellow's converted church filled with household furnishings and art. At one point I noticed a toy helicopter and asked about it. The host set me up with the battery controls and away it went. I asked if we could borrow it for that night's performance? He said yes on the condition that he would operate it. So we three actors plotted. I think we informed Geoff who ran the lights and sound only that we had a planned surprise. No, we did not tell the other four actors. Of course Tanushka and Sarah and I were wetting ourselves with anticipation the whole show never was one (or three) so excited for the final solution. As we acted out the final battle scene we three would glance at each other like Cheshire cats grins and all. Finally the sound effect of recorded helicopters began .... and finally to our trios greatest theatrical ratbag pleasure .... lo and behold from the back of the theatre where our seven pairs of eyes were always choreographed to look ..... here comes an ACTUAL helicopter albeit a small one. We three died with laughter inside and the other four had a gentle theatrical trick - a once in a lifetime experience. Thank you Bron, Liz, John, David, Geoff. Sorry. Not. :)

Our last shows of the tour were in the Republic of Ireland. The very last was in Tralee where we performed in the national folk theatre of Ireland "Siamsa Tire". This is a most unusual theatre company founded by Father Pat Ahern who grew up on a farm in a nearby village. He grew up with all of the archaic farming practices as well as the culture of their native Celtic language, the church, and folk songs, dances and traditions. When he became a priest he understood that all of the threads of the culture were about to change forever due to technology and economics. Thus he set up a regional cultural education that included song, dance, story telling, and a new technique which he felt would make their shows translate visually which was mime. I think Father Pat also mentioned the he took some inspiration from Marcel Marceau. I apologised for asking but wondered if there was any connection with Siamsa Tire and River Dance. He said there certainly was as the founders of River Dance saw Siamsa Tire and thought they could make a more commercial style and according to Father Pat River Dance continues to have a thank you to Siamsa Tire in their program notes. Father Pat devised the first shows which became their classics. All children were thus educated in the performance skills at an early age. Those who wanted could go onward through several levels. Finally those who emerged over years of training became the new professionals into the highly skilled company which toured the world.

Father Pat had recently retired before we arrived. After the show I met the new Artistic Director and he said I'd be welcome to chat with him further the following morning, but, we were to leave quite early to get our second hand rented old van back for its return deadline in Brighton. After an early breakfast, the van would not budge. We needed a mechanic at least. By the time it was 10am it was clear we may not be leaving at all. So I headed over to the theatre and said hello to the artistic director and he said that Father Pat happened to drop by this morning would I like to meet him. So we three met standing in the foyer for about an hour and Father Pat and I had a remarkable conversation. I mentioned that I was completing my doctorate and at that time I was focused on culture being in ones body. That theme was our focus so primarily we discussed that culture is the body. I used to say "there are no saints in the theatre", but, then I met Father Pat. I think one commedia actor in the 1600s may have been anointed?

CLOWN THEMED SHOWS? CLOWN THEMED LIFE!

As mentioned in the beginning of this chapter some of my own creations examined the inner life of a clown. One thread of that life is as Max Wall said of his philosophy of life "One thing leads to another". There was a clown named Frankie Daily who came to Dell'arte School to do our makeup for our student show "Stravaganza". After I had left Dell'arte and revisited for a day one of our Dell'arte teachers Jon Paul Cooke suggested that when I move the next day to San Francisco I could give Frankie a call. I called when I arrived in San Francisco. Frankie remembered me and asked me if I wanted to be in a clown show he was directing. He told me to meet the next day at Cafe Flore and he would introduce me to the clown he would pair me with, David Pearce. The cafe was across the street from the theatre he would use the Eureka Theatre of San Francisco.

I used to always arrive for any appointment, meeting, audition, or interview at least 45 minutes early. At Cafe Flore on Market Street I ordered a coffee and sat in the back of the cafe and where I could see the door to see when Frankie came in. First in came a man with raven black curly hair and a thick beard. He was wearing a dress and carried a purse. I had never seen anything like this. As he greeted his friends who he knew in the cafe which seemed like he knew everyone he gave them a kiss. All men. He kissed the fella working the counter and making the coffees. As he turned in my direction I froze. He didn't know me so he simply turned away and then went and sat with some of his friends. Honestly I was a bit in shock simply because I had never seen a man in a dress and such behaviour so I just did not understand what was going on. A tall man came in and just after him Frankie came in and they both saw the bearded laddie and kiss kiss kiss. Then Frankie saw me and walked the tall fellow up to meet me. He introduced David and I and went to get coffees for himself and David. David and I started talking and joking immediately. What a wonderful fellow! They had the simple idea for our act which was David was the clown tight rope walker with the rope on the floor and I was his assistant. It was a funny physical act with some patter (clown dialogue). The whole show was called "Parachute" as it started with all of the clowns laying down underneath an opened flat parachute. Later I did three more shows at the same theatre. I didn't know it but it was a fairly famous local theatre and years later it commissioned Tony Kushner for the creation of his masterpieces "Angels in America" and "Perestroika".

One thread of my San Francisco life was related to Frankie, David and the Eureka Theatre.

OMENS, COINCIDENCE, SYNCHRONICITY, TIMING .... ONE THING LEADS TO ANOTHER

WARNING: I am about to disclose some experiences which like love or hope do not exist within the known limitations of scientific proof. Yet, as a human phenomenon, as an experience they certainly do exist. A human or an animal can sense, of course, when a person is happy or sad or scared or upset. Feelings are palpable inside and from the outside. There are other things in life which one can not share as an experience with another person. One person may feel the temperature outside rise and another person may not sense the change or the phenomenon. So, as clearly as I can, I'm going to tell you some layered stories which are about experiences which are imperceptible to some but vivid to another person.

To be very clear - I use the word 'phenomenon' which means that the experience itself is real though the force may be illusional or a creation of the brain. The brain and mind is a world of study unto itself. Many older cultures understood already many aspects of the brain and mind.
Similarly as a scientist of cell research informed me, until recently science actually thought just about everything was known about the 'hidden' (microscopic) world of the cells. New information became available and now science estimates that about 1% is known of what is hidden within the world of cells.

Back to my one day return visit to Dell'arte. Also visiting that day was a female clown Misha and her boyfriend who was a clown. She understood that I had no place to stay so she said I could stay in her apartment on the living room floor. Beggars can't be choosers. On the same day at Dell'arte one of the former students was there, Janice from Canada and she was going a day later to the Marin County Renaissance Faire. So I met her and others there. At the faire there were a lot of outdoor street style entertainers such as jugglers, acrobats, musicians. There were also all sorts of healers with herbs, massage, but, one was different. It had a small tent with an open side so people could look in. I looked at it from a distance and two people sat in chairs and one was waving his hands around and talking. I went closer. Then closer. Then a woman in a white dress and blonde hair suddenly appeared in front of me and said "Can I help you"? We spoke but I kept trying to look around her as I was very curious about the hand waving. Finally Lady Godiva held my attention and explained that there was a healing and aura reading going on. Would I like one? How much? It was not much but I had very little money. She said well you can come to our free healing clinic tomorrow. She gave me the address in Berkeley. That evening at Misha's tiny basement apartment she got a phone call from a friend. Misha told that she had a fellow clown visiting and soon put me on the phone. The woman said she desperately needed a live-in babysitter for her 6 year old son. She could give me my own room in her house and food and a small payment and I would be needed to stay home some evenings so she could go out. Sounds pretty good. Plus the house was in the Sunset District at the end of the N-Judah tram line and was ocean front. She was desperate, insistent, would I please just give it a try starting in a few days. She was a bit forceful but I understood she just wanted to be able to go out in the evenings.

Boy did she! Misha then told me I can stay in her apartment as she was going to move overseas and I could have her business. She too was desperate. She started to teach me about having a clown business in one hour. The most important thing she said was "When people offer you a gig, no matter what they want you can do it". Huh? "Even if they want a clown who can unicycle just tell them you have a flat tire so you can do mime instead".

The next morning as I awoke I had an extreme stiff neck. A locked neck. I lay in bed, i.e. on the little mattress on the floor. I thought it could be from having such a thin mattress on a concrete floor. But it was too painful. I asked myself what could it be. The pain was from the woman who needed a live-in baby sitter. A pain in the neck. Still it was an amazing offer for someone who just arrived in a city with no money, no work, no place to live other than this basement apartment. Now I had two places to live and one was on the ocean.

I remembered then about the free healing clinic in Berkeley. I went there. When I was paired up with a healer I was told to sit in the chair and that the process was that the healer would stand. What I had seen at the Renaissance was a full aura reading and for that the reader also sat in a chair. Right away the healer said "You've really got a pain in the neck". I said wow and whipped around stiff neck and all and asked how she knew that. She calmed me down and told me to sit still and face forward then said "Hmm, she really wants you". Wow and whipped around. Face forward. Then she started to tell me about the woman who I had not yet met. I asked some questions then the healer moved the energy in my neck back to the woman and my neck had no tension within a few minutes.

I moved into the ocean front house. To get to the ocean I had to walk a few minutes to the little pedestrian tunnel that went under the small highway. The other side of the tunnel was only sand, beach and the wild

Pacific Ocean. The water there is cold. But I began swimming the first day and every day. I also went to the free healing clinics in Berkeley which were twice a week. Each healing clinic the teacher would also explain some of their meditation techniques and I would practice every day. I told my girlfriend from Dell'arte about this amazing place. She informed me that she and two of the other women at Dell'arte had told me about this healing centre 2 years before the very first week we met at Dell'arte. Oh. Duh. Well better late than never.

On the third day of Dell'arte those three women invited me for dinner for that Wednesday evening. I didn't need to bring anything. They lived in the small apartment within the school's building. Lenka, Michelle, Marlene. The dinner would be vegetarian. Whatever. At dinner they talked about all kinds of strange things in theatre and spiritual stuff. I knew nearly nothing about either. It all seemed very strange. It was. They started talking about psychic stuff and it turned out that all three had heard about the Berkeley Psychic Institute (BPI), and they all had an interest to study there. Maybe when this ten week course at Dell'arte finished they could study at BPI. I asked, study what? Past lives. I said it doesn't make any sense. Michelle said after dessert she would show us an exercise to see past lives. Dessert? I'm hooked. I was to sit opposite Michelle while Lenka sat opposite Marlene and in between each couple was a lighted candle. One of each couple was to look at the opposite person's face and to describe that person's past lives. Whatever. Michelle told me to go first. Whatever. I looked beyond the candle and onto Michelle's face. Within one minute I start to see very clearly different faces or apparitions of faces over Michelle's face. One after another. First I was just staring and stuck staring as I was amazed to see such a phenomenon with my eyes wide open. After 2 minutes I shut my eyes. Looked away. Said I have to go. What about dessert? Another time thanks .... and I was out of there like a flash. I was quite upset as I had never experienced something like that, whatever that was. The house I rented a room in was just minutes away. I went to the bathroom to brush my teeth. As I looked in the mirror I saw a bright flashing rainbow around my head. I closed my eyes, rinsed out the toothpaste. Looked away from the mirror and went to bed. I had seen my own aura reflected in the mirror. Whatever.

Two years later I get it. Phenomenon of the mind such as the illusions we name as auras, psychic matters, or past lives exist in the same way that love or hope exists. Such phenomenon manifest at least through one's visual perception which is an illusion in the mind anyways - our visual perception is partially an illusion of the mind. It is as Macbeth says in Act II "Or art thou but a dagger of the mind, a false creation, proceeding from the heat-oppressed brain"?.

One day at the healing clinic I was told I could get a free reading which would take 2 hours and that was for the students to learn to read auras but was guided by one of the teachers. In that reading they told me about a special man I knew. They described David before I told them anything. They said that we had shared a past life. Whatever. Whatever other than the use of the dirty words 'past lives' that they told me seemed specific and accurate. So the next day I told David. He asked if he could go with me to the next clinic. Lenka went with us. This day Michael Tamara the young Japanese teacher at BPI explained to us that today he was training a "trance-medium". As he explained it, that is a person with psychic ability to allow another entity to enter their aura or being and to give more advanced information to the person being read. Michael guided the reader and the entity. Is this real or not. Well, depends. We could see changes take place in the reader. Eventually there was not only a change in the pitch of her voice but in the manner in which she spoke. There is no scientific detector deciphering what takes place. Soon a volunteer to be read is chosen. Whatever :). Now I am sitting opposite this big woman with a fairly manly voice. Michael walks us through the communication warmup. That warmup is about to get very hot. Gradually my body starts sweating, and twitching, and something is starting to move emotionally. What transpired was witnessed by my two friends and about a dozen people there for the free healing clinic. They got their monies worth this day. I was guided through what was essentially a vicarious birthing process. The story that unfolded is that on the day I was born my Mother had a big challenge because she wanted to be out dancing. I don't know the details except that I was born New Years Day. I think late in the evening. So some people would call what they witnessed at the clinic either a rebirthing or an exorcism. I was by the near end completely soaked in sweat. During the pinnacle I was heard moaning like a woman giving birth. Another way this could be viewed is a purging of a trauma. At any rate .... as shocking as it was to me to go through it was also shocking for anyone who witnessed it. Michael said I needed to go for an energetic walk to get back into my body. He also explained that it would be much better for me to at least enrol and attend their basic meditation course because I come consistently to the healing clinics and it seems like I am too open and can use the techniques they teach to close down psychic energies and then to be able to open in a controlled and safe way. I told my friends I'd see them later. I made it to the end of the block. There was a house with a very nice lawn. I laid down. And passed out and woke up a few hours later as the Sun started to go down. I walked back to the healing centre and spoke briefly with Michael so he could see I was still amongst the living. I then got something to eat and went home.

I enrolled in the first course. I met the Founder of BPI and liked him. Soon I enrolled in the full-time course and began to attend BPI every day with most days all day. For full-time students there were the set classes but there were at least two more sessions of readings which one could also participate in as much as one wanted. It was a great experience being inside this organisation which had several centres in the Bay Area. There were hundreds of students all developing their practical intuition. So it was a remarkable and positive experience for nearly two years from the free healing clinic weeks to the intensive period of study.

Near the end of my training I was offered a job in the clown theatre company that my Dell'arte friends Gale, Jim, Hannah, Janice, Paul were collectively a part of. Paul wanted a break. The troupe was based in Blue Lake as is Dell'arte the troupe was formed by graduates of Dell'arte. The troupe, Kit 'n Kaboodle American Theater Company was founded by Gale McNeely who was a brilliant extremely funny clown but he also had been a professional classical actor. He was briefly in the US Navy but found a way to get out. He then went to university in Ohio, at Kent State and was a witness to the tragic event memorialised in the song "Four Dead in Ohio" by Crosby, Stills, Nash, & Young.

So I filled in for Paul. Paul Klustermann and Jim Stephenson earlier that year had been in my ensemble clown theatre show "Zealous Zanies" at the Eureka Theatre. In Kit n Kaboodle my first tour was in a five person show. Then the two women decided to take a break so Gale, Jim, and I did a long tour as a trio. That job was wonderful timing for me. That company toured the Pacific Northwest primarily and sometimes as far south as Arizona. Once we went to a convention where performance groups gave a 10-20 minutes version of their show to representatives from universities who would buy a performance. The representatives though were only first or second year students so it was a big party and the partying definitely effected the bookings. It was at that convention that I saw the clown Howard "Buffo" Buten perform. He was austere and highly skilled. Like myself, it was that year he decided to get out of the USA. He has lived primarily in France since then, 1979, and has done profound work for children with Autism. He has a doctorate in psychology and has toured as a clown throughout France.

On my second tour with Kit n Kaboodle after a few shows I decided to quit. I felt like we weren't having fun and I could not see the point of being a clown troupe and not having fun. That choice to quit caused a bit of catharsis and lo and behold the next show we started to have fun. But something inside me was seeking something further. I wrote a fine scenario for the three of us, Gale, Jim, myself. After a few days I just felt I had something else further to find. I quit even though it was well paid work in a region with little work so it was easy that the next day one of our local friends was able to take my place. I didn't know what to do but I felt free but with a lot of time on my hands. Suddenly, one week I got three offers. One was that my second application to attend Ringling Clown College was approved. They gave each person a 'scholarship' as they needed trained clowns to fill in low paying contracts every year. I was also offered a weekly fee to attend the course. I don't know if others were offered that. The same week Circus Vargas offered a double contract to a) be in their clown troupe and also b) to be trained to do the classic Frog in the Barrel contortion acrobatic act. And the third offer came via a postcard from the clown Bill Irwin who I knew in San Francisco. He had come to see "Zealous Zanies" a few months earlier. He asked me to be his stage partner for his first New York City show. I figured that was his destiny and not mine. By the time this unusual week of three offers occurred I already thought I would like to go to Europe to see the classic clowns who performed in the traditional European one-ring circuses. I knew that some of the old men were still alive and performing and I wanted to see the tradition I had read about. During this 'in-between' period another Dell'arte friend Bernadette Sabbath suggested that I talk with her boyfriend who was a musician and played with clowns in Europe every year. He was very supportive and informative. Bernie suggested we make a duet clown street show because she was going to go to Europe to be with her boyfriend. So we made an act that was juggling and acrobatics. Our big trick was doing a row of double backbends while holding each other upside down.

I tried to sell my VW station wagon. As the days neared I still owned this car. Finally my friend Hannah suggested she could trade me a box of rings from Bali for the car and I could sell the rings in Europe. Done deal.

On the plane over the Atlantic, Bernie came over to my seat and told me she got me a job for a week in Vienna teaching clown. I went and spoke with the fellow and made the deal. In the plane. Over the Atlantic. I took it more as omen of 'being looked after' and 'things will work out'. When we arrived at Heathrow and we got our bags Bernie's boyfriend said 'seeya' and took Bernie up, up, and away to their journey.

I had written letters (1979 pre-email!!) to two friends to say I was coming to Europe. I gave them each other's information and said when I was arriving. I phoned the English fellow and he said meet at The Cutty Sark the sail boat on display by the Thames River. I stood there and suddenly see the other friend, the Dutchman and was so surprised. But he had called the Englishman so all was organised. We all went to a pub and then the Dutchman and his girlfriend Clare (or Claire?) said we would go the next day to the Festival of Fools in Cornwall for a few days and then we would drive to Edinburgh for about a week, then we would take the ferry from Hull to Rotterdam and then drive and stay at his parents for a few days and then we'd drive to Paris and I could stay at Clare's apartment on Place Clichy. Whatever. Talk about friends looking after you!

SOME KEY PROJECTS

At Festival of Fools I improvised doing clown, mime, acro, juggling. My friend Bernie was there. There is a beautiful photo of her in George Speaight's 1980 "The Book of Clowns" on page 18 playing around outside a circus tent and holding 3 of our matching 6 clubs and with rainbow socks which we also had matching. Those clubs and socks were fairly standard clown items in those days.

When our trio got to Edinburgh a few days later I was introduced to the Dutchman and Clare's newly graduated fellow classmates of Lecoq school - those who graduated in 1979. We were shown a section of the mouldy, dank, dark, cold squat house in which the whole lot were staying. I was told that the whole group was going to perform a 15 minutes version of Macbeth up near the castle and I could join them and play the Son of Banquo and they would tell me my entrance and the fellow playing Banquo was John. We agreed on 'what to do' but it was all very simple and nicely ordered so everyone simple knew when to enter, more or less what to do or to say, and to exit. Then to bow and pass the hat for donations. The Banquo's entered and I clowned and did 'something(s)' and the audience laughed and we soon exited and soon bowed and soon passed the hat. When we were done all of the graduates surrounded me and said I was very funny and asked where I trained and a few asked if I could teach them acrobatics, or mime etc. So we hung out for a few days and they were all good to me. I did a few of 'my own thing' improvised performances including jumping into the gigantic parade. I took a place in front of a full-kit kilted Scottish marching band with drums and bagpipes. I danced to their music for the entire parade. Heaven.

We then drove to Hull, ferried to Rotterdam, drove to Maastricht for just a few days. One afternoon we went to have a coffee at a very nice cafe with tables outdoors. There was a wonderful lithe waiter. Suddenly, a big rain began and everyone ran for cover. But the waiter stayed and collected some of the drinks. But, I don't know how, he did not get wet. Totally impossible but I saw that happen. I once saw a car drive trough a overhead highway railing and spin and fall from the height of about 30 or 40 feet, land on its roof and a whole family of Black Americas all opened their doors crawled out from being upside down and stood up and walked around their car as people came to see if they were okay. I was in a car with my Sister Faye. Our light changed and she drove onward. In Berlin one time when I was there inside the Wall to perform my solo "A Clown's House" and to teach a workshop, I went to a bank to change money. 1980. There were several bank clerks. But for some reason there was a line of people waiting for one particular clerk. All ladies were waiting for him. He had a short chat with each of them and they each went away very happy. He was very upright and handsome and pleasant. I went to him. He was very nice even though I only spoke a few words of German. But, when he counted money he was like a high speed machine. I have no idea how he could finger and count the money so neatly and fast. He was like a mystic in a bank.

I think much of life is simply mechanical common sense and logic. But I think there are other aspects of life which are mysterious. Not miraculous, not outside of nature and science, but I think there are things in life which are natural but mysterious. I have witnessed these and many other anecdotal phenomena but I can not prove any of them. I think being an upright walking human on this planet while it spins around so fast and hurtles within our galaxy through the known universe into the unknown universe is mysterious and the grandest phenomenon of our lives other than birth, death, love.

I think actors and clowns are simply symbols of that big mystery. The root of Western theatre stems from the English Mystery plays.

WORST CLOWNS

The two worst clowns I have ever seen were each wonderful. When I was a young, agile, funny, physical clown with only a few years experience in the performing arts I would often see a fat old clown sitting in a chair making balloon animals for people and getting money handed to him in exchange for his balloon animals. He had a regular out of the way spot where he was allowed to sit. He always had a few people waiting for his balloons. Finally one day I thought I would go see what this clown says to people that must work as they always looked happy. I went and stood close enough to hear what he said. He was so nice, and kind, and witty. He was excellent at making the balloon sculptures while he talked to each person. He gave each person his undivided attention. He gave them attention, love, wit, and wished each of them a good day. He was wonderful. The other worst clown was a Ronald McDonald. As an arty, intellectual clown I thought the worst imaginable job as a clown would be to play Ronald McDonald. One day in San Francisco I saw a poster for a local street fair and it said you-know-who will be there. So I went to see him-who. Wow! First of all his costume and makeup were utterly immaculate. Impeccable makeup. His presence and way of dealing with each person was so positive and grounded. When he did his short performance of magic he was the consummate professional. Warm, welcoming, energetic, joyous.

I do not think there is such a thing as 'the best clown'. I think those two 'worst' clowns are amongst the best, I saw what they did, their genuine warmth and humanity and kindness and generosity. I think the clowns who are amongst the 'worst' are actually the best, those are the kitsch commercial clowns who go into peoples homes into intimate spaces such as family, community, and business events and make people laugh or even are there to be the butt of the wicked humour of someone who wants to be the centre of attention, those clowns hidden from the arts councils and art critics and famous theatres, those clowns in private spaces bring the heart of clown close enough to touch. Of course the hospital clowns and crisis clowns do this as well. At the same time, so did Marcel Marceau do so within the limitations of the fancy theatres he brought the spotlight right to the heart and soul of the individual human as symbolised by the clown and actor.

"CHAPLIN'S EYE"

During my six years in Frank Theatre inspired by Tadashi Suzuki the company directors made a project to let members of the company make their own short pieces of about 20 minutes. I was still fairly new compared to those who had been in it ten years. So John was kind enough to ask me if I'd like to make a piece. Sure. Do you know what you would do? No? Could you use Kristin? Sure! She was fab. Quiet. Although she didn't get the roles like the main members her technique was excellent and she had her own unique softer qualities. Then he said what about Jane, could you use her? Sure. So it went and John basically cast my team each of whom was fab and fine but none were the main company members. The project was to be at the Powerhouse which was originally a power house by the river and had many unique spaces. We were encouraged to each use a different space and to create with that space in mind. I chose the very long foyer it is perhaps 25 meters long. One enters via automatic sliding glass doors. There were two stairwells which also connected to the foyer. I sat the audience at the end of the foyer opposite the glass doors. The first two people entered via the doors. Three more from the upstairs and two from the downstairs. They entered in different timing and the two men had some martial arts experience so I exploited that in the choreography. Several people came up to me at the end of the evening's pieces and said they liked my piece. One person was Andrew who also did occasional clown performances. He said he had Metro Arts theatre reserved but didn't want to create a new piece and he had $5000 that he would put up to produce a show for me and if there was anything he could act in then he'd be happy to be one of my performers.

I got an idea to 'make a star' out of Kristin to make her the lead character, but the star bit was up to her stars. Andrew said he knew a talented young actress named Kate and maybe she could be in it. I also asked Jane to be in. I called it "Chaplin's Eye". Partially I was aware that so many clown teachers have stopped referencing Charlie Chaplin. I felt his work needed to be reignited within the clown teaching network. I would enter last in the piece, as "The Ghost of Chaplin". I wanted to explore and play with something I saw a Korean woman shaman do with five colours which represent the principle of five in Asian cultures. So each of the five clowns was to be a different colour. I wanted the first four clowns to be 'real' clowns who then treat Chaplin like a windup toy doll and play and taunt him. I wanted him to be "He who gets slapped" i.e. the clown at the bottom of the pecking order.

I also had recently seen Slava's Snowshow for the second time. First time was 1999 in Montreal and the second was in Brisbane. I ran into Slava and Lena his wife at Southbank. We chatted briefly and they offered me a ticket and to meet them and their son after the show. Snowshow reminded me to return to my original clowning which was silent and a story. So I did not want to imitate Slava but I was reminded to emulate the simplicity.

Tiffany Beckwith-Skinner made the four costumes and mine was to be simply classic Chaplin. It happened that sometime before a clown/actor named Jack decided he wanted to focus on acting and stop doing his Chaplin impersonation so he gave me his handmade Chaplin boots. Kristin would enter first in a Flamenco dress that was rose colour. I named her "Femmla". Then Jane entered in lime green dress with a fat suit underneath making a big bottom and big top (breasts) and a big yellow clown wig. She was called "Zophtie" from the Yiddish word for a big elegant woman like the Australian Maria Venuty, or Dame Joan Sutherland. The Yiddish word is 'zophtich'. Then came Andrew who is tall, in a yellow one piece like a toddler's sleeping suit. Referencing of course Slava's yellow clown. I called this character Lanky and we explored long lanky movement like a Great Dane puppy. The fourth to enter the stage was Kate as Pierroutte in a dark powder blue costume referencing Jean-Louis Barrault's Pierrot in the film Les Enfants du Paradis. The four actors had never seen the movie so we had a movie night at Andrew's apartment where I rented a room. I knew a musician and composer named Carla Thackrah and I asked her if she could help with music. I wanted a music theme for each character which would come on each time they entered. In the end she said just take the music she had made for a mutual friend's short film. That film was "Frock" created by the dancer Rosetta Cooke. The film was very short so Carla suggested I could simply repeat the music. With that and some other recorded songs I selected I cobbled together a sound score.

The story was that Femmla had a favourite small suitcase. She enters with it but can not figure out where to place it. This is a parody of the cliche of a woman wanting to rearrange the furniture periodically but not being able to decide. As Kristin was a dancer her action was done through a type of mime or clown dance. She leaves the small suitcase in its right spot and exits. Zophtie enters and discovers the suitcase and likes it and as no one is around she takes it. Femmla comes on with a larger suitcase and is shocked that the little one is gone. She leaves the bigger one and exits. Zophtie comes on very proud with her new suitcase and small rainbow umbrella and new long boots. So she's quite the dandy and Femmla enters with a third suitcase which is the biggest. Zophtie sees that and wants it. There ensues a layered struggle over the biggest suitcase they each exit. Lanky enters to his music and discovers the smallest suitcase and takes it and the other two clowns re-enter and the three clowns have an encounter over the suitcases as to who is going to get which one. They exit. Big music change and light change so the stage looks in lighting terms like the pantomime scene in Les Enfants du Paradis which is itself meant to look like we imagine the stage lighting in the 1800s. The music matched. Pierroutte enters with the big floaty steps like the movie. She discovers the little suitcase and looks around the theatre to see that no one is around and she slowly starts to steal the little suitcase. Suddenly the music and lights change and all three other clowns enter and a choreographed chase ensues between all four clowns and the suitcase. Three of the clowns fall on the floor siting in their bottoms and Femmla ends up with the little suitcase and dances over the clowns and sits on her bottom. The music and lights change to an eery mysterious tune. The clowns are sitting in a row and all look up towards the back of the theatre behind the audience and already The Ghost of Chaplin has begun to descend the steps in the middle of the audiences seats. He is walking slow motion Suzuki style like a ghost floating as he nears the stage the four seated clowns spiral around to standing. Chaplin moves near them all are moving in slow motion. He is then in a line with the others and with the spin of his cane the music changes to a very up tempo tune like a circus song. The four clowns fully come alive Chaplin moves like a lively mechanical doll as his hat, cane and the little suitcase are continually taken and he retrieves them. Magically his hat gets hid inside the suitcase and finally he gets his hat and cane and the real slapstick between the five clowns ensues with kicks, falls, stunts. Finally all settles and Chaplin magically reveals a flower and presents it to Femmla. She is happy but in the next moment is abandoned by her new friends each disappeared behind four on stage exits. Suddenly a flower appears at each exit held by one arm of each clown. When she has all the flowers the clowns enter and take a stylised bow and exit. The suggestion to have all the clowns give a flower after Chaplin had, came from an audience member Karen Tuney who since then I have called "my flower girl". The show was a metaphor for coveting, greed, and with a resolution of sharing and generosity.

SOME KEY PROJECTS

MY SHOWS AND THE INNER WORLD OF CLOWN

The clown shares what they feel. They express their feeling or thought and impress that on to the audience. The clown is a direct conduit of emotion in the same way a conductor is a conduit for a symphony. The clown plays the audience. It is a two-way street. Stanislavsky called that transference of energy between the actor and the audience, prana, the Sanskrit word for life-force.

Several shows of mine explored the inner world of the clown. My first clown theatre show was *A Clown's Show* at the Eureka Theater of San Francisco. Each show explored that inner world in a different way. For example my first touring solo show was called *A Clown's House*. The stage metaphorically is where the clown feels at home. They feel more at home in performance than in everyday reality. The show which immediately preceded and led to *A Clown's House* was called *Getting Into Struggle*.

Getting Into Struggle happened in March 1980 after I had been teaching in Stockholm already since October 1979. I came to Stockholm to help my friend Ole Brekke start his Commedia School which was first called Clownskolan. At the same time he helped me by giving me an opportunity to teach even though I was only 27 years old. We had done one fun clown duet when we were at The Dell'arte School. We made a piece for the end of a week showing which were on Fridays. We made a short duet that revolved around a park bench that was part of the studio furniture. The payoff was when Ole's clown was sitting on the bench with a hat on and reading a newspaper. This was in our second semester in early 1976.

In late 1975 I had moved to Sarasota, Florida to become a clown. In Sarasota I found my clown teacher who was Danny Chapman and he sent me to learn acrobatics from a master teacher named Willie who taught evening classes mainly for the children of circus performers. Their level was extremely high and mine was pre-basic. When I was at Dell'arte I felt the classes were not particularly functional and of course compared to Willie and Willie's students our theatre acrobatic classes were in fact shameful. So even though I was still pre-basic I thought I would be better off learning from a book and practicing on my own. I progressed steadily and took myself past pre-basic into basic.

Thus in the duet with the bench the finale trick was a trick right out the book. Right out of one of the three books I had borrowed from Humboldt State Library. Those books had not been borrowed in several decades. One had 'every trick in the book'. Another was an olde school gymnastics text. The third was an even older book for handstands. The duet's finale trick was as said Ole sitting on the bench with a hat on reading the newspaper. The bench had a wooden back. I ran a few steps and did a dive-roll or what Grotowski called "a cat spring" and in midair I grabbed the hat, put it on my head and still in the dive now with the hat on my head I grabbed the newspaper then landed via a roll with the newspaper in my hands and the roll continued so that rolled to standing reading the newspaper.

The trick, so to speak, was to grab the hat on the first part of the dive going upward and to grab the newspaper on the beginning of the descent. It is possible that I had a mat placed in front of the bench to accomodate my roll. However, Dell'arte's 'mats' at that time were very old judo tatami mats of straw which had been pounded down in whatever judo dojo they were from. The mats hardly were better than the worn out carpet on the wooden floor. So, even if there was a mat, it was only a step up from landing the roll on a wooden floor. My friends "Price & McCoy comic acrobats" only practiced their routine on a wooden floor, as did our Australian Knockabout teacher Clete Ball, so that when they performed on stage they never used a mat. Such practice conditions your muscles, joints, bones, ligaments, and tendons for normal stage work. The benefit of training on mats though is so that you can practice a trick more times before your muscles start to tighten for the day. Eventually of course gymnastics developed the sprung floor. But at Dell'arte the mats at that time 1976-77 when I was there were of no benefit to most learners who could hardly do a proper low basic dive roll. So that is where Ole and I met and became friends.

Two years after Dell'arte I left the USA for three-weeks to see the old European clowns doing their classic acts in the European one-ring circus tradition. Soon I had friends in Paris where I could 'crash'. I stayed in the apartment of a friend's girlfriend Claire Tyson. An American actress who shared the apartment with an Italian actor. They lived at the main plaza of Pigalle. One day Claire and I decided to try busking and improvising a 'show' at Centre du Pompidou. There was a Romany busker who did fakir stuff and had a knife and shooshed us away so that he could build an audience. It took three shooshes and swooshes with his knife until we were far away enough which was not favourable to gather an audience. In this period September 1979 was when such great buskers as Pony the Mime, Rene Bazinet, David Shiner were very successful creating real clown and mime acts that earned them plenty of money. Philippe Petite would have already have cracked the code there and in NYC and Robert Shields had long been discovered at Union Square in San Fransisco. Claire and I didn't have a clue. We tried once. Got threatened by the knife wielding Gypsy or maybe he was just a ruffian, and exiled to the furthest part of the plaza.

A day or so later I decided to find a nice park to train some acrobatics. An olde school gendarme (policeman) came and shooshed me off of the nice grass without a swooshing knife, just a pouted lip a nod and a wave of the hand. I could take an unsublte hint. I had been shooshed from better places. Well from one place better so to speak. That was 1977 when my cross country Greyhound Bus (Boston to San Francisco) made a meal stop in Salt Lake City, Idaho. I went to check out the Morman temple and lo and behold they had a very nice acrobatic lawn. An Arnold Swarznegger-like security guard in his Morman suit gave me the shoosh Morman-style. I dutifully stopped my acrobatics and just as well got to the bus in time.

After my Paris knife shooshing I decided to send Ole a telegram (very pre-email days!) to say I'm in Paris and seeking work as a teacher. He sent one back that said "You're hired". He then instructed me to apply for a work visa at the Swedish embassy or consulate and that their rules at the time were if you applied you could actually work in Sweden until the bureaucracy ruled yes or no. The woman at the counter, that is the woman who sat at a desk behind the counter stood when I came to the counter and who hardly moved from the desk. It was very weird coming from the USA where one comes directly to the 'customer'. Then she came close enough only momentarily to give me the form and close enough only momentarily to take the form when I completed it. I took the train then from Paris to

Stockholm. When I arrived in Stockholm I had approximately $3.50 in total to my name and my whole existence.

So. The show. That show. *Getting Into Struggle*. To be sure, I was already experimenting with reality for several years. Testing our normal perception or parameters of reality which can be viewed in many different ways. Our perceptions are socially influenced. I simply suddenly had awoke one morning and had an idea to do a show that involved an image of a home. I pictured a small refrigerator, a bed, and a few other things. At the time I was living at the house and home of Ole and his wife Maria which was a yogic household. Originally I was to stay there very briefly for a few weeks until I found a place. I was harmonious enough with the environment so I was welcomed to stay through my first year of teaching. At breakfast I told people that I was going to do a show in ten days. I was asked where and told that it would not be so easy to find a place. At the time, I had a healing clinic within the new age centre Galleri Medmera near Slussen. I taught evening classes in meditation, healing, and psychic development. I had a free healing clinic on Sundays which was always full with a flow of people waiting to see me. Also by appointment during the week I would do individual psychic readings for 45 to 60 minutes. This day I had a morning appointment. When I got out at Slussen instead of walking the way I walked every other time I decided to take a different route and I wondered why. Then after just 2 blocks in the new direction and very near Galleri Medmera there was a dumpster and on top was a small refrigerator and a bed and some other household items. I thought I would come back and get those. I did one or two readings that morning and then decided I would try a theater I had heard about - Teater-9. I went there and spoke to the one person working there and asked about the dates I wanted and they said those dates were fine and we made a deal right then.

The show was in my mind and my imagination. I had very little worked out practically. There was seating for about 60 people. I made a drawing and photocopied it as an A-4 handbill and poster. On the day of the premiere of the three night season I arrived four hours early to warmup and practice. When I 'worked through' the show it took only about 10 minutes. I had only ten minutes of prepared material. The show in performance lasted 90 minutes. I improvised and played. The audience entered and the only thing on the stage was a small rug in the middle. At the timed moment for the show to start the audience heard some knocking. Like someone knocking on a door to come in. They soon realised it was coming from under the floor. They began to laugh. The location traveled until the knocking was in the middle of the stage under the rug. Then the middle of the rug started to move upward and the audience laughed a lot more loudly. The rug moved upward a few inches at first, then a foot, then a full meter upward and the rug then started to disappear into the now opened trap door. Much more laughter. Then my hands appeared. Then my head, then my foot and thus began after at least five minutes thus far my first bit of slapstick which was improvised around me trying to get out of the hole. Eventually perhaps ten minutes later I was fully standing. At some point I brought a suitcase on to stage. I had a wonderful old steamer travel trunk which opened to an L-shape and the top part had wooden hangers for clothes. In that I could keep lots of things including my juggling props of five orange lacrosse balls which were the norm for my generation of jugglers and clowns, and three white plastic juggling clubs which were also the norm at the time. Then I think Dubay juggling company in NYC had started to manufacture much more aesthetically pleasing clubs which are now the norm. At some point I brought out a doll and played with it in various ways. Some moments I treated it like a baby, then a football, then a witness to my tricks of juggling and entertainment. At some point I brought out a chair and newspaper and did my slapstick routine with those which involved a lot of pratfalls and playing with and eating some of the paper. Quite a lot. Not swallowing it though. The show went very well and various friends came including my then new friend Manne af Klintberg who is essentially the unofficial national clown. He certainly deserves to be the official national clown. On the last night the theatre could not provide anyone in the box office until close to the show time. So I sat in the box office and sold a few tickets early. One woman asked if the show was good and if the performer was funny. So when I was first fully on stage and she realised our conversation she was dying with laughter. In those days I thought a clown was to be funny and physical. I was extremely funny and physical. A few years later I wrote a short article for a little local journal in New Zealand when I lived there. I was writing about technique versus being. Naturally as is important for the new clown .... one should invest in hard skills such as juggling, dance, acrobatics, music, singing, circus skills, vocal skills, magic etc and the basic crafts of makeup, costume, gags; and, a knowledge of clown history (international, national, local). However, one must also hone ones soul and sensibilities. So as I kept developing my skills I also understand presence. I understood that early on but as I built skills I also studied and lived the soul of the clown.

From this show I got a gig on a variety TV show *Confetti* and that came directly from Manne. The show was filmed at the theater which he performed in regularly, The Comedy Teater in the Stockholm tivoli called Gronalund. It was in that theatre I met Clownen Manne. I had seen a tiny ad for a clown show in the newspaper and went within my first week of being in Sweden. The next morning I taught my regular theatre class but the students were all excited and told me some had seen me on TV but also that people on the trains and buses were talking about "the clown" they had seen on *Confetti*. I did my chair and newspaper routine which was structured but improvised using schtick or comedy bits which I had developed either in rehearsal or in performance. My falls involved slipping in various ways on the chair and on the newspaper as it fell apart onto the floor. I took the classic image of a clown or person "slipping on a banana peel" and took it into absurd proportions.

HOW THINGS HAPPEN

From *Getting Into Struggle* I got a manager Mike who was from England married to a Swedish woman named Anna. He managed bands. He got a photographer and I had photos taken in Teater-9. I asked my friend Sharon to come along as the audience so I had someone to clown for while the photographer worked to catch me in action. Mike had already said he would like to manage me but first to simply help me get bookings. He had a book *Theater Festivals Around the World*. He suggested that I make a publicity brochure about my show, my work and myself to send to any festivals listed in that book. Then if any offers came he would help me negotiate the contracts.

Getting Into Struggle I did that 3 times which was enough become a much more refined idea that was called *A Clown's House*. So the publicity was for a show that I had not created yet. I transformed elements of *Getting Into Struggle* into a succinct storyline and clearer skill sections with the result of a repeatable show that was about 50 minutes. Just long enough for a complete one-man show.

A Clown's House was non-verbal, no music either. I wore an oversized tails suit, with a red & white Marimekko cotton shirt; a small bow tie and red Converse All-Star tennis shoes. I had my steamer suitcase with which I entered the stage. It would take 5 to 10 minutes for me to fully enter the stage. If I entered via the audience I would struggle and struggle to get up to the stage. If there were steps up the side of the stage I would fall and fall. I would try to get my leg onto the stage and often would solicit someone's help. How bizarre is it to be a clown. As I write and was about to say that this gag is used in *Slava's Snowshow* at interval to start the 2nd half of the show ... and lo and behold the song which is used just started playing in this cafe in Potsdam, Germany.

I would do all the usual schtick of getting an audience member to help and push me up while at the same time not letting them succeed and falling about them. As Carlo Mazzone-Clementi would say to us as students "Nothing is original so don' worry about it". Jerry Lewis did this type of schtick with Dean Martin at the Copacabana and on their TV show. Eventually though in my case I would finally put my hands on the stage and jump up to a handstand. That required jumping to a tuck or ball and then elongating to the handstand. Then I walked on my hands a bit. Eventually though, I still had to get my suitcase which allowed more comic business. Next I would leave the suitcase on stage and exit then return wheeling in a very small refrigerator. Then I'd bring on a small table and two chairs. At this stage I would take items which do not belong in a suitcase i.e. a banana and three apples. From the refrigerator I would take non-belonging items which were a tablecloth, tin plates, and some cutlery. Set up the table first by opening the tablecloth and running around with it over my shoulders like a cape then suddenly I'd leap onto then off the table and when I jumped off I left the tablecloth to float onto the table.

A CLOWN'S HOUSE

Bill Irwin saw me do that stunt in "A Clown's House" around 1980 at a small theatre in the Mission District of San Francisco. Jael Wiseman was with him at the performance. That stunt Bill then did when he played the servant in the Pickles clown trio theatre show "Three High" (with Larry Pisoni and Geoff Hoyle). A wonderful show!

I juggled with the tin plates and cutlery and set the table for two. Then I juggled the apples eventually I pulled a wooden mallet from the refrigerator and smashed the apples on a third tin plate into a mush (creatively). Then out came the banana and into the mush mash it went. Then like a waiter I served the mush dish to two invisible diners. Finally I sat in one of the chairs now as a diner. I tried to make myself comfortable but I looked forlornly at the empty setting for the missing dinner date. I'd start to look casually towards the audience. Then more intent.

MORE TIME OVERLAPPING

Eventually a woman in the front row would connect with me non-verbally. With my body language, subtle and ambiguous at first I would eventually nod or look in such a way that she would beam a big smile, or a questioning smile, or might point to herself or point to the stage and I would smile or blink my eyes .... eventually she would silently rise and come to the steps of the stage or walk onto the stage and I would go to greet her and offer my elbow as in the old fashioned way of walking with ones spouse. Then near the table I would become the waiter until I sat down. Then we would improvise looks. I would divide the mushed up apples and banana onto each of our plates. Certainly throughout all of this there were things I did which made the audience laugh, and they would laugh at my partner's situation. Finally I would go to feed some mush on a spoon to my partner and of course this became a very funny game and the timing was unique each show.

As mentioned before Bill Irwin and Jael Wiseman (who directed comedy and commedia) saw this show and spoke with me after and they were trying to figure out how the timing was so good. It was certainly better timing than most clown duets. They were convinced that I had 'planted' the woman i.e. rehearsed with her. So they had been trying to figure out if I just met her the day of the show or before to rehearse. They were impressed. I was improvising but I based most of my timing on whatever the 'volunteer' did. She and I had never met until the moment in the show when I took her as a volunteer. When a clown does such work several hundreds or even thousands of times they accumulate a bag full of reactions. That is understandable and admirable. I had not done the show enough to find that necessary or useful. I certainly never felt that I did this show enough. I was just starting to get more offers for it, and, then life took me in another direction .... south .... very far south as in the Southern Hemisphere.

From the theater festivals book that my manager, Mike, in Sweden gave me, I selected 100 festivals to write to. A handwritten letter to each with my new brochure "Vincenzo". That was what my teacher Carlo named my character. Only one festival even replied. That was Moomba Festival in Melbourne. The director was Mark Sasellea. He made a modest offer and as I was just starting with this show I thought it was fine. It was understood that I would be flying from San Francisco. Part of the deal was that I would buy my own air ticket but would be reimbursed. But by the time February of 1981 rolled around I was fairly broke financially. So I asked Mark if he would front the money. He did so with hesitation as the festival was not really set up to do that, but he did it. I was also waiting on my visa which was to come to the Australian consulate in San Francisco. Whenever I would check it had not arrived. Finally as I was to fly on a Saturday, I phoned Friday morning and they explained that they close at 330pm and if it had not been cleared there was nothing they could do. They said to come in at 315pm and if it arrived there was still time for them to process. It had arrived.

But.
Qantas Airlines was going to have an employees strike. So it was not sure that the flight would leave, and, I was also told that if the flight did leave it may not be allowed to land in Australia due to the influence of the strike and empathy from other unions in the flight industry. We did take off. There were no hostesses. There were only men who were stout hearted

blokes. I don't know how they got permission to host us because they certainly were not air attendants. We stopped to refuel and then it was not sure if we would be able to land. On our descent into Melbourne the 8 year old boy who was seated next to me kept saying "We're going to crash". We didn't crash but did land. I was to have been met by someone from the festival but there was no one. So I took a taxi to the festival office address that was perhaps on Collins Street certainly near Swanston.

I said to the receptionist that I would like to see the director Mark Saselea (I'm not sure of the spelling of his last name) she asked for my name. When I told her she had an odd suspicious reaction. She phoned Mark and said "There's someone here who says he is Ira Seidenstein". She told me to wait. When Mark arrived he did not come close enough to shake hands but stood at a distance. He said "Can I help you". I said "Hi Mark, I'm Ira". Mark replied "Excuse me" and still did not come closer. So I added "I'm Ira. Ira Seidenstein. You know "Vincenzo the clown". He looked shocked and asked "How did you get here"? "I took a taxi". "No. How did you get in the country? How did you get through Customs". Clearly I did not understand what the issue was.

Mark then lit up and stepped forward to shake hands and laugh and explained that he did not think I would get through Customs as he had been informed that the actors union had decided to use me as a test case to block foreign artists and had even warned Customs that I might try to come in on a tourist visa. However, I had a legal short work visa from the San Francisco consulate. From that moment Mark and the staff treated me like gold. I was put up in a small hotel on Little Collins Street. I was informed that the intended plan to have me perform my show on an outdoor stage had been changed as the city turned down the festival's plan for such outdoor performances. My performances and others had been reassigned to perform on indoor stages in shopping malls around the city. I explained that my show was not made for such venues and was told I could do whatever material I felt would work in the malls. The festival would arrange taxis to and from each venue. Mark invited me to the staff pre-opening party at a night club this night. There the receptionist came over and asked if she could talk with me. She asked me a few questions about where I was from and she said "You don't know what it's like here" and began to explain that she was from Greek parents and began to explain about the issues that ethnic people faced in Australia.

Fourteen years later two Greek heritage sisters and their business partner from Iceland hired me in Sweden. It was then I looked back and realised that nearly every time I was hired it was either by someone foreign to whatever country I was hired in; or, someone married to a foreigner; or, someone gay. In other words it was someone who subconsciously was an 'other', and, was I suppose more open to hiring another 'other'.

Though I viewed Mark and the receptionist as Australian though of ethnic heritage, and, I viewed the Greek heritage sisters and the Icelandic woman as Swedish, they all viewed themselves also as 'others'. In the United States when I grew up it was assumed that everyone was both American and an other. Yet, the USA seemed to also have the worst racism.

I made a few tours to Australia and in that process four people encouraged me to relocate from Auckland, New Zealand (Aotearoa) to Sydney, Australia. I did so by fluke in May, 1985. Two of those four people were Indigenous Australians and two were white/Anglo Australians. The four people were: Ted uGaboo" Thomas a mix-race Indigenous elder; and, Neville who was a former tap dancer then a mentor and elder for the National Aboriginal and Islander Dance Academy (NAISDA); and, Stephen Champion who was part of the 'original' (2nd wave) Circus Oz; and, last of the four was Ian Tasker who was for many years the Stage Manager and Assistant to Barry Humphries as well as the director of Kinselea's night club.

Stephen and I met when Circus Oz had their first overseas season in Holland. When we met I was already contracted to go a few months later to Moomba Festival in Melbourne. After I saw the show in Holland, Stephen invited me to come the next day and so we could do some acrobatic training together and it was then that I met the rest of the cast which included Robyn Laurie, Jon Hawkes, Sue Broadway, Tim Caldwell.

When I was in Melbourne Circus Oz was on holiday but I taught a 2-hour acrobatic workshop for Robyn and Jon at the Pram Factory. We did some partner acrobatics and they liked that and Robyn arranged for me to teach another workshop for them and others who they invited. That was a few days later and in my method that combined movement/mime/clown. It was at a contemporary dance studio. I created my own exercises and improvised as a teacher. However, I had already developed my "Core Mechanics" and usually started with that. The workshop went well and Robyn, Jon and the others suggested that I should return 7-months later to Melbourne in October 1981 to teach an 8-weeks physical theatre course in my method for the members of Circus Oz and for members of the contemporary dance community in Melbourne, And to then continue immediately with 4-weeks to create and for me to direct a new show for Circus Oz.

For the physical theatre course we were to use the same dance studio. Several months later the studio lost it's fire permit and had to find the money to build a fire escape or loose the permit to teach classes so my course and directing was postponed indefinitely.

2 months after Moomba I was at a small clown festival in southern Sweden and performed my solo show "A Clown's House". There was another mime/clown there named Michael River Lynch. River who had lived in Sweden but was then only visiting for the festival and for his Swedish wife's family. River now was living in Nelson, New Zealand (Aotearoa) and offered to help me to tour in New Zealand with "A Clown's House" and to teach my method.

"River" provided me with a letter of introduction, as well as names and addresses of people who could hire me. The day I received the letter from Circus Oz (likely from Robyn or Jon) of postponement due to the dance studio loosing its fire permit, I also received the first of many letters which were to come from River's contacts in New Zealand.

Each of his contacts wrote positively and provided dates for performances and workshops. The first little contract was to be in October, 1981 was performing 2 or 3 evenings per week in Robinson Family Circus. That was for

SOME KEY PROJECTS

their Auckland season of October and November and was connected with their work during the school term. The dates Robinson's offered happened to be the same as the intended dates to be in Melbourne.

Each few days I received other letters of dates for New Zealand performances and workshops. Usually one performance on a Friday or Saturday and a weekend workshop. A number of these were in art galleries of small cities such as Hamilton, New Plymouth and others. These galleries were also adaptable venues used for the performing arts and workshops.

BEFORE NEW ZEALAND

Just before the clown festival southern Sweden I had arranged a little bit of work for two friends: Barbara and Jodi. They were the last remnant of The Great Salt Lake Mime Troupe and had changed their performing name to *Heroes and Regulars* which were two types of sandwiches in New York City where they resided half of the year. The other half was based in Amsterdam. I arranged for them to perform their show at Teater 9 in Stockholm and to teach some workshops. On the Friday of their show they invited me to come in to the theatre and train with them.

Then the two dancers suggested that the three of us should do some street performing as a trio on Saturday, the next day, and pass the hat. We performed in front of Konsert Huset. It was 100% improvised but made use of our abilities as mime, clowns, dancers. I was not a dancer but could move well whereas they were both trained dancers who were also good clowns and mimes.

There was a small stylish woman watching our performance and she had on a small mink stole around her shoulders. When we finished the performance and put a hat out to collect donations the woman came up to me and exclaimed "You are a real dancer"! To me. Not to the two dancers. They frowned. She went on explaining what she saw in me and continuing with compliments and then said she wanted to bring me to Helsinki to teach her dance company "Raatikko". My partners were fuming.

She, Maria Wolska, and I traded contact information (address and phone - this is 1980, 19years before I had my first email address). She followed up and hired me to teach a ten days workshop for Raatikko and for some members of the Finland national ballet. One night Maria invited me to accompany her and see a performance at the opera. As we sat on a bench in the foyer people would walk by and bow to her. I said "I'm sorry I had no idea that you were famous". She said "Oh fuck them!!".

Maria had also arranged for me to perform my solo show "A Clown's House" one night in a beautiful old university theatre that held about 500 people. There was to be a contemporary dancer in town so she made it a double bill. The dancer performed first. The show was sold out. There was a review in the main Finish paper. The dancer's name was Mary Prestige and she had some connection to Ballet Rambert. Later that year I also taught a one week workshop for the national ballet school of Norway in Oslo.

Before I went to Helsinki in September, in the summer of 1980 I teamed up with the two dancers and we became "Heroes, Regulars, and Jerks". As a trio we performed 100% improvised with the only set bit being that the lighting technician was to bring the lights up on stage at the scheduled starting time and 55 minutes later, 5 minutes before the hour long show/improvisation was to end the technician was to begin a slow fade of the lights over the 5 minutes so that we could bring the performance to an end on time. We performed four nights in the Eureka Theatre of San Francisco with a standup bass player who also had total freedom to improvise. When we performed at the Omega Institute our trio was accompanied by the then famous cellist David Darling. When we played in Holland and Germany other solo musicians would join us including the wonderful saxophonist Michael Moore. With him we did one performance in an out of the way tiny studio located on the 2nd floor of an office building. Nobody came, not even the ticket seller. We did the show and had a ball.

As a trio we once performed in Aachen, Germany with no musician. The show was our normal excellent. The audience applauded enthusiastically at the end. However, above the applauds someone was shouting in German which none of our trio understood except if he had said "Eine schtuck der

SOME KEY PROJECTS

kuchen und eine tasse der kaffe" (i.e. a piece of cake and a cup of coffee). As the applause died down other people started yelling at the man yelling at us. Within minutes most of the audience was arguing and gradually their arguments continued as they walked up on to the stage. Within about 4 minutes we were surrounded and separated from each other by the whole audience which now was on stage shouting and arguing in German. Finally someone explained that the man complained that we were clearly physically skilled but we didn't use enough techniques but for most of the audience they didn't care as the show was fine and we were highly skilled improvisers. Eventually as normal the audience departed the theatre we changed clothes and did my preferred norm after every show which was to go to an Italian restaurant and have a pizza or spaghetti and a salad and a glass of red wine then go 'home' to the host or hotel. In the process of touring, very soon Barbara and I became a couple and also a performing team.

During our few days at the Eureka Theater several things happened. The three of us were each 28 years old. We were each living on the edge artistically, financially, psychologically and emotionally. Not good. I was quite disciplined and was training one day on my own in the theatre. The two dancers came in and as far as I could tell completely wanted to interfere with my training process by interrupting it with no care and no sensitivity and I told them as much, directly. That night after our performance Barbara and I were walking 'home' to our host's, which was the apartment of my friend David Pearce. Very near to his apartment we got mugged. Four young men each pulled a knife on us. They separated us - two with Barbara and two with me. They wanted her leather jacket and they wanted my backpack. I didn't know what to do so as they jabbed me with their knives only enough to scare me but hard enough so I could feel the point of the knives so to stall I moaned as if they were cutting me. Barbara thought they were killing me. Suddenly she jumped out of her coat and those two fellows were standing holding the jacket while she ran and yelled "Help! Help! They're killing my boyfriend!". Then my two attackers left me and the four of them were gone like a flash. I ran after Barbara and a car had stopped to help her and the man who helped her into the car saw me running and thought I was one of the attackers. So I stopped and yelled "I'm her boyfriend". He was not convinced then Barbara came out of the car and confirmed. We got in the car and were driven the mere 2 blocks to David's apartment. We called the police who came quickly and drove us to look for the fellows and the leather jacket which they abandoned as they just wanted cash.

We were unharmed theoretically. We were 28 and living on the edge and tough. However, the next day we had off and were walking and as the sun began to set we were both hit suddenly with a deep panic and needed to get home. This happened two more evenings. Then we began to recover from the shock of being attacked. The recovery is a long slow process. But one never forgets. It seems to me it was this time we began a process of several years of a dysfunctional relationship. We tried. We failed. We tried repeatedly. Eventually I saw a very specific pattern that we were fine about 3 weeks per month. Unfortunately, as every woman knows and no man does having the menstrual peak each month is painful, taxing, and can be for some a dramatic challenge. Our difficulties happened like clockwork as reliable as the cycle of the Moon. I was awful because suddenly it would dawn on me and I would say something to try as the last resort to acknowledge what was happening. Not the best strategy, not a good one, but the last one was to 'pipe up' and say "You're going to have your period in two days" or "You're going to have your period tomorrow". Awful. In English there is a saying "Damned if you do and damned if you don't". Finally after 4 years of "Struggle Street", we were able to give up. Thank God!!!! We would see each other three mornings a week in Ballet class. After a month, one morning after class she asked if I would like to go get a coffee. From that day we were able to rejoice once again in a pure platonic friendship.

Every night we would go out to a movie or dinner and part our seperate ways. In a very short time I started to get unusual work related offers. One came from the One Earth Gathering that I attended. That was held at the new age Tauhara Centre in Taupo. The Tauhara Centre was one the places the mime River recommended me to and they were one of the first to write to hire me while I was still living in Sweden. So I had taught there a few times.

SOME KEY PROJECTS

The Elder of that Gathering was the Australian Indigenous man Ted "Guboo" Thomas. There was an invitation of course for the local Maori's to attend and to have one of their Elder's join Guboo. Down the hierarchy one Elder after another could not attend. Finally it fell upon the shoulders of a younger man who was distant from his culture. It was put upon. Guboo designated a series of ritual tests for the younger Maori man. The Gathering was scheduled for what was considered astrologically an auspicious planetary alignment. The alignment was mathematical, and not 'rocket science' as the saying goes. The meaning of the alignment can be argued or fobbed off or meditated upon. Nonetheless a peak group meeting was set to time with the peak alignment of the planets. The meeting was deemed to be run like the Maori tradition where anyone can speak in any way the feel to and for as long or as short as the choose, nobody can interrupt the speaker. This tradition was explained to our group of about 100 people. The resident astrologer was a brilliant English man who had also set up the first full Tibetan Buddhist centre that brought a Geshe and two other monks to live and teach at the centre. I was also at the formal welcoming for the Geshe and monks. The astrologer spoke briefly and said he would occasionally speak only briefly to inform us of the placement of the planets at any particular moment. Again, note, the placement and movement of the planets is mathematical and scientific and NASA and the Space Station all nations sending interstellar missions uses the same math and science that a good astrologer uses. The message and meaning if any can be argued.

So we were off to the races. The Maori man who had been through Guboo's obstacle course had told us a few things that shocked him. Of course going up a mountain and deep into bush with Guboo one of the first things was a ritual cleansing in icy mountain water, fully immersed, and he had to stay in until Guboo said enough. One of the last tests the man had to go into a tract of land near Lake Taupo. He had vague instructions to go via a gate and to follow his guide. This fellow up to this point was still totally cynical but was trying to do the right thing by his community. When he went through the gate to look for his guide, a small bird called a willy wagtail appeared and flitted about in front of the man. Soon the man understood this was his guide. He simply followed the wily wagtail further and further. Suddenly the bird stopped. It stopped on a small rock. The rock split and the bird flew up. Inside the split rock was a crystal which the man brought to Guboo. Suffice to say the man turned from a sceptic and cynic to someone who had just passed through various tests. A few others got up to speak briefly. Each rising after a previous speaker had sat down as per the protocol of no interruptions. I felt moved to speak and stood up and spoke. After about one minute Guboo the gathering's Elder stood and yelled at me and told me to sit down. I stood as I understood the protocol and whatever it is I felt to say still was to be said. Guboo sat down. I continued and Guboo tried two more times to interrupt me and tell me to sit down. I stood. After the third time Guboo stormed out of the room. Now a Maori woman who was the senior Maori person began to speak to me in Maori. I just looked and listened not understanding one word she spoke. Then she said "I just said you keep going boy he's just testing you. Keep going." I did. When I finished whatever it was I felt to say I sat down. The astrologer stood up and explained that the various things that happened including when I stood and when I sat were exact according to his charts timing. Soon Guboo came in and sat down. Others spoke and the evening meeting/ritual was over.

When I awoke in my tent the first thought was I have to find Guboo and apologise. Not that I knew what I did wrong. I headed up to the main building which also held the dining room. On my way an older Dutch man stopped me and told me what I did last night in relation to Guboo was disrespectful and awful and that I should turn around get my belongings and leave the gathering. He then said that young people like me should spend time in the military and that people like me were just dole bludgers. I told him how old I was which was quite a bit older than I looked. I told him that I had been in the military for four years. I told him that I refused to even register for the dole. (It was three years later that I needed to register and did so). He was very apologetic. I went into the building and immediately saw Guboo. He saw me and said "There he is"! He had been looking for me. He wanted to apologise. He said he was just testing me. He said let's get breakfast. When we sat together he said "You should come to Australia". He was encouraging me to move there. I said I had been there a few times. I said I'd like to ask him something. He was fine with that. I started to tell him that the first time I was in Australia I was hired by the Moomba Festival in Melbourne. He looked down and stopped eating. I asked "Is it true …." and he started laughing uncontrollably and nodding his head. I said "So it is true"? He nodded. "So moomba means 'asshole'"? According to him it does. I was told that by someone I knew when I was first in Melbourne. As I understand it people wanted an Indigenous name for the festival and consulted some Indigenous people. Moomba was put forth as they said it meant 'festival'. So the festival would be essentially Festival Festival with one word from the Indigenous and one from Non-Indigenous.

When I moved to Sydney I contacted Guboo and he wanted to show me a sacred site. So as planned one day he took me to a spot in Centennial Park and showed me a rock formation which he said was sacred. First he had me look at it straight on and it simply looked like a standard large rock, perhaps sandstone? Then he had me look from the side and it was a perfect classic profile of an Indigenous man. The face looks out over the whole of Centennial Park. I tell more about this in my show "Harlequin Dreams" which is on youtube in 5 parts.

CHAPTER 4

SHENANIGANS AND CHAGRIN

PRELIMINARY EPISODE - LEARNING

One of the first episodes of my life that seemed to set a pattern or revealed one, occurred when I was about 3 or perhaps 4 years old. This event I remember like a film. I was driven by my father and with my mother to Tiny Tot Nursery a daycare centre. My parents had jobs to go to and it was time for me to be in a centre during their working hours. I remember very little about my time in nursery but the first day was a doozy. My Father parked the car on the inclined driveway and my parents walked me into the nursery and introduced me to the teacher. She was very warm and welcoming. My parents and I were at ease as we went our separate ways. I waved to my parents and the teacher took me in. My Father drove my Mother then to her job.

My Tiny Tot Nursery teacher took me into the main room and sat me down in an empty chair in the front row. There were a dozen or so other children. A little boy on my right side then leaned over and bit me on the neck. I was hurt and upset and went up to the teacher. She told me to bite him back. So I did. He cried and that was the end of that incident. I don't imagine that a teacher telling a child to bite another student was politically nor professionally correct even in the mid-1950s when this incident happened. Still in retrospect unfortunately my lesson was - if bitten out of the blue then bite back.

My Mother worked as a sales clerk at Kaufmann's Department Store that was located at Fifth Avenue and Smithfield Street in downtown Pittsburgh. Many nights I would travel with my Father to drive and pickup my Mother after work. Years later after I had my driver's licence at 16 years old, I would occasionally pickup my Mother via my sister's red Dodge Dart.

My Father was a traveling salesman whose territory was the greater district within 100 miles of Pittsburgh. In the Summer I would go on some of his routes with him for a few days. Sometimes I could hold the steering wheel or do some simple task related to lights etc while my Father drove.

LIFE LESSON TWO LEARNING TO DRIVE

My first real driving lesson, with me in the driver's seat allowed by my learning permit, so I could see over the dashboard I had to sit on large phone books. My Father in the passenger's seat. A disaster. We lived on the corner of Wilkins Avenue our street, and Beeler Street that was the angled street running behind our row of houses. We only lived one home away from the corner. The corner was about 20 yards/metres from our front door. After I rounded the corner which was not a 90 degree angle but on a diagonal about 45 degrees. I held the helm too hard after turning the corner. Although I could see the immanent crash coming, I was too scared to shock my Father by slamming on the brakes. So I just eased the brakes. Letting the steering wheel return to neutral.

However, alas, alack poor Yorick ... too much too late and too easy. With tasteful ease our Dodge which was not just the family pleasure car, but, was also his office and source of his livelihood as he was a traveling salesman, yes this very precious commodity melted into and along one of our neighbours' cars. Demolishing the driver's door and front fender of the neighbour and damaging Dad's front side panel as well. The neighbour's car side melted like butter. I feel it all in my cellular memory or in my mind's eye. Both Father and son were devastated. One of us then parked the car. We then had to go to the neighbour and inform them of the accident and damage. They were exceptionally kind. So too was my Father even though such a prang was tragic. It could have been worse and that was my Father's understanding and generosity.

LESSON THREE

Soon, at 16 years old, I had my licence and the first day that I borrowed my sister's Dodge Dart - I crashed it. A fender bender only. That was in the parking lot of Carnegie Tech. In the parking lot I had backed out of my parking space easily. Then I stepped on the gas pedal to go forward. Only the gear was still in reverse. I put a small but noteworthy dent in the middle of the trunk which made the trunk temporarily unusable as the dent was on the lock. Again, minor damage and nobody bruised except for ones ego.

Carnegie Institute of Technology is where Andy Warhol studied classical painting. C.I.T. In 1967 it was renamed CMU - Carnegie Mellon University. Now CMU is where Bill Gates invested a rumoured one billion dollars for the university's I.T. research centre. (The Drama Department has been directed for a number of years by Australian the fabulous Peter Cooke.) My next and last accident (touch wood) was several years later.

LIFE HAS MYSTERY

So far I have told three very short stories about learning situations. One of those was day one of nursery school, then first real driving lesson, and the other my first day borrowing my Sister's car.

This next short story was my first day at public school. I was five years old. Again due to the need for both of my parents to work simply for basic household needs it was decided that although young, perhaps as much as one year too young, for the family it was best that I start school at five years of age. I may not have been the only one to do so.

This story may or may not be verified. That is up to the sole witness other than myself. Not only up to her choice but up to her memory of a strange, upsetting, and unusual event.

I had two wonderful sisters seven and eight years older than me. The younger of the two sisters was Faye and the older was Sheila. Faye then would have been about 12 or 13 years old. Faye and Sheila were both at the Junior High School of Taylor Allderdice and likely started school a little later than my Elementary School - Wightman. Or because of the circumstances Faye had permission to be late to school in order to walk me to Wightman for my first day of primary school.

I can remember us starting to walk together and remember her leaving me at school. My memory is that she left me at the entrance which I was to walk up. Left at the steps and walked up the steps. So not mollycoddled, nor babied, but set in the right place with instructions where to go and what to do i.e. to go to the First Grade Class.

Apparently, according to family stories, I walked and talked at 9 months old. That is now possibly more common? Maybe in some places that was always the norm? However it seems that at the time it was not so common so young? Anyways what I am piecing together is that I already was capable of some independent thinking especially if I was given some instructions.

To be sure, I was home alone in the afternoons from 5 years old. My sisters both worked at retail stores from a young age. Thus my parents worked and my sister's worked. So I was taught how to make three different instant meals so I would eat when I came home after school. I think school let out about 330pm. I could walk home in 10 or 15 minutes. Solway and Wightman Street to the corner of Wilkins and Beeler and that further 20 yards to our front door. I think in the beginning the back door was left unlocked. Then later a key was left for me between the front door and the screen door in front of that.

So Faye left me at the front steps of Wightman Elementary and headed home first to get her books and then likely caught the school bus that day to Taylor Allderdice High School. However, when she arrived at home to get her school books, I was sitting on the front steps. That's not scientifically possible unless someone gave me a ride home. I don't remember getting a ride home. I don't remember walking home. I only remember walking up the steps of school then turning around to leave and then suddenly calmly waiting for my sister to arrive home. The distance is about one mile between Wightman school and home. There is no shorter route than the very simple direct route. I would have had to have passed up my sister if I ran. At 5 years old I could not run that much faster for such a distance.

This can be a family myth.

MYTH VS MYSTERY

However, I'd like to point out that I once witnessed a similar inexplicable occurrence of a person 'jumping' from one place to another faster than the car we were in could travel the same distance. There were two other witnesses with me. That story is told within this book.

In many Indigenous cultures this type of 'space jump' is common amongst shaman and their witnesses. There may be no scientific evidence. Yet it is known to occur in many cultures and I am a witness to it at least once as an adult.

But I will tell you one more short story of my youth that is equally uncanny or absurd. It went on for a period of about three months.

The three-months incident started with a distinct action and finished just as abruptly with another distinct action. I was about 10 years old and was outside during a school recess at lunch time. Somehow an older and larger boy and I happened to bump into each other. With the bump, somehow his wallet popped out of his back pocket and I caught it while moving in the direction opposite of the other boy but in the same direction as the flying wallet. I looked at the wallet in my hand. I opened the wallet and saw a ten dollar bill. That was around 1962 and $10 for a child was a lot of money, at least to me at that time. I took the $10 bill out and got rid of the wallet - somehow. Somehow seems to be the operative word with these inexplicable incidents. I am only reporting what I know and what I remember. What I don't know is then skimmed over with the word 'somehow'. It was so much money I didn't know what to do with it. I was stunned by what happened and didn't have the insight to simply return the wallet immediately to it's owner. It became a petty crime by circumstances. I'm guilty of misinterpreting those circumstances and should have returned the wallet immediately as I would most certainly do now. But at 10 years old

I could not understand how something could pop out like that and into my quick and agile hands. So I went to the candy store on South Negley Avenue around the corner from Wightman school. I bought a lot of candy and gave most of it away to other children.

Somehow. Somehow I understood that if I bumped into a person once and this happened then there was a way it could happen again. I learned instead, quickly, inexplicably quickly as in suddenly, how to bump into a person as a form of misdirection and to take the wallet from their back pocket. This went on over a period that I estimate at three months overall. Not every day, but frequently I would pick someone's pocket. I was an adept. I could take a wallet, take the money, and put the wallet back. There is no way that I can explain how I was so adept. There was no lead up to this except that I did have very fast reflexes as a child. This period is the closest I have experienced to say or to imagine that yes there is something to the idea of "past lives". The musical Oliver based on the novel Oliver Twist has the characters "The Artful Dodger" the young pickpocket and "Fagin" the master of the urchins who were a variety of young thieves. So certainly Dickens recorded, artfully, that there were such youthful thieves and pickpockets at least in London in the 1800s. So why not Pittsburgh too?

The first incident was and is completely explainable. As I said it came from an innocent incident of two people accidentally bumping into each other and something jarred as a result. Now that Pandora's jar was opened, it became a youthful sport for me. One in which I excelled. I didn't really want the money at all. I only enjoyed the experience which was like a physical form of chess. So when I would get the money I would treat a number of kids to candy some days but on many other days I would treat children to a bag of french fries from Sodini's Restaurant one block from the school. Mind you I've never tasted such delicious french fries as Sodini's. We would buy them in a very small brown paper bag only big enough to hold the individual order of fries that cost 25 cents. The extra money I didn't want so I gave that away each day. So perhaps some people will read this and may have a memory of a one dollar bill or a five dollar bill or even a ten dollar bill 'disappearing' mysteriously in 1962 at Wightman school. If so I have no intention of returning any of the money as there is no way to verify who lost some mysteriously or how much. But I'd gladly shout (the Australian and English term for 'treat') someone to a beer, glass of wine, a cup of coffee or a tea for anyone who makes claim to such a mysterious event in 1962.

The last thing I pick-pocketed though was extraordinary. Again it happened via circumstances that simply presented themselves and I chose to capitalise on them in an immoral way. Maybe in a childish or adolescent way only? One day at the end of school as I started to walk home, at the first corner, at the corner of Solway and Wightman we had a traffic policeman stand to cross the children. On this particular day I happened to simply stand on the policeman's left side waiting to cross. As I was short, right below my eye level was the policeman's gun and holster. It was the usual sweet fat policeman who looked like a moustache-free Oliver Hardy (of Laurel & Hardy the cinema clowns). Well, I spied with my little eye a unique opportunity. As opportunity presented itself I unclipped the holster and removed the pistol and pointed it at some kids across the street who were waiting for the friends in the next group to cross. Michael Herman a school chum lived across the street. He being the Michael Herman who invited me home one day after school to see his father's pistol and who then offered me and he a whiskey which we drank a sip of. It was way too hot for me, but, he had practice and could drink a whole shot.

So I had the policeman's gun and pointed it at kids across the street and then put it back, unclipped and then crossed the street and went home quite satisfied with my sojourn into pickpocketing. Taking a gun from a policeman and putting it back in the holster was a peak experience for a ten year old and thus ended a brief episode into a Dickensian reality.

PERFORMING LIFE

My parents met when they each with their separate friends went to see two clowns perform on New Years Eve in Pittsburgh. That would have been in the early 1940s.

My Father born in 1905 would have been at least 35 years old. As was common at the time for New Years Eve there would be various venues and social clubs that hired a big band, a singer, and some variety entertainers including comedians as well as perhaps jugglers or acrobats to complete the program. As my Mother told me, she was standing with her friends and she happened to turn when the entrance door opened. A man walked in. My Mother turned to her friends and she said that she was going to marry that man. So she did. I knew too from her story that the headline act was the clown & comedian Red Buttons and there was a support act. Both of my parents loved clowns and comedians and Red was the main attraction until they met that night. I knew all of that since childhood.

My Mother was a very grounded, practical and loving person. She was also strong and forthright. She was also a healer. Her healing situation though was at her normal 9-5 job as a simple salesperson at Kaufmann's Department Store where she worked for 40 years in the women's lingerie department. She was noted as a type of counsellor who was used to hearing the most intimate confessions while helping women to select their under garments in the private booths of the fitting room. She never told me the specifics as that was secret women's business. But she explained that she did listen a lot and gave beneficial support and advice. She understood that for many women over many years they were repeat customers due to her listening ability and compassion.

Years after she retired, for her 80th birthday I made an extended visit to be with her more and talk with her more and hear more of her stories of her life. She lived in a small apartment that my sisters provided for her near them in Florida. She had beautiful paintings that she made. When she retired she fulfilled a lifetime's desire to paint. Her paintings were from photographs but her way was semi-expressionist realism. Simple use of colour, basic form, but her sensitivity to light made each of her paintings alive and vibrant. On this visit one day on the beach we spoke about spirituality and I explained and acknowledged that anything I understood about spirituality came from her.

A little while later she was back in the waves and then when she was standing where the waves hit the sand suddenly a surprise larger wave came and swept her feet out and up making her almost sitting in the air for a moment just like Buster Keaton and then crash onto her bottom for a great pratfall. I jumped to go to her but she was already laughing still sitting in the sand with the water around her. When we were at her apartment she talked about her Mother who was somewhat eccentric and who translated letters for people as she spoke and wrote in about six languages. She also went around with two paper shopping bags with herbs and was lay-person 'doctor' also known as a healer. And her Mother, my Great-Grandmother was known in their Czech village, shtetl as "The Mother" as she was bonafide healer. My Mother was born in New York City, in Haarlem. My Grandmother, "Boubie" Gussie (Gertrude) was born in a Czech village. Her married name was Marcus and maiden name was Mahler. Only when I was 27 did I find out that my Mother had extensive training in classical piano. It was she told that her Czech Mother who we referred to as Boubie Marcus (Grandmother Marcus) had the maiden name of Mahler and in theory was a cousin of the composer Gustav Mahler. This can not be proven as I don't know the name of Boubie Marcus' village. On this same day my Mother also explained that she was the one on the piano for her friends' singalongs at parties. She also said she used to clown on the piano "Like the kinds of things that Chico Marx did".

My Father was commonly known as "a clown". He was, quiet, funny, knew a lot of comic tricks, but, he was not an ideal salesman at all. More than anything it seems he loved to drive out into the country and in between calling on customers, he liked to read the newspaper, smoke his pipe, and listen to sports on radio. He once took me to the office of a friend of his. They had known each other as youths likely early 20s. Perhaps they went to Peabody High School together or maybe the met through work? The meeting had been arranged and his friend had a film set up to show me. We chatted a few minutes. The film was of a house in a rural area just outside of Pittsburgh. They and several other friends had built a summer house on a property. It would have been mainly a timber house. The first shot of film was the outside of the house and the property and forest behind the house. The next shot was of the front porch then close up on the screen door. The door burst open and my Father bounced out like a drunk Charlie Chaplin clowning around. The next shot was their baseball game, it was set up as there weren't enough men to play 9 on each side. My Father was batting though this was not a real game and was set up for the camera. The pitch came and he slammed the ball far away and ran a Home Run. He was a phenomenal cook. He and my Mother had a side business to do something with his culinary gifts. It was only a part time business for some weekends. They were Kosher caterers. My Father also decorated every dish that he cooked. My Sisters and I would help with a variety of tasks. I went with my Parents occasionally to deliver the food and set up the food table mostly for weddings. Whenever he catered even for family affairs it was incredible to hear the delight of people tasting his cooking. He also had a 'green thumb' and when and where he could grow things they excelled. I think he won an award once for a Japanese maple tree that he grew. He also briefly had been president of the Pittsburgh aquarium society. We always had a fish tank and cats. He also made things called "planters". They were similar in appearance to bonsai potted gardens. So we had some in our home and he also made planters as gifts for family or friends.

After I had been a performer for a few years, my Sister had a wedding and at the reception after all the formalities and after dinner, I watched my Father playing tricks on the group of kids who all wanted "More! More!". He was like the Pied Piper. One of his favourite little bits was to tie the shoelaces of a child's two shoes together and tell the kid to "go have a walk". Of course the child knew what would happen and they would fall over and over again trying to walk with their shoelaces tied. That's how he made me a slapstick clown.

When he needed to drive someone he would often double up on errands. So if you went with him to do one thing he usually also had something else to do as well. The last day I saw him, I was about 27, he was to take me to the airport for me to fly back to California. Only he said he wanted to go shopping first, on the way to the airport. We went in to the super market. He got the large shopping trolley. He opened the kiddies seat that was in those days at the back of each trolley at the handle which you pushed the trolley around with. When he pulled the little seat open he said "Get in". So I squeezed in. He pushed me and the trolley around and did his shopping. When we got to the check out he said "Get out". We put his shopping bags in the car, drove to the airport gave a kiss and goodbye. That was the last time I saw him.

Not long after, several months, he took sick. Besides smoking his pipe, he had been a chain smoker of around a pack of cigarettes a day. Maybe more at times. So he was going. I was living in San Francisco with Lenka. One early morning from being sound asleep I was in an instant calling out as if in pain and awake in the same moment already standing on the bed sweating. The next day the same happened. The third day the same only I caught myself and only sat up but still let out a loud gasp and was sweating. The fourth day as the same moment happened I awoke but was in control and the sweat was less. It was then I understood that my Father was going. I adored him and was deeply connected. That morning my Mother phoned and said she thinks he's going but doesn't know how much longer but I should be ready to come. Fifth, Sixth, Seventh day the same awareness during the moment and being able to control my reaction. After arising though from the seventh awaking I said I feel really weird in my stomach. I said I did not feel sick but it was a very strange feeling. All this while, about 15 minutes I kept rubbing my stomach. Suddenly, my eyes widened and I ran to the toilet and evacuated like never before in my life. When I came out and sat down I was exhausted and said that I cleared out like never before in my life. Soon the phone rang. It was my Aunt Phyllis who was at the hospital and explained that my Father passed away 15 minutes ago and that she was with him.

I flew home to Pittsburgh. My Mother told me that when she was at the hospital with my Father on that last day, she decided at one moment to walk out of the room just to walk up the hall and back. When she headed back Aunt Phyllis was standing outside the room. She told my Mother he was gone and that she should go in. My Mother said she didn't need to see him as he had recently depleted so much and that she had a treasure of memories. My Aunt was insistent so my Mother went in. As she told me, it was the most remarkable thing she had ever seen. My Father looked completely radiant and with a huge smile on his face. She explained further that because of that she felt free. After the year of traditional Jewish mourning and at the end of which a memorial stone is laid, then my Mother moved to the small apartment that my Sister's provided for her.

I soon made my overseas journey intended for three weeks which is now approaching 40 years living outside of the USA and now a longtime citizen of Australia.

However, to tie in the stories above with some things that happened later …. In 1980 during the time I was living in Stockholm teaching clowning, acrobatics, physical theatre - I also had a healing clinic. That was within a new age centre called Galleri Medmera. I offered three services: a free healing clinic on Sundays; short courses in psychic mediation and psychic healing; and individual psychic readings for one hour by appointment. That work was all energy based. That means I would describe the energy of the client as I perceived it. I would sit down with a person seated opposite me. I would close my eyes. I would then ask them to simply say their whole name three times. The moment they finished I already had a 'fix' or an image that came to me and I would start by describing everything I perceived about this person. Normally I would talk non-stop for about 30 minutes and then would ask if they had any questions. Then I would answer the questions only by describing the energy as I perceived it and any images that popped in my mind's eye or in my imagination. My intuition was, and is, good and accurate. When I was a child I already had this gift but as I was a wild child. Some things were best left unspoken. Many times I said things that I should not have. I am still trying to improve on learning what not to say in any social situation. Mostly I'm fine, but, sometimes I say too much about things that are best left unspoken. The centre where I trained in California for over a year focused on reading the energy and images and definitely not on predictions! However, the Founder passed away and eventually the centre has changed in various ways. My friend David Pearce ran the centre very successfully but then eventually he left and for more than 20 years he and his wife have run their Intuitive Way centre outside of Oakland, California.

GALLERI MEDMERA & GEORGE CARL

I was alone one evening in the Galleri Medmera. I would sometimes practice juggling in their storefront space that had a large wall size window. This evening a VW beetle driver sees me juggling stops and drives the car into the curb with its lights shining on me like a spotlight. The driver mimes juggling and shrugs his shoulders as if to say "Nu, so why are you there juggling"? Then I imitate him and he waves for me to come out. He says ";Who are you? What are you doing juggling here"? So I told him. He asked if I knew George Carl. I said no. He showed me a small leaflet with George's name on the Bern's Casino publicity. We traded names and he said he was Francois Bronnet and he was bringing George here from Paris' Crazy Horse Saloon for a short season and that he'd like to invite me to the opening night. So I asked my friend Carina who was a mime.

When George did his first number I was taken aback because he was doing some body moves that people would consider "Ira's moves". When he later did his second number I understood that I must have seen him on TV when I was a child. I certainly would have imitated him as I did with Chaplin, Jerry Lewis, The Three Stooges, Red Skelton and many comedians and actors on TV. At Bern's Casino during interval I read the program and it said that George had performed numerous times on TV including the Ed Sullivan Show. My parents and I watched the Ed Sullivan Show every Sunday. Well George was great. Certainly he is easily one of the greatest clowns our generation has ever seen. He's the fellow that does the comical act with the microphone, coat & hat, and harmonica. He was for some years in the great clown musical act of Johnny Puleo!!

After the show in Stockholm 1980 I was to meet Francois and he took me and Carina to George's dressing room where George immediately fell for Carina. He said right away the classic showbiz people's line "Where you been all my life"? And threw his arms around her. He then asked her to come to Paris with him. He gave her a hotel room or apartment for a week. He was also acting in a quick setup short film and invited her to act in it. I saw it once long ago. It was set at a Paris bistro sitting outdoors.

In 1986 George was hired to work at Australia's then new casino "Jupiter's" located on the Gold Coast. The Gold Coast is like a mini Miami Beach and the Sunshine Coast is not like a Riviera. My friend Terry Price was hired to be a featured acrobat in Jupiter's opening season. I was going to stay with Terry for a week and see the show and meet George Carl again. When their Jupiter's season started I was performing at Sydney's Belvoir St. Theatre in "An Imaginary Life". I had a scheduled solo commercial to act in then. Then I was to fly to stay with Terry and his partner Henning. In the commercial I was to play an Indian fakir. At the time they could not find an Indian contortionist who could also act and whose English was clear enough for Australian audiences, so I got the gig. I had to do a subcontinent Indian accent which of course was over the top and a bit like Peter Sellers. When I showed up I was sent straight to makeup. There I was informed that I would not only have 'blackface' but will have body colouring on my whole body as I was going to wear only a dhoti and turban. That was for a product called Selley's Simple String. The job was not simple. Not at all. The exceptional young director was Alex Pyros. We shot various short setups throughout the day. The last hour was hell. Starting around midnight after a full day of acting, filming, and contortions I was informed we now need to do the final shot and this was to be with the whole text and only one leg behind my neck at the same time. However, as I recall the timing was so precise that it included a quarter of a second! The text portion was to last precisely 27 and 1/4 seconds. The first takes were around 26 and 28. Some takes were 25 1/2 or 28 1/4. Out of sheer desire on my part and insistence and patience on the part of Alex we started to get 27 and 27 3/4. Finally it was 27 1/4. I was able to have a shower and remove the grosser amount of body paint. I got home after 130am and tried to get the rest of the body paint off. It was in the pores of my skin still. Early that morning I had to catch a flight to the Gold Coast to be fetched by Terry.

I spent much of the week around showtime chatting with George in his dressing room. On the second day he said to me "Where the hell are you from anyways"?. Pittsburgh. "Pittsburgh"! Have you ever been there I asked. "Been there! I was stranded there for 7 years". When? In the 50s. Many people in the Jupiter's show commented about how much I was like

George. We don't particularly look alike except for being short, ethnic, acrobats and clowns. At the end of the week I went to my next contract in Canberra with Jigsaw Theatre in an acrobatic clown show called "Building Blocks" directed by my friend Stephen Champion. I was curious if my Mother remembered ever seeing George Carl in Pittsburgh. The first day in Canberra I phoned my Mother. After a few opening standard lines: How are you? Fine? And how are you? Fine? What's new? Not much. Any you? etc I asked outright "Do you remember a clown named George Carl"? "You know I don't remember those things. If your Father was alive he'd remember. He knew all their names.". Then we talked for ten minutes about anything related to family or work. We were saying our goodbyes and suddenly my Mother exclaims "Oh my God"! What? "Oh my God, who did you say that clown was"? George Carl. "Of course I remember him!! He was in the show the night your Father and I met. Red Buttons was the headliner and George Carl was the other one we went to see".

This is a story. Another true story. Does destiny call before one is born? Or before one is born is it arranged to be born into a clown friendly family? Or simply because my parents loved clowns does one take to clowning by the age of 5 as I did?

With my parents love of clowns and growing up during the 1950s as TV began to flourish in the USA I watched (as did most of the clowns of my generation) a great variety of top level clowns every day from the time I was 5 years old when the TV was my babysitter. I would come home from school by myself. My family taught me how to heat a TV dinner in the oven. I would have one of three meals; a TV dinner, a pot-pie, or a mini pizza all stored in our refrigerator for me. I think school finished at 3:30pm pop a frozen dinner in the oven, and most likely The Three Stooges TV show came on about 4pm. That was my constant routine until it was time at 8 years old for me to begin Hebrew school in the afternoons to prepare for my Bar Mitzvah. I went by bus from Wightman Elementary to the Hebrew Institute and later from junior high school to Hebrew Institute - Monday to Thursdays. My parents would come home from work about 6:30 and we would have dinner. In the evening there were the clown shows such as Red Skelton, I Love Lucy, Jackie Gleason (Saturday nights?), and many others including Amos & Andy, Molly Goldberg, George Gobel, etc. Sunday night was the Ed Sullivan Show - a variety show that always had comedians, circus acts, singers, and musicians including Elvis Presley and The Beatles. On the weekends during the day were regular films of Chaplin, Keaton, Laurel & Hardy, Ma & Pa Kettle, Keystone Kops, and others. This was also the period when Jerry Lewis' films began to flourish.

I did not study much school work. Although I saw a lot of TV, I did also play a lot outdoors, up trees, in streets, riding on my bicycle, playing games such as Release and Red Rover and Hide & Go Seek, at a young age also playing soldiers and cowboys and Indians (I always chose to be an Indian). I played all neighbourhood sports in season - baseball, football (gridiron), basketball. We would play in our local laneway Beelermont Place and move when cars came through. The corner house was owned by a Mr. Hornberger (yes his actual name) who was the local pervert with a playful attraction to the young ladies. I doubt if he ever did anything illegal. Rude, perverse, but not malicious. In fact he was exceptionally kind to us all and let us play for years, outdoors, on his front lawn! There we would create magnificent snow forts from where we would pelt cars, buses, and trucks with snowballs. We would also pelt each other and would make snowmen. Mr. Hornberger allowed all of these constructions to stay until the early Spring sun melted them.

It was on Mr. Hornberger's lawn that we began the adolescent discovery and research into the differences between the sexes. This was done ritualistically in a game called Release played in the late Spring and Summer nights. There was a single person who guarded a 'Jail' on Mr. Hornberger's front stoop of a tiny porch and about 4 steps. The Guard would go searching for hiding people and if he caught one he would bring the captured back to the Jail. Then the game shifted for the hiding people to try to get to the Jail to tag the prisoner without getting tagged by the Guard. If the prisoner(s) was/were tagged they were released, thus, the game's name Release. People could hide together and if it was a boy and a girl they could huddle and cuddle and depending on the mix they might do some exploring of petting, necking, kissing, hugging, leaning together giving a subtext to the word 'release'. Doing-a-what comes naturally, whichever ways one is inclined.

When I wasn't playing games and sports and climbing trees and cycling around the neighbourhood of Squirrel Hill or the bordering neighbourhoods of Shadyside and Oakland, then, I was home and certainly not doing any school work. I am pretty sure I could read before I started first grade. I would read at home but not study so much. Rather I was studying my main interest which was clowning, performing, entertainment, and acting. I learned how to do pratfalls and slapstick and funny looks and double-takes by watching dozens if not hundreds of such masters of those crafts acting in television shows and films shown on TV. I would 'watch' while standing or falling. I was acting out what the clowns or stuntmen were doing.

We also had a wonderful small old cinema in Squirrel Hill named The Manor located on Murray Avenue in the main shopping street along with Forbes Avenue. The owner of The Manor I think was Jewish as were the majority of shop owners in a Jewish neighbourhood. However, the owner of the cinema sported a small moustache so he had a minor resemblance to a particularly nasty clown named Adolf. On Saturdays when we should have all been in Synagogue and celebrating Shabbat and all of its wonderful accoutrements including chanting and incanting of weekly parsha of the Torah. Instead those of us who were overly and overtly secularised as well as all of the non-Jewish kids who comprised most of the neighbourhood, would fill the cinema many Saturdays for the "Double Feature" as well as the "17-Cartoons" all for about 50 cents. Of course we bought the treasured candy boxes of gummies, mint chocolates, popcorn, soda pop, ice creams. Hazarei is the Yiddish word for 'junk'.

My first date was to The Manor. Somehow I managed to get the courage to ask my imagined sweetheart Nancy to go on a date to The Manor. I certainly would have asked my Mother's advice about what to do when I was so attracted to my classmate. My Father then on the arranged date and time drove me over to Nancy's and we were both dressed up. I would have rung the doorbell and would have been introduced briefly to her parents. In my mind's eye I can see my father's car waiting. I can watch me going to the door and seeing Nancy dressed up and then walking together to the car, knowing to open the door for her and sitting together in the backseat. Then my Father drove us about 3 minutes to The Manor. First Date. Normally I was the 'class clown', a trickster, or prankster, who was unpredictable to say the least. Although most of the time I was still and quiet and watching and listening. On this date I was polite, well mannered though I remember knowing I was meant to try to put my arm around or to try to hold hands or to see where those first steps led to. We explored a few innocent avenues briefly, tentatively, and from my end clumsily. I was enormously attracted to her and I wanted to show her not only was I polite but that I was a forthright man. The two of us were munchkins. The smallest students in our age group. Out of my depth, this was the limit of my depth that took everything I understood to have one date. There was no understanding from me that there was a process on how to proceed to date. Seeing her at school the following Monday was overwhelming and embarrassing without knowing how to followup. This is of course unrequited love. Pure, simple, adolescent, honest and bittersweet for eternity. This is the inner world of a clown. The source of compassion and empathy. The vulnerability on stage of not knowing how to proceed. Being dumbfounded and awestruck at the beauty of a being outside of oneself might be one of the deeper aspects of being a clown. It is the clowns' humanity.

I had occasionally gone with my Father to a magic shop in the Downtown section of Pittsburgh. He bought me some of the smallest and simplest tricks. One was trick handcuffs and another was small box in which one could make a coin disappear and reappear. In 6th grade at Wightman Elementary School I decided to do a magic show of my few tricks. I asked the teacher's permission. For the trick handcuffs I asked for a volunteer who was a boy named Alex. He was a bulky, staltworthy lad. So I did the set up and then put the cuffs on him and asked him to try to escape. He broke a link and thus the show ended on a quite flat finale. I then unlocked him.

I did however have a 'party trick' that I developed that year during my very brief fascination with magic. My Uncle Moe had been a magician briefly when he was young. He did only close up and card tricks and specialised with memory 'tricks' as he had an innate photographic memory. But he kept doing magic for family and friends for the rest of his life and he lived to be 94. When I last saw him he was 90 and completely healthy and he did several card tricks for me. He had a great ability especially with kids to fail doing the trick and asking the child to say a magic word or to blow magic air on the cards and then the trick worked and the child experienced 'magic' and Moe was in awe of their ability. So on the very rare occasions when I saw him he always did magic tricks. For him it was like offering a guest a cup of tea.

My party trick. I saw a movie on TV about Houdini starring Tony Curtis. I taught myself to be tied up in a rope and to escape and my main party trick was that I could be punched in the stomach by any other boy and not get hurt. I was tiny. There was a huge size difference between me and most boys my age. If they were very strong or big then when they punched me in the stomach it would knock me backwards a bit but the punch did not hurt my stomach. So if it was a big or strong fellow then I would get someone else to stand behind me and hold my back so I wouldn't be moved. Then wham. No problem.

About 2 years later my friend Art who I usually called Jackie decided with me to play a trick on a young fellow who was a bit 'up himself'. So Art (Jackie) asked the kid if he thought he was as strong as me. I was tiny. So the other boy was in. I could also punch full force and fast, but, I could also do the stunt punch where one stops on the receiver's stomach thus only appearing to punch them. Plus there was a way of moving forward to cover the 'punch' completely. So we were to trade punches on each other. So we set it up so that Jackie and the other kid punched me then I would punch them. So Jackie and the other kid punched me. Then I 'punched' Jackie with the feigned punch/slap. However, I also in addition to being able to take a punch had what is called 'good leverage' and was able to punch extremely hard. So I punched the other kid and of course as planned he was completely winded and down for the count which also succeeded in taking the wind out of his sail.

GETTING SERIOUS

I did not like school and did not connect with the approach to study and learning, unfortunately. When I was 21 my Mother told me that most years when I was a youngster, the new teacher each year would phone my parents after the first few weeks of school and express that they were concerned that I was such an extreme daydreamer. My Mother informed them "Oh he's fine. That's just the way he is". There was ample reason for concern though as to what would become of me after I would graduate from high school. Certainly I did not want to go to more school i.e. a university. Nor was my terrible academic record leading that way. One day I was looking out of the window - daydreaming in Mr. Welle's superb English class. How I ended up in the elite class in my senior year is a total mystery to me. So on this particular day I realised that I should join the U.S. Navy after graduation. At home that evening I informed my parents of this idea. They were understanding and supportive and simply felt that if I thought it was the best thing then it was. The following Saturday my Father took me to speak with the Downtown naval recruiter. I had an instant medical examination. I was five feet 1 inch tall. One inch too short to legally enter the Navy at that time. But the doctor understood I would grow so he said "Looks like five feet 2 inches to me". Meaning he was going to fudge in a '2' instead of a '1'. I was in. I weighed 103 pounds or 46.7 kilos. As I was 17 and a minor, my Father had to sign over my Guardianship to the U.S. Navy. The deal was sealed and I would go to boot camp on July 21st, 1969. The day after the First Moon Landing which I watched with my parents. Also I happened to watch a detailed documentary about the near sinking of the U.S. Navy ship the USS Franklin - aircraft carrier CV13 - during WWII. There was incredible film footage and the damaged ship was towed by the USS Pittsburgh until it was able to steam again of its own accord into port. My parting date was July 21st and was also my Mother's birthday - she was 58. As I left home she stood in the door way and said "Smooth sailing". She was strong and encouraging to me, but, I am sure she would have then shut the door and then cried and 'talked to God' on my behalf.

CHAPTER 5

IN THE NAVY

The first day of Active Duty into the Navy starts at home. Travel to the Recruiting Office downtown. Assembly of the group in alphabetical order. 120 men. I was clearly the tiniest recruit in our mob. I was a bit younger then most as I was 17 and many would have been 19 or older. I was 5 feet 1inch and barely more than 100 pounds. We loaded into buses to travel to the airport. Flight from Pittsburgh to Chicago there to board buses to Great Lakes Naval Station to the Recruit Training base. In our group's alphabetical roll call Rogers came just before Seidenstein. Early on the journey Rogers befriended me in our unit of Recruits. Like many in the Navy he found that my last name was 'too long'. Added to that I was from Squirrel Hill which was known as the Jewish neighbourhood as it had the largest Jewish community in Pittsburgh. Rogers said "How about if we call you Juju"? Fine. I had never had a nickname. Except that my Father called me by a 'pet' name. He called me "Thack" as he loved the writing of William Makepeace Thackery who wrote Vanity Fair.

After Boot Camp I was nicknamed "Sid" as a mispronunciation of my last name. My last two years I was almost always called by my first name Ira and in formal situations I was Petty Officer Seidenstein. During that period I was stationed in the South with many Southerners which meant there was a wonderful musical twang to my last name.

Traditionally, one of the first rituals of initiation at any Boot Camp is to have your hair cut. Short. Quickly. The shaving of the head takes about one minute. There were at the time 120 young men put into a unit, to start with for the first week. We met our Recruit Drill Officer who was a Chief Petty Officer. He gave us a rough and tough short talk. He explained that we would be in the first camp for one week to get our uniforms, learn to obey the commands, learn to march, learn to wait. He said "For the next 3 months I'm going to be your mother and your father". His way of speaking was to set the rules and shake us out of being civilians into being in the military. He was quite tough like in the movies. The first evening we were each allowed 3 minutes to phone home to let the family know that we arrived safely.

We were always set, even during marching formation, into the alphabetical order with Rogers immediately before me. Thank God. He was my Guardian Angel. He was a few years older and a lot more worldly. He understood that I was naive and he kept an eye on me and for me. On the first day one also has to get your military uniforms. This is done ritualistically. In alphabetical order you are measured for each general item of shoes, boots, hats, shirts, pants, jackets, socks, and four pairs of underwear as in small, medium, or large. After being measured you are given a seabag and then you proceed to receive all of the measured items, plus a ditty bags which are netted bags to hold your dirty laundry in. A label is made and sew on the bags. Thus dozens of bags of laundry can be done in one wash and can be quickly sorted after bag by bag from the labels. Now with the seabag full of new uniforms we are marched into a huge drill hall which is about the size of an aircraft hanger or giant gymnasium. We are told to stand in a certain number of rows and a certain distance apart. I end up in the middle of a row. For the ritual process of checking that each recruit has every item the drill petty officer in charge stands on a large podium and calls out orders to raise the items one at a time. Or if given 2 or 3 or 4 of an item then all of us had to hold the required number of items aloft or were instructed to put one of the items on to also show that we received the correct size. First put down the seabag, next is "Attention" stand straight with arms by the side, then is "Parade Rest" feet a metre apart and arms clasped behind your back to receive the next instruction.

We are now ordered to lay the clothes out so we can see all of them on the floor in clear groups. Then we have to strip out of our civilian clothes. We have to put on one pair of boxer shorts (underwear) and hold the other three pairs in three locations of one in each hand and one in the mouth held by the teeth.

The boxer shorts were pressed tight at the factory. So one has to pull them apart to step in. There is a flat opening in the front pressed tight.

When we did this first step with one pair of boxer pants on and two held held high and another held in the mouth. At the moment of gathering the four boxer pants and getting into one pair, there was a big laugh from the drill officer. We turn around to face front and he is still laughing. He calls out to me and then tells everyone to put down their spare three boxer shorts. He pointed me out and told the other 119 young men to look at me. He tells me to bend over. As I do there is a huge roaring laughter from the group. I had put the pressed boxer shorts on backwards so that when I bent forward the pressed fly opening in the front which was now in the back gave a 'bird's eye view'. I was then told to put my shorts on correctly.

We then proceeded ritualistically so that the drill petty officer can see that each Recruit had every item necessary for a complete seabag. This included summer and winter uniforms. Dress shoes and working boots. A toiletry kit. Belts. Sailors kerchiefs that are tied around the neck.

Each morning Reveille was about 4:30am. Lights out was by 10pm.

HOLDING COMPANY

We are informed that each unit of 120 men is only for the first week only. This is reduced to 90 before going to the main camp for the formal Boot Camp. The 30 man difference is because some people suddenly find or disclose in the first week that they have health issues - mental or physical. Or dental issues. Or issues with their sight. Or issues with discipline. The average is about 30 people who need a little special attention. In some cases it may be deemed that a Recruit is actually unfit for any of those reasons and is sent home. So during the week various tests and examinations are carried out. At the end of the week if there are not 30 people then extra people will be selected to comprise the 30. The 30 will then go to a holding camp. There were 28. Each was called to step aside out of the main group. Then it was said they need to take 2 more. They called out for Rogers and Seidenstein to step out. My name would have been mispronounced in any number of ways such as Saidestew. We 30 were to pack our seabags.

When we were assembled outside it was a motley group. Except for Rogers who was sharp as a tack and me who was very cute at 5'1" and barely over 100lbs. We were marched over to the section known as Holding Company. When Rogers and I entered the Holding building .... it did not look good. We saw people meandering about like in a mental asylum. We said this doesn't look good. Rogers said "We gotta find a way out". I asked "How". He said "I don't know, but, we'll find a way" and he looked towards a wall with a bulletin board and we walked towards it and he said excitedly "Here it is"!! It was a tiny notice saying that tomorrow there will be an audition for the Drill Team. So in the morning at the appointed time and place we were there!!! We wanted out. ASAP.

The Drill Team petty officer introduced himself and explained that we were now to follow his commands. So he drilled us with a lot of commands to turn "Left face" (90 degrees left) and "Right face" (90 degrees right) and "About face" (180 degrees while standing at Attention) and "To the rear, march" (180 while marching). Right out of Chaplin, Keaton, Jerry Lewis, Lucille Ball ..... almost every time he said left I went right and right I went left. I was just a bit nervous. I certainly had no coordination issues but I got a bit flustered yet it never stopped me and if I turned left for right I recovered in a second and fought to get OUT of Holding Company!!! Plus I knew who my Guardian Angel was and I was not going anywhere without Rogers!! Next command was "Readyyy, halt"! He told Rogers he'll be on the Drill Team.

'Sarge' asked me a few questions and gave me a few commands only for me. Then he asked me "How would you like to be the Guide-on"? I asked "What's a Guide-on"? He laughed and explained that it is the person who marches with the flag and that they usually give the flag to the smallest person. Would I like to do that? Done deal. Pack your bags now. He marched the two of us out of Holding Camp and over the 'river kwai' to the main camp. We were taken to the performing arts dormitory for the Recruit Drill Team and the Recruit Marching Band.

DRILL TEAM

I was assigned a top bunk and was introduced to the fellow who slept in the bottom bunk. He was very friendly. As is very common in the military amongst the nicknames are the place the sailor or soldier or marine is from. My bunk mate was "Arkansas" or "Alabama". I told him my name and he said "How about I call you "Sid" as derived from another common mispronunciation as Sidenstein. We chatted and asked about each other "what do you do" and he informed me that he was a member of the Ku Klux Klan. He surmised and asked if I was Jewish. Yes. He said "Don't worry we ain't got nothing against you Jews". I didn't worry. He was a nice guy. The petty officer who auditioned Rogers and I was the assistant and close colleague of the main Drill Petty Officer who was Black/Afro American. We learned to march to his 'soul' cadence. We marched to a Black beat with a down beat on one side and a slight swagger. There were 51 men on the Drill Team. The 51 was divided into two squads of 24 men with an old wooden rifle with a fixed bayonet. The combined rifle bayonet was about 8 pounds. With each squad of 24 there was a Leader who marched with a curved sword held by the handle. One of these men was Black/Afro Jamaican and he mostly was the person who called our cadence which was both rhythm and rhyme.

Rogers and I were the last taken into the 51 man Drill Team. We were all gathered and told that we will train every day for 30 days no break and 8 hours of marching per day. We will have the 8-minutes choreographed 51 man routine at the end of 30 days. I was told that for 30 days I was to train with the rifle and bayonet. However, whenever we marched to chow (meals) and any classes that I would always march with the Company flag. Whenever we assembled before marching we would start with a loud stomp on the right foot which counted as a '1'. We would go right left right left or 1,2,3,4 so every other step with the right foot was a stomp while continuing to march. The Drill leaders would sometimes call cadence "Sound off" and we would reply "1,2" then "Sound off" and reply "3,4" and more classic lines including "Biddy biddy don't down ain't no pussy on the ground".

After our 30 days I was presented with the performance flag. I was told by the head Drill Officer that I could now create my own routine as I would now march in between the two teams in performance. This was officially then my first choreography and improvisation. I was like a duck in water. In my element. We now did much less drill and began to attend more standard Boot Camp training classes or whatever was required. Another standard Boot Camp ritual was getting a battery of shots. We marched to the medical drill hall. We were put in a single file line with one step less than a metre between each two Recruits. There were two rows of men with air pressure medical guns that were connected each to a different mix of shots/chemicals. There were about ten men in each row. The rows were one metre apart. In between each 'gunner' was one step. With each step we would stand in between two 'gunners' and get zapped with an air pressure needle. No hygienic change of needles. If you moved or even jerked the needle would slice you a bit. Of course I imagine that we were guinea pigs for medical research. I have no idea what we got zapped with.

Just after our 30 days we had our first performance. Each week we would perform our drill routine as part of the Recruit Graduation. This was all more ritual and ceremony which included our 8 minutes. Once we were in a city parade doing our routine in front of the parade Reviewing Stand. The biggest gig though was to be the Halftime Entertainment for a football (gridiron) game at the huge Soldier Field which was a stadium in Chicago. At the time we were there the capacity of the stadium was 100,000 people. The game was tapped and played on TV the next day. Our Drill Team sat together to watch it. Each of our two squads were placed at each end near the goalposts and I was placed at the 50-yard midfield line. On the signal the two teams and I marched to the centre. I had less distance to travel. But, when we watched the game the halftime was only shown for 30 seconds or so and the only camera shot was of me marching with the flag blowing. Somewhere there may be footage? It was likely early October 1969.

One day one of our Leaders was a bit prickly about something minor so I told him to "Fuck off". He tried again and I told him again. So he said he was going to Report me. About once a week we had a practice Military Court. Besides our performance Petty Officers who were actually only with us for Drill practice. We had a Company Commander who was a higher rank. He was a big fellow like Orson Welles. Sonorous deep voice too. Court would involve him telling us about the week's schedule or any changes etc and was also to give voice to any questions or grievances. So, this day my Case was on the agenda. The last part of the Court. Orson was seated at a little table like a Judge, which he was actually within this context.

Deep sonorous voice says "Seaman Recruit Sadestia step forward". Seaman Recruit (Leader's name) step forward. Orson read the report and asked each of us if this was true and accurate. Yes Yes. "Seaman Recruit Sadestia do you know karate or some goddam shit like that"? "No sir". "Well then you're a little too goddam small to be telling anyone to 'fuck off'!! Is that clear Seaman Recruit"? I squeaked out another Yes Sir. Then Orson bellowed "Now if I hear of anymore goddam trouble out of you I'm going to unscrew your goddam head and shit in it!! Is that clear"??!! Yes Sir squeaketh I. "Now your punishment is at 4pm everyday you will have an hour of military drill commanded by Seaman Recruit (Leader's name). Is that clear"? Yes Sir squeaked. Orson added "And I better not hear about any other shit either. Is that clear"? Yes Sir. The hour of discipline drill started that afternoon and the Recruit Leader was very kind and tried to add in bits of leniency. He would have been advised what type of drills I was to do. It was all drills with a rifle and included all the classic movements and held positions, only, I had to hold them longer than normal.

Our Drill Team practice from the first day included juggling the rifles with fixed bayonet in various ways while marching and many turns and crisscross formations. There were also various rhythms including banging the bottom of the rifle on the ground and hitting the rifle with our hands. If anyone dropped a rifle they had to drop out and do 10 pushups and then hustle to get back into the moving group. Sometimes we had to all "hit the deck" and give ten. Many of the wooden drill rifles broke from impact of being missed from a high toss or fast spin. I had a bit of gung-ho and relished the whole experience even the thrill of that kangaroo court with Orson. In fact I even liked the extra hour as it was an extra challenge. I considered it an accomplishment much more than a punishment. Every day through Boot Camp in the evening I did an extra set of 60 pushups non-stop.

I had a high score on the tests to find what job a Recruit should be trained for. So I was offered to have the longest training which was in electronics. Computers were coming so electronics was a great field to get into. But as the training was longer one had to change to six years active duty instead of four. I didn't know what to do so I went with my instincts and said I would stick with the four years and took the option that I was offered which was to train as a Radarman, a radar operator rather than the one who fixes their electronics.

My first Leave, a short vacation after Boot Camp and before job training. Rogers said his friends were going to pick him up at the airport in Pittsburgh and that they could give me a ride home. When we got in the car there was beer. So, I had a beer. I couldn't drink much. I would not have had a drink but it was the social thing and being a sailor now etc. So by the time I got home I was 'under the influence'. From a single beer. Unfortunately that was the last time I saw that Guardian Angel. He was to train as a Seabee since he had some experience in construction. When I arrived home I was tipsy and giggly. But the first thing my Father said, as always was "give me a kiss" or "you got a kiss for me"?. I said "Dad I'm in the Navy now" and he said "You're never too old to kiss your Father. Gimme a kiss. You smell like beer. Wait til your Mother sees this". All was fine. Of course I wanted to see my friends Art and Richie who were both at university. Art in metallurgy and Richie in law.

FIRST LEAVE

Richie invited me to go out with a couple of friends of his as one of them had a car. We drove out of the city centre and towards some hills. It was a young man driving and a young woman in the front seat and me and Richie in the back. As we neared one big hill the woman started to roll a cigarette. The car which was a station wagon turned up the big hill. At the top of the hill was a radio tower. The woman lit the cigarette. Took a puff and gave it to the driver who took a puff and gave it to Richie. I had never smelled this odour. I didn't know what it was. It smelled like burning grass. I thought oh, I know what this is, its that stuff. I was given the cigarette and didn't know what to do socially but I took it and did what the others did only tried to take as little a puff as possible and gave it back to the woman. It started to go around again and suddenly there was a police car light and then a siren and the driver opened all the windows including the back window. The Police stopped us. I was already off my face. Tipsy. I was upset because I liked having a career in the Navy and this could end it. The driver had his licence out before the Policeman got to him. He presented his licence but added who his influential father was which stopped the policeman who then asked the woman who she was and the driver named her father who was running for Mayor. Next question from the policeman was to ask my friend Richie who he was and he replied immediately that his family are friends with Frankie Bruno who was then boss of the 'syndicate' a mellow mafia. So the Irish and Italian mafia kids saved this little seventeen year old sailor son of a schlepper (traveling salesman) i.e. the cop gave up and never asked about me.

Radar training was long, probably around three months. So I moved from Boot Camp to the normal Camp which had barracks with rooms with a maximum of four men. Great Lakes base was on the shore front of Lake Michigan which is bigger than Switzerland. They have a big Winter with very strong winds. Chicago which is also on the lake is called The Windy City. The base had a club for Enlisted Men. There were other clubs for the Officers as with any base. I would often go to the club and dance to the taped music playing. I was always the only one dancing. There were no women there at the time, or at least at the times I was there. One would have Guard Duty on a rotation basis at night. So in the middle of Winter the wind-chill factor made it often 40 below freezing in Fahrenheit. For Guard Duty one simply walked around the perimeter of ones barracks or duty building.

I enjoyed the study of Radar and excelled, although, if there was something I didn't quite understand there was an older student who I would ask for help and chat with. I think he was actually going to be a Chaplain but I think they had to also have a technical craft. I can't remember. I do know that he had been a Jesuit Priest .... or maybe he still was. Fab fellow and great to talk with.

The Navy changed Radarman title to Operations Specialist during the early part of my service. After I graduated from radar training I did not have a duty assignment immediately so I went into the regular base's Holding Company which had its own barracks. Again, take one look and one wants to get out asap. There was an old WWII cinema on the base. I went there one night and while I waited for the movie to start, there were two sailors in front of me who were from the country or the South and they were discussing what a Jew is. One did not know but the other did and he explained that they were like people but they had horns on their heads. So I butted in. I said excuse me but I overheard that you are talking about Jews and I'm Jewish. They were quite excited to meet a real one, without horns. We had a nice chat and I answered some of their questions and then the movie started. Four weeks in Holding and my Orders arrived.

FIRST DUTY ASSIGNMENT

I was assigned to the USS Ingraham (DD694). But it was at the end of a North Sea cruise and I was to first go to holding aboard the USS Puget Sound a supply ship. The port was Newport, Rhode Island. The Puget Sound was a huge, brand new ship. Wow. Plenty of room in the sleeping quarters! The food was excellent! As I was just a transit for two weeks until my ship came in I was given the job of cleaning the toilet at the gangway, at the ship's entrance where a Duty Officer and a sailor stood 24hrs on security watch to check anyone who walked up the gangway. Most of the day I stood outside of the 'head' (ships jargon for toilet). Fortunately it was a very small head and seldom used. One day there was to be a ship's inspection by the second in command who was by rank a Captain (one step below Admiral). I had to be inside the head while he conducted the inspection with a junior officer by his side. That was the highlight of my 2 weeks. I did LOVE being on a ship and being in port and being at a base which I didn't leave. The morning my ship USS Ingraham was to arrive at 8am, I was long waiting on the pier. Here it comes. Closer. What? It was like an old rust bucket! It certainly needed a paint job! So for the first time I saw the docking ritual of the ropes being tossed and a sailor on the pier tying down the ropes (lines as they're called). Upon being connected to the pier there is a whistle, mooring announcement on the loud speaker, and the changing of flags hoisted. The tiny narrow gangway went across and suddenly after six months cruising in the North Sea half of the ship's crew had leave and left with their seabags on their shoulders and a quick salute to the Duty Officer and the ensign (flag) and those salutes were done in a flash but each sailor had a personal way of doing it. Their wives, girlfriends, newly born children, and others were awaiting.

Finally the last one left and I entered with my seabag on my shoulder and my formal Orders packet in my hand. I did everything by the book and the Petty Officer couldn't care less. I was set aside and his aide called to C.I.C. (Combat Information Center) where the Radarmen worked and told them the new arrival was waiting. A few minutes later a speedy Radarman took me first to show me my bunk in the sleeping quarters so that I could leave my seabag on my bunk and then he would take me to CIC. The ladder (stairway) down was very narrow and not big enough for me and the seabag at the same time. The sleeping quarters was highly unkempt! The bunks were as the rest of the ship .... from World War II. Canvas bunks tied with rope to an aluminium frame. Then back up and through the extremely narrow passageway where sailors have to turn halfway to pass each other, then up and up ladders to the tower where CIC is located right behind the Captain's bridge. My escort opened the steel door and on the ground was another sailor also in uniform, squatted on the ground pretending to be a monkey. The monkey took my escort. Another monkey man sailor hopped quickly over and took me monkey style by the hand and walked me in. My jaw dropped my eyes widened. There all of the Radarmen were monkeys. This included picking nits from each other's hair and hanging from the rafter and hopping across the various radar and navigation equipment. Inclusive of monkey, ape grunts and cries etc.

Part of my reasoning to join the Navy in addition to just a flash intuition in Mr Welles' English class, and besides not knowing what to do after high school as I had no direction or specific ambition, but, I also knew I was 'the class clown' and knew that if I didn't do something seriously in life and very soon then I could be in big trouble for the rest of my life. I clearly thought the military would sort me out. I was right. Up to a point. Being in the military with a lot of other young men was absolutely wonderful. I ate up the discipline even the kangaroo recruit court and the week of extra rifle drill. It was all a boys and young man's adventure. Including having the shitty responsibility of cleaning a nearly never used head/toilet. I was on the road to recovery. Until coincidence, synchronicity, karma, God, the universe, arbitrary life events brought me together with this group of iconoclast, outrageous, unruly, madcap monkeys, apes, Radarmen.

LIFE'S PLAN FOR YOU

It was all over for me. I was assigned to the Sixth Fleet's known 'clown' troupe. The M.A.S.H. of the US Navy during the Vietnam War, aka, the Radarmen of the USS Ingraham (DD-694). I did not join in. I did not play a monkey/ape. I did have my hat taken and imaginary nits picked from my hair and monkeys pulling for flash moments at my uniform or arm or .... pulling my leg. The origin of that saying "pulling your leg" was literally manifest. Then one by one the sailors, my new buddies in life, each came over to introduce themselves and say "welcome aboard". What a great group of men. As I write this I have a bit of "Teardrop the Clown" going on. I thank my lucky stars for delivering me into that most beautiful group of actors. At least half of those twelve, with me as the new 13th, had been in Vietnam for the obligatory 13 months. Some were on river boat assignments on patrol and in combat on and in the Mekong river and delta. One was on the Newport battleship bombing up and down the coast. One had an absurd 13 months as the bar man on a base which included Seabees. Seabees are the Navy's construction workers. The bar was the safest place. It was a below ground bunker, custom built by the Seabees to be so safe in order to be able to enjoy a beer or a dozen in peace in a war zone. In addition to being below ground it had reinforced concrete walls and roof.

DAY ONE INITIATION

My initiation was about to go a step further. Unbeknownst to me. Soon I was told that when lunchtime came we were not having lunch on the ship but were going to head up to the canteen on the base. One man had to stay behind on duty. So off to lunch we marched. Only we did not march. Not at all. As we went to leave there is a formal ritual at the gangway to salute the Duty Petty Officer or Officer and then salut the ensign (flag). With this motley group .... not on your life. Though some of the Radarmen did deliver the proper ritual. Others did whatever variation they liked and some did any kind of hand jive. As we walked up the pier and if we as enlisted men were about to approach an Officer we were obliged to salut. Not this pack of wolves! I was quite excited to have the chance to be a real sailor and salute the oncoming officers. As I raised my arm abruptly my nearest Radarman grabbed my arm and prevented me from saluting. These guys were rebels that ruled. As far as they were concerned officers were below their dignity. The rebels would look away as if they hadn't noticed the officers. They taught me the tricks of the trade immediately. One also said "Don't ever let me see you salute an officer". I loved these guys. This was fun and absolutely fascinating. We ordered hamburgers and fries. They ordered pitchers of beer. Several of them. At once. I can hardly drink. I was in danger zone. Drink, drink, fill 'er up. Maybe, possibly, I would have had a total of 2 beers. I was now 18. First day on my ship. We have to cut lunch. And drinking. Short. There is a radio communications drill for all of the ships in port. We now headed downhill. I was totally giddy and clowning and running down hill. This was really fun. Until they marched me up, up, and away and into C.I.C. where they informed me that I was to carry out the radio communications drill. I had been a very diligent student in my training. So I stood by ready to start, but wobbling, and leaning on the navigation table. One of the seniors stood by me. The others were plopped all around and with their feet raised up on the various pieces of equipment. I was told our ship's code name. And bang the drill starts with acknowledging that you, your ship, is present and tuned in. Only problem was I in my very lugubrious state of a non-drinking 18 year old under the influence happy go lucky fellow found this absolutely hilarious and .... my replies over the military radio gave away all of my secrets. I was inebriated by less than 2 full beers, and running and jumping downhill. So after a few bouts of giggles galore .... my senior pal took over and someone got me a coffee and I was from that moment definitely an 'in' member of this zany outfit. And this was just day 1. Oh boy, as the song goes "Hey diddly dee a sailor's life for me".

ANCHORS AWEIGH

Soon we had a supply day for armaments. This was my first day at sea. Which was just upstream further up the bay to the armament island where we went in a single file line and each picked up a bomb and carried it like a baby as instructed and then up the gangway and along the outside of the ship to the bomb loader. One at a time we were to wait our turn. When the bomb in front was received its special loading apparatus lowered the bomb below decks to the bomb bay, then the person who deposited the bomb could leave and the next bomb carrier stepped forward. My first bomb was placed as I was told, but, at the start of its descent which did not succeed, it jammed. So I had to stand right there until it was unjammed or whatever. After a few starts and stops of the automatic switch it was unjammed and I was free to go get another bomb. I liked supply days when trucks would come to our pier and we would off load and load food and other supplies. It was the long single file line and each sailor took one case off of the truck and up the gangway and into the hold (supply storage).

At some point I had a Liberty which is a day off. Leave means a few days off. So on my day off I ventured to see the town of Newport and to see the famous seaside mansions.

Then finally was our first training cruise for a week or two. We were to head down the Eastern Seaboard to have manoeuvre exercises off of Cape Hatteras. Naval exercises could involve normally a dozen or more ships. Ships from different ports would rendezvous. Hatteras, off of North Carolina is just south of the large port and base of Norfolk, Virginia. During the exercises the ships do all sorts of general drills including, importantly, signal practice which changes the geometry of the formation of ships, their speed changes, and intent for actions. As Radarmen our job was a central part of the communication which is what CIC Combat Information Center is for. In the back section of CIC in a seperate room for the Sonarmen and their equipment. We also had a small room for electronic espionage and this was early days in terms of electronic warfare. CIC was wonderfully mysterious because of the different equipment areas but also it was a darkened room so that we could easily see the radar scopes. We would rotate positions during a normal 6 hours watch. Our unit CIC was within the Operations Department and the head of that was Commander Schultz. He was not at all like Sergeant Schultz of Hogan's Heroes (TV sitcom) but the Radarmen were similar to Hogan and his colleagues.

So, shiver me timbers and blow me down, anchors aweigh at last for me. The first signal sent indicated the geometry of the formation once into the open bay and the speed. Outside the port the ships align in their first travel formation which is normally a simple functional line. When all of the ships are aligned the next signal will be given which will increase the speed and possibly set up a new geometry. We had a signal book which was fascinating to look at but also had all of the information for each signal. There were standard signals which everyone knew well, but, sometimes part of the game was for the Squadron or Flotilla commander to test out more rare signals which we would have to look up. All part of the training. Normally of course there would be any level of drills including the call to Battle Stations. It is normal on exercises that the crew for a few days goes into Port & Starboard rotation which means all working units have half its sailors at work and the other half eating, resting, sleeping, or spending their time recreationally.

It was smooth sailing until we arrived near Cape Hatteras known as "The Graveyard of the Atlantic". It is always rough seas. There are said to be hundreds of ships sunk off the coast there. There the other part of training kicked in which is how to cope with rough seas. So it wasn't long before I was topsy turvy with a feeling I had never had, seasickness. Oy vey. Not nice. First though I was managing. But the body has its own mechanism and there is not a lot one can do when it kicks over. It feels like all of your special body parts involved with getting rid of anything are about to kick into overdrive and all at once. You hold. You can tell your face has gone blank and pale. Your concentration has gone. Your eyes notice every possible thing that hangs or moves. Cups start sliding on tables. You're walking straight and suddenly the ship tilts and you just want to stay leaning against the bulkhead (wall) that you just fell into. You start to lose dedication to your job, craft, ship, military, nation, and actually in the final crescendo preceding the cascade about to pour out of your mouth like a geyser at Yosemite park, you first wish death upon yourself. It is fascinating. The first time. You are like a puppy that has been hit by a car. You just don't understand what is going on nor what to do. You try as hard as possible to do everything as normal but nothing is the same anymore. Not work, not walking. Not eating nor sleeping. This is really really bad and this is Cape Hatteras Hell. It was rough so very very soon it was not at all just me with 'the look'. It was really rough seas. A big Navy ship like ours, a Destroyer is unbelievably huge compared to most millionaires yachts. It is over 300 feet long. But Destroyers are also nicknamed "tin cans". Destroyers are fast and agile, but, when the seas are rough the destroyers bounce and bob like a tin can. All of this time you are still in one long week long or two weeks exercise in various stages. Fun and games though have stopped. Most of the crew was 'down' with seasickness by this stage. Everybody works but not everything inside the body is in working order. Finally at one stage I went into the mess area where one can eat or hang out and I was a visible mess but fighting on. There was one other sailor in the mess. He was seated part way and laying on his side. He watched me try to eat. I gave up and turned in my tray and dishes and tried to walk away in a very forlorn state. The other fellow was a Boilerman who worked in the bowels of the ship where the engine was. Deep down like Dante's Inferno. A frightening place. We had met before and he called over to me, in his deep Black Southern accent "Syd honey come over here and lay down next to Mama Spruel. Don't you worry. Mama Spruel goina look after you". And he patted the seat next to him and I lay down part way and he put his arms around and said "Don't you worry honey this is going to be over soon". If I put it in a movie or on stage no one would believe but that's what happened. Like a movie.

When we were back in calmer waters we ran exercises again in earnest. One afternoon I was on duty and near the large navigation table. It had long wide drawers inside which were the sea charts for the world including coastal and local landmarks. These charts were not just for sea navigation but also for land bombing. Atop the navigation table was always the local navigation chart for the area we were in. We kept an update on our current location. This table was also a key radio communications spot. Suddenly a call on the speaker came over "Man overboard. Man overboard." It would have also been said either "Port side" (left) or "Starboard side" (right). For CIC for "man overboard" it is the navigation table that is our main point of action. I reacted immediately changing the setup of the table and its gears accordingly and plotting moment by moment where the man went overboard and our ship's evolving relative position. The sea is big. A single person can be lost in one minute. The faster the ship is going the bigger the turn around is so the Bridge and Captain or Duty Officer and the Botswains each had our jobs to do immediately. In a few minutes, when the ship came around, we were told it was a drill. In CIC it was my 'coming of age' moment. I did everything by the book correctly, fast, and accurate. The motto of Radarmen is "speed and accuracy".

That was north or south of Cape Hatteras. We were only off Cape Hatteras about 4 days on that cruise. Good and necessary training in itself i.e. cruising in inclement weather and rough seas. Little did I know, the worst was yet to come.

Back in port the ship was getting fresh paint and various things had to be repaired, replaced, or upgraded. It was on the schedule that we were preparing for our six months Med Cruise starting in October. One week before our 10-days cruise across the Atlantic to enter the Straits of Gibraltar, suddenly about 3am a urgent call came over the speaker "All hands on deck! All hands on deck! Emergency stations. Emergency stations. The ship is sinking!". It was indeed. As we got out of our bunks we stumbled as the ship had a terrific list towards one side. So getting out was like jumping down a steep hill. We urgently dressed and went to assigned emergency stations. We were sinking along side the pier. One of the repairs that had been on going was below sea level. There was a patch being made on a section of ship's side. The patch was overnight being held up in part by air pressure and the air pressure machine had dropped out, the patch went off, the water came pouring in. We were only able to assist with the moving of pumps and hoses. Multiple pumps were gathered and put in place and when there were enough the immediate danger was abated and in a few hours began a slow reversal.

As it were, the water was removed, the ship straightened, the patch job completed, so we heard, and the decision was made. Our ship was considered sea worthy patch and all. We were leaving with the rest of the Squadron on time. The Navy had to also decide if those sailors who were near the end of their enlistment were to be flown back from the Mediterranean/Europe or get out early or reassigned. Verdi was our senior radarman at this time. He was wonderful. He was a brilliant Radarman which included our duties in Air Control when assisting the flight operations of Aircraft Carriers. He had a lot of experience with that off the coast of Vietnam around 1968 and 1969. Another fellow also from NYC was deemed not to go on the Med cruise. He was a very gentle fellow who originally trained as an electrician and for submarine duty. However on his first cruise for about 3 months under the sea, after a short period he wasn't coping very well. One day was his liberty his 'day off'. Under the sea. As he explained to me, liberty on a nuclear submarine was 15 minutes of looking out of the periscope. Approximately 15 minutes per week. Depending on what was the sub's assignment. The sub does not always come near the sea's surface. It does not always surface to put the periscope up. As the subs are to be unseen, they don't want to surface when other ships are around. So whenever your liberty comes up, for those 15 minutes you see the sea. So after one of his early liberties he lost the plot and had to be sedated for the next two months under the sea. He was reassigned to our ship to our USS Ingraham, and now before our Med cruise his enlistment was over.

In the process of researching for this chapter I found there are alumni groups for each ship. The alumni are for the whole of that ship's commissioned life. Like many alumni groups only a few join. The organiser, Doug Genereux, signed me in and got me in contact with a fellow whose last weeks were my first, Larry Koehler. And Larry got me in touch with a fellow who was a good friend during our year together aboard the USS Ingraham. Darrel Bahner whom we called "Bear" ... and he was strong as a bear and came from rural Kansas. We have begun to write to each other. We also had a year with another fab fellow from NYC who we called Neanderthal who could have shaved about three times a day.

CROSSING THE ATLANTIC

The morning the cruise was to start I was informed that I had Mess Duty for the first month of the cruise. It was explained that this was normal for the junior member. I was assigned to be a food valet for the Chief Petty Officers. They were the real old sea salts. Men who came up through the ranks to the highest level as Enlisted Men. They each were total experts in their fields. They were very Earthy and intelligent. I loved my jobs in CIC but I was excited to be around the sea salts. There was another fellow assigned who was from the Boatswains. He was Mexican heritage, but I am pretty sure he was actually born in Mexico. His name was Garcia and he was very nice and a bit chubby. We would get along fine. So, we weighed anchors. Once the ships left port and started to proceed Garcia and I were to leave our normal jobs and head to the Chief Petty Officers Mess. They lived and ate in the most forward section of the ship. They lived and ate in the bow. The bow has the most movement. On a Destroyer, a tin can, the bow is constantly busy going up and down. Up and down. Up and down. If you get the picture. So one of the Chiefs explained to us in no uncertain terms what the lay of the land was. We snapped to and set up their table for lunch. Lunch and Dinner were to be from the main ships galley and cook. Breakfast was to be cooked by us two innocents.

The first night, something went kerplonk. The Destroyer has two screws which drive the ship. One dropped dead. More than 100 nautical miles from shore. Investigations began below decks. The ship now had quite a list (lean) to one side due to only one screw operable. Up and down never stops. We cleaned the dishes and set up for breakfast. It was late. I went up to say hello to my friends in CIC. The deal is the rest of the Squadron is proceeding on schedule but with one screw we can't keep up. It will be decided overnight or in the morning whether we are to proceed, on our own, or to return to port on our own.

Cruising with one screw is wonky. Garcia and I were up about 5am and had to have a full breakfast ready for the Chiefs early. At 6am the Chiefs look like gods. All dressed sharp. Looking real good. Garcia and I looked and felt like shit. We were out of it. Totally seasick. I decided that one of us should serve and one cook. I gave it a go to cook. On the flattop Navy grill. Lots of eggs and bacon and toast. Anything else I don't remember. We listed and rock-n-rolled and up and downed. Constantly. During breakfast though, Garcia and I were hanging on by a thread. Sometimes he'd have to go out and puke so I would deliver a Chief's breakfast, barely, trying to manage my gut I still had to manage my sea-legs while pretending to be a waiter while going up and down but walking sideways so I remember plonking down someone's breakfast and that person naturally wondering if they were going to get a geyser worth of some extras. I can remember one Chief leaning far away but dead set staring at me to know which way he should move. In the meantime the fried eggs would pour down the griddle depending which way the ship rocked. I put the eggs and bacon on then would dash to the head and puke and dash back without washing and flip the eggs over or plonk them on a plate. It was horrible. Again if I put in a movie, no one would believe, but that is the way it happened. We two little Indians and the Chiefs made it. Just. We began to clear the dishes to wash up and I told Garcia I gotta go but I'll come back. I walked right into the Officers quarters and hunted up Commander Schultz. His door was open. He was shaving facing the mirror. He stopped mid razor stroke and stared into the mirror seeing me and he froze. He then turned around and said "Finish whatever you have to in the Chiefs mess and I'll have you off of mess duty this morning". Garcia and I cleaned up and puked. Finished and wiped out.

I was back in CIC. Barely. This is early morning of day two crossing the Atlantic. Eight days to go. Plus the rest of the six months.

The rest of the crew was going down. With one screw we were screwed. The plan was that in port the other screw could be repaired. We did our best. But at one point I was the watch on the radar scope. I could hardly see. I just lay my head down. On the radar scope. Our section Officer, a young tall, handsome Lieutenant came in on his rounds to check on CIC. He too was gone. All he could say was "Syd could you sit up and at least look like your watching the radar"? Sometime on that 2nd or 3rd day I decided I'd just carry a bucket with me wherever I went. To work, to eat, to sleep. I took my metal bucket. Once I was on duty in CIC and the urge to irk came upon me so I headed out to the nearest open air spot which was the Bridge. I was on a direct trajectory and when I got to the outdoor wing seated in the captain's chair was the Captain and I had a little heave ho right by his side and back I went to work.

In CIC we also had those big vertical clear plastic boards which we stood behind with earphones on and wrote in colour on the board backwards so that the Officer on watch could read and see the updated information on the sea and air traffic. My Hebrew lessons paid off as we write right to left in Hebrew which is the same as backwards in English. Perfect training for Radarman. After about a week the seas calmed and there was a huge relief. Chitchat, shooting the breeze was back in. Unfortunately the junior Lieutenant who looked like Woody Allen came in while doing his rounds on duty. He was a very shy and very nice fellow. Unfortunately, a few of our senior Radarmen were all hanging around this day. One of the guys, Hanson, was very handsome and sported a classy handlebar moustache. He was ultra slick. Could talk his way into or out of anything. He was like a movie star stuck in a uniform. Also from NYC. So he went up to junior in a very seductive way. Junior got giddy. And Mr Moustache started to go in for the kill and others joined in. They smooched and teased junior who was ticklish as well as giddy. And one, two, three before you know it junior was completely stripped of any respectability as well as his hat, shirt, tie, shoes, socks, pants. They were just playing so they left him in his underwear. More or less he had to beg a bit i.e. "promise to be nice" to get his uniform back and to be allowed to put it on before stepping out and onto the bridge. I can't say that my colleagues weren't entertaining. And we hadn't even hit port yet.

MEDITERRANEAN

Our first port of call was Palma, Majorca. Fantastic. The other ports of call were Barcelona, Toulon, Genoa, Naples, Valletta, Athens, Souse, Lisbon, Gibraltar. Naples is the NATO Headquarters and we spent a lot of time there. In fact we were in port a lot as this was the beginning of economic rationalisation due to price wars on fuel. Naples was like 'my city'. I had a good time in every port. It was a huge adventure, every day, and, every night, as I was 18 and turned 19 during the cruise. Naples was dangerous for sailors to be robbed, mugged, or stabbed. In Naples at the time the "Hey Joes" would offer to sell you anything. Joe comes from WWII as the American soldiers were known as G.I.s (Government Issued). But the Italians had a way to make it more friendly as in G.I.Joe. So in my time, men who had something to sell would would call out to you as you walked "Psst, hey Joe, you wanna buy .... ". They offered everything from their 'sister' to guns, weapons, even a tank. One of the trinkets that nearly every sailor bought was a lead necklace with one of the symbols of nearby Pompeii. This was the "flying cock and balls" which was a small lead flying cock and balls. I suppose if you google it will come up. I will look after I write this. So most sailors would have their full uniform plus the flying cock and balls neck lance. At least for one day. In Napoli our ship was not at the pier but was anchored in the bay. So we would ride ashore and back on our small escort craft which could hold about 20 or 30 people. The boatswains were the sailors who operated these. Cinderella Liberty meant the sailors had to be back by midnight. It was normal for me to never come back until the last minutes of Liberty.

In Napoli there was a bistro just near where our liberty boat dropped us. There were plenty of "Hey Joes" always waiting for the sailors. One day I asked a buddy Bertoldi to take my video camera and film me with the Hey Joes at the bistro. I had a few cigarette lighters my Father had given me so I could sell them as soldiers and sailors did in WWII. Such selling still occurred in my time. So I did a clown act if you will, and reversed the whole Hey Joe thing. I had my few items and I stood outside the cafe and called to the men outside and inside who were looking, "Psst, hey buddy, you want to buy ..." and I improvised while they crowded around me for a few minutes and we all had a good laugh. I had that and a few other of my comedy movies on super 8 film. Those few films disappeared long ago, though in my mind's eye they are still vivid and clear.

In Tunisia our port was Souse. On the way to visit Tunis we also got to ride camels. We visited Carthage. In Athens we visited the Acropolis. Each night when I came home to the ship moored in Piraeus I would go into the tavern at the pier and dance with the old men and I could dance with a drink balanced on my head. However, one night when three of us arrived at the pier there was a queue of people going aboard a huge ship behind ours. I said lets go see what they're doing. We would have had civilian clothes on. It was an Italian cruise liner. We went up and aboard. Days long before the security needed today to board such a ship! We walked around and soon went to look for a bar and ordered a drink. Just after our drinks were poured the music changed to the Tarantella and everybody got up to dance.

As I went to dance I realised the ship was moving! I said we gotta get off. Our liberty would be out any minute. We ran and looked down the first hallway at the end we could a building passing by, the ship was underway. We ran straight through the hall and the cruise liner was already moving at a good pace but only about 50 feet from the pier. I said let's jump. Fortunately one of the three of us said he could not swim. We ran to get the Captain. We ran into a small old Italian room service man. I told him "Capitano Capitano!!! Americano Americano!!" He shuffled along quickly but not quite a run. We went up a few ladders and onto the bridge. He called to the Captain in Italian. He came over, very calmly said you do not have to worry the Pilot is still onboard so you can get off with him and he will take you to your ship. We waited and when the ship was past the pier the Pilot came over and said to wait and in a few minutes we would be in open water and we can go with him. The water was open and now turbulent. We walked with the Pilot and his boat pulled alongside. He went first. Down a VERY long rope ladder. It was about 30 feet down the rope. But the water was rough so the boat would pull in and out as necessary. Then we sent our non swimmer pal. Then the other buddy. Then I went, but, when I got halfway the boat had to pull away a bit. So for about two minutes I was left hanging. Finally I was told to proceed down. With all three of us aboard the Pilot said "You should have stayed on the ship! It is going to Mykonos!!! Your Captain could do nothing against you. And you could have had a few days on the beautiful island.". We explained to the Duty Petty Officer what happened and why we were late and there was no hassle.

In Barcelona where we were anchored one day we had to muster topside in our dress uniforms as Spain's Generalissimo Franco was going to come via boat to Inspect the Fleet so we had to stand at attention and when his boat passed we had to salute. In Lisbon one night I had Duty so I had to stay aboard, fortunately, there was a riot with our fleet's sailors and local sailors and the police. No one was killed but there were police beatings and brief arrests. Like Spain, Portugal was under fascist leaders. In Napoli Hey Joes would also come by small wooden boats and pull alongside the Navy ships and offer to sell things and offer to buy brass fittings. So, yes, some sailors took off brass fittings and sold them on the spot, down the side of the ship. One morning it was discovered that the most precious and big brass item was gone!! Someone had sold or someone had stolen the Ship's Bell - the heart and soul of the USS Ingraham was gone. The day we sailed from Napoli to Souse the sea was like glass. Yet still I felt seasick. No more of the violent variety but still it was an undesirable feeling. I told one of the old salts and he said "Hasn't anybody told you the secret"? He told me. Before the ship pulls out of port have a big breakfast really stuff your self and keep your belly full through out the cruise. I went down to eat then even though it was 'too late'. I never got seasick again. Consequently on our return voyage - with two working screws! When we hit the hugest sea, the biggest waves I have ever seen I was able to enjoy the thrilling passage. The waves were enormous so that even our Destroyer could only encounter them directly at a right angle heading directly into them. The ship would rise upward and then periodically depending on the timing of meeting the wave the ship would face downward at a steep angle like going down a slide. The speed had to be adjusted to a pace in harmony with the roll of the waves. It was the same as surfing but on a huge dimension. That huge sea only lasted two days. When we would hit the big wave a huge amount of water was sprayed to the top of the ship so when I watched I had to stay near a hatch (door) so that when a big splash came I could duck inside. In such seas if anyone fell overboard the ship could not turn around.

Soon the USS Ingraham (DD-694) was deemed too old to serve the US Navy which was overhauling its systems and ships. During my early period Admiral Zumwalt was the admiral in charge of the Navy and he set in many policies to modernise all aspects of the organisation including pay, allowing long hair, as well as upgrading all military standards. Our ship was to be sold or given to the Greek navy. We were to put in a Dream Sheet that is each sailor could put in a request to be stationed anywhere and if that met with the Navy's needs then you had a chance to get the type of duty or place that you requested. We were to give three requests. I got one of my choices which was Florida.

During the my last month though half of our crew was sent elsewhere and an equal amount of Greek sailors came aboard to train on our equipment. However, they had a very different culture. Apparently the Greek sailors sleep together. In what sense, I don't know. We do know that our Botswain Mate First Class who was a bulldog of a man .... on his rounds found two lads in bed and immediately threw them on the deck (floor). It seemed generally that for those weeks the Greeks and the Yanks were living in parallel worlds except when training on equipment had to occur or shared duties.

NEXT DUTY ASSIGNMENT

I was onward and upward. Flight to Jacksonville, Florida and then transport to the Mayport Naval Station and my new Orders were to be on the Admiral's staff of COMCRUDESFLOT-12. Commander Cruiser Destroyer Flotilla 12. A flotilla is made up of squadrons and a fleet is made up of flotillas.

We were stationed in an old Quonset building on the base. Our enlisted mens barracks was ocean front. The Flagship was the USS Albany - a Cruiser which is similar to a destroyer in form but much larger and a cruiser is smaller than a battleship or aircraft carrier. The barracks were quite new and modern and the food was excellent. The office was about a 10 minute walk from the barracks. The Admiral's staff had about 50 people. 1 admiral, 1 Chief of Staff (a Captain), several Commanders or Lt Commanders, a few other officers, several Warrant Officers or Chief Petty Officers, a few First Class Petty Officers, and others. I was an other. I was a Third Class Operations Specialist (Radarman as a term was now passé as there was a new technological process underway including computers and advanced electronic warfare). I had already passed my exam for the next rank up Second Class Petty Officer also referred to as Second Class

Operations Specialist. But the date for the official award was a little time away. When that date came it would be time for my uniform shirts and pea coat (Winter jacket) to go to the tailor to have the new merit rank sewn on. I advanced at each step at the earliest date possible.

Our unit, COMCRUDESFLOT-12 also had valets which included cooks for the Admiral and Officers and two drivers for the Admiral and the Chief of Staff who each had an official car. The cooks and butlers were Philippine men who were also US Citizens and sailors in the US Navy. They were each small and tough. Rumour was fact - do not mess with them. In theory they carried switch blade automatic knives as weapons and knew how to use them. I got along with them perfectly well. We liked each other but were in seperate social circles. The drivers were two Marines. One of the things about being assigned to the South, as Florida is south of Virginia, the Carolinas, Georgia, and Alabama, so, as most of my mob on ship in Newport, Rhode Island were Northerners so those in Mayport were primarily Southerners and when announcements were made on the base it was a Southern accent. So not only did I get stationed on a beautiful beach with palm trees, but I got to experience aspects of the Deep South especially through many of my new colleagues. Curt was from Chicago and Cliff was from Cincinnati, Larry Joe was from Detroit, Chief Allen was from the North and just about everyone else was from the South including my main two supervisors Chief McCoy and Petty Officer First Class Dan Doyle. I think they were both from Alabama. So, as we worked in an office there was always radio music on and it was only ever on a station that played Country music. Fortunately I attuned instantly and as my new colleagues and supervisors were all wonderful so I have a soft spot forever for shitkicking music!

One of my buddies from the Ingraham, a Botswain named Cassidy also was assigned to Mayport to the USS Albany. So we could catch up and go to dinner and get drunk and laugh. He wanted to be a poet and looked a bit like a handsome James Cagney and he had equal charm galore. He would always speak in a poetic way and would also quote various poems spontaneously. Dan Doyle was another of my Guardian Angels. In fact, in my life, there has been an ongoing flow as if one or more Guardian Angels has handed me to the next, and in many periods it is that several Guardian Angels at once step into the breach and cooperatively look after me. In some way each of my colleagues has always done that. Except for a few.

PROMOTION

My date arrived for my rank advancement to officially commence. I was informed that it is the tradition that the new ranking person should buy drinks for the others. So everyone was invited but it was known that only the enlisted men will come and maybe your chief or perhaps even your section head who was a junior officer. With an admiral around everyone is like a junior officer. So we had a large table reserved at the small enlisted club. We were to be in the upstairs room which was simple and purely functional but it did have a view of the ships. My chief and even my section officer were there and they insisted that on this day I was the one being honoured even though I was paying for the drinks which was part of the honour. They insisted I was to be the Head of the Table. So everyone decided on beer and several pitchers of beer were ordered. We had a toast and a few nice words. Down went the first beer so that meant I was immediately two sheets to the wind. Under the influence. We were all chatting and suddenly one by one down the table, my celebratory pals went pale and mum. And in an instant they all stood up. I had no idea what was going on so I just looked in the direction they were starring at, around behind me. Shiver me timbers and blow me down .... shit! It's him! Mr Comcrudesflot-12 himself! Admiral, "oh captain my captain". So I quickly start to push my chair out to stand up and offer my chair to Mr HeHimIt. But he said no, no, no and indicated for me to sit down first, in my throne of the moment. Of course the person on my right did actually give up their chair which HeHimIt took. But he was not alone! There were a few other officers and one Marine as always with the Admiral. The Marine was allowed to sit as well. Nobody knew quite what to do as apparently this was quite unusual. I think this was Admiral Wallace. As with most commanders of flotilla's his official rank was Rear Admiral.

So I went to pour him a beer, but, instead he poured me a beer. Sheeesh. I was flustered. I had no idea what the protocol was. Not to worry the Admiral was in charge. We chatted. So those near participated by listening and those at the other end could also chat. So this went on for the duration of our beers and then the Admiral and his closest aides departed.

As Operations Specialists our job on base was to keep a continuous update of ships locations and to update manuals or paperwork. I also made boards for the officers operations presentations. A type of simple graphic design. Part of the work of the whole staff, Admiral included was to practice transferring our command center from land office to shipboard. So we went on several short cruises. The transfer was by packing about 50 cruise storage boxes and putting them onto a truck and then taking them onto a ship and setting up the various offices in the quarters provided. Additionally we would take our packed seabags from our barracks or homes and then onto the ship and into the sleeping quarters provided. This was also a good adventure as I enjoyed experiencing working and at sea conditions on the different ships. We made a cruise as far as NYC and actually docked in NYC aboard the USS Yosemite which was an old supply ship. On that cruise we once had whales alongside the ship for a few minutes. We were on water rations and there were rain swells so the ship was taken under one and the crew was encouraged to go on the top decks and have a rain shower. Hi-diddle-dee a sailor's life for me! Being docked on a Navy ship in New York City continued the imaginary game.

But when we walked through the pier's security we were right in the action. It was Summer and there were kids who had opened, or had their parents open the fire hydrants and were playing in the water. In a matter of minutes I heard a little girl about 8 years old tell a boy about the same age "Fuck off Johnny" and if he did not heed that as a warning she was ready to clobber him. A fair number of sailors got mugged i.e. robbed at knife point when they neared the dock late at night. The small group I was with wanted to go in near Broadway and Times Square but at one stage someone knew where the hot spot was which then was 8th Avenue so we did a detour. We went into what was proposed to be a massage parlour. The one we chose had a barker outside that is someone who barks out to wandering men who are wondering. He barks at them to come in and see the hot women etc. We went in en masse and I took one look at the inside of hell and walked out with a buddy who also wanted to leave. The barker was gone. We had to wait for our pals. So I jumped in and started to bark at people to hustle them to come in. I couldn't understand where the barker went, but, I could see some police coming down the street. So I stopped and in a moment our buddies were exiting so the word was out and as we left the cops went in. Then we walked around Times Square and back got back to the Yosemite.

Another cruise was aboard the cruiser the USS Albany which was fairly new and spit-spot. This was to be about three weeks of drills and exercises including firing missiles in the Caribbean. That meant we would go through or around the Bermuda Triangle. We would sail around parts of Cuba and would have a few days liberty in Puerto Rico and then a few days in Martinique. There we were anchored and took ship launches (small boats) back at night. One night I was with Cassidy and probably Curt Baumann and we came back 'under the influence' but for me that meant I was more influenced than others. I am quite prone to clowning anyways, and influence influenced me more especially as I was just enjoying the night and the night was still young though we had a curfew to be back and lo and behold as we were walking through the lower decks to get to our sleeping quarters we happened to cross paths with the Duty Officer on his rounds with two assistants. Only this officer was one everyone knew including me. So in my jovial cheery way I yelled out, to the young Lieutenant in charge "Heyyyy!! Eisenhower!!! How ya doin'?? And gave him a right ripe coupla pats on the back. He was absolutely fine with have an authentic sailor moment rather than being treated with kid gloves. The others froze including his aides and my buddies. Then off we all toddled. Oh, that was former President Eisenhower's grandson who was at that time married to the current President Nixon's daughter Julie. That little slip in discipline could have landed me in the brig in the olden days. David Eisenhower was simply an obviously benevolent soul.

During our exercises off of Puerto Rico it came time to practice the procedures for missiles lock on and launching. On the Albany we had NTDS, Naval Tactical Data System which included a radar lock on system. Once the radar operator identified the target they moved a lock-on cursor over the radar location and click, lock-on, the first step for someone else to push a firing button and that Dr. Strangelov-esque equals bombs away. We had our very own Dr. Strangelove in the form of Rear Admiral Wallace who spoke in a falsetto. He also, when we were out at sea, and when we were running exercises was prone to wearing his pajamas and slippers and his bathrobe. WOW this IS what I call fun. As it so happened when it was time for launcharoodles with nuclear missiles .... without the warhead on (unloaded) ... Operations Specialist 2nd Class Seidenstein happened to be the operator on duty on the Admiral's staff radar. So with Panama Man standing by my side and leaning over and asking questions he would also squeak out quiet commands to me to "lockon" ... "aye, aye, Sir" done. Then he would call the command squeakily to "Fire". And so it went on for as many times as he deemed fun. It was all fun to me.

Back in port I had decided that with my pay raise which came with the promotion to Second Class I wanted to buy a car. I was going to invest and get a new car, but, one of my Southern Guardian Angels in the form of a wonderfully chipper benevolent junior officer heard that I was going to get a new car and came into the office and had a chat with me and asked a few questions and said don't do it! "Don't get a new car! You just needed a little car to cruise around in and go to the beach and get sand in it and spill beer in it." I sometimes had use of Larry Joe's coolmobile when he went home up North for a few days. LarryJoe was a Black American with a sinus condition. A permanent sniffly condition. He was wonderful and funny and we were good friends. I really did not go out much in port but a few times Larry Joe and I would go in his car and get something to eat. I didn't understand, or didn't realise that some places that I might want to go my friend would feel uncomfortable in. He understood that and scooted around the issue. Although we could have a good laugh about 'issues'. I bought a 1964 yellow Ford Fairlane for $500. I could spill as much beer on it and sand in it as I wanted. I could now hoon around with Cassidy. One long weekend we drove to Miami Beach. It was in fact a very long drive and it was the old Highway which was a slow way. We went once to Daytona Beach for a weekend during the university break onslaught. For me everything was simply fun and interesting and things I had never seen before. I know Curt also went with me a few times more in the evenings.

A few of the staff were flown up to Norfolk base for a few days to be on an aircraft carrier. It was the FDR and it was already out to sea so we were flown in a helicopter and landed on the flight deck. There was a new fellow with us briefly who was Mexican and looked like my 'brother' his name was Rodriquez and he was also Petty Officer Second Class. We were to be on the ship for a bit less than a week. It wasn't the whole staff so were were to fit in with the ships Operations team who had to find work for us to do. Rodriquez took me aside and came up with an assignment. We were going to do some vacuuming. So we had to walk around to find the equipment. Rodriquez made sure we walked around a lot. And far. And took a few breaks near the cafe. Eventually we had to find the necessary equipment which we had to inspect thoroughly and then we had to take our time looking for a plug. Then when we started, Rodriquez detected a serious malfunction so we had to sit down right there and take the vacuum apart. Then he knew what it needed but we would have to go and get 'it'. To find 'it'. He said we can leave the vacuum right in the middle of the floor as we would be right back. As we passed out of sight he started to giggle and explain that there is no work that we need to do. So the trick is to do anything right in front of everyone so everyone thinks you are busy. Our search for 'it' took us so close to the cafe again that we decided to sit down and have another coffee.

MEDITERRANEAN #2

Back home in Mayport we were then told we will be going on a six months Med cruise. Six months was the normal period. We would be going on the USS America which was then a fairly modern aircraft carrier. To prepare I would be flown to the base at Norfolk, Virginia to do a three-weeks specialist course for the advanced Naval Tactical Data System. At this stage, I was having such a good experience three years into the Navy and I was excelling in my job, with each promotion in the minimum time allowed, and, all along had wonderful friends and colleagues. So I thought maybe I could just stick it out and stay in. Go from short-timer now with less than a year remaining of my enlistment to become a "lifer", a career sailor. Of course I was thoroughly enjoying the beach, Florida and Southern ways. So I was quite excited to have the most advanced training and to go on a modern ship for an extended period. Half way through the course I was told we would not be going on the aircraft carrier with NTDA. Instead we would go on the USS Intrepid which was a decrepit i.e. old carrier without NTDS. This struck me as a moral setback. I wanted to shoot for the stars but this was another WWII ship that had seen better days. I was told to complete the course anyways. When that cruise would finish soon would follow my end date for my enlistment. For the first time, I thought, what will I do?

The day before we set sail I sold my car to a used car dealer. Several of our Operations Specialists went out for a 'night before setting sail' dinner and drinks (my usual maximum of 2 beers). The bar we went to that afternoon had its band practicing, particularly it was practicing one song. We ordered a drink, played pool, and chatted. In the Navy chatting is called "shooting the shit" which has a literal origin. The day I learned how to "shoot the shit" was aboard the Destroyer whose head (toilet) had about six sit-down toilets in two rows facing each other. No doors. One day I sat to do my deed. Just after I sat one of my colleagues, Taylor, sat directly opposite me. There were 4 other empty stalls he could have chosen which were not directly opposite me. As soon as he sat he started "to shoot the shit". Blah, blah, blah but a nice conversation. Such a thing was not my thing. Not at all. But, I cottoned on and chatted and it was an interesting conversation. I learned my lesson. The Lord works in mysterious ways. This was confounding, but, I got it, I need to just learn to chat more with people. It was from that day that I changed and became a much more open communicator. Not my thing, but, it changed my life for the better. That happened out at sea in the Atlantic before I went to the Mediterranean cruise #1.

Back to the night before sailing Med cruise #2, our bar party. At the pool table it came my turn to break. To break is the first shot. To shoot the white ball into the neatly stacked triangle of 15 numbered and coloured pool balls. On my break, in the initial hit, I sank six balls!

Early the next morning the USS Intrepid set sail with Comcrudesflot-12 staff aboard. The Admiral or the Captain of a ship is officially referred to in the Third Person Singular as the name of their command which may be a ship, a staff, or a base. When such a person who has a command job boards a ship there is an announcement such as "Comcrudesflot-12 boarding", and when they exit the ship "Comcrudesflot-12 departing".

By this time we had our third Admiral. Mr Pajamas was gone. We had a brief replacement. Then we had a new fellow whose first name was John and he preferred to be called by the casual form of 'John' which is "Jake". He walked and talked and looked like - John Wayne. He was very nice, very down to earth. Where as Mr Pajamas was a bit of a Prima Donna though friendly, Jake was a man's man. He was great with the enlisted men. Apparently, as the Philippine valets told me, he insisted on washing his own dishes and the Marines had similar reports as in he would open his own door. He was a 'good guy', but, he was a bit of a scoundrel. In fact I think three of the Admirals whose staff I was on had Congressional investigations into something amiss in their bureaucratic behaviour. In Jake's case, he ordered one less combat ready fighter jet aboard the carrier for our cruise. In its place was a training jet because during the six-months he wanted to complete his training hours so he could earn his flight wings (fighter pilot qualification). He was replaced and the next Rear Admiral had his wife meet him in every port. This may have been seen as compromising our security i.e. the ship and fleet movements (schedule).

The day after the Intrepid pulled out for our six-months Med cruise a shipboard notice went out that a rat had been sighted so all were to be on the alert and to report further sightings so 'it' (them, those, they) could be trapped. On the other hand an aircraft carrier has a 24 hours a day donut shop. Then again, one day while we were early in the Med, a mysterious helicopter quickly arrived while we were out at sea and quickly left. What was that all about? Lo and behold, and blow me down, a sailor had been serving the fleet. Apparently our staff was informed, he had set up a nifty little business on the fantail. The fantail is the back of a ship and on a carrier there is ample room and covering to operate covert shenanigans including drinking, gambling, drugs or anything that was deemed illegal. Apparently, so we were told, for five bucks a pop there were many happy endings going on. At the time I was in, homosexual activity, which is a norm throughout human history, was out. Well not out of the closet but out of permission. Also women in the Navy known as Waves were not allowed to sail aboard ships, yet.

Our first port o' call was as is common, Palma, Majorca. This was my second Med cruise but the first for some of my buddies so I was now a newly seasoned sailor. A few of us went to a bar I knew which was owned by a Black American who formerly was a professional baseball player. A few of us were sitting in a classic American style booth. We had been drinking. My close buddy Curt who could drink a lot more than me, simply put his arm up on the back of the booth. But, in so doing he happened to knock one of the neighbouring booth's customers' arm. That neighbour took offence and immediately retaliated by harshly knocking Curt's arm. Curt was a very straight shooter and responded equally and that 'did it'. The neighbour made an actual threat and Curt was more than ready to take him on. However, the neighbour's mates started to move and we were about to have a bar brawl over nothing. I stepped in and made some quick jokes and said it was just an accident etc etc anything to divert and dissipate the tension. I also offered to buy the neighbours a round of drinks. As we chatted we found that they were four lads, men a few years older than us (this was in October and I was 20) and all from London. Although not all were offical Cockney's two were. They asked if I could take them on a tour of the carrier. I could but only an escorted tour i.e. close by my side. They arrived the next day on time. They were already a little bit pushy as if they were the guests of the Admiral. I signed them in and off we went. They were tremendously curious and well read even though working class, typical of that era. One of the them was a pilot on the Thames and was very proud to show me his license. In a very short time, he went astray. I was now in a pickle and damned if I do and damned if I don't. I did. I told the other three to wait on the spot I had to get find the straggler. Got him. Came back. The others were gone. I was summonsed over the speaker to come to the gangway. I was scolded and the others were already kicked off the ship and the straggler had to get off immediately. We five made arrangements to meet that evening. During our remaining mutual days we met a few times. We kept contact and we would meet again someday.

The remainder of the cruise was non-eventful and good work and fun. Each day ashore that I had duty I would sit forlornly in the office. Shortly after I was sitting there depressed that I couldn't be ashore venturing around, after about an hour with a long face, my general supervisor Dan Doyle would come in aggressively say "Get out of here"! I would light up "You mean it". He still wouldn't crack a smile but would add "Go on and you better have one for me". I was changed and on my way within minutes. Dan, from Alabama, lived with his wife in a trailer park just outside of our base in Florida. Dan was always ready to go home.

Two incidents from my first Med cruise are worth sharing here. On that cruise aboard the USS Ingraham, a fellow who befriended me told me just before we got to Toulon, France that he was going to take a few days liberty and was going to take a train from Toulon to Paris and stay there 2 or 3 nights and he asked if I'd like to go as well. Paris! Dream time. I got permission to take leave. I can not remember his name. He was several years older. Very slick. He initially had joined the Navy to become a SEAL (special forces). He passed the tests and training far along but in the end fell short of confirmation. We went up in the Eiffel Tower, and walked all over the centre of the Paris. I bought a beret. I asked him to make a comic movie of me playing the French outdoor bowling with the old men and they were fine with that. On the first day however my pal said he wanted to go into a department store and look at some mens clothes. When we got into the men's clothing department he looked at a variety of clothes. Then he said he would be right back and when he comes out of the dressing room we were to walk out together and not say anything until we were outside. He was an expert shoplifter did his shopping and came out wearing the best that a Paris department store had to offer in 1970.

ODD INCIDENT

The other incident that I'd like to note before I finish this section about my 4 years in the Navy and that occurred while I was on that first Med cruise aboard the Ingraham. Our ship was assigned to scout at the edge of International Waters off of the coast of Libya. This is in 1971 towards the end of the six-month cruise and still during the height of the Cold War. It was like MAD Magazine's cartoon "Spy vs Spy" as the USA spied on the Soviets and the Soviets spied on the USA. The Soviets constantly had a ship trailing the USA's prize ships the Aircraft Carriers. Each carrier traveled constantly with Destroyers as escorts who could intercept attacks before the carrier was hit. This also meant there was time for the carrier to launch its fighter jets. So each carrier had a small flotilla of escorts. Usually a single ship which we would refer to as "Igor". One of our radar jobs was to keep a constant watch on the position of each ship in our squadron or flotilla. If our group included a carrier then we included "Igor" as part of 'our' squadron or flotilla. In this case our ship the Ingraham was to leave our flotilla and was sent to track and follow an important Soviet ship. The ship would have been important either for its own spy equipment or if it was a command ship or most modern ship. Espionage information knew the Soviet ship was soon to leave a port on the coast of Libya near Egypt. We were informed that it would leave in the pre-dawn hour. When I assumed the watch it was shortly before suggested departure time. I was to be the radar operator and was informed which ship in port was believed to be the Soviet ship of concern. We also had to stay at least 12 nautical miles from land i.e. to stay in International Waters. I was to notify the bridge the moment the Soviet ship of concern started to pull away from the pier.

On the radar ships close together could appear to be one. That also depended on ones distance from those two ships. The further one was the more the ships appeared on radar as a single radar blip. Ships in port are close together. In all fields of work, information does not stand on its own, information needs to be interpreted. I saw, interpreted that two ships were suddenly moving at the same time. They moved in such a way, a simultaneous rotation, so they blended on the radar. That single blip headed to the port entry. When they entered the Med they parted and one could not visually tell which was 'our' ship. I had watched the whole thing with fascination because I had never seen nor heard of such a manoeuvre. The ships parted the port at the same time. My interpretation was different from the bridge's radar operator. Our CIC officer, a Lieutenant burst in and towered over me very angrily saying it was the other ship. I was solid on what I watched. I didn't blink. I was able to surmise which ship was 'ours'. The Captain was on the bridge and this Lieutenant was his radar operator at this crucial moment. It was still dark outside.

If these were two Soviet destroyers then outside the naked eye could not tell the difference i.e. which were we to follow. We, the Captain, had to decide which ship to follow as they parted in opposite directions. I didn't waiver on my decision. Mr Hothead Lieutenant said "Goddamit Syd if you're wrong I'll have your ass". I told him my choice. He then had to go back to the bridge and tell the Captain. They followed my choice and then we and 'Igor' began a cat and mouse chase with the Soviet ship trying to lose us. This was a Cold War opportunity which allowed one nation's navy to practice evasion and the other to practice following. When dawn came visual sighting proved I was correct we were on the tail of the correct ship. Soon it was time to change the watch so I was off duty. As the light came the helmsman and Captain could make instant change of directions and finally like a game of chess we were able to close in so that the chase was over. At this point soon there was an announcement on all of our speakers "Attention all hands. Soviet ship off the port bow". Everyone who could grabbed any binoculars or cameras and rushed topside.

This was a great life lesson.

There we were hundreds of USA sailors and officers waving and jumping towards the Soviets while the Soviets were also waving and jumping facing us. Both Captains allowed and encouraged this. 1971 thirteen years before Gorbachev and Perestroika. So for those few minutes when we were so close together we each got a glimpse of our shared humanity. We then found our traditional distance as "Igor" and Joe? But I am positive each sailor on both ships treasures that glimpse into the truth that we humans are more similar than different.

Let's now skip again to the end of the second Med cruise. During the cruise I discovered the ship's library and read and read. I read a lot of books on psychology and philosophy and I read historical novels by Mary Renault. I soon passed my First Class Operations Specialist exam and in a few months at the earliest allotted time I would be officially promoted. I was now an asset that the Navy had invested in. I was given the official offer if I was to reenlist. Upon signing I would not have to wait the allotted time to receive promotion. The promotion to Petty Officer First Class would be immediate. The promotion was a significant pay raise, which also meant if I became a lifer at retirement the retirement pay was higher. In the military one could retire after 20 years. I would be 37. I could also apply to be stationed anywhere the Navy had operations including overseas. I was also offered a cash bonus of $10,000. Which at the time and for an ordinary and young enlisted man was a small fortune.

I was asked by my supervisors what were my plans. I decided I would 'get out'. Half of my seniors totally supported that and half started to have little 'casual' chats with me. For the most part, I think each was simply trying to help. I was now 21 and was still naive about how the world worked. I still don't know. I still maintain a valuable naiveness. One officer tried to get me to start in Amway so I could have a way to earn money. One wonderful Chief Petty Officer suggested I should take the bonus and take the opportunity to be stationed anywhere and go to Saigon (July 1973) and get the extra pay that would bring. One Captain had a great chat with me and asked if I had managed to save any money. Yes. He asked how much. He said "If I were you the Navy will fly you anywhere in the world when you leave. I'd take that money and see the whole world while young and single." Some others including the Amway officer tried to explain to me that we had a steady pay and accomodation and food in the Navy but the "outside" was very tough. I didn't know what I would do.

CHANGE

I understood I could be flown anywhere. More significantly I understood something inside that I was still very close to my family and my parents in particular. I understood that if i could be free near them then I could be free anywhere in the world. I also felt like I would like to study generally to repair what I missed from my years of attending school. I wasn't sure if I could study well enough for a major university but I knew that the 2 year programs at Community Colleges helped with life and study transitions. Also following full time military service I was entitled to the G.I.Bill if I attended a college or university. The G.I.Bill provided four years of monthly payments for anyone who enrolled in a college or university. This was one of my main reasons for joining in the first place. I felt I would try the adventure of college/university.

I let my parents know first. A few weeks after I spoke with my sisters who lived minutes away from each other but when I phoned on schedule they were together. Then my sister Faye said her husband Bob wanted to speak with me. Bob worked in his cousin's real estate business, and, explained that he had an inexpensive apartment reserved for me in my home neighbourhood. He also had a job waiting for me as a landscape labourer at a huge apartment complex that he managed. Then he said my other Brother-in-Law, Bobbie, wanted to speak with me. He said his Parents had moved out of their house and the furniture was stored. If I took the apartment offered he would arrange to have it furnished with some of his parents furniture.

EX-NAVY. CIVILIAN LIFE.

In a few weeks, on schedule, I competed my 4 years Active Duty and flew home. My parents had sold our tiny house and moved into a wonderful apartment building where my Father also had a garden. I stayed the first night at my sister's and the next day I was taken to my apartment of Fifth Avenue on the border of Squirrel Hill and Shadyside. I was now a rent and utilities paying, employed civilian who was also in the US Navy Reserve as part of the enlistment contract. I bought a brand new VW Super Beetle so I had a monthly payment for that and insurance which would soon come in very handy!

A few weeks later new friends said there was an annual Xmas in August party at a bar in Oakland the inner city university area. The owner went to Florida every year for Winter so he missed Christmas with friends and customers so he created his own ritual. I drove there. When it was closing time I offered to drive friends to their homes. We packed the VW. I was QUITE under the influence!! We were to drop the one gal off first. She and the fellow giving directions were the two in the car on my first leave after boot camp when we got caught by the police with their grass. At one point the navigator yelled turn here. I was on military reflex timing, an order was an order. The timing of the directions was late. I held a sharp turn. But it was too late. In the sharp curve the car went briefly onto the sidewalk then still in the same arc briefly onto a hilly lawn and finally into a pole. Head on. Dead center of my brand new VW. The young woman was bleeding in her mouth and all the rest were fine but ruffled and the rat bag navigator immediately was talking about whiplash and suing me and how the young woman should sue me. He was a shit. He had just graduated with a B.A. in Law. He soon became a politician. Very soon was elected to the State Senate. Jumping back a few years to my first Leave after boot camp when we got caught by the police, he got us out of being arrested in part because his Father owned the Irish mafia funeral parlour, and the young woman was the daughter of a Mr. Flaherty who was then running for Mayor, and my pal Richie pipped up to the police about being family friends to Frankie Bruno who was the godfather boss of the local Italian syndicate which was a mild form of mafia. In those days almost all policemen were Irish or Italian. So they never bothered asking my who my Father was, a poor, independent, traveling salesman. The police had to let us go because of the triumvirate's family political clout in the Irish and Italian sectors.

I started work with the two supervisors who also worked physically. One had been in the Marines and his job in Vietnam was as liaison between new or visiting officers and the mountain's Indigenous chief. With each visitor he hiked them up the mountain to have a ritual welcoming meal with the chief. He was married now with children. The main supervisor had been in the Army but had seven children! So everyday after our labour job he would go home have a meal and see his children then he soon went to sleep and about 11pm he awoke and did his second full-time job as night supervisor for IBM computers.

ACADEMIC PLEASURE

I enrolled in Liberal Arts at the Community College of Allegheny County - Boyce Campus. In a previous chapter I had told some of what transpired during my time at Boyce and how I fell into theatre, and became close friend (drinking buddy) with my German professor of Sociology and Political Science, Peter Dittrich. I also had wonderful teachers in French, Literature, Psychology Dr. Bernstein who was also born in Germany. He would have been born during the peak of fascism. Peter was born in the late 1930s in Hamburg. His Father was a merchant ship captain and was primarily at sea. Peter's older brother was a Brown Shirt (fascist youth).

During the war the family moved to Berlin and they had to go on several evacuation marches and back. While in Berlin late in the war, in between bombing raids the children were sent out of the bomb shelters to gather food and other items off of the dead soldiers.

The London lads whom I met in Palma wanted to visit me and see something in the USA. So the timing could not have been worse. They arrived at the worst possible time, the start of my academic studies. Every night we partied which included staying in the bars until they closed and then coming home for night caps. I had to get up about 7am to get to my first classes each morning. We did have fun. It was a great learning experience spending a month with four working class Londoners who absolutely loved politics. They were shocked to see televisions in bars which of course inhibit conversation. At the time British pubs rarely had televisions and if they did they were reserved for special sports events. Whereas the USA had started just keeping the TV on! Also they were shocked to see so many security guards even at fast food places, and that these fat fellows working in security all had loaded guns in a holster. One of the fellows who came was not in the original Palma quartet. He, Colin, who was Irish heritage, worked in security and was an amateur boxer. Many evenings particularly when we were standing at a bar, he would suddenly say "Oh dear". One or two of the other Cockneys would say "Ere we go".
Colin: I'm sorry to announce this my dear friends
Cockney: You're not going to
Colin: Yes, I'm afraid the urge has definitely come upon me
Cockney: Well let's make room. Go ahead.
Colin: Make room lads
Cockney: Go on, get it over with
Colin: Well, gentlemen please bare with me for a moment
Down they'd go. His trousers. And there he would be for a few minutes while we continued to chat and drink. Then
Colin: Well gentlemen. I'm sorry to disappoint you but the urge has passed. In a moment I shall raise me britches.

After their month stay in my apartment I was quite happy to see them go! Then I could zero in on my study. When they left I was deeply excited to immerse myself in study. It was thrilling. The rest of this saga and how it lead me into the theatre is briefly told in a previous chapter. There I mention a horrendous rain storm that suddenly came one night when I was on my way home in my VW. There were two people getting completely drenched at a bus stop. I stopped, opened the door and yelled get in. Inside I offered to take them wherever they needed to be. They were friends, young women, who were each going to their own home. I dropped one. The second one became openly seductive. As I dropped her we exchanged phone numbers. I phoned the next night. Then she said that the following night she was rehearsing in a play so how about if I picked her up after rehearsal and we could go out. When I dropped her she invited me in to meet her Mother. The daughter and I soon became an item and had dates several nights a week. So civilian life was looking better than ever on all fronts. I was 21 and she was a few years younger but drastically more mature than I was, or, at least she was highly educated, worldly, arty, and scholarly. She had attended a special school based on the principles of A.S.Neill and Summerhill which I was studying within Sociology. She also was in a theatre group based on Grotowski's Laboratory theatre philosophy and method. One evening when I fetched her and we got back to my apartment she asked if she could smoke. Sure.

She rolled a joint and said do you want some? Sure. Not really but what should I do? If I was a "two beer screamer" who had no resistance to alcohol, well, let me tell you .... one small puff was all I needed when it came to marijuana. I can readily remember every time I smoked and each time it was the doing or offer of a friend. Except for one occasion did I have more than two puffs. It was about ten times between the age of 17 to 34 that on single occasions I had a puff or two. A single puff was enough to doom me. So as usual I would drive my friend home. Only this night I was still well and truly under the influence. It was scary. I was floating and could not feel the clutch pedal. The driving was fine, but, I was very glad to get her safely home, and myself too.
Her play came up and it was only the second play I had ever seen. The first was in ninth grade as a visiting troupe came to our high school and performed Ionesco's famous "Rhinoceros". That was an absurdist play and I remember nothing except staring at the actors and at one point a

rhinoceros appeared. This second play was just as avant-garde. It was The Balcony by Jean Genet.

Soon by flukes I fell into the theatre world at CCAC-Boyce Campus. The theatre teacher and director was Trudy Scott. The first piece I was in was one in a selection of guerrilla theatre pieces.
I was in "Telephoney". That script was from the San Francisco Mime Troupe and the piece taught audiences how to cheat the phone companies. This was the beginning of two years of theatre while studying Liberal Arts: Sociology, Psychology, French, Literature, Acting, Modern Dance.

CHAPTER 6

BEING AUSTRALIAN

At the moment there is a political and social discussion about "what it means to be Australian" and its corollary 'to be un-Australian'. Given the variants and extreme opposites voiced in those discussions in the newspapers, TV, radio, in person, there is no set conclusion.

I am Australian. I am an Australian citizen. I am dedicated to being Australian and to understanding, learning, and living more each week as such. Like virtually all Australians I live in at least two worlds and play in the liminal energies of the those worlds. Dare one say, that even for the Indigenous people they exist in at least two worlds. They are Indigenous and also they have their specific people, clan, family, and totem. Their Indigenous family origins may be from any of the more than 350 Aboriginal language groups. They are also Australians. Like anyone else they may also be a part of other communities based around a religion, occupation, artistic form, intellectual or spiritual or creative or athletic or political or social based interests. The show I created by writing the scenario and giving the title "A Play On Worlds" was then developed with my full participation with the three Australian actors. We each understood clearly that all Australians live in - at least (!!) two worlds.

There must be variants even within the Indigenous sectors whose living circumstances differ broadly from inner city, small towns, rural, farmlands, bush, and remote communities. There are also notable differences within related Indigenous groups around the world by geographic generalities such as people of the mountain, plain, valley, or sea. For those of us who are non-Indigenous Australians most of the same variants of location exist, but, are often different experiences due to issues of heritage. The variants exist for the 'white' or perhaps whiter Australians including the whiter-than-white and the who-says-who-is-white and what-does-white-mean and what-does-black-mean clusters of people.

So who am I to speak about being Australian? I'm Australian enough to recognise that very Australian question, mate. Or should it be maaaaate? I'm Australian enough to take the piss out of you, and, me. I'm Australian enough to have-a-go-at-ya. I'm Australian enough to 'stick-it-right-up-ya'.

How Australian is Australian enough? What flavour Australian are we talking about? What flavour Australians are there? These basic questions exist in a similar way probably in every or most cultures in the world. Even where they did not occur 50 years ago these questions now exist virtually everywhere. There are 3 billion people more on the planet in the last 60 years. There are multiple tides of emigration world wide. Things have changed.

Being Australian has changed in the mere 30 plus years since I first arrived in Australia. Yes, like the majority of Australians I am naturalised, or as in many cases either the parents or grandparents or great-grandparents were immigrants to Australia. There was a huge influx of immigrants immediately after World War II. They immigrated for two reasons primarily. First to get away from the war torn regions to try a fresh start in life, and, to help build up the growing nation that once again needed immigrants' knowledge and willingness to work hard to build such schemes as the Snowy River, The Sydney Opera House and multiple areas of development in construction, manufacturing, arts, science, medicine, universities, and sports.

The contribution to Australian sports by coaches from overseas has never been broadly recorded nor researched. That hidden information is all part of a new 'religion' (sic) called "Denialism". In Denialism anything which does not support a set of beliefs is ignored or even actively denied.

Sometimes, it seems, that in the arts and intellectual domains, being Australian shows the same signs as nationalism in every country. It feels like one needs to live in permanent state of denial with regards to whatever your field of interest is. It seems like ones field of perception is meant to narrow down along national lines rather than to open up. In the artistic and intellectual fields it seems there is a constant need to prove how Australian one is which immediately brings about acts of nationalism and begins to establish a new myth with its own truths and un-truths (Denialism). Pierre Bourdieu explains such social contrasts in his theory about culture and particularly heterodoxy vs orthodoxy in every field. His was the social theory I used in my Doctorate Thesis.

One of the paradoxes of being Australian, I experience and know clearly that Australians are very curious creatures. Now 'curious' can mean interested in anything or it can mean odd. Being Australian to me means a group of people, a nation who as a whole are bright pennies who are infinitely curious about everything under the sun and who are notorious world travellers and adventurers seeking to experience to create what is wonderful in this world. Yet, and here is the 'curious', part 2, they (Australians per se) and by 'they' I only mean some as in s-o-m-e can deny that anything or anyone in any field from any other country can be equal or better or much better than any particular Australian in the same field. The Australian can be the best at denialism.

The legendary books accredited to Nino Cullota (the pen name of John O'Grady) included the most famous "They're A Weird Mob". That book, movie of the same name expressed how strange the Australian must seem to a curious immigrant trying to make sense of this wonderful new world.

And Australia is an astonishing new world. My oath it is! No matter what field of human endeavour one can find Australians excelling. Though in a high percentage of cases they will be excelling in lands other than The Land Downunder. Their genuine curiosity just takes them beyond the horizon of these shores. To be sure, I like Australians - a lot!!! That's why I live here. I like the people, the multicultural society, the political and social systems, the progressive spirit, the ancient and modern histories, and of course the nature. The Australian nature outside is fascinating and sensitively varied. Its nature inside has a type of tolerance and a 'have a fair go' attitude that still exists.

Naturally as in every country there are special obstacles and barriers and particular prejudices that an immigrant must encounter and seek ways of by-passing or undermining or getting around or through. This could, I suppose, without knowing specifically, happen even within a wide and varied Indigenous world(s) if an Indigenous person from New South Wales decided unannounced to move up to the more remote region of Kakadu to set up a home and business they may very well be asked 'so who do you think you are suddenly coming up here out of the blue'? I don't know and am going out on an invisible limb to push the limits of a thought. Has such an incident ever occurred? I don't know.

Maybe it is more likely that an Indigenous person from outside of a remote area would simply know that such a sudden move unannounced and without proper protocol would not be a good idea. In fact, if I understand correctly a person from another area could not cross the new land unless they knew the language. There were formal exchanges made when Bangarra Dance Company was established. Such exchanges were already begun by NAISDA the school out of which Bangarra was born. Additionally the Indigenous 'nations' had ways and protocols for visiting and crossing each others territories.

It is said that Gondawannaland was invaded by the British first fleets. Particularly by the First and Second fleets. That is historically true since England had an established process for exploration which happened to require invading every nation they were curious about. That was how the British Empire (now called the Commonwealth) was established. The French, Dutch, Spanish, Portuguese, Arabic, Romans, Vikings, and many other nations did exactly the same thing. They were curious, adventurers, ambitious, greedy, blood thirsty, whoring, thieving peoples who were also developing intellectually in other ways. So too the Australians as the newest and luckiest members of the British Empire (Commonwealth) have used their very fortunate circumstances of time, English language, higher education, and Commonwealth connections to 'invade' any bloody place and situation they got curious about. Monkey see monkey do. It's a free world. Nothing ventured nothing gained. At the same time English/British/Australians like each of the other venturing nations brought with them human developments that the newer lands had not yet achieved. The Romans, Norse and Normans brought new knowledge and crafts with them when they invaded, raped and pillaged the British Isles.

However, before the British First and Second Fleets invaded the Australian continent there were others who got onto the land first. Those known to have arrived earlier were the French, the Dutch, the Chinese, the Indonesians and perhaps the Indigenous people themselves as some say theoretically. If the original people of the land did not come from Indonesian then where and how did they arrive or evolve or appear? The myths of Australian Aborigines or Indigenous people usually refer to their Creation stories which revolve around the Rainbow Serpent and Dreamtime legends. From a scientific view it is said that the Australian Aborigines have been on the continent or from the continent at least 50,000 years. Some say 60, some say 100 thousand years.

There were Indigenous peoples around the world. The modern nation-states began mainly in the 1700s! England which was invaded by the Romans and the Vikings and others is very much a mixed race of people. A brief look at the history of three great Western European nations; Germany, Italy, France, shows that their construction is very recent. Italy was until the 1800s, city-states. France and Germany were composed from distinct regions based on geographic elements. In England, Germany, France, Italy until only recently (1950s,1960s, 1970s) each of their regions had such distinct dialects that those people were speaking virtually a different language than the regal national language. An English person can not understand the actual languages of Wales, Ireland, or Scotland. Similarly in Sweden there were absolute distinct dialects even between villages at least in the far north into the 1950s. Today each regional dialect of Sweden is still distinguishable immediately from Stockholmska. The Australian Indigenous people are divided by approximately 350 language groups.

Each nation lives in a myth about 'who they really are'.

In high school I did a project about Rwanda which included learning about the diabolical wars amongst their own people who had distinguishable heritages.

"There is nothing new under the Sun".

The Native Americans seem to have some connection with the Mongols or Indigenous Chinese. There were and are Indigenous Indonesians of many 'nations'. The Japanese and Taiwanese are in denial that they have Indigenous people. A very large percentage of Palestinian people have a specific history noted by their last names of people who started coming to Palestine (as it was then called) as recent as the 1920s, 30s, 40s from Kuwait, Egypt (such as Yasser Arafat), Lebanon, Syria, Jordan. By their last name it is clear not only which nation they came from but in which period in the 19th and 20th centuries. Although the Torah is a collection of indigenous myths the vast scientific evidence through archeology is increasing. According to B.S.J. Isserlin the evidence shows clearly the layers of settlements which in part like all human settlements varied at least into three general groups of people of the hills, plains, seas. In recent years there is an accumulation of material evidence that there was a race of Indigenous people on the islands of what is now called New Zealand, before the Maoris arrived and possibly invaded, between 1250-1300 and became the Indigenous people. The name "New Zealand" is derived from the Dutch explorer Abel Tasman for whom the Australian state of Tasmania is named.

I don't like it when Australians of late are saying and insisting that Australia is a racist country as if it was the only place that has any racism. As I've just tried to point out, even a nation such as Rwanda i.e. an African nation has prejudices or racism. Within their own people so does Sweden! And Italy! And we can assume that such prejudice exists nearly everywhere within any large group. Perhaps there is some truth to Australia having racism, but, probably one group of Amazonian Indians does not like certain of their neighbours' habits. In Australia there is a quiet little known annual award - the Australian Ethnic Business Awards. If you want an example of what a deeply, wonderful, and profound experience it is for people such as myself, ethnic people, to come here and try to offer goodness in our own fields of interest you will see in such a very simple awards ceremony some of the most uplifting, generous and spiritual stories of this great nation. In recent years this has included a category for an Indigenous award. Even though this is a televised event only a small percentage of Australians will know that such an award exists.

I never heard anyone in Australia say that they wanted or were shooting for an AO, however, a large part of the upwardly mobile Australian's certainly read the awards list each year.

So, I'm Australian. But what flavour Australian?

Becoming Australian also means becoming oneself, or, for some it may mean avoiding ones self?

For myself I am on a learning path in part to understand more on a daily continuum about Australia, about its Indigenous cultures, about the depth of being Jewish, and about the depth of being Human, and about artistic expression. Particularly I am inspired by where those areas crossover. My show "Harlequin Dreams" was an experiment in doing just that. In my next book I will tell more about the process of that and other shows which I touch on in CLOWN SECRET.

A book "Writing the Nation" discusses Australian writer Patrick White's inclusion of Indigenous characters in some of his novels one of which is "Riders in the Chariot". In reference to that novel this is said in reference to the novel's Indigenous character Alf Dubbo:

"Alf's most sustained encounter is with the Jew, Himmelfarb. Through his observation of the treatment of Himmelfarb, Alf is brought to recognize that the blacks are not the only recipients of white cruelty. The Himmelfarb narrative brings the Holocaust and awareness of a much larger theatre of human cruelty and suffering into the text. Historically, Fanon shows that the Jew and the black have a shared space of common suffering" (Pg 141,

Writing the Nation: Patrick White and the Indigene, by, Cynthia van den Driesen 2009)

Driesen explains White's body of work as a "contribution to enhancing his Australian people's awareness of a transcendental dimension to experience, of the need for a spiritual awareness to counteract the increasing secularism and materialism of the contemporary world" (pg. 177).

Stories are an important part of the human experience. Myth is how knowledge, wisdom, and understanding is passed on. Myth is more than information. It gives meaning and context to information, facts, science. Myth is in the same method that the Indigenous Australians and the Jewish people and all people pass on the most important information. The language of origin though stores the secrets of those myths. The stories themselves often make no sense outside of the language of origin. So a proper translation must also include references specific to the language of origin. The English translations of the Bible start off on the wrong foot from the first sentence, the first paragraph, the first section, the first chapter. The Hebrew word for that book (actually a set of five books) is not 'bible' but is 'torah' which means teaching and instruction as in law, law as in how to live or wisdom. One of the teachings is that a story/myth had four levels. The one usually considered is the most superficial. It is the fourth level 'sod' which carries the most important meaning. Sod implies secret or that which takes learning or insight/intuition to understand.

The following is the normal, classical, actual teaching about the four levels known as 'pardes' which itself means 'orchard'. Note that the p-r-d-s are also the first letter of the four levels. This is a common indicator that a translation needs to have a special consideration that relates back to the original language.

Peshat: often inaccurately translated as literal, it comes from the root which means simple, although peshat is sometimes anything but simple! Peshat correctly means the intended, explicit meaning.
Remez: alluded meaning (reading between the lines). Remez in modern Hebrew means hint. Traditionally, remez referred to methods such as

gezera shava (equivalent language implying equivalent meaning) and gematria (word-number values).

Derash: Homiletical or interpretative meaning. The word 'midrash' is from the same root. The drash is an interpretation that is not explicit in the text.

Sod: (literally - secret). The mystical or esoteric meaning.

"There is no conclusion. There is only further discussion".

CHAPTER 7

CLOWN VS GOD...NOTES ON THE CLOWN MOVEMENT

<u>This is an essay in final draft form and was originally on my blog in 2016. Some of it is theoretical about words and ideas. There is one section that has many names as sources for you to research which can start with youtube and google. You are welcome to write to me directly and to view my website that has pages for ISAAC, "Creative Mentorship". You are welcome to write generally, anytime.</u>

INTRODUCTION

My writing meanders like an actual conversation. I suddenly throw in an anecdote, personal or otherwise. I come back to themes previously mentioned. If you are interested in understanding what really works to become a clown or to become a better clown - I provide dozens of hints. Even though it is a matter of "seek and ye shall find", in fact, I present open advice for artists at any stage.

Chaplin was the ultra and consummate professional and he said "You can never be professional enough". One of the most remarkable modern clowns is Steve Martin - he is on par with Robin Williams, Woody Allen, Jim Carey - none of whom are officially 'clowns' according to some clown teachers. Yet on almost all levels those four people are among the greatest of modern clowns. Martin's deeply personal autobiography is one of the greatest disclosures about what it takes to be a clown and a great clown at that. The 2012 documentary on Woody Allen is another of the greatest sources about the inner/outer world of being a great clown (the complete DVD is 2 and a half hours).

So even for fully professional clowns - one can go further. This article is intended to openly and freely assist those out there who are what I call "Seekers" who are 'looking for something'. For many who think they've 'found it' - they still need to rethink and deprogram themselves and those whom they teach. I provide mentorship for artists at any stage of their career or vision. My work is to assist your process. "Creative Mentorship" is the formal process that I offer and there is basic information on my website about that.

SECTION 1 - General discussion about words, ideas, current discourses

"Clown of God" was how Nijinsky the dancer viewed his life. I follow Nijinsky's inspiration to juxtapose those two words in the hope this article might give you food for thought to readdress the small word 'clown' or the more challenging word 'god'. Food for thought may be viewed also as fodder for complaint.

Shakespeare says via Hamlet "Nothing is either good or bad only thinking makes it so". With thinking in mind this article is an attempt to give us a chance to redefine those loaded words 'god' and 'clown'. Let's see what happens as a philosophical exercise when the juxtaposition of those two words is used for the purpose of enhancing our understanding and compassion.

Clown and god are simply words to express an idea or phenomenon. 'God' by the way, or to get it out of the way, is simply a word for an inexplicable phenomenon. Some might call that inexplicable phenomenon "the big bang", or, "the universe", or "the Tao", or "The Rainbow Serpent". 'God' is a word. It is a powerful word since it can easily provoke anger and hate in some whereas for others it provokes love and empathy.

For some people for whom clown is treated sacred, the word god is considered vile like a four-letter curse word. For other people for whom god is sacred, clown is considered vile.

Some contemporary clowns and clown teachers insist on clowns wearing red noses. Yet those same people abhor the classic clown who wears a red nose, plus makeup, and big shoes and garish costume. It's a bit of damned if you don't and damned if you do. Clowns and clown teachers can be as dogmatic as fundamentalist preachers.

Here is a quote from The Makers of Magic, a chapter in Ronald Harwood's book *All The World's A Stage* (1984). "The theatre is one of man's most ingenious compromises with himself. ... because the theatre is something that people need."

Here is the longer version of that quote:
"The theatre is one of man's most ingenious compromises with himself. In it he performs and entertains, shows off and amuses himself, and yet it is also one of his most powerful instruments for exploring and attempting to understand himself, the world he lives in, and his place in that world. The theatre can be controversial or reassuring, subversive or conservative, diverting or enlightening: if it chooses it can be all of these, and more. .... it is able to provoke deep, often subconscious emotions, and to embody those drives and forces in the human mind which set both individuals and society most at risk... because the theatre is something that people need." (Ronald Harwood, 1984)

Thoughts of words and logic.

I propose to use freeform logic to find fresh perspectives behind the words 'clown' and 'god'. In philosophy one learns that the word 'chair' is not the chair itself. A word represents something else. A word represents an object, a person, or an idea. Logic implies using words to develop one's clarity in thought processes to enhance discussion of any subject. Logic can occur from many angles.

A word is just a word, yet, in some circles the word 'clown' is loaded and sometimes provokes strong emotions. Those reactions may be positive, negative, or sometimes dogmatic. Within the clown profession such reactions may be valid or flippant. Opposing reactions seem to be unreasonable, illogical and emotional reactions. They occur for some reason other than the simple meaning of a word. Ones definition of the word clown becomes virtually theological when forced to adhere to an ideological framework.

By juxtaposing two words or concepts we have the potential to rectify confusion and illusions imposed on each word. Clown, humour, and parody are common in most cultures. Reverence toward some form of ideal being is also common. Such idolising can be towards a sports hero, national hero, great politician, artist, or nature itself. That instinct is to 'worship' something 'higher'. Such reverence is so common that it may be a logical norm of a healthy, instinctual and psychological human need.

Stories and myths in literature.

In literature a warning about idolising any person is given in the story of The Emperor's New Clothes. In that story we are advised against idolising even if it is someone we respect such as a king. Another warning via literature is about worship of any thing. That is found in the myth of The Worship of the Golden Calf. Humanity is warned even if the object of worship is our own collective creation. The story and the myth teach us to discern. That story and the myth teach us to use our critical faculties. They initiate a dialectic or discussion about reverence even if it is of our own design.

A child learns to discern between two animals by juxtaposition. A child sees two objects moving in the garden and asks "What are those"? The adult looks and sees two animals, a snake and a dog. Both animals are moving in unison. The adult says the one in front wriggling is a snake and the one walking behind is a dog. Then the child sees two other moving objects, one wriggling and one following, points at them and says "Snake and dog"! The adult sees where the child points and says "Those are a lizard and a cat".

At the first level of learning the child may have assumed the lizard was a snake because it was wriggling in front and that the cat was a dog because it was following. The mind always follows a form of logic, but, not always a linear logic. The human mind readily jumps to conclusions or confusions before it has clarity. Too much clarity such as in one's beliefs about science, god, or clown leads to misguided yet well intended worship of a deified definition of science, god, or clown. Formal and complete definitions can create an illusion as in the emperor's new clothes which were non-existent. Worship of something of one's own creation such as one's definitions, concepts or humour signals the message of the myth of the Golden Calf.

When discussing concepts such as clown or god, often the first thing to leave the room is logic because sometimes there is no clear context of terms being discussed. Sometimes in a discussion the first thing to enter the room is emotion. Clown and god are words loaded with expectation, assumptions, illusions, no matter what side or angle of the discussion you are on. Consequently when one discusses those words there is a tendency for emotion to enter the room while logic leaves. In the science vs god debate some have suggested that science is the how and god is the why. Clown: is clown a person, an art, an artist, a performer, an entertainer, a business, a movement, a culture or even a cult?

Science vs God debate

I enjoy the science versus god debates, books, and discussions. Those discussions are fun, fiery, and often dysfunctional. Even debates around clown disclose a type of fire and brimstone orthodoxy or dare one say a fundamentalism bordering on religiosity. The paradox is that many participants in The Clown Movement, and theatre and the arts, have a formidable and obvious antagonism towards religion or those who believe in some form of 'God'.

It seems that sometimes the words 'clown' and 'god' invoke debate. The people involved on most angles of the debates around those words appear to have vested interests in their own claims and we witness that they appear to say their way may be the only way, the only right way, or the only best way.

In the science versus god debate even those on the side of science fail to see the dogma in their camp as they revere Richard Dawkins and David Suzuki as if they were saints or godlike. In the discussions about clown there are arguments about whether the greatest clown was Chaplin or Keaton. Some will say they are not even clowns because their work was not live but in cinema. Then someone might say that Chaplin and Keaton were each live entertainers for 15 years or more (both were born into performing families) before they worked in cinema, thus for some they were still clowns. Either camp might become righteous in their reverence for their preference of one clown over another (Chaplin vs Keaton devotees) or one method or one school or one teacher over another. These things one can witness go beyond preference and go into dogmatic reverence, which rather than opening the scope of the field close down the minds, creativity, imagination, potential and possibilities, debates and discussions within a field.

Dogma in acting, theatre, clown, performing arts

To counter dogma in acting, theatre, clown, or performing arts, I evolved a method that can work with any other method or training. This method can enhance any other method for acting, theatre, clown, or performing arts. It is not that this method is better or best, but that it is different. The difference is the intention to close the gaps in other methods. I think all acting methods are good. It is just that most don't work for most actors. The only method that really works is when an actor/student is 100% engaged with their own unified sense of body, voice, creativity, performance, no matter what the exercise or technique. In the end it is not that any method works, rather it is the participant's commitment and discovery that works. Carlo Mazzone-Clementi, one of my teachers, said that his method "was the art of discovery".

Returning for a moment to the clown-god paradox, some people view those who believe in god with a capital 'G' as being clowns (fools, idiots, or worse terms). Some people active in The Clown Movement believe in the power of clowns to have a godlike power to change the world. As if healing throughout the eons in infinite ways had never existed. This is part of a new 'religion' that I have named "Denialism". In Denialism a person will deny any obvious fact that doesn't support their own social group agenda.

To be sure, clown as a healing agent existed in many cultures and was in some synonymous with a shaman, healer, dancer, priest or priestess. Since the Western world has removed most of its cultural practices, those who 'believe in clown' appear to believe with a fervency of born-again religious zealots. When presented with other thoughts outside of their particular clown dogma, one can suddenly see flaring nostrils, venomous speech, glaring eyes, self-righteous indignation and all the signs of fanatic, fundamentalist religious zealotry.

The instinct of worship

Freud's life research was an attempt to recognise that the invention of religion to worship or revere something larger than the mundane happens in all cultures and all strata of a society. His early book "Totem and Taboo" explained how for one group a particular object may be considered sacred or a totem, whereas for another group that same object is considered forbidden or a 'taboo'. He also explained that the 'totem' can become 'taboo' if certain elements are added or taken away.

As a liberal-minded artist I can be viewed as belonging to the group of Left-wing, Liberal-Minded, Union-supporters, of the Labor or Green parties, artists and intellectuals. It seems in this day and age most of my fellow mob of such folks are non-believers in any 'god', they may however believe in atheism, agnosticism, or their preferred spiritual guru, or their most respected politicians, or they may be followers in the beliefs of socialism or communism. From someone who does not believe in those social options as the ultimate wisdom, one can see those who do believe in their guru or teacher or anti-religious philosophy do so ironically, with a religious veracity with the same tendency as any religious fundamentalist. Sometimes they seem to merge into a group of believers in Denialism.

SECTION 2 - CLOWN
A summarised overview of the history of TCM - "The Clown Movement".

To further enhance the discussions within the fields of acting, theatre, circus and dance with reference to clown, I have coined the term "The Clown Movement" or TCM.

TCM's history is complex and not linear.

TCM has overlapping circles of influence.

TCM's influences are from general categories such as: nation, media, timeframes, and individuals within those categories.

This essay is about 'clown', and some of the same ideas may apply to any of the performing arts and perhaps other fields in society. Clown is a metaphor for discussing intellectual discourse. At the same time there will be thoughts about clown as an art-form. A discourse ideally can include divergent opinions and experiences in a peaceful manner.

Defining 'clown' can be as difficult as defining 'god'. Both words can be defined many different ways depending on one's own perspective or desires. What is interesting is that both words (clown, god) have people adhering to their proscribed beliefs about those words.

Here are a few brief ideas about what I mean by "The Clown Movement". It is a rebirth of clown. In some circles that rebirth, The Clown Movement, is thought to have occurred only since the 1970s. In part due to the 'cultural revolution' of the 1960s/70s. It was during those years when various clown groups started to appear with an agenda to provide an alternative to straight society and straight theatre. However, those groups were preceded by other factors which I will soon mention.

Clown can mean many things professionally speaking and can be interpreted in infinite ways artistically. That it can be so varied professionally and artistically is the greatest aspect of clowning.

For example, clown can imply a red nose and funny costumes, or, no false nose and no clothes. Clown can also be used to imply some altruistic things like the shaman/clown/healer found in some indigenous societies. It can mean the clown doctors or clowns without borders, or other forms of social activism clowning. Clown can mean the professional entertainers found in circus, theatre, festivals, parties. Clown can mean a person in your family who likes to joke, play, or kibbitz. Clown can mean anything. It has a notable history that is too complex to be linear. An interesting aspect is the factors, elements, and people rarely included in discussions about The Clown Movement and its history. I will bring in some of those obscure facts and you can see for yourself that "The Clown Movement" perhaps is perpetually only just getting started.

Here are some angles on the history of clown. There are indigenous clown traditions in most cultures. Some cultures not considered officially 'indigenous' are indigenous in other ways. Some of those have clowns integrated into their social and cultural networks. Carnevale, Feast of Fools, Purim, Mardi Gras are some of the celebrations within religious cultures when people could do the opposite of the norm in social behaviour. In the folk dances of many European cultures there were some clown and slapstick dances. In the Western world there are two cultures which perhaps have the richest variations in clowning. Those extend the definition of clown to its siblings of comedians and clown characters within the theatre. The two cultures English/British clown tradition inclusive of the Irish native humorists and storytellers, and the Jewish culture within its 1000 year old European traditional humour. A third culture extremely rich in clown is the USA which I will cover in a bit more detail.

Generally speaking those cultures English, British, Irish, Jewish for example, are not officially considered 'indigenous' with a capital 'I'. However, even until the 1950s England (like most European nations) had absolutely clear and distinct regional indigenous cultures that included complete dialects, songs, dances, foods and festivals that were part of the local folk culture. They may not have been Aboriginal peoples but the were indigenous. Into the 1960s the west coast of Ireland was still fluent in native language as were the northern Scots, and the Welsh were speaking Welsh.

In France and Italy also, regional dialects were so different as to constitute different languages/cultures/people.

In the Jewish culture there was the wedding clown, called a 'badchen', who was expert in verbal wit combined with improvisation on sacred texts mixed with song, music, sometimes juggling, acrobatics, dance; there were the Purim Schpielers; Klezmer bands which often hand 'tumlers' or comedians; some Hassidic rabbis had an associated fool or 'naar'; and there were various fools in their oral story telling traditions. Such fools were not the schpielers, naars, badchens, nor tumlers but were called schmendrake, schlemiel, or kuni lemels.

The 'tumlers' were the professional clowns who combined verbal and physical comedy. The tumlers continued until the 1960s in the summer resorts of the Catskills mountains. Once air-conditioning got established the resorts entertainment, including tumlers, flourished in Florida and Las Vegas. Jerry Lewis's father was a tumler in the Catskills as was the father of the great musical star Joel Grey. Lewis and Grey cut their teeth in the Catskills in the 1940s and 50s. That tradition branched away from the Catskills tumlers to people like Henny Youngman, Rodney Dangerfield, Myron Cohen, Marty Allen, Steve Allen, Woody Allen, Phyllis Diller, Joan Rivers, Totie Fields, Jackie Mason, Billy Crystal, Jerry Seinfeld, as well as notable comedy writers Mel Brooks, Steve Allen, Carl Reiner, Neil Simon, and many others.

"The Clown Movement" - TCM

The recent history of Western and Westernised 'clown' that I call "The Clown Movement" is occasionally assumed to have its beginnings in the 1970s in Paris, when in fact that is a minor part of "The Clown Movement". Paris was important decades earlier because of notable professionals working as actors and directors in the new mime/clown rebirth, primarily: Copeau, Decroux, Saint-Denis, Barrault, Marceau, and Tati. However, like artists in other fields such as music, dance, visual arts, these people were not the most influential. It is more that the artists were reflections of other more dynamic events in other fields such as science, technology, war, literature, scholarship, anthropology, physics. Genius may be a phenomenon in which individuals emerge from a much greater movement of time, place, technology, conflicts of ideologies, and discourse of ideas. An example is presented in the book *Constellation of Genius 1922: Modernism Year One* written by Kevin Jackson (2012 Hutchinson Press). That book was given to me by playwright and theatre practitioner Andrew Cowie.

Paris was already steeped in the artistic avant-garde where Cubism emerged by 1910, and where Gertrude Stein wrote many of her 80 experimental theatre pieces. The Paris avant-garde of art and writing was stimulated by Stein. From fervent conversations artists and writers alike were challenging themselves and others. Those included Picasso, Chagall, Calder, Giacometti, James Joyce, Samuel Beckett, Eugene Ionesco, and numerous others.

Earlier the clowns Les Fratellini, were leading lights and inspirations to the world of art, literature, and theatre. Copeau hired Les Fratellini to help teach his theatre and mime students. Copeau's curriculum was broad and included philosophy, Noh Theatre, mask, and much more. His nephew Michel Saint-Denis then combined Copeau's work with Stanslavsky's and created the most successful training that is still the basis of most university programs for actor or theatre education in Western countries including England, USA, Canada, Australia.

Paris was also the city that really launched revolutions caused directly by Russians, in dance (Ballet Russe), music (Stravinsky), theatre (Stanislavsky). art (Chagall). Paris embraced the great clownesse Josephine Baker, famous for her humour, pathos, as well as song and dance. She was also a respected intellectual and activist in social causes.

An expansive view of what a clown can be

The 1960s had already seen an alternative clown in the USA called "Wavy Gravy" based in California and who appeared at rock concerts and protests and happenings of all sorts. He was a social activist who became a clown to develop his activism. There were other types of 'clowns' working as musical bands: The Beatles, the Monkees (originally the cast of a TV show who became a band), Alice Cooper and the theatricality of rock and punk bands were types of musical theatre clowning. At the same time there were tremendously great variants of clowns such as the boxing-poet-activist clown Casius Clay, who changed his name to Muhammad Ali; his one and only banter partner worthy of his dexterous mind was the commentator clown Howard Cosell. There was the nimble spiritual basketball clown Meadowlark Lemon, and the all singing, dancing, chameleon clown Michael Jackson, who so greatly admired two of the few master clowns: Charlie Chaplin and Marcel Marceau.

Around the same time (the late 1960s and early 1970s) there were clown groups forming in numerous other countries such as England, Australia, Czech Republic, Russia, and New Zealand. One of the earliest workshops in clowning in England was held at Oval House in London. But by this time such great clowns as Morecombe & Wise, The Two Ronnies, Peter Cooke and Dudley Moore, and Monty Python were well and truly causing a clown revolution following on from The Goons. The Frost Report was how the two Ronnies (Corbett and Barker) began to work together with an unknown John Cleese. Some of their trio sketches are on youtube. Cleese along with Michael Palin, Eric Idle and Graham Chapman, who became Monty Python, began professionally as comedy writers on David Frost's satire and revue show on TV.

Counter-culture

San Francisco and California had been the counter-culture hotbed and this social activism crossed over with the new comedy, new clown, new vaudeville, and new commedia. With the action around Haight-Ashbury, U.C.Berkley, Esalen Institute and the cultural revolution of the hippies, the 1960s effected even theatre and clown. The Living Theatre was based in NYC while the West Coast yielded Wavy Gravy as the Clown Prince of the cultural revolution. Wavy Gravy was brought to California by Lenny Bruce in 1962. Wavy Gravy formed a group of political activists named The Phurst Church of Phun (The First Church of Fun). He also founded Camp Winnarainbow, a circus camp for all ages and families that continues today. An odd anecdote is that it seems Wavy Gravy as a child used to go on walks with Albert Einstein. Those walks occurred over several months.

In the late 1960s a new West Coast influence in commedia and clown was Carlo Mazzone-Clementi and his wife Jane Hill, and eventually their Dell'arte school. Dell'arte School was initiated in San Francisco when Jane taught across the bay at U.C.Berkley and then finally established in the rural town of Blue Lake in Northern California.

Two groups which are frequently left out of the discussion of "The Clown Movement" and which were established by the early 1970s, were: The Great Salt Lake Mime Troupe (http://theatrex.net/theatre/mt_pt7/gslmt_outline.htm), and The Friends Roadshow (http://theatrex.net/theatre/mt_pt7/friends_international.htm). Both were primarily American groups and were comprised of people who after university, dropped out of the 'system' (capitalism) and were creating their own alternative ways of surviving in the given Western society. Those two troupes performed throughout the USA and Europe and offered workshops as they travelled. Jango Edwards is the one who emerged as the most dominant of those two sibling troupes, but for sure they were collectives of extremely talented people who also were incredible adventurers.

As a fluke of life I saw both troupes one afternoon, first Great Salt Lake Mime Troupe and after a short change over came Friends Roadshow. This was a huge experimental theatre festival in Ann Arbor, Michigan in May 1975. I decided then and there to 'become a clown'. I also met the theatre's counter-culture legends Julian Beck and Richard Schechner at this festival.

On the West and East coasts were also troupes who were more local or regional such as The San Francisco Mime Troupe (a political commedia/clown group), and The Pickle Family Circus (a social activist troupe), both based in San Francisco with tours on the West Coast, and both troupes had an emphasis on clown. The Big Apple was more conservative, but, none the less it was an alternative circus and theatre company based in New York which developed its touring to be less local and more regional with occasional tours nationally.

In 1977 a small theatrical clown circus was begun: The Kit 'n Kaboodle American Theater Company. Founded in California by one of my Dell'arte classmates Gale McNeely along with other classmates Jim Stephenson, Hannah Lomden and Paul Klusterman, they were wonderful clowns and Gale excelled as "Captain Plunge". After they were established, touring California, Oregon, Washington, Idaho, I did two tours with them in 1979 as the clown "Vincenzo Furioso".

Carlo, our teacher named me "Vincenzo". Several years later an Italian man roared when I told him that "Vincenzo" was my clown name. He had already been laughing that I was walking to a clown gig for which I was walking towards but had to ask him, a stranger, for directions. Then he asked if I knew what "Vincenzo' meant, and I didn't, so he laughed with tears coming out of his eyes. Apparently, according to this Italian stranger, a 'Vincenzo' implies a fool. The English use the term "Wally" as a 'name' that implies a fool. In Yiddish such a name was 'Kuni Leml'. Gale added the last name to Vincenzo - thus Vincenzo Furioso.

Another small USA troupe focused on clown was The Royal Lichtenstein 1/4 Ring Circus, established by the early 1970s and toured continuously for decades. Usually as a three-person circus performing on stages, halls and parks of hundreds of university campuses throughout the whole of the USA. Uniquely The Royal Lichtenstein was started by Nick Weber who was a Jesuit Priest. So in a very practical and blatant way this was Nick's pulpit from which he created a unique combination of clown and God if you will. His autobiography was published recently and of late he has taken to working with elderly patients and uses Shakespeare with them.

Clowns scattered wide and far and varied

Canada had the TV show *Kids in the Hall* and England had *The Young Ones* and earlier, Australia had *The Auntie Jack Show*. All three were indeed forms of clown shows. More traditional clowns also existed in Australia including: Zig & Zag; Daddy Longlegs; Theo Zaccini was in Ashton's Circus; Edgleys had begun to bring the Moscow Circus with Yuri Nikulin as the star clown; at the same period the Australian Dougie Ashton was a clown in Ringling Circus. Gary Grant emerged as the long standing clown in Ashtons. I last saw him performing about 2013 when he was about 80 years old, he's a truly hilarious clown!!!! The Ashton family has 3 circuses and one of them, married with the Rodrigus family of Brazil, have a daughter who is a fabulous clown and juggler. Lennon family also have three touring circuses. One is *Stardust* with four fab clowns led by Matthew Ezekiel Smith, Lee, a roustabout who doubles by clowning in drag, and the M.C. who plays the role of Monsieur Loyal for the clown acts. They are fantastic fast and funny clowns. *Lennons* currently run The Great Moscow Circus with its three fantastic clowns: Matthew de Goldi as "ZoBo the Clown", Rafael Nino, Jr, and Ashley Brophy. Nino the Clown is 6th generation circus, and Ashley is the son from the famous Brophy Boxing Tent touring show. Tim Caldwell was the long time clown in Circus Oz but in its original form it was like a clown troupe. Two of the outstanding clowns within Oz's later incarnation were Nicci Wilks, and, Flip Kammerer who had to be one of the greatest female slapstick clowns.

Queensland, Australia though, has had some of the most outstanding clowns such as Amanda-Lyn Pearson and her partners as "The Crackup Sisters" shows touring throughout the state; as well as Annie Lee and The Kransky Sisters; Mark Winmill and his colleagues Fez and brother Natano are also wonderful clowns. Last but not least from Queensland, are the most divine ratbag clowns in the world Wacko & Blotto. There is Jester the Clown entertaining and bring joy into homes and events, and Jane Barber-Lacey who is a creative wizard clowning in aged-care facilities. Jane is a Graduate of RADA, and former touring actress in the UK now longtime Queenslander and excelled as "Zophtie the Green Clown" in "Chaplin's Eye". Also in Australia another outstanding clown is Mr. Snotbottom who is surely one of the funniest. Clare Bartholomew and Daniel Tobias have worked together as a fab team. Maryke de Castillo of The Tutti Fruiti had for years one of the greatest street clown duet clown shows with their comedy 'water skiing' act. Penny Lowther was her longtime partner in that act and both are excelling in solo clown work again. Flloyd Kennedy and her clown "Bessie" are emerging via the gentle show "Yes, Because" about the 7 or so stages of being a woman. Gentle, or family, or general public shows such as: "Yes, Because", The Crackup Sisters, Mr Snotbottom, Jane Barber-Lacey, Jester the Clown, Slava, Clownen Manne, or Sam Starr who specialises in birthday parties, should all be applauded for what they bring to the public.

Return to radical clown history

In the 1950s the Beat Poets who were a form of intellectual clowns began in Venice, California and later shifted to San Francisco. One of their headliners was Jack Kerouac who wrote *On The Road* which certainly spurred on the cultural revolution. California was a place where 'things were happening' on so many social, cultural and creative levels including seeming opposites of the Esalen Institute and the New College of San Francisco with its mime course.

The San Francisco Mime Troupe was the primary alternative professional troupe out of which two members created Pickle Family CIrcus. Those two were Peggy Snyder and Larry Pisoni. Where the mime troupe focused on active politics and modern commedia, the Pickles were more social activists and there was an emphasis on clown led by the incredibly skilled and artistic clown Lawrence 'Lorenzo Pickle' Pisoni, who then teamed with Geoff Hoyle and Bill Irwin. Irwin's then wife or partner, Kimi Okada, was one of Pickle's and Bill's secret weapons. Kimi excelled in theatrical and comical choreography. From the influence of the Mime Troupe and Pickles another fine group formed: Make-s-Circus.

Okada was an outstanding performer herself who had a profoundly mesmerising clown presence. Kimi and Bill met at Oberon College. Bill studied for several years with Herbert Blau and when Blau transferred from a university in California to Oberon, Bill stayed with this master theatre teacher and was part of Blau's troupe, *Kraken,* along with fellow student Julie Taymor. Blau is the person who brought plays such as Waiting For Godot to the USA. So somewhere in Blau's mind, who was one of the most brilliant scholars in world theatre, there was also room for clown albeit via absurdist writers. Blau's acting approach combined intellectual & physical training. On the physical end he preferred Tai Chi as one of the keys to Kraken's experiments.

In San Francisco there was also a wild troupe called *The Angels of Light*. I trained in acrobatics with them and was soon invited to join their troupe. I sat in on the first meeting discussing their new show and that discussion was wild. I said thanks but no thanks. Whereas other groups in San Francisco were professional clown troupes, The Angels of Light were like a living clown troupe 24/7. This is where the New Zealand eccentric theatre maker Warwick Broadhead learned his craft.

In New Zealand one of the first alternative clown-theatre groups was *Red Mole*. They preceded the other great Kiwi teams of *The Topp Twins* and *Flight of the Concords*. But even preceding Red Mole were two unique clowns, Fred Dagg (John Clarke), and The Wizard of Christchurch. Billy T. James was like Clarke, a comedian/clown. There were non-theatre clowns such as circus clown Russel Middlebrook, known by his two characters "Byko" and "Madame Fifi". Middlebrook was New Zealand's original highly skilled and contemporary clown from the 1940s until the early 1980s when I first saw him perform in *Ridgeways Circus*.

The mime/clown Michael "River" Lynch took his clown and comedy to every small town in New Zealand and taught workshops in mime, juggling, and clown. He brought me to NZ in 1981 to take the clown training further. By this time The Topp Twins were starting to excel. In the early 1980s in New Zealand in Her Majesty's Theatre, I was able to see the most exemplary clowns perform their own concert theatre solos: Spike Milligan, Rowan Atkinson, and Barrie Humphries. There were a small variety of clowns in New Zealand then, including the wonderful Two Englishmen: Jonathon Acorn and Dave Sheridan. Female clowns besides The Topp Twins were: Debbie Wallingford who partnered Acorn, and Barbara Doherty who partnered me as "Heroes, Regulars, and Jerks". At this time the most skilled clown other than Middlebrook was "Crunchie the Clown" (Peter Newberry?).

Coast to coast clowns

San Francisco's North Beach District had been the home of new comedy, radically so from people such as Lenny Bruce, Phyllis Diller, Mort Saul, iconoclast politically incorrect comedians reinventing comedy with direct attacks on the status quo of society as well as the status quo of comedy. Later more physical comedians such as Steve Martin and Robin Williams were able to pursue their creativity that changed clowning and comedy forever in a similar way as did Monty Python. Robert Shields, perhaps the greatest street mime ever, was in San Francisco already, and teaming with Yarnell to create their own TV show. Sam Shepherd was churning out plays creating a new theatre of dark clowns in the tradition of Beckett, Brecht, and Valentin, with characters who were underclass folks. This city's creative energy eventually commissioned Tony Kushner's first play *Angels in America* at the alternative Eureka Theater of San Francisco. That is where I was part of four clown theatre shows including my own "A Clown Show" solo and collective show "Zealous Zanies". The first show I was in there, "Parachute", was created by Frank Daily a profound true urban clown.

By this time the New Age Movement had taken root with San Francisco as its mecca. So there were all types of yoga, meditation, healing, health food, martial arts, and alternative living being developed that changed every major city's lifestyle in the Western World. So 'clown' was only a small but useful part of a changing society and San Francisco and California were central to those.

At the same time the theatre and acting teacher Jane Hill and her husband who was expert in commedia, mime, clown, Carlo Mazzone-Clementi, relocated to the Bay Area. Jane taught at U.C. Berkley that happened also to be the main campus for counter-culture revolution. Soon Jane and Carlo sought a way of 'retreat to advance' as Carlo worded it, and they headed for the hills of Humboldt County. There they co-founded the Dell'arte School and connected with the great Joan Schirle, who was the key triumvirate of Dell'arte.

On the other coast were the developments of The Big Apple Circus in NYC and Tony Montanaro's vision of clown, mime, and commedia called *Celebration Barn*. The Bread and Puppet Theatre had its own take on 'clown' and physical theatre.

In Chicago one of the world's greatest teachers of improvisation and theatre Viola Spolin had developed work that could easily improve most clown 'trainings'. Out of her work a new clown/commedia/comedy energy gestated to form *Second City*!!!

In the north, in Canada, there was an extraordinary clown duet called Simon & Schuster. They worked mainly on TV and I saw them numerous times on USA TV shows such as the Ed Sullivan show. Ed Sullivan also hosted Oleg Popov and the Moscow Circus annually, as well as Johny Puleo and His Harmoncats, a musical slapstick ensemble that at times included one of the greatest of modern clowns, George Carl. The closest clowns to Simon & Schuster that the USA had were The Smother's Brothers who did play live but also had their own TV show. I'll come back to TV clowns of which the USA was host to the most abundant and varied.

The sources of "The Clown Movement"

However, all of these clowns were all preceded by various professional clowns, what some people might say were 'real' clowns, the circus clowns. Red Skelton and Joe E. Brown had been circus clowns. The Ringling Brothers' Barnum & Bailey Circus saw that its old clowns were dying or at least ageing and getting less active. There was an experiment to have a clown school run by RBBB in 1967 led by my original clown teacher Danny Chapman. But, according to the official story the RBBB Clown College started in 1968 which is when it was formally setup and well organised by Bill Ballentine. By 1975 Clown College was taking in 50 students for its very intense 8-weeks round-the-clock immersion into clown and circus. About half of those people were then offered a 2-years contract as Apprentices touring in one of the huge RBBB circuses either the Red Unit or the Blue Unit as they were named. As a side note, there was a significant event in the influences of "The Clown Movement". In 1966 the U.S. Postal Service launched a postage stamp of the great circus clown, Lou Jacobs, thus a clown became a national icon. What this indicates is that clowning was well and truly established and respected in the USA by 1966.

The renowned Moscow Circus School started in 1927 as part of the Soviet propaganda machine which used the arts for its own purposes as did the

CIA with its funding of American artists after WWII. In the CCCP/USSR, Karandesh was the most notable clown in that period and presumably the school also trained clowns shortly after opening. Certainly by the 1960s Moscow had a special program for clowns. Popov was one graduate of the school who became a revered and extremely skilled circus clown. He would have graduated in the 1940s. In the 1960s Slava Polunin began to study mime where he met Nicolai and this led to them establishing a clown theatre troupe *Licedi*.

A few key and potent influences in The Clown Movement - IJA, Marcel Marceau, Les Enfants du Paradis, Jacques Tati

In 1947 a clown named Art Jennings helped form the influential IJA (International Jugglers Association). This was to function similar to the magician conventions in the USA for the purpose of trading professional information and to network professionally and socially. TV had not yet come in to fruition but the musical movies were flourishing and they included novelty acts within their stories.

In 1947 several important factors in the development of clown occurred in Paris. Three premieres: Marcel Marceau's solo show; Jacques Tati's first clown movie; the film about a sad clown *Les Enfants du Paradis*, were all released in 1947. Most significant was Marcel Marceau who began to perform publicly as a mime and a clown with immediate success which took him on a one-year performing tour in Italy, with his stage assistant bringing the sign titles for each of Marceau's mime pieces. The assistant was Carlo Mazzone-Clementi, and each sign title was accompanied by an instant encapsulation of Marceau's sketch to follow. In the second half of the program Marceau performed as his clown character "Bip". Generally speaking for the next nearly 60 years Marceau performed as "Bip" in the second half. Marceau had an effect on the public's imagination like Cirque du Soleil had nearly 40 years later. The Paris *rediscovery* so to speak, of clown, mime, and commedia was in gear.

Film, vaudeville, Pantomime, Music Hall - sources of TCM

The film industry had a large body of circus films which of course also had clowns as part of the stories. To mention a few: The Greatest Show on Earth, Sawdust & Tinsel (Ingmar Bergman), films of Nils Poppe, and Fellini's I Clowns. Decades before however, the Soviet directors such as Meyerhold, Vahktangov, and Tairov, had their theatres rebirthing mime, clown, and commedia in Moscow.

Before that the English Music Hall, Pantomimes, and Variety were all flourishing with their own variants of mime, clown, and commedia (*pantomime* as they called it). One of the central characters in Pantomime was named "Clown". The famous Pantomime Theatre in Copenhagen's Tivoli has been playing their form of mime, clown, and commedia since the early 1800s. The main character of their Pantomime at The Tivoli is the clown "Perrot". Even that was pre-dated marginally by the deer park Baaken which also has a "Perrot" in the same guise and interpretation though he performs solo.

The USA of course had one of the richest traditions in its own way of combining mime-clown-commedia as established by the founder of the *Keystone Kops*, Mack Sennett, who was a Quebecoise-Canadian. This was the birth of Hollywood's vast array of clowns including the most notable ones: Charlie Chaplin, Buster Keaton, Fatty Arbuckle and the many women who clowned with them: Mabel Normand, Edna Purviance, Georia Hale, Merna Kennedy, Virginia Cherrill, Paulette Goddard, Martha Raye, Claire Bloom, and Dawn Addams. Harold Lloyd, Snub Pollard, Charlie Chase, Laurel & Hardy, The Marx Brothers, W.C.Fields, Mae West, and The Three Stooges, were all derivatives of that same combination of mime-clown-commedia without any of the archaic restrictions; they were the most contemporary clowns already in the 1920s and 1930s.

As part of the process to use the arts to revitalise the citizens in the USA during the Depression, acrobatics and clowning was taught in an advanced, creative and technical way in the YMCA. L.L. McClow created the elaborate curriculum and codified it in the book *Tumbling Illustrated* published in 1931. I got this book in 1976 and started to teach myself as many of the tricks and combinations as I could without killing myself in the process. In 1984 when I was performing a duet circus clown act, I saw another team perform many of the advanced tricks from that book. We met and became friends. They were the original "Price & McCoy" - Terrence Price and Tim Freeman who had been trained by Cletus Ball. Clete is the world master of Australian Knockabout which is Australia's own clown art form based on an arduous acrobatic and tumbling skill level. Terry Price took me to meet his teacher Clete, who began to train me in Knockabout. Clete is the person "who knows every trick in the book" i.e. in *Tumbling Illustrated* (1931).

The treasure chest of "The Clown Movement" - the influential TV clowns

Of these rich sources of clowning I will briefly list some of the clowns in the USA who had their own TV shows. My generation of clowns was profoundly inspired by those TV clowns. Some of my generation includes: Bill Irwin, Jango Edwards, Avner Eisenberg, Barry Lubin, Larry Pisoni, Joan Mankin, Robin Williams, Steve Martin, and David Shiner in the USA. I can not say that it is true for each of those, but, I can say for most of us, we had 'the best clown school in the world' by watching the American TV clowns.

Not all of us watched these shows, but most of us did regularly get to see on a weekly basis a selection of the following Master Clowns: Red Skelton, Lucille Ball, Jackie Gleason, Soupy Sales, Carol Burnett, Clarabell the Clown, Shari Lewis and "Lambchops", Paul Winchell and "Jerry Mahoney", "Kukla, Fran, and Ollie", Liberace, Dick Van Dyke, Howdy Doody, Sid Caesar, Imogen Coca, Phil Silvers, Groucho Marx, Jack Benny with "Rochester", Martha Raye, and there were many more depending on one's age and if the family had or allowed such viewing. A few other clowns who earlier had their own TV shows include: Milton Berle, Ed Wynn, Buster Keaton, Red Buttons, Ernie Kovacs, Bob Hope, George Gobel, Morey Amsterdam, Jimmy Durante, Martin and Lewis (Dean

QRw2w

Martin and Jerry Lewis had 6 seasons on TV), plus there was the Colgate Comedy Hour.

Kids were not 'couch potatoes' in the 1950s and 60s. No computers, no mobile phones, TV for those allowed was limited to the evenings. Kids were rambunctious, respectful, risk takers and baby boomers. So the clowning one watched spurred some of us into action and antics. "Denis the Menace" may have been another influential show. There were also a variety of TV shows that were actually the showing of short films previously made including: Amos & Andy, Ma and Pa Kettle, The Dead End Kids, The Bowery Boys, The Little Rascals (directed by Hal Roach!!), The Three Stooges as well as the airing of most of the movies of Chaplin, Keaton, Laurel & Hardy (directed by Hal Roach), The Keystone Kops (created by Mack Sennett), Mae West, W.C.Fields, and The Marx Brothers.

Before Kramer (*Seinfeld*), before Pee Wee Herman, before Soupy Sales, there was Pinky Lee!!!! Pinky had been one of the greatest Burlesque clowns also known as comics. He had a TV series: *The Pinky Lee Show*, plus his duet show with a singer. In the 1960s and 1970s he returned to live performances.

Shari Lewis was another type of clown. She worked as puppeteer and ventriloquist mainly on TV for which she received 12 Emmy Awards and was the artist who replaced the long standing *Captain Kangaroo Show* with its resident clown *Clarabell*.

There were in the 1960s and 1970s a variety of then new sitcoms which were basically episodic clown shows such as: F-Troop, MASH, Archie Bunker, The Beverly Hillbillies, Hogan's Heroes, Sergent Bilko, I Dream of Jeanie, Bewitched, The Adams Family and many more. These could be viewed as 'clown' or certainly clown based or physical comedy. There were other types of shows that were variety shows often hosted by singers such as Johnny Cash, and Dinah Shore that frequently had comedians and variety artists as guests, as well as doing sketch comedy with the host and great comedians i.e. clowning together.

There were clowns galore: Richard Pryor, Nipsey Russel, Moms Mabley, Amos & Andy, Ma and Pa Kettle, to name a few. There were numerous birthday party clowns, professionals who focused on children and family entertainment. So it was no surprise that by 1966 Lou Jacobs was honoured with a postage stamp. The Clown Movement was certainly recognised by then. Even Ronald McDonald had a real part to play in TCM!

England of course was an incredible centre of clown, equalled only by the USA. England had Max Wall, Norman Wisdom, Spike Milligan, Peter Sellers, Coco, The Crazy Gang, Monty Python, Peter Cook n Dudley Moore, Ken Dodd, and oodles more. Charlie Chaplin, Stan Laurel, and Bob Hope were also from England.

Clowns from different cultures

So The Clown Movement is to an extreme not from a school, nor a teacher, nor even a particular nation or culture. The Clown Movement I am referring to is generally within the Western nations. This is in part due only to the imperial force of the English speaking world dominated by the British Empire and American global influence. Notably, though the USA is a melting pot and openly hired people from every culture, Lou Jacobs and Otto Greibling were both German artists before they emigrated to the USA. Coco the Clown, who was like England's national clown was from Russia.

I don't believe that there is any such thing as 'the greatest clown'. The closest would have to be Chaplin on so many levels. But there are many people who much prefer Buster Keaton. Then there are those who prefer Laurel & Hardy and others who prefer The Marx Brothers or The Three Stooges or Monty Python. Or who prefer their local clown who performed in their own language such as Yuri Nikulin of Russia, Toto of Italy, Cantinflas of Mexico, Nils Poppe of Sweden, or the array of comedies in Bollywood for example.

In the early 1970s a great clown emerged in Sweden, Manne af Klintberg, whose stage name is Clownen Manne. He had trained in Grotowski's acting method, the mime method of Etienne Decroux taught by Ingemar Lindh; and significantly, in clown with members of the Italian clown family "i Colombiaoni" (there is a video clip of i Colombiaoni teaching slapstick around 1970 for Eugenio Barba's *Odin Teater*). The process Manne was involved with were three groups of acting students following three different paths in theatre. Their retreat hired a hall. Blacked out the windows and each group took an 8 hour section of the day and practiced on their own and explored their own creative impulses. Manne's studio time was with one other actor with similar interests. Each emerged with a solo show - Manne's a clown show. Part of Manne's personal and professional life included Sign Language for the Deaf which he uses in all of his shows including his former TV series'.

Manne emerged as a clown, a great one who focused on children and family entertainment. In the early 1970s he began a series of his own TV shows. In 1975 he performed for the first time in the city parks of Stockholm. He has now performed in those parks for 40 years each summer and for at least a decade has performed with two of his children. Recently he was awarded lifetime support for his achievements in and via clowning. His famous solo show *Min Bror, Min Bror* was performed at least 10,000 times and throughout the whole of Sweden. I met him after Min Bror at the Comedie Teatern in Gronalund in 1979.

A year later in Gronalund, I saw Charlie Rivels perform his solo stage show assisted by his son and daughter who were each about 60 years old. Charlie was 86. After watching his show four days in a row, including the last day of his season, I went backstage to meet him. We chatted briefly and he introduced me to his fiancé. Across the road from Gronalund is the Swedish circus building that was turned into a TV studio. One of the last performances there was a clown festival which was filmed by the Bronnet circus family. That show included solos by Charlie Rivels, George Carl, Joe Jackson Jr, and Fantini. At this time the two sons of Francoise Bronett had evolved to be two wonderful modern circus clowns.

In 1976 two clown books appeared: *Clowns* by John Towsen, and *The World of Clowns* by George Bishop. Those books were preceded by two masterpieces: *The Fool and His Sceptre: A study in clowns and jesters and their audience* by William Willeford, and *The Fool and His Social and Literary History* by Enid Welsford; both books were published in 1968.

Local clowns

Some people have a more favoured, more local clown. Australia is where I call home, though Pittsburgh is my birthplace which I also love. Pittsburgh's local clown was a policeman named Vince who was a traffic cop and who did mime, clown and dance while directing the downtown main traffic intersections. My Father took me to watch him direct traffic a few times. Vince also appeared a few times on TV shows like Candid Camera.

Australia has one of the greatest modern clowns, Barrie Humphries, and many in the profession say he is not a clown. Bert Lahr (the Cowardly Lion in the *Wizard of Oz*) had a son who is a noteworthy drama critic John Lahr. John Lahr wrote a book about Barrie Humphries and considers Humphries the greatest modern clown. I have seen Humphries numerous times live. Utterly incredible. I've seen him as Dame Edna, Sir Les, Lance Boil and Sandy Stone. He possesses a most astonishing rapport with an audience. His longtime Assistant/Manager/Director Ian Tasker was one of the four people who arranged for me to move to Australia. Only recently have two clowns appeared, via TV, to top Humphries legacy. They are Chris Lilley, and Pauly Fenech. Fenech has one of the only 'slapstick' film troupes since the Keystone Kops; a different genre of slapstick of course but an ensemble of broad comedians.

In addition to seeing Humphries live numerous times, I've seen several of the other greatest of Australian clowns in live performances such as: Reg Livermore, Mark Trevorrow (Bob Downe), Mary Coustas (Effie), Wogs Out of Work, Garry McDonald, Sue Ingleton, and Nancye Hayes, all in live performances. One of the greatest clown teams though, is the STC Wharf Revue team of Phil Scott, Jonathon Biggins, Drew Forsythe with their newer muse Mandy Bishop. There is a VERY wide array of other clowns of all types in Australia. Generally speaking only a very few of the 'better' clowns attended a 'clown' or 'physical theatre' school. Instead, most of the best clowns either forged their own path via arduous self-discipline of practice and persistence, and another common beginning for the clowns who excel was to train in a conservative 3 or 4 years acting or theatre program.

Many of the people in Australia who teach clowning have rarely if ever seen the greatest Australian clowns live such as Barrie Humphries, Reg Livermore, Nancy Hayes, Mark Trevorow, STC Wharf Revue inclusive of Mandy Bishop, Matthew Ezekiel Smith, Gary Grant, Amanda-Lyn Pearson etc. There is a huge pool of 'clowns' in Australia within the touring large scale musicals. Many musicals from the USA and England are close to being clown shows albeit all singing, all dancing, all acting. In 2014 I saw *Anything Goes* and it IS a clown show!!! Twenty-two exceptionally funny characters played by the most talented and skilled performers. There is an apathetic crossover of professionals not seeing others' work if it is not in their preferred genres. When I first saw Circus Oz, which at that time (1980) were in their first overseas contract in Holland, they were like a wonderful clown troupe: very physical, very skilled, very funny and eccentric, and eclectic. By the time I met them in 1980 I was already contracted to perform a few months later in their hometown of Melbourne for the Moomba Festival. My solo theatre show, *A Clown's House*, had been playing in Scandinavia, Germany, USA.

The dichotomy of teaching clown and the business of clowning

As many great clowns have found, teaching clown is possible. That means one can teach skills, gags, routines, makeup, history, but teaching someone to be a clown is almost impossible. The person has to 'discover' clowning themselves. Thus Carlo Mazzone-Clementi described his method as "The art of discovery". Most of the so-called clown and physical theatre courses make a lot of money theoretically 'teaching clown'. Really what they teach is how to do exercises and how to please the teacher.

One can teach skills such as juggling, pratfalls, mime, slapstick, makeup, props making, business basics, simple magic or any other performance skill which a clown might call upon. One can teach the history of clown. One can show movies of the great clowns and films of clowns performing in live situations and one can discuss all of those. Unfortunately many clown or related physical theatre courses are forms of socialisation that seem to narrow the learners mind and in some cases even encourage cult-like behaviour.

Some of the more known teachers of clown were clowns for about "half an hour" briefly sometimes 20 or 30 or 40 years ago in the 1970s, usually not with a wide variety of experience, and rarely since. Other clown teachers are top notch professionals but they will almost never give away any of their 'secrets'. Especially, they will almost never tell how very hard they worked when they were very young. The social theorist Pierre Bourdieu explained how important one's early years in family, school, and community deeply affect one's habitus or embodied attributes. One can use all of that personal fodder along with one's inclination to 'become a clown', and to train, practice, work hard and learn about the highs and lows of the business, art, and craft.

Why won't most of the actual professional clowns, who occasionally teach for extra income, tell how very hard they worked? Because their 'students' who are their paying customers will not continue to study (pay). There are a whole range of youngish professionals doing gig after gig but the majority succeeding are very simply skilled crafts people in very nice costumes. So they think they have learned to clown and love saying their teacher was "incredible" or a "master" when in fact it is rather obvious the student has let them self be conned by falling into awe. Many of these young, able, skilled 'clowns' lack a sense of humour. Even more important are they funny? Does a clown have to be funny? No, not unless you choose to be dogmatic and fundamentalist about your definition of clown. Certainly the greater clowns could create tremendous laughter, but, the greater ones could and did also make audiences cry: Chaplin, Keaton, Marceau, Toto, Slava, Theirree to name a few.

I have always respected the hidden clowns, the entertainers - the birthday party clowns. They go into several homes or private celebrations or events each and every weekend and make people happy. They do some skilled things, they do some silly things, they memorise many funny quips which they can quote endlessly; for me they are some of the most real and wonderful clowns. They have forever gone into hospitals to perform, usually around Christmas or Easter, decades before the great Patch Adams began the phenomenon of "clown doctors".

So what has happened, largely due to Patch Adams' creation of a fine altruistic, benevolent, money making and respectable job for clowns, and due to Cirque du Soleil's extraordinary financial and popular global success, is that many more performers saw that one could actually make a living by being a "clown doctor" or by being a clown-like performer in Cirque du Soleil. Thus the abundance of 'clown schools'.

However, behind that form of avarice and capitalism disguised as altruistic empathy is what I call "Clown Culture". "Clown Culture" is the hidden dimension of TCM "The Clown Movement". I think, believe, or imagine, or hope, that people are drawn to participate and learn about clown because they generally either lack a formal culture or because they rejected their own culture as limited or inhibiting or conservative, they lack culture and thus seek it.

Many of the best, talented, skilled, and funniest clowns are not 'officially' seen as clowns. This can include a fine range of comic actors such as Will Farrell, Jack Black, Adam Sandler, Peter Sellers, Dan Ackroyd, "Stuart" and his Mother from MAD TV (portrayed by Michael McDonald and Mo Collins), "Homey D. Clown" (portrayed by Damon Wayans who co-created Living Color), Mike Myers (Austin Powers), and lest we forget two of the greatest "Little Britain" creators and stars Matt Lucas and David Walliams and their team of actors. Previous generations of clowns who were actors included Danny Kaye, Dick van Dyke, and Norman Wisdom.

Most of the Pythons graduated either from Cambridge or Oxford in English, History, or Medicine. John Cleese had been for a period a school teacher in Latin, History, English. One of the most violent ideas in clown teaching has created a myth that a clown should be stupid. Obviously this may be so for a clown character, but a clown that is, the artist/person in the case of the greatest and funniest of clowns are the antithesis of 'stupid'.

Cleese, Pythons, Corbett, Barker, and the creative writers and clowns such as: Norman Lear, Mel Brooks, Woody Allen, Yuri Nikulin, Slava Polunin, James Thierree, and Mary Coustas, are anything but 'stupid'. True, their characters can be naive, dumb, innocent, foolish, idiots and even stupid. However, by saying a 'clown is stupid' or a 'clown is an idiot' has fooled many people into a shutdown of their intellects. Rather than studying clowns they simply perform theatre exercises and games. As Carlo Mazzone-Clementi warned "You can not be a fool to play a fool". The Pythons, Ronnies, Morecombe & Wise, Goons etc, were highly intelligent people and people who engaged with social changes, and problems in society. As Corbett tells in the 'autobiography' of The Two Ronnies in relation to *The Frost Report* where the Two Ronnies first worked with Cleese on weekly episodes "on a different subject - politics, authority, religion, class, the countryside, etc".

One of the greatest theatre minds in the 20th century, Bertolt Brecht, apprenticed a clown for two years. That clown was Karl Valentin, and his partner Liesl Karlstadt were anything but 'stupid'. Samuel Beckett in his black clown masterpiece *Waiting For Godot* has the character Pozzo yell at the ultra fool Lucky "Think!!".

If you truly want to learn about clown and to develop your clown character and career as a clown .... think! In this case the gist of this article is simple: to remind us all to think again about what we think we know or believe about subjects as mundane as clown or as lofty as god or "On the Nature of the Universe" as the ancient writer/thinker Lucretius titled his book written around 55 B.C.

The best chance an actor has to start in the business of theatre is to attend a straight conservatory for acting in which one is taught in the Cartesian framework, divided classes of movement, voice, acting, rehearsal, and performance of plays. Usually these courses are 3 or 4 years with a complete full-time commitment. As mentioned earlier, those programs have their root in the system devised by Copeau's nephew Michel Saint-Denis in the 1930s in France and England, and established later in the USA, Canada, and Australia. I think for most people who want to be a fully professional clown attending a full university program in acting, theatre, dance, or circus will give them some form of stable foundation.

On the other hand, I continue to offer non-degree courses and consciously, openly, mentor those interested in developing their career, to develop a discipline not only of training physically but also of reading, study, and observation, and most importantly, thinking in a fractal or a quantum way. Additionally, I provide a unique and effective warmup process for daily training not only as a clown but as a performing artist and actor who wants to rekindle their career or to develop their own new material. That process is "The Four Articulations for Performing Arts" which I sometimes refer to as "Pushups for Clowns".

Three or four year degrees in acting and theatre programs not specific to clown provide exposure to some other aspects of performance such as voice, dramatic texts, character relationships, movement, and choreography. Along the way or after, they can seek technical books on clown and begin to practice on their own. For those who haven't attended a normal, straight, conservative actor training program which includes classes in the following: Movement, Voice, Acting methods; History of Theatre; Scene Study; Rehearsals and Performance of at least 3 plays per year of study, then you need to 'find a way' of filling in those voids in your general study of acting and performance. In the third paragraph below I offer 7 simple points to consider as a way to begin your own study of clowning.

In 2010 Bill Irwin and I had a chance to catch up on Broadway in NYC for an hour chat. We discussed the subject of teaching clown which he, like most professional clowns, found near impossible because most of the students did not have basics in classical acting. Not to mention a general lack of physical training. As he said to me near the end of our chat "You trained as an actor didn't you? I'm so glad I did." His acting and theatre teacher was Herbert Blau!

Even the so-called clown courses attached to circus schools really are only going to churn out skilled technical performers albeit ones who 'want to be a clown' but in reality are not clowns. Rather, they are skilled performers who choose to also learn something about clown, make a weird character, good costume, choreograph an act and sell it. Still, are they really clowns or more likely people who want to be clowns? The original Moscow Circus School that ran until about 1990 in its original form had weekly lessons in classical acting and classical ballet. The circus students had to read 10 plays per week. TEN!! They had tickets continuously to see theatre of all types including plays, opera, puppetry, and ballet. If they wanted to be a clown or circus artist they had to study classical acting.

What did 'real' clowns ACTUALLY do to learn their craft?

1st - In most cases - first and foremost - they trained physically in anything from dance, sport, gymnastics, or martial arts. Some were simply highly physical as youths and later studied dance, acrobatics, or martial arts.
2nd - they watched many many many films of Chaplin, Keaton, Tati, Toto, Laurel & Hardy, and TV show footage such as that of Lucille Ball, Vivienne Vance, Carol Burnett! They imitated some of those master clowns. They studied the films and tv shows of the great clowns.
3rd - They watched as many live clown shows as they could.
4th - very often they were naturally very funny or weird or prone to playing 'tricks' on people or entertaining people for a laugh or attention during childhood.
5th - they imitated people and the clowns they saw live, or on TV, or in cinema.
6th - they stole any small gag, movement, or trick that they liked and repeated it and 'made it their own' with a twist.
7th - they constructed a short act of a few minutes and found some situation to perform it in. Then they created another short piece of a few minutes and began to perform it etc. For example one of Slava's earliest acts was 'simple' mime of a runner in a competition. It is on youtube. Short and sweet and beautifully done. It was a start.

Samples of outstanding contemporary clowns reinventing the genre

One of the most astounding clowns, besides Slava Polunin, is James Thierree. Now I have already heard clowns and clown teachers say that Slava is not really a clown even though he and his colleagues have created the most successful clown show since Marcel Marceau. Why do clowns and clown teachers choose to say one of the most successful clowns is not a clown? They sit on their so-called 'expertise' and their banal definitions while Slava and previously Marceau could not tour enough to fill the public demand to see these great clown shows. Slava along with his wife, several directors, and a wonderful team of colleagues masterminded over time the phenomenon of Slava's Snow Show. Next to the decades of tours of Marcel Marceau, Slava's show is then the most successful clown show ever. Grock was at his time the most successful and his work overlapped with the arrival of Marceau. Slava was profoundly inspired and influenced by Marceau's show and its success to make people laugh and cry, like the work of the ultra clown Charles Spencer Chaplin. Now the shows of James Theirree are the top demand from his growing public. Other highly successful theatre clowns have been Avner Eisenberg, Bill Irwin, and Dimitri the Swiss clown. The Swiss group *Mummenschanz* was also a type of clown show and tremendously successful in continuous world tours.

It is via fluke, fate, DNA, hard work, authentic talent, and a family circus, in which James Thierree grew up that now we have 'the next greatest phenomenon' in The Clown Movement i.e. the next generation of Chaplins. The most prominent is James, but his parents still tour. One of his Aunts has long had her own theatre company that specialises in comic plays, and James' sister, Aurelie, is equally talented. James and Aurelie's early self-devised shows were directed by their mother, Victoria, who was also the head of design for their unique artistic creations.

A professional anecdote - "Chaplin's Eye"

Slava has already inspired a variety of theatre clowns such as KGB, Licedi, and even one of my own shows *"Chaplin's Eye"* since that was in part inspired by Slava's work. Of course I did my own thing, but the inspirational aspects were for me to return to my silent clown work and to make another of my shows which had 'spiritual' or altruistic themes. Additionally I was at the time in the middle of a six-year period of training and study of the *Suzuki Actor Training Method*. If SATM was yang, then my method was yin. Suzuki's method was strong yet included sensitivity whereas mine is sensitive but includes strong practice. In *"Chaplin's Eye"*, I experimented with combining my method with SATM and with sensibilities I identified with from Slava's show. It was to be an ensemble show. I was testing out the idea of forming a troupe with a show that could allow other actors, dancers, or clowns to take over any of the five roles including mine as "The Ghost of Chaplin".

"Chaplin's Eye" was also to serve as a launch of my traveling school ISAAC. Additionally the idea was to bring Chaplin's name again to the forefront of discussion, education, and training of clowns. I had explained to the actors that I was making the show for those reasons and with that intention and explained that if the show went on long enough then someone may want to take a break or may have other contracts. This is how Snow Show and Cirque du Soleil (CDS) operate.

After a few months of intentional slow development of *"Chaplin's Eye"*, suddenly just a few weeks before the premiere, one night around midnight I got a phone call from Yves Sherrif the Head of Clown Casting for CDS. Yves said that I had been chosen via a video of my general audition 3 years before. I was to be the Lead Character for the new show. It was to start with their normal one-week show development. That timing worked 'fine', but, with not much breathing space. I was to fly in a few days for a one week stay and then return home to Brisbane only a few days later to open *"Chaplin's Eye"*.

The timing worked out for that week in Montreal and to be home in time for a solid premiere of *"Chaplin's Eye"* in Brisbane. However, at CDS, things always change until the show is finally set. The financial principle in CDS is that a show lasts ten years of constant touring to cover the huge expense of creation, touring, and to finally return a huge profit while paying about 140 people's salaries within each show. However, out of the

17 people brought to Montreal for that week of creation, only 1 person actually ended up being in that show called *Kooza*.

Nearly 2 years later I was brought back to CDS to join the show named *Corteo* on a Replacement Contract with a pre-planned end after the last performance of 2007. During that contract's rehearsal I became friends with the clown who had replaced Slava in *Alegria*. That was the phenomenal mime Yuri Medvedev! As the story goes, Slava was in NYC and took a taxi and the driver was fellow mime Yuri. In that ride Slava asked Yuri if he would like to replace him. Better than driving a taxi. Slava and family were with *Alegria* for its first 2 years. Yuri was in nearly 15 years, along with another of the Russian mime/clown 'mafia' Nicolai, who was one of the original Licedei clowns with Slava and Peter. Nicolai is a master of music as well as a qualified opera singer and it was he who suggested they make a clown number to *Blue Canary* around 1980 in St. Petersburg.

Another aspect of teaching clown

Professional clown teaching happens beyond hammering in skills, craft, know-how, 'improvisation' and 'play'; even though each of those topics are some of the elements of clown 'teaching', certainly most, if not each and every highly successful clown focused on the skills, craft, and know-how above improvisation or play. Whereas most clown workshops and even longer trainings offer very little in the areas of skills, craft, and know-how.

A hidden part of clown teaching occurs if the teacher was actually a highly experienced clown. The teacher who was an actual professional clown will often relate first hand anecdotal tales of training, touring, and performing. That is the oral tradition in clowning.

Many clown 'teachers' generally have a limited breadth of actual professional performance experience. Paradoxically, being a fully experienced professional clown does not automatically make one a good teacher, nor a teacher for professionals. Even further we have seen for decades that well-established clown 'teachers' have manipulated the minds of their students to follow some form of clown dogma and fundamentalism usually focused on 'improvisation' or 'play' or 'games'. Another detrimental fallacy in the training of clowns is when the teacher pushes to give or name an actor's 'clown character' much too early. The actor is then stuck for years trying to fulfil an imposed 'character'. Carlo Mazzone-Clementi was honest and direct to us on the first day at his school which at that time offered sequentially 10-weeks courses. He said "You think this is a ten-week course. It is not!! It is a ten-year school." He then explained that most clowns of great significance took 10 to 15 years before the character that they became famous for emerged.

SECTION 3 - god
Clown yields to another discussion.

This article will now transition from that brief discussion of 'clown' and particular areas of concern within The Clown Movement, with a jump to a briefer discussion of how the dogma of clown becomes like a cult, one of many in the modern society, replacing 'god' themes.

There are many clowns with 'a mission'. Nothing new under the sun. As Carlo Mazzone-Clementi said "Nothing is original. Do! Don't worry. Just do.". The 'missions' of clowns are diverse. I don't know Eloise Green personally in any depth, but her street act of a wedding is a spiritual expression - warm, meaningful, hilarious. I do know Amanda-Lyn Pearson and her mission for many years has been to bring love and harmony to the hard working folks of outback and regional Australia - to farmers and those in the associated businesses and lifestyles via her *Crackup Sisters*. The Wau Wau Sisters are certainly two of the worlds greatest female clowns. They are wild and part of their mission is to counter restrictions on personal freedom seemingly and sometimes actually imposed by religious zealots. Finn Johannassen "Klovnurin Bubu" is as dedicated to his understanding and belief and brings a hilarious yet gentle clown to his people and those near and far from the Faroes Islands. He recently extended to film clown story telling of a few biblical tales, on location where events were said to have happened and in some places with archeological proof of such events in Israel. His video clips are only recently released. He has a huge following on youtube. He's a natural clown. Nils Poppe made a film regarding faith and God. As he explained to me, he had his acting teacher play God. The acting teacher was like a surrogate Father to Poppe. Poppe also played The Fool in one of Ingmar Bergman's masterpiece films and played a priest in another film. As Poppe explained to me - he was an Atheist. Sometimes the outward labels of Atheist, Agnostic, Religious are not at all far apart except with particular obvious outward differences. It appears to me that 'inside' all are zealots for their own fundamentalist beliefs.

We live in an exciting time when the Science vs God debate (sometimes referred to as Science vs Religion Debate) is one of the healthiest discussions about 'WTF' or 'What's it all about'?. This depends on your perspective and as mentioned to me today by a young colleague educated in the History of Science - many of the current debates have their roots in a Victorian way of thinking. The Victorians asked questions pertinent to the Victorian era. This is the subject of the book *Victorian Anthropology* (George Stocking - 1991)that explains our ways of thinking on many issues in society may be stuck in Victorian England. This can be seen to be so when analysing both Right and Left Wing politics today. It's as if we are in Dickensian times on both sides.

The Science vs God debate may also be harmoniously dealt with by a simple adage that Science is about the "How of existence" and the "God" is the "Why of existence". I enjoy the debate because it challenges both sides and you can see this by your own reaction right now while you read this. Your own drama is occurring inside your head which ever side of the debate you favour.

In the past, including the fervent Victorian era, many or perhaps most of the scientists were also people of faith or religious people, or people who were educated and faithful within a structured religion. Others of course rejected religion sometimes for personal, logical or private reasons. Some rejected the concept of God, or at least rejected the idea that there is a single, particular all-knowing being who was capable of actually listening and responded to ones pleadings, needs, or demands. Understandably.

Sir Isaac Newtown was a believer in faith. As part of that he became fluent in Hebrew to understand what the books of the Torah actually said, and further, what they actually meant. He searched greater understanding about the world hidden in story telling. Indigenous people use stories to store their community's knowledge about herbs, plants, husbandry, seasons, and elements which led to pure science that we know today.

Indigenous societies also have a very clear moral code. Incredibly this is openly discussed in the beginning chapters of the book *Totem and Taboo*. Most ancient communities had already found harmony of the Science vs God debate albeit sometimes simultaneously with other unscientific beliefs.

Darwin, and most of his associates and competitors were people of faith, i.e. full believing religious practitioners. Ironically, yet not surprisingly, Richard Dawkins was raised and educated within a fully religious family and upbringing. So, paradoxically, not only did he reject religion, God, faith etc, but somehow it is likely that the mental and imaginative training of bible and study of ethics may have influenced him to develop his scientific imagination. That is plausible. Even the creators of the comedy film *Life of Brian* were steeped in an intellectual training based upon Biblical discourse. There is a fantastic discussion on this subject with two of the Pythons and two pastors on youtube discussing *Life of Brian*.

We in the modern Western nations believe we live in highly secular time. That is being in denial and excluding the 2 billion Christians including Catholics, and excluding the 2 billion practicing Muslims, and 1 billion or so practicing Hindus, and the multi-million practicing Buddhists, and multi millions of Indigenous people who have their own religion.

I propose that there is, metaphorically speaking, a secular religion albeit one that rejects God but has deified its own 'saints' such as: Darwin and Dawkins; Chomsky and Trotsky; Lenin and Lennon; Marx and Mao; Brand and Branson; Pilger and Pizza. If you get my drift? This secular religion has developed its own rites and rituals which includes highly capable, intelligent, savvy, astute and successful hipsters with their obligatory beards and/or tattoos and piercings. Other Secularists worship via their own politically correct, secular religious fervour for partying or artistic expression.

Why clown? Shakespeare used images of 'actors', players to represent humans and humanity. The clown is a more essentialised symbol of a human. In a sense Krishna, Buddha, Moses, Jesus, Mohammed, Oedipus, Lady Di, can be seen as forms of 'clowns' i.e. humans (be they mythical or real) who symbolise humanity or Everyman as the Medieval playwrights devised it.

I am writing to offer or perhaps to request rethinking one's own beliefs about clown. To do that I have offered some of my own thoughts, experiences, understandings, beliefs, dreams, hopes, and considerations about clown and what it is and what it can be.

Again lest we forget the warning about adhering to one's own beliefs, about anything including clown, in a dogmatic and fundamentalist way, may as it does in some cases become a cult. Even clown cults have their own taboos and totems, and their own myopic inability to see the whole 'truth' about The Clown Movement. Clown becomes your religion even though you may claim to be anti-religious. As mentioned at the beginning of this article there are two literary warnings from the story of The Emperor's New Clothes and the myth of The Worship of the Golden Calf.

Part of my own interest in clown is that the phenomenon of The Clown Movement like art, theatre, music, literature, and scholarly research, is a psychological replacement for the absence of religion, ritual, rites and rites of passage. For some, clown is their religion and is dogmatic and fundamentalist in practice. My specific interest in these areas I have termed "Clown Culture". This reflects my theory or idea that underneath The Clown Movement is the use of clown to fill in the gap left by a lack of meaningful ritual and rites in ones life. That may imply a void of religious practice as well, but not necessarily so. There is also a community and social gap where previously cultural practices existed even in the Western nations which included folk or cultural dance, song, food, and notable seasonal festivities. Those included all of the Indigenous practices of pre-religious cultures and included celebrations for the change in seasons, new and full moons, and the two seasonal solstices.

The 'problem', as I see it, is that even a topic as secular and safe such as clown or the arts has become as fundamentalist as the religions which so many of the secular, leftwing, liberal minded folks criticise. So in reality, the 'problem' is not religion but the human tendency towards fundamentalism which seems to be a glitch in the human psychology.

Freud loved jokes, that was one of many sides to his complex personality. His spiritual instincts led him to attempt to explain or understand why every culture has 'religious' impulses to create practices that include specifically totems and taboos (The Hidden Freud published in 2015). In The Clown Movement 'totem and taboo' operates when one clown or one type of clown is revered and others are reviled.

I propose we try to understand or even just think about the underlying human condition of a need to 'worship' either emperors with nothing on or to 'worship' something of our own design. This applies to any field of human activity including clown where there is an observable tendency to make a totem of some clown, or way of clown, or method of clown, and the need to revile or make a taboo of some clown, or way of clown, or method of clown. Clowns en masse are no more harmonious than gatherings of scientists, scholars, or theologians.

Perhaps by making our own thoughts transparent even to ourself, perhaps The Clown Movement participants can have a meaningful re-evolution within the 'community' (or communities). Jacques Copeau, who was one of the people who initiated the original modern stream of The Clown Movement, was already creating a complete education and curriculum that included subjects of health, movement, clown, mime, and Noh Theatre.

My M.A. Thesis was examining the pure scientific nature of the body in performance in its most essential way, of the body in space. Further I reduced that to its core of energy in the bio "The Body of the Actor in the Space of the Theatre".

There is no conclusion. There is only further discussion. Let the discourse begin.

CHAPTER 8

SHAKESPEARE BITS

The following articles appeared originally on my blog ACTOR-CLOWN-ACTING

ARTICLE 1

THE QUICK WAY TO IMPROVE MOST ENGLISH SPEAKING SHAKESPEARE PRODUCTIONS.

For the purposes of improving English language productions which are understandably rooted in the words I am providing: a) a list of words which actors habitually point on b) suggest that if one does not point on those words then one must find the appropriate body language before/during/after those particular words are spoken.

To begin, here are a few ideas and observations, followed by a few practical principles which can assist at any point in any rehearsal, production, or training.

IDEAS AND OBSERVATIONS

I like to see Shakespeare plays performed in any language including English. Numerous times I have been amazed at the quality of foreign language professional productions, yet surprisingly occasionally disappointed by many English language professional productions.

Could it be that something in the language, or more likely the use of English, restricts many English language productions of Shakespeare? Perhaps the ingrained reverence for Shakespeare's richness is what actually inhibits many directors and actors in the English speaking theatre environment? Not always, of course. Often in the weaker productions the actors are just as well trained and talented as they are in the stronger productions. This paradox seems true in the UK, in England, Australia, NZ, and the USA, even in many national level companies.

Of course I can give examples of excellent English speaking productions which for some reason have tended to account for the pitfalls which I list below. For example, I have seen three excellent productions recently directed by Gregory Doran at the RSC. Yet, I have seen several productions of Shakespeare recently, which were notably weaker and which were subject to the pitfalls I list below.

Here I will provide very direct, simple suggestions that can improve virtually any English speaking production of Shakespeare at any point in its rehearsal or performance or touring season.

In fact anyone can read the pitfalls I list, get a copy of productions most available on DVD or even scenes from many professional productions found on youtube, and within the first few minutes it is quite obvious what I point out below is observable and true.

If you experiment with or use the ideas I list, please acknowledge where the list or points are from.

If you experiment or use the ideas perhaps you can let me know the results via iraseid@gmail.com

THE PRACTICAL PRINCIPLES ENDING WITH TWO EXERCISES IN VIDEO DEMONSTRATION

Although it is easy for me to observe and point out these particular pitfalls, the solution as I mention within the notes below takes a renewed effort by each actor and director, as well as the teachers of text, speech, and acting of Shakespeare's works.

- Each actor needs to stop generic gestures such as pointing to another actor, for example, on the word "you". Why? First the author has already written the word 'you' so the actor must speak the word 'you'. Additionally the actor speaking 'you' is very likely already looking at the actor/character to whom the word 'you' is intended. Thus, in - most instances - the audience does not need a further clarification via gesturing.
- One's gestures do not have to be a literal embodiment of the word spoken. So when speaking the word 'you', for example, rather than the habitual norm in many English speaking productions to point when saying 'you' one could choose other more effective actions such as: a nod, or a shrug of the shoulders, or turn away, or stomp one's foot, or lean forward, or raise one's eyebrows.
- Do anything except point on words such as 'you'. If the actor does not point on 'you' (or the other particular pitfall words provided below) then the actor has to face the problem of what to do, physically, in terms of body language to express the inner monologue (so to speak) of the character.
- Speaking of character, most of Shakespeare's characters do anything to get what they want and they will act or deceive or seduce or antagonise the other characters.
- The Shakespearian actor needs to be: exploratory, explicitly physical, a playful drama queen, wickedly provocative to oneself, to the director, and with one's fellow player. "I know thou wilt say 'Ay'... I'll frown, and be perverse, and say thee nay" (Romeo and Juliet Act II). A Shakespearian actor needs to be willing to frown, be perverse (contrary), pout, yell, shrug, do a quick jig for joy, glare, stare, turn ones back on a fellow player/character, misbehave, take offence, show shock or remorse, plead, beg, be coy, cantankerous, obstreperous, be goofy, flare one's nostrils, dilate one's pupils, step back startled, or gasp for example.
- One must drive the text through to the end of sentences in particular, as well as drive through to the end of phrases, and to the

end of the lines in verse work. One has to learn and be sensitive to whether sentence, phrase, or line end takes priority in each moment of speaking. Some will say that each section of text has specific renderings of those priorities, however, that is still relative to the actor. The variations depend upon the actor's breathing, and their interpretation of the text at any given moment, and, in any particular performance. Much of a text can be mechanically resolved but to enliven the theatre one still needs to involve a measure of spontaneity. In "The Lee Strasberg Notes", Strasberg explains that the only thing he added to the Stanislavsky System was spontaneity. Vahktangov got his understanding of spontaneity and the importance of gesture, and the hands when he directed *The Dybbuk*. In the ideal a Shakespearean actor is also a player.

- In a practical sense some production choices usually need to be taken well in advance so that the costume, props, sound, set designers can have materials ready in time for dress rehearsals. None the less, Shakespeare's texts and dramatic intrigues are completely elastic. However, the actor needs maximum freedom to stretch the parameters of the protocol definitions of texts and characters. However, actors, due to their trainings and experience with directors limited by time constraints, cut back the freedom/exploration/play and soon the professional actor learns to cut back themselves before a director has a chance. Some directors understand to push and provoke and challenge and cajole an actor so that together they can mutually drive out a creative interpretation that neither actor nor director had foreseen. The limited view is due to text analysis or particular angles the director is driving within their overall production's interpretation.

- No matter what the actor does or how the text is interpreted the actor must always integrate: arms, hands, legs, feet, torso, feeling, face, eyes, breathing, voice, imagination and creativity. For this purpose I have defined a key to body/mind integration for acting as: "The Principle of Four"; body, voice, performance, creativity.

- That integration is trained initially via the ISAAC exercises - "The Twist Choreography", and, "The Creative Twist".

- The Twist Choreography exercise is physical, not creatively exploratory, but is choreographed and is not vocal. The Creative Twist exercise while being physical has a structure but not a choreography and is vocal but not verbal.
- The sound/voice element is the final step in that exercise and is intended to assist each actor to accept that the voice actually is physical and comes from the body, and upon hearing the voice then becomes creatively stimulating. Then text/verbal work is integrated to make any text embodied and grounded in the feet, legs, pelvis, torso, arms, hands, face, and eyes whilst one is speaking. Speaking from the body of which the vocal cords and oral dexterity are but one part of acting with complete integration body, voice, imagination and creativity.
- Now returning to the Land of No-No's i.e. what NOT to do which by NOT doing will IMMEDIATELY improve almost any Shakespeare production in English and possibly many other productions in any other language. As indicated by the example earlier, one of the worst no-no's is for an actor to point every time they say the word "you". That does not mean one never points when saying "you". In Shakespeare, occasionally but rarely, it can actually be effective to point when saying "you". It is more rare that on occasions the text may require that the actor MUST point when saying "you". My guess is that "98%" i.e. most of the time "you" is written in a Shakespeare play, one must absolutely not point when saying "you". By pointing to the other actor on "you" you avoid a need to discover what your character is feeling.
- Admittedly one must then find "the damned thing" and find the deeper meaning of the text/character and what body language can be integrated in such a way that the word comes after the body's engagement. Many people and cultures have tried to explain or understand where language comes from. Two notable researchers were the theatre director Peter Brook and the linguist Noam Chomsky.
- In terms of acting, one reads the words on the page first and those words are meant to trigger the actor's intellect, imagination, creativity, feeling, and body. The word is the input to the actor. The

SHAKESPEARE BITS

word needs then a reverse cycle for the actor's output to be real in rehearsal and performance. THE WORD COMES AFTER THE BODY'S ENGAGEMENT. Perhaps thought or feeling precedes an energy moving in one's body that stimulates the spoken word. Perhaps there are three sections of verbal action: a) Thought or Feeling, b) Energy or Desire or Need (impulse) in the body c) Speaking what is thought or felt.

- Besides "you" as a word to almost 'always' avoid a pointing gesture that mimics the word, there are several other words which English speaking actors far too often insist on pointing when those words are spoken. Mind you most actors will think they don't point on those words. Directors are generally ambivalent of noting the over use of pointing. Some directors actually think one is supposed to point on those words. Again sometimes one must point on those words but that is extremely rare. For example if one has a letter in one's hand and is to say "This letter" there is no need to point to the letter. One can simply raise or lower the letter or simply look at the letter at the appropriate timing. However, the one who says "That letter" may need to point or can simply nod towards the letter or take a step towards it. The problem is that most English speaking actors almost ALWAYS point on the following words: you, I, me, my, him, he, she, we, they, them, those, these, that, there, thine, ye, and this.

- Another very useful principle is, generally speaking, the actor should not indicate offstage when discussing a character who is somewhere else other than the present scene. On the other hand of course usually one does have to indicate (ideally without pointing) when one 'sees' a character approaching i.e. before they make their entrance.

- As a counter argument one should not stand for prolonged periods speaking with one's arms dormant and dangling.

- Here are two simple exercises from The Four Articulations each then used with a snippet from Shakespeare https://www.youtube.com/watch?v=a5ORazuNvR4 (from The Four Articulations - The Indian Club Swing Exercise) You can cut and paste each exercise which is purely physical but as a demonstration with a snippet from

Shakespeare how the physicality can be immediately used with ones spontaneity, imagination, and creativity. Below is another exercise with another quick demonstration of the body as a tool for interpreting texts https://www.youtube.com/watch?v=i8Z541X-mPrE (from The Four Articulations - The Jo-Ha-Kyu Exercise). www.iraseid.com / iraseid@gmail.com

The Madness of King Lear with Ira Seidenstein (Fool, director, dramaturge). Review - https://www.ayoungertheatre.com/edinburgh-fringe-review-the-madness-of-king-lear-c-venues-cw-productions

ARTICLE 2

THE SCIENCE OF IMPROVING SHAKESPEARE PRODUCTIONS IN ENGLISH VIA I.S.A.A.C.

One of the central principles and techniques in The Seidenstein Method is the integration of the Body-Voice-Creativity-Performance. The two preliminary exercises are The Twist Choreography #6 movement from Core Mechanics. That 1 minute exercise provides a way for an actor/performer to practice body-mind integration head to toe to finger - while moving, training, rehearsing, or performing. That is 'mechanical' and not yet 'creative'. So the extracted exercise is The Creative Twist that gives the actor a short practice to integrate the body-mind awareness when applied to improvisation and creativity.

One of the central points of these exercises is related to the use of the hands and arms as related to the whole body, the text, and the voice.

In the following clip from The Globe Theatre 2012 production of Henry IV Part 2 I will note 4 moments and the foibles of these very fine, very experienced professional actors.

The minor corrections I suggest are only in pinpointed moments. My view about the whole scene is that it, like the rest of the production, is feeble. Yet this is a VERY high standard production compared to most companies around the English speaking world.

This article is only to point out 4 simple constant habits that the majority of experienced and less so actors have, not matter who directs, no matter which Shakespeare play, no matter which character.

Generally speaking of course.

This all falls into the schism I term "Actors acting like Shakeseparean actors acting like actors acting like Shakespearean actors".

So here are 4 simple moments and a general habit that the majority of actors are subject/guilty of and which most directors overlook or ignore.

The Globe 2012 production of Henry IV, Part 2 Act 3, scene 2 with the characters Shallow and Silence opening it. I did see the 2014 RSC production of the same play and generally speaking the acting and direction was far superior and such habitual errors as I shall point out were much less common in that production.

1). At 1:57 Silence says "This Sir John, cousin, that comes hither anon about soldiers?"
Falstaff does enter 3 minutes later, and he enters after his soldiers. (i.e. Bardolf and his Boy).

So the actor playing Silence in the Globe production indicates with his hand the gesture of 'this' when he says the word "This". However as I like to say to actors "There is no 'this'" i.e. the subject or object to which the text seems to refer is not yet present. At The Globe it is QUITE possible that Sir John (Falstaff) has entered The Globe arena but not yet the stage itself. None the less it is amazing how many actors always or very often indicate while acting in a Shakespeare play every time they say the word "this" or "that" when in fact there is not yet a 'this' nor a 'that' to be seen. IF on the other hand the actor wants the audience to actually look in the direction then the actor needs to be more conscious and needs to also sustain the gesture for 2 or 3 seconds.

2.) 4:57 Bardolph says "... but I will maintain the word with my sword to be a soldier-like word and a word of exceeding good command." The actor puts his hand on his sword by his side for the moment of saying the word "sword". It becomes a distraction and is an indicator that a) the actor is being a literalist and b) does not know what to do with his hands generally. Though he has likely been programmed by his acting teachers, other actors, other directors and the present director "Do not saw the air too much with your hand" to quote Hamlet's speech to the Player(s). Of course he, Hamlet, then goes on to say "Be not too tame neither". IF on the other hand the actor had established his hand on the sword by his side earlier i.e. at the beginning of the present speech which actually begins "Pardon, sir, I have heard the word… ". By placing the hand there at the beginning the word "sword" would not stand out in this short speech about "word" as 'word' is used 4 times in a few sentences and follows the word play immediately preceding (and following) on the word "accommodate" which occurs 7 times in variants within a minute of text. The actors do a moderately good framing of the play on the word "accommodate" and its variants - accommodated and accommodo.

3) 5:36 Falstaff gives Shallow a shallow 'hug' (not). The actor makes what I term "A False Gesture". That is a gesture on stage that has no meaning or value and often the actor only does it half way and then cancels out the body's expression by withdrawing the arm, hand, and gesture before it completed its task.

4) 5:49 Silence wipes his hand. It is an 'idea' that perhaps the actor and director had that the character Silence has not a clean hand to shake hands with Sir John (Falstaff). It is a type of "False Gesture" because we did not see the actor eating with his hands or working with his hands earlier to indicate that his hands were dirty. Or if they thought this would be "A Bit of Comic Business" then something had to be made of it. As it was done it was a type of nervous action of an actor who doesn't know what to do with his hands nor how to integrate his hand and body language. Or he is "Telegraphing" the comic business involved when he does actually shake hands with Sir John (Falstaff). That 'comic business' is "A False Gesture" since neither actor nor director knows how to honour the comic intention.

These are minor quibbles however my point is precisely that it is the minor quibbles that occur hundreds of times in most Shakespeare productions in the English speaking world that I have seen. These minor moments and "False Gestures" for example are indicators of much more gross weaknesses in the actualisation of the text and characters' relationships as told through body language.

https://www.youtube.com/watch?v=V9PsELU9YtQ

Here is a short documentary by a film editor examining the physical work of Robin Williams. He has a question about how did he do what he did. No one can replace Robin Williams' unique genius as a comedian, entertainer, actor. However, there are other ways to see into elements of his ability that one can study and use to improve one's own acting or productions. The editor talks about his use and general use of gestures that he has to observe within the editing suite. https://www.youtube.com/watch?v=I8lQKL-jmoWI&list=TLubYg_m0fGzgUw5lh0w_Y_4Yu89YSs074&index=5

ARTICLE 3

ACTORS COMMENTS ABOUT ANTONY & CLEOPATRA 2013 (My comments are Article 4)

There were 18 actors and one stage manager.
4 of the actors were youths and their drama teacher Ms. Lopes was acting in the production and was co-producer (Punchbug Productions).
Everyone was invited to contribute their thoughts about their own experience and Ms. Lopes was able to write on behalf of the youths.
Below are the comments of those who chose to contribute their thoughts.

First here are comments from a Director **KERRY DWYER** (original member of The Pram Factory, freelance director):

Ira Seidenstein's production of Antony and Cleopatra opened the text to me in ways I had never known before, even though I had studied it closely at school and at university. The actors playing the lead roles found nuances in their relationship that made emotional, intellectual and political sense of their relationship. Cleopatra emerged as a cunning political operator as aware of the intricacies of Machiavellian politics as Antony and their lust only served to sweeten the intrigue. The portrayal of Antony as louche and dissolute opened up many layers of their relationship that I had never seen exposed on stage before. This was a most articulate and detailed portrait of a doomed political affair driven by lust and ambition.

The actors were all very open emotionally, and very expressive physically, and at no time were they overawed by the fact that they were working with the great master's words. Actors in Australia often put on a "Shakespeare" voice, but these actors found their own voice from a close and visceral connection with the text. They allowed the emotional level of the scene free reign to take them where ever the impulse drove them, and as a consequence, their work held a very varied audience in close attention for three hours.

On the opening night, when I saw the production, there were a couple of actors who still had not quite found their way in to the text, but they clearly were working with precision to a deeper connection to the innermost truth of their characters, and would, I am confident, have arrived at a very powerful embodiment of that personage.

The staging was very spare, with screens upstage with several alternative entrances and exits allowing for snappy and fluid scene changes. The actors were dynamic, well-trained and quick to respond physically to the impulses of the scene. Although they were disciplined, at no time was there any sense that they were puppets moving around the stage at the whim of the director. They always moved with purpose and intense focus.

BERYNN SCHWERDT - Antony

I doubt I'll say much that hasn't already been said by brighter people than me. One of the big things for me was how the play keeps upsetting expectations. It is not a tragedy complete, nor a comedy, nor even a tragi-comedy. It discourages an emotional wash for the audience, as each scene trips up what might be anticipated style-wise. We see the great queen and triumvir having a domestic quibble over responsibility and pleasure, with Cleo teasing Antony and Antony playing along to some degree. The first scene is like Who's Afraid of Virginia Woolfe (was pleased to see someone else thought so in that analysis you linked a little while ago), the next A & C scene like Benedick and Beatrice in Much Ado, but far more cutting. Most of the scenes are domestic in nature, referring to the larger world of the Roman Empire. Fulvia's death is mourned for a moment, but used as an argument for the security of Antony's departure from egypt, and later Fulvia's 'garboils' are used as an excuse by Antony. We see that the response to what might otherwise be reflected on as a tragic event is various depending on context. Spek well of the dead? For a moment maybe. And this is but one example of Antony's ignobility - there is no honour in how Fulvia's life and death is used by her husband. And this kind of behaviour mirrors real life. Shakespeare seems to be taking the mask off nobility, calling our attention to the difference between myth and reality, and how and why that separation arises. Cleopatra is described in different ways at different times, from the pomp of her meeting with Antony, her capriciousness of character, and none of these do justice to the character that is, finally realised throughout the play. Public perception and private reality seems to be a strong theme of the play.

I always enjoyed the unlikely humour in Antony's decent to dishonour, even to his botched suicide attempt, on what we know (but he doesn't) is a false pretext. Shakespeare doesn't let us off the hook. The tragedy of Antony is not that he becomes ridiculous, but that he fights against it or doesn't see it. He is unknown to himself, or tries to escape the fact of his decline - as can be seen in the turnaround after the first naval defeat. In the final moments of death, there is a strange nobility in his insistence that he is noble, even when we know he is not. It's not one or the other, but both at odds - a disquieting experience for the viewer, happily. this is the great strength of the play - we are not allowed to settle on an expectation, and thus become more engaged. Cleopatra's death, elsewhere perceived as the great lovers gesture (Romeo and Juliet), is turned into a Brechtian scene with a clown robbing the event of its sentiment. Over and again the rug is pulled out from a comfortable, one note experience of the play, forcing the audience to reconsider their impressions. From what I have read, most productions cant one way or the other, or maybe combine the humour and tragedy, but avoid or overlook the many avenues the play trips down in literary style.

There is an absurdist element to Antony and Cleopatra - another genre that seems to be incorporated, albeit way before its time. All in all, though, I would say that the play does not conform to any particular genre, and defies conventional analysis. It is an intriguing challenge to put on and for an audience to view. The elements themselves are finely done, but they are not consonant to any particular style. Still, the whole piece seems balanced in the playing, which is a tribute, perhaps, to Shakespeare's theatrical instinct as much as his literary skill.
END

BRON LIM
Bron Lim's thoughts on rehearsal and performance experience of Antony and Cleopatra – June 2013 King Street Theatre - Punchbug - Directed by Dr Ira Seidenstein
Alexas, Varrius, Diomedes, Seleucus

Pre-rehearsal influences
Read
Antony and Cleopatra - Arden text & RSC text
Watched
- Steven Pimlott's 2001 RSC production at the Barbican with Frances de la Tour and Alan Bates in the title roles
- Jon Scoffield's 1974 made for television version of the Adrian Noble 1972 RSC production with Richard Johnson and Janet Suzman in the title roles.
- Jonathan Miller's 1981 made for BBC television production with Colin Blakely and Jane Lapatoire In the title roles.
- Morcombe and Wise with Glenda Jackson spoof of the characters of Antony and Cleopatra
- Excerpts of Charlton Heston's 1983 film with Lynn Redgrave and Timothy Dalton in the title roles.
- Excerpts of Warwick University's 2011 production. Directed by Clare Byrne & Joshua Elliott.

I note title roles for identification purposes.
Listened
1963. The Shakespeare Recording Society / Caedmon Records. Anthony Quayle and Pamela Brown in the title roles.

Preparation
I read through the Arden text which was useful for meaning, references and notes on how roles had previously been played.
On receiving the RSC text, I was able to mark up the text according to stresses, making notes of scansion: shared lines, regular vs irregular lines – short and feminine endings, and variance from the Arden text with editing.
Characters
Alexas:
Act 1 Scene 2
The scene opens with Charmian badgering Alexas for the whereabouts of the Soothsayer. After some flattery he relents. This indicates Alexas is privvy to some information which Charmian, Cleopatra's closest confidante, doesn't have access to. As such, he wields some limited power within the court. The dynamic between Alexas, Charmian, Iras and the Soothsayer as servants to the Queen was fluid throughout the rehearsals and performances. We needed to function as a chorus and as individuals. In terms of playing this opening, the shared lines after Charmian's intial speech indicate a speed, which given the right attack could be thrilling. Of the six initial speeches, five of them are shared lines.
Initially, I took the Soothsayer to be a parlour game to Alexas, much as the other characters within the court, however after some review, I realised that it would be stronger to acknowledge that the consequences of the Soothsayer's words would sway Alexas, and that he would have a vested interest in the fates of those around him. He could believe the Soothsayer's words to be absolute. As such, the lines:
Vex not his precience: be attentive
And
Nay, hear him
Bear more urgency and by contrast could heighten the frivolity of Charmian and Iras, whilst giving the Soothsayer more weight. I was toying

with playing a Malvolio character, but I think Alexas is more aware of his standing amongst his "peers and betters". Also, unlike Malvolio, there is more of a knowing sexual predator about him.

Alexas is made fun of in this scene for being a knave. It seems in Charmian's line:

O that I knew this husband which you say must charge his horns with garlands!

that there is some sexual tension between the two of them, with Alexas referring to himself as the adulterer, or at the very least, they are on flirtatious terms.

I made the decision that the vehemence that brings Charmian and Iras' wrath indicated a past sexual history with both of them.

He shrugs off their humiliating prognostications by calling them whores.

I decided Alexas lived by his wits and by keeping his ears open within court. He is an opportunist, eager to be of service to those who could ensure his position.

T S Eliot's The Love Song of J Alfred Prufrock came to mind when unravelling this character:

No! I am not Prince Hamlet, nor was meant to be;
Am an attendant lord, one that will do
To swell a progress, start a scene or two
Advise the prince; no doubt, an easy tool,
Deferential, glad to be of use,
Politic, cautious, and meticulous;
Full of high sentence, but a bit obtuse;
At times, indeed, almost ridiculous—
Almost, at times, the Fool.

The scene's tone changes upon the entrance of Cleopatra. The servants return to their positions as servants.

The Arden places Cleopatra's entrance after Enobarbas remark:

Not he, the queen.

The line is attributed to Charmian in the RSC text.

In retrospect, there was an opportunity for Cleopatra to be in the same disguise as Antony in order to walk about the city, and this is why there is a visual misunderstanding.

Alexas' salutation to the Queen, nine speeches after her entrance, is perfunctory and deferential.
Here, at your service. My lord approaches.
The RSC performance text places the comma after 'Here', unlike the Arden, which runs on. The former allows for a little more personality to emerge. Following on from the 'heel clicks' in a later scene, I inserted them here also, to further express the formality and protocol of meeting with the Queen.
Act 1 Scene 3
We see Alexas briefly in this scene; he is sent on an errand to find Antony. This could be completely unremarkable, however, Ira broke up Cleopatra's lines:
See where his, who's with him, what he does:
I did not send you. If you find him sad,
Say I am dancing; if in mirth, report
That I am sudden sick. Quick, and return.
With each addition to the inital order, Alexas was to leave and return. Upon finding Alexas' costume shoes, I realised they made a very satisfactory sound when clicked together, so this punctuated each of the orders before attempting to leave Cleopatra's room. This routine was repeated in a later scene, in a slightly different way.
Act 1 Scene 5
In this scene Cleopatra is pining for Antony. Alexas enters with news of Antony's departure and is keen to exploit this knowledge to gain favour with the Queen.
He greets Cleopatra in an outlandish fashion:
Cleo: ...With looking on his life
Alex: Sovereign of Egypt, hail!
The shared six syllable lines allow for overlap, or a nice pause to make an entrance, indicating a change of pace.
Alexas is quick to sweet talk the queen, referring to her familiarly with
Last thing he did, dear queen,
This is a short line, and I could have made more of the flattery.
I made the decision that the description of Antony kissing a pearl many times before giving it to Alexas was an outright lie; likewise his following speech. I thought it would be amusing to concoct a story to alleviate

Cleopatra's sadness, whilst furthering Alexas' standing in court. He begins with:

'Good friend', quoth he

Antony's favour would no doubt annoy both Charmian and Iras.

He goes on to describe the precious pearl as signifying a promise to gain kingdoms for Cleopatra to reign over upon Antony's return. This text is exquisite, it makes full repetitive use of plosive p's and is almost entirely regular excepting the change of subject to begin the description of Antony and his horse. Everything is grand about Antony in this speech, including his horse and his horse's neigh. I wanted to indicate this referred grandiosity in my performance style. Ira had me playing out and it reminded me of the Morcombe and Wise sketch I had seen previously. He took this further by referencing Vaudeville, and expressed the need to create a 'turn'. In essence, it was a snippet of a self-contained performance within a performance designed to impress both Cleopatra and the audience. This stylistic reference allowed me to free myself from the desire to be naturalistic.

Cleopatra questions Alexas:

What, was he sad or merry?

This line has only seven syllables. So I allowed myself a pause to make up the ten. This gave me an opportunity to come up with an answer that would not only seem plausible for this non-event, but would also not run the risk of being an answer Cleopatra would detest and thereby punish Alexas.

Conversely, Cleopatra's following question and Alexas' reply:

...Met'st though my posts?

Ay, Madam, twenty several messengers.

Why do you send so thick?

Is met with Cleopatra's ire, showing her changeability. It was also an opportunity to physically allow Cleopatra's superiority over Alexas, which I had the opportunity to punctuate with a Suzuki inspired mini backdown. This routine is immediately repeated by Charmian when she dares to taunt Cleopatra with having previously loved Caesar before meeting with Antony.

The court are shown to be at the mercy of Cleopatra's whim, and the uneasiness brings a underclass solidarity to the servants.

Act 2 Scene 5

In this scene, Alexas has no solo speeches, but it is pivotal to the character. Initially, Alexas is enjoying the intimate surrounding of Cleopatra's inner circle, until the arrival of the messenger bearing news of Antony's marriage to Octavia.

In this scene he witnesses Cleopatra threaten to kill the messenger and sees her hit. I believe it is here that Alexas fully realises the uncertain nature of being associated with this court. Cleopatra's lament:

These hands do lack nobility that they strike
A meaner than myself, since I myself
Have given myself the cause

Does little to ingratiate her to him, as he knows the sincerest words from her mean little when tested.

At the end of the scene, Cleopatra bids Alexas to discover and report on Octavias features. Again, Ira insisted on using the heel click exits after each section of the request:

Go to the fellow, good Alexas, bid him
Report the feature of Octavia: her years,
Her inclination, let him not leave out
The colour of her hair. Bring me word quickly.

Cleopatra recalls Alexas after having left the room completely:

...Bid you Alexas
Bring me word how tall she is.

I found great difficulty in turning and clicking heels up to three times at some points in the text. It became easier with practice, but within the middle of the run, my personal frustration at my own ineptitude led to a revelation of Alexas' frustration with Cleopatra and I allowed the character to crack, and go a little mad with a maniacal laugh on the last bidding. The big question with Alexas was always, why does this man choose to defect,unlike the others within Cleopatras inner sanctum? And I think this breakdown allowed a little foreshadowing to Alexas' revolt.

Act 3 Scene 3

Alexas was cut from this scene due to rehearsal constraints. But his lines in this scene are in defence of the messenger's unwillingness to come before

Cleopatra. He also mentions Herod, whom he later visits on affairs of Antony before defecting and being hanged by Caesar.

Act 4 Scene 2
Again Alexas has no solo lines, but this is the last time we see Alexas before he defects and is hanged by Caesar.
The court are disturbed by Antony's erratic and over-familiar behaviour. When Antony begins to speak of defeat:
Haply you shall not see me more, or if,
A mangled shadow. Perchance tomorrow
You'll serve antoher master. I look on you
As one that takes his leave.
My inner dialogue was urging Alexas to make plans to leave, culminating in him leaving the stage by crossing severally from the rest. In doing so, he notices Enobarbas looking at him as though he may be planning on a similar course of action.

Varrius
Act 2 Scene 1
Varrius is seen once, with only one speech. But his speech is remarkable in that it makes full dramatic use of the caesuras within it:
This is most certain that I shall deliver:
Mark Antony is every hour in Rome
Expected. Since he went from Egypt 'tis
A space for further travel.
The initial line has a feminine ending, indicating a conflict within the following lines.
The following two lines are regular, however in playing out the caesuras, it allowed for an unexpected twist at the beginning of the third line, and an implied revelation in the fourth short line.
I needed a reference for the audience in order to understand Varrius quickly, so I donned a film noir trenchcoat and did my best to affect an indeterminate European accent. Ira took this further by suggesting taking my 'spy acting' to a Pink Panther extreme. I played with this throughout the run, taking it further and pulling it back. Together, with the quick change revelations of text from line to line, informing the absurd pauses

and wariness of Menas when speaking with Pompey, this was a fufilling gem of a character.

Diomedes
Initially when reading Diomedes, I thought he must be a loyal and honourable fellow staying to the end to aid Cleopatra. The text would support this, and all the other versions I've seen and listened to, show this interpretation. It was easy to fall in love with the meter of Diomedes largest speech with its inbuilt dramatic pauses and momentum of sincerity.

Over the course of the rehearsals, it occured to me that maybe it wasn't honour that was keeping him in Cleopatra's court, but a sense of fate similar to that of the Gravedigger in Hamlet. This is crystallised in Cleopatra's line:

...young boys and girls
Are level now with men: the odds is gone
And there is nothing left remarkable
Beneath the visiting moon.

At the time when an empire was crumbling around him, I wanted Diomedes to embody this anarchic notion. So he turned from a young girl in Cleopatra's service to a drunken sot of a guard, neccessarily lower class in order to highlight the levelling nature of the events surrounding everyone. There is no real support in the text for this reading of this character. But there is none to the contrary either. I chose to play Diomedes drunk, bottle in hand, coming to terms with the end of the world as he knows it. Rather than Diomedes simply explaining or sympathising with Antony's situation on finding him mortally wounded, I chose to have him admonishing him or even, for some performances, taunting him. However I alternately played the lines:

...and I am come,
I dread, too late.

As horrified with Antony's situation and being more concerned about the admonishment he would get when he tells Cleopatra the news.

During the following scene, Act 4 Scene 15, Diomedes is bemused and disgusted by the over-the-top reactions of Cleopatra. Bruno Lucia suggested Diomedes be rolling a cigarette during the scene, which I incorporated with a casual delight. Antony's pain-wrecked body was carried across the stage several times according to Cleopatra's whim, and hauling Antony's dead body offstage like a piece of meat further emphasised the anarchic principal of death.

Seleucus
Seleucus is another character who underwent a large character shift throughout the rehearsal period. All of my other characters were indeterminate gender (although I've been referring to them as male throughout this write-up) but Seleucus was the only definite female in my mind. As such I chose a skirt and a tailored jacket, to indicate that she had been treated very well by Cleopatra during her service, and may have enjoyed her station.
She begins with a short line:
Here Madam.
The remaining beats allowed for a hiatus as she was called onto the stage. Originally, I played her as being timid, aware that there was no real way of getting out of this situation alive, in having to confront both Cleopatra and Caesar with her findings of Cleopatra fiddling the books. However, this reading gave nowhere for the character to develop in the short space of time she was onstage. Playing her as a sympathetic character also lessoned the audience's sympathy with Cleopatra as she threatened yet another equivalent of a messenger. So instead,I made Seleucus' admission a brazen attempt to curry favour with Caesar, demanding acknowledgement from him for her sacrifice within Cleopatra's court. The outright contempt Seleucus shows at twisting Cleopatra's own words against herself is astounding:
Cleo ...Let him speak, my lord,
Upon his peril, that I have reserved
To myself nothing. Speak the truth, Seleucus.
Sel Madam,
I had rather seal my lips *than to my peril*
Speak that which is not.
Although urged by Cleopatra to leave earlier, Seleucus remains onstage until Caesar gives permission and some nod of asuurance is given to her safe passage. This is the first time we see a character change their allegience in the prescence of Cleopatra.

In parting
This quartet of characters seem to be unified by notions of loyalty and allegiance. Alexas, although the most intimate with Cleopatra, defects. Varrius garners intelligence for Pompey and is suspicious of everyone surrounding him. Diomedes admonishes Antony for his lack of belief in Cleopatra and his leaving her. However in my interpretation, he is ultimately outside of the loyalty dichotomy. And Seleucus chooses to change sides out of necessity, but also with lashings of joyous self-preservation.

One of the many interesting things working with Ira's acting method, was spotting how each of his warm-up exercises fed into the dynamics of scenes on several levels. How energy moves about the stage and within the bones of the text could be found in the fall or thrust or reach of each of the exercises. I found the natural timings of the swings allowed natural pauses within the text, allowing it to breathe. The problems encountered with achieving a bridge more fully supported from the legs are not unlike the mental exertion required to prop up a particularly demanding piece of text. I have no doubt that being pushed beyond my ability with those darned heel-click turns, allowed a greater understanding of Alexas to come to the fore.

Ultimately, the sense of play I experienced physically, when I allowed it to take me over in front of an audience, was beyond anything I could plan, and I thank Ira for the amazing experience. Thank you!
END

NATALIE LOPES - Charmian
Nat's Thoughts
This project found me. Denby and Berynn came to see 25Eight at the end of 2012 and from that evening grew the plan of Ira to direct them in Ant and Cleo. Ira then brought me into the project as producer and actor.

The relationships between the people involved in the project were varied and interesting. Denby and Berynn were past in relationship. Berynn taught Denby, Brinley and Robert. Ira taught Berynn, myself, Erin and Yiss. Erin and I studied together but had never been cast to act together before this show. Denby and Brendon work together. Bruno and Ira are old friends. Lara and Berynn are siblings nineteen years apart who had never acted together. Four of my current students in high school were in the show. This completed the three generations of theatre.

Wearing my actor/producer/teacher hat during this project was at times complicated and stressful but also greatly rewarding. Each person came to this project with enthusiasm, professionalism and dedication despite a lack of pay. My students grew immensely from the experience, and it was a unique experience for us to do a show together. That may never happen again. I felt a great deal of pressure for the show to be a success as producer. The cast were a joy to work with and I found I wanted to spend more time with each cast member and get to know them. By the end of the run it felt like we still hadn't really scratched the surface.

It was a very quick rehearsal period which in hindsight I would have liked it to be at least four weeks rather than three.

The character of Charmian was at times perplexing. She would say things to others, especially Cleo that Iras and Alexas would not and at times would "obviously" make Cleo look silly. i.e The brave Caesar, the valiant Caesar….

Charmian doesn't let Cleo get away with much in the text but she also knows her place. She doesn't challenge Cleo when Ira's does at the end 'No more…It were for me to throw my….'

Charmian is use to role playing the drama of life with Cleo. Cleo remarks numerous times 'Mark him/her Charmian' or 'Cut my lace Charmian' Is it any wonder that Charmian continues to play along by challenging Cleo to her most dramatic performance of faking her death 'To the monument'. When performing the servant scene where Charmian mimes the news behind Cleo's back I found I was often met with confusion from the audience. Only 2-3 audiences laughed in that scene and seemed to understand the pressure to please Cleo was what motivated it. Sometimes it felt in that scene that the audience didn't want to laugh behind Cleo's back. The previous servant scene they would always laugh a great deal at Cleo's attempts to make the truth not so.

All in all I had a great experience working on this show with the wonderful cast and with Ira as director. I feel I discovered some interesting things about Charmian, but I also would have liked more time to explore the play.
END

YISS MILL – Soothsayer, Mardian, Clown – and accompanying musician interspersed throughout the performance.

I will do my best to express my experience and discovery. Firstly, I think that you are truly an amazing educator and through your direction, taught us all so much. Your direction is very concise and little explanation of why, which I think gave us the opportunity to really think about what you said and discover for ourselves the importance of doing certain things overall and in the context of the play. Personally, I feel that i gained a lot in terms of learning stage craft. I haven't nailed it yet and still have lots to learn but as you say, which I believe "it's all in there, it's all the same thing". I feel that in time and with more experience I will understand this more and derive more from what I have been taught, shown.....

Before going into my characters, I would like to mention Cleopatra. There was much to think about during the production in terms of how the character was portrayed and how I guess one might assume the character should be portrayed. I'll be more specific with one particular scene, Antony dying. "Noblest of men woo't die?" I thought about this line a lot. I guess my uneducated take would be that Cleopatra would be heart broken and would cry these words out in pain, and yet Denby's voice was so "you fucken serious?" I think it really tied the whole character together and made the rest of her make sense this way, after much thought. I think it is really in the text the whole play that this is her personality, even though at first glance it seemed so Romeo and Juliet. (I hope that made sense)

I don't have much to say on the soothsayer. I guess his role calls for a serious dude that can be taken seriously when prophesying the future. But then he grabs Iris' arse. I guess he is in the company of royalty and therefore has a certain boost of confidence on top of the fact that he is a seer. I also felt that he wasn't too awed by royalty or status anyway as a seer would hold himself with an above mundane status. This does come from the text as he is witty with his line " a million" and wont be treated like a servant with his line "I have said". It also shows with his confidence in telling Antony to go back to Egypt. Firstly, he is straight to the point, secondly he is so persistent with his message. It's like; what I'm saying is so real, you better listen to me!

Mardian, the awesome :) I reckon he was such a fun role to play and a real challenge to stay true to the text. But he is referred to a saucy eunuch which doesn't translate exactly but I feel definitely infers that he is sexualised in his mannerism. I received comments from some friends that saw the show along the lines of "you needed to take your shirt off and hump the queen on stage to fulfil some Hollywood porn desires which had nothing to with the play; it's a modern take so you guys chucked that stuff in there" which are things I never thought about before opening night at all. It's all there in the text dummies! Mardian doesn't say much and in the first of his three conversations the queen asks him about his take on sex and he says that he thinks about it. This may mean that he doesn't act sexual at all if the queen needs to ask him, but after getting to know Cleopatra and her drama queen ways, it seems as if she is invoking the topic and what better way to get on topic than getting her saucy eunuch ignited. Otherwise, from the text, Mardian seems subservient and loyal.

As an actor there was much freedom in character, especially with Mardian which allowed to bring out the clown in him, and also the occasional fighting stance'd male ready to protect and take one for the team. Your direction helped me find this in him, getting me involved in Cleopatra's outbursts at times, which at first made no sense to me but quickly sank in and allowed me to find what I should be doing on stage and how I should react (with no text).

The clown, I'm still unsure about. Obviously a lot of innuendo but I wasn't sure how to bring that out. His appearance is short but yet a really important moment, as it is the point in time which makes Cleopatra's suicide an actual reality. Why then a clown? I don't know. What in the text shows him as a clown? I guess the fact that he is a blabber mouth, but still not necessarily a clown so again I don't know. However, old Willie calls him a clown and so more important than understanding the reason for this, is to do the ensemble justice and be a clown. A red nose and colorful wig? Why not? Mardian wears a wig and blows a comically long horn, and hey, even the soothsayer gets to clown about, sorta..But there is something special and much much deeper in this character, but I cant put my finger on it. Having lots of freedom allowed me to try different walks and movements which I thought were clown-like. I read a fair bit about the clown to understand him better but I didn't get much out of it.

Maybe he is called a clown as he represents the thing of disguise; He shows a basket of figs but in reality is delivering asps. A simple view.
END

PAUL MCNALLY – Agrippa

I finally have time to write about working on 'Carry On Up The Nile' sorry 'Antony and Cleopatra.'

In spite of being a week away from the play and travelling, I can't stop thinking about and missing that time and group of people, more so than anything else I've worked on.

We're in Hong Kong for the weekend before Tim starts work in Shanghai tomorrow. He had to go into the HK office today so that coupled with the pouring rain has given me some free time to write.

The week before I auditioned for you I had decided to pack in the acting thing as I'd been auditioning left right and centre for two years for TV, musicals, films and getting nowhere. I'd always get great feedback but no re-calls or gigs, which is hard to put into perspective and I wondered if, at my age, the Universe was trying to tell me something.

So, out of work for a total of four and a half years, since I left the UK and then the opportunity to work with you came along, which was the only reason I auditioned in the first place having seen some of your You Tube videos.

It was a fantastic experience and learning curve both as an actor and an individual.

It's only now in retrospect that I've discovered how much I've changed as a person since I last worked with an acting company in the UK in 2008/09 when I was morbidly obese and as a result a very different character.

I could have stayed in that rehearsal room for another three weeks doing all those 'group exercises' and learning the many techniques you introduced us to.

You created a very tight team of actors who moved both as one and also as individuals to create a very unique and varied journey each night called 'Antony & Cleopatra.'

It's one of my least favourite plays, I can't relate to or find sympathy with any of the characters, but I've come to have enormous affection for some of them in the guise of the people who played them.

The work itself:

In spite of being such a physical person and always wanting to push myself to develop my physical abilities and in spite of the physical being so much of what you were teaching us it was the one thing I struggled with, wildly! I couldn't, couldn't, stop theorising EVERYTHING.

The swing exercises, the plastic exercise, I loathed them because they took me so far out of my comfort zone, I just couldn't stop pre-empting what I was about to do or what shape I would take or noise I would make before doing it. I only succeeded in letting go once and allowing the physical to take over and it was in a warm up in the first week at the theatre.

I've since realised how much I react physically in day to day life with other people and it feels so liberating just knowing how real that is or should be on stage.

When we get on stage, for one reason or another we employ a stillness, well I do, it's appropriate in certain situations but it's not real all the time. Even sitting in the hotel lobby and looking around myself now as I write I can see how animated everyone is as they communicate with each other. Yet when art imitates life some of us take on a very weird surreal interpretation of what we feel we should do or be rather than just bloody well 'DO' or 'BE.'

I always try to find reality and truth in what I'm doing on stage or with any character I play, that's the whole point of what we do, isn't it?

To find that from the physical happened quite a few times in performance which I'm pleased with, mission accomplished perhaps, even if it only happened a few times it happened and it was honest and real and in the moment.

When I went to see 'Richard III or Almost' there were many moments when I didn't believe either of the two actors, it had nothing to do with the writing or direction or their character and it was only some time after seeing the play that I realised I didn't believe their physicality or their physical reaction to what was happening.

To then experience 'Slava's Snow Show' and see a troupe of honest to God clowns 'DOING' it was inspiring. Even Tim said it was one of the best things he'd ever seen!

The whole point of 'taking ones time' was magnified tenfold watching that show!

Anyway, I'm going to take a break now and see if there is anything more to add to the thoughts above but I'll come back to that, most likely in Shanghai in a few days time.

……………………So; Shanghai, two weeks later and I've had plenty of time to 'mull' further.

Agrippa:-

What an angry head fuck that guy started out as.

I found him emotionally draining for those first two weeks of rehearsals but didn't realise this, nor did this manifest itself until after the run through on each of the two Saturdays, where, because of the way I was playing him at the time, I was in full on guard dog beast mode, angry and tense, physically and emotionally and I knew it wasn't right.

Each of those Saturdays ended in tears at some point in the evening, a rare occurrence for me. The second time it happened it was triggered by something joyous so I knew it was due to the work and my heightened emotional state at the time.

Then in the third week you, Ira, gave me a note to 'ease up' on Lepidus, Brendan, which changed the game for Agrippa and opened doors I wouldn't have otherwise considered. Agrippa didn't have to go around barking and scowling at everyone, he became aware of himself and his capabilities rocked back on his heels and laughed at the world and my God it was liberating!

So beast mode in check and testosterone levels receding………slightly, I was able to play with him more (and everyone else) with greater openness and roundedness rather than the dog with a bone approach I started with. The most significant aspect of playing Agrippa was the casting of Brinley as Enobarbus. It allowed a relationship and presented opportunities for Agrippa that weren't in the text. (I would imagine)

A fairly insignificant character, his main, probably only, plot contribution being the 'Antony should marry Octavia' speech, whole worlds of possibilities opened up with the Godsend casting of Brinley. It was this and only this that allowed Agrippa such significance and relevance in this version of the play.

After that first week of rehearsal, finding our feet and wondering who these characters are and how they relate to each other we had the weekend to ponder. Then out of left field a thought struck me, forcibly, we have to have sex, Agrippa and Enobarbus have to have sex, it was obvious, why didn't I see it before?

Monday, back in the rehearsal room, Brinley and I start talking, I've had an idea, we each say to the other, but it's a bit 'out there' we also both say to each other............we should have sex, in that first scene when we first meet we should have sex.

'BOOM' I had no doubt we were on the right track when both of us independently came back on Monday with the same idea, but I didn't want it to be gratuitous, in spite of the scenes eventual climax, so I suggested we 'Tango.'

Our meetings, rehearsing, talking, discovering, abandoning and searching for what we wanted to bring to the Tango continued in several different venues developing and growing as it did until the final ingredient was added in the form of Yiss.

Not only did he bring his musical skills to our aid but his eye and attention to detail took our basic premise of a passionate but animalistic reunion between two soldiers to a whole new level, both in the Tango scene and in the boxing scene.

I could waffle on and reminisce for hours so it must be time to let go and hit send.

So, in closing, moments (In The Woods) there are many but those that are constantly with me:-

meeting Berynn at that first read through and the wonderful compliments he paid me having heard my audition,

just being in a rehearsal room, LOLLIES, fucking LOLLIES, dancing/working with Brinley in any space we could find, that first conversation with Yiss in the car and hearing his lyrics, Jonathans' sleeping tablets episode, Jonathan and the rubber chicken episode (he knows) Roberts' 7 seconds You Tube videos and the terrifyingly uncontrollable 'waiting in the wings' at the interval giggling as a result- Drop it like it's hot, getting to see it happen on the TV in the foyer bar each night, talking to Miss Lobes' Troupe about ICE CREAM, Satay chicken from the Thai opposite the Theatre, talking to Denby about Rock climbing, what Finn said and the lovely Tammy taking the piss out of me for calling Jonathans' kitchen, 'a country kitchen' at the wrap party, I know what I meant.

Last but not least this photo which a friend took on the last night and sent to me after we closed, I see it every day and smile.
END

BRUNO LUCIA - Philo, Silius, Ambassador/Schoolmaster, Scarrus

I read though almost all of your blogs today - seems I did have time OR shall we say I made time to soak up your thoughts & indeed ignite mine! Well as you already know, the experience as a whole working with you and cast on my first ever Shakespeare Production was nothing short of miraculous! I have gone from fear to bravery (love!) one could say! When I use the word fear I don't mean sneaking up behind someone boo hoo fear - fear of the language, fear of failure, fear of the unknown, fear of not being worthy to even speak the words and language of shakespeare! I know it's ridiculous BUT these are the blocks we put for ourselves as we get older! In my case, you know it's the fact that I have immobolised myself and it's taken your constant reminder as a friend to look & explore more as an actor. I feel like I have started out in the business again! Only this time with experience and wisdom under my belt. A perfect segue to the fact that working with four school children and the way they stepped up to the plate - to use a baseball analogy - was also nothing short of miraculous!

When I think about your reference to the 3 generations in theatre I now can identify what that exchange was about in some ways, ie: the exchange of energy for experience, for enthusiasm and passion for technique and much much more! With every performance came something new. The text became clearer, the connection between my fellow actors. I played four characters. Philo being the narrator almost with a wonderful monolgue that allowed for even more than what I touched on! Silius was the most challenging of the shorter characters again with only one scene BUT rich in possibilities and obvious "silliness" that I took to a new level on the final show as I realised that even though my connection with fellow actor Lara playing Ventidius was always improving, it was this scene that opened up the importance of a deeper understanding and memorising of text for the whole scene as a way of opening up even more creative possibilites! As you put it - each "scene" in itself is a monologue!

TO BE CONTINUED...
It was OUR production. There was a sense of community with the "all walks of life & all age group " cast! With our limited time your guidance, microscopic eye and radar sensitivities we were allowed free reign to create - this was as you say a traditional theatrical co-op!

STILL MORE - TO BE CONTINUED...

Continuing on from my last email in regards to text and character (s) ... my third character being the Ambassador / Schoolmaster was extremely satisfying and again on my last performance felt like I really nailed it, not only from a personal perspective but in really connecting with my fellow cast members! I guess the two go hand in hand! With constant reminder via your direction - (and my perfectionist tendencies!) - to keep working & tweeking and feel alive with the other actors on stage - I was able to find even more comedic moments and connections with every actor in my two scenes! The first scene with Caesar, Agrippa. Dollabella, Proculeus, even though my lines/dialogue were with Caesar, once extremely comfortable with the logic and delivery of the text I was able to engage with every actor on stage even with just a look while bringing in the audience as well! It made me realize how important our time on the floor was with our limited rehearsal. It made me think/question my generosity as an actor and/or lack of? The second scene for the Embassador/ Schoolmaster with Antony even though only brief was equally satisfying - the notebook/prop which I'd thought about BUT instigated by you ended up being a wonderful bit of visual, physical exchange with Berynn who was a real team player - wonderful comic moment when after ranting & dictating he takes the notebook and pencil from me and exits leaving me with two empty hands and a glance to the audience - what the? His timing fabulous and again generous! Again in this scene came the importance of REALLY listening to my fellow actors text - I had a lot of this with Berynn /Antony and in this scene it brought up a couple of wonderful comic moments that would otherwise have been lost! ie: ...one of them being as I'm frantically writing he states, "tell me him/caesar to lay his gay comparisons..." I then stop gaze at the audience and ask with a look and mouthing gay?

My fourth and main character of Scarrus gave me a more well rounded feel of what acting in a Play / Shakespeare production was all about. I was able to explore relationships a little deeper, mainly with Antony, but also Enobarbus, Eros, Agrippa and to a lesser extent Canidius. I don't mean that they were more important - all scenes and characters and your realtionships are important - I mean that I had two or more lengthy scenes with them and our characters were emotionally linked to the whole story.

From my first scene - (originally a random soldier...) - given to Scarrus to come in to warn Antony of the perils of fighting by sea, where the audience has just heard Enobarbus trying to persuade him not to fight by sea, the importance of setting up a connection with Enobarbus in this scene which was not in the script made for a deeper connection for our next scene; "gods & godesses, all the whole synod of them - the greater cantle of the world is lost etc.." it was just a shared glance but I think vital - ie: ...we then shared the pain and frustration - which in turn set up the difficulty for Scarrus in delivering the news to Antony later that he had been betrayed by "one ever near thee" call for Enobarbus!

My exchange with Candidius in the earlier scene about the perils of fighting by sea set us up nicely here - in that Robert/ Canidius came in drunk and slagging off Antony which made me lose respect after we;d set up a mateship also. All my scenes with Antony and Berynn were shear joy - I really did feel like his right hand man - he made me feel like he was my brother in arms! From the returning of the battle scene which was also with Eros there was an honest / believable connection between us I feel that drove that scene. Our scene of celebration and meeting with Cleopatra became all the more joyful again as the "art of listening" to the other actors and the scene as a whole solid! By the time we got to Antony's death I really felt the pain of losing a great friend, brother, master which is what the script and writer obviously intended!

My final scene with Caesar, Agrippa, Proculeaus and messenger was my most difficult in that it required a deep emotional concentration. The text was also I think the most difficult. It might sound weird BUT originally it was to be played as Dercetus - (a fifth character for me...) - and when I first read the play and kept going back over my lines, I kept reading him as a Greek! I remember emailing you about the characters that had sprung up for me in the dialogue once I was on my feet. It really did happen organically. Consequently, sometimes I would wander between him and Scarrus as it was in the last week of rehearsals that you suggested to give his lines to Scarrus! It was only a couple of times I had this issue. Having said all this, it made perfect sense to do give the lines to Scarrus - logically, technically, emotionally - one less costume change!!! Maybe this was due to the brilliance of the "character dialogue" that Shakepeare had given each of his characters??? The way my lines read as Scarrus had started to sound like they'd be delivered by Scarrus! So then when I went to deliver Dercetus's lines as Scarrus certain phrases made me disconnect? I could just be talking out of my arse BUT - just now that I'm writing / dissecting it is interesting?

For nineteen or so people, ego's, personalities from very diverse backgrounds and upbringings to work together for five weeks, intensely I might add, and produce what we did was astounding! No one but us REALLY can understand that. You mentioned about the freedom of the actor - we could do anything! You did give us free run - this is rare I know! The fact we warmed up each session together, including our ritual etc... I think made us even more connected as people which essentially means more connected as actors / players. I did my best to keep the friend / director relationship separate / respectful if you know what I mean - and for the most part I think you'd agree it was great - you were hard on me when you needed to be, maybe once (ort twice?) over the top BUT that's all relative and probably necessary from your perspective as you had an enormous task (as we all did) of steering the ship and the last thing you needed was a comic cynicism! Which I can assure you even with the occassional reflex action I was so committed!

This is it I think? There's probably more. I'm sure there's more. I'll keep this aside for me also and read it in six months! Be interesting to see what else comes up - I'm sure a lot more!

Thank you once again - words of thanks are not enough!

Ciao for now

Bruno x

ARTICLE 4 - Notes from Ira Seidenstein
Antony & Cleopatra 2013 Directed by Ira Seidenstein, PhD

How did this project begin?

In 2012 I had directed the third play by Valentino Musico in Sydney. A friend and former student from NIDA, Berynn Schwerdt said he would come to see the play, and did so. He came with his friend Denby Weller. They liked the direction and we chatted afterwards. Berynn and Denby said they had a whim to act as Antony and Cleopatra. We discussed that briefly and did a Three-Musketeers - "all for one and one for all" type of agreement. We followed up on it. I asked Natalie Lopes who was acting in and assisted in producing Musico's play if she may be interested to help produce A & C. We discussed the possibility of her also acting in it. I said we should have a workshop asap. Denby said she had a friend Brinley Meyer who was interested to play Enobarbus.

At the workshop was Denby, Natalie, Brinley and another associate of mine Alice Williams. The workshop that dealt with the relation of movement, voice, acting and Shakespeare and my creative method of interpretation on the part of the actor. Berynn could not make the workshop so at the end I read in for "Antony" in the single scene I selected to examine as an example of how I approach discovery of a text in an ensemble context.

After a few minutes some bits started to fit into a mise-en-scene/staging logic. At least a few possibilities. This was Act 3, scene 11 that starts with Antony and Attendants, shortly Cleopatra, Charmian, Iras, Eros enter. My main edition of the play has Iras listed thus "[Iras]", another edition has Iras listed thus "[and followed by Iras]". At any rate we started to make headway to see some 'humorous' possibilities. For example, we see that

Cleopatra's attendants actually cajole or perhaps even argue with her. We saw that Antony is a 'case'. I went so far as to say that he may be bi-polar. He is pouting like an adolescent. The attendants of Antony (Eros) and Cleopatra (Charmian and Iras) are trying to get the lovers together. It is absurd, sad, pathetic, comical, a slice of a domestic kitchen drama. Shakespeare lets us see in this scene the total vulnerability of the super elite.

That was the beginning. The next phase was the casting. I could see that Natalie would be the ideal Charmian. We set a date for the auditions. As soon as the first notice went online within a few minutes Tammy Brennan who had recently completed my Quantum Clown Residency #4 wrote and asked if she might be considered for an audition. She was cast as Octavia.

Section Two - Casting/Audition
Even the folks who I asked to be in the production I also asked to present a Shakespeare monologue. They were free to choose any monologue/soliloquy. In auditions I try to work with each actor about 10-15 minutes. In that time I run it as a workshop and also explain that I am auditioning for them. I show them a sample of how I work and if they don't like that way then please do not do the production. In recent years I have joked that I am a "prodologist" that is I prod and provoke the actor to give more of what they are really capable of rather than just giving what they were taught to give. Remarkable things can happen in those 10 or 15 minutes. So even the few folks who I asked to be in the production have not been directed by me before in a Shakespeare play so the specific issue was around the combination of Shakespeare, the actor, and my method(s).

Denby (Cleopatra), Brinley (Enobarbus), and Natalie (Charmian) had already been in a Shakespeare workshop with me and we knew what they would play. Natalie was teaching the day of the audition so Denby and Brinley assisted me by welcoming people, handling the CV/Photos, and being witness to each audition. More importantly, I wanted them to assist to witness the transformation that each actor would make in a few minutes - to see what would be possible in our few weeks of rehearsal. I worked each actor 'hard' thoroughly. Each actor gave a lot, was challenged and was positively supported by me.

The others who I asked to be in the production included Bruno Lucia, Bron Lim, Erin. I asked my friend Aku Kadoggo who was newly returned to Australia to play three parts however she had a work commitment exactly during the time of our performance season. Then I thought I could play those three parts and was going to, but, Slava Polunin the Russian clown, asked me to fill in for a few weeks for one of the Russian actors in his "Slava's Snow Show". The first week of that gig was the second week of A & C and I thought it would be good to give the actors a break from me seeing every show. It also had the potential to be good publicity to be involved with the two shows. But also I realised this coincidence was an ideal way to celebrate my 40 years in theatre and to celebrate one of my key philosophical ideas of the value of relating acting (classical acting as in A & C) and clown (classical as in Slava's Snow Show). Then I had to get someone to take that set of three characters: Soothsayer, Mardian, Clown. So I asked a young actor I had taught one day - Yiss Mill. He had never really been in a full play with professionals. But I suspected he would offer something unique and he certainly did.

Bruno played four characters and Bron played three. So in a way Bruno, Bron, Yiss became a triumvirate of character actors. A character actor in olde school acting was a type of clown/actor who could transform themselves completely into a role.

There were other actors who also played several roles but they are a different nature than the classic character actors. And each of those who played several roles did fine jobs!!! I think the character actor is one who will simply radically shift their body language and vocal tones. Yiss was the least experienced but he travelled a huge creative and technical distance in rehearsal. The others who played several roles were Brendon, Robert, Lara.

Already early in the casting process Enobarbus, and Alexas (Bron Lim) were going to be played by women. I cast one man as Eros but he could not adapt his financial work for the artistic as we were doing a co-op and likelihood of earning anything with 18 actors and a stage manager and a director were slim. Then Berynn wrote to me that just in case - I should know - that he had a sister who was an actress and had fairly recently graduated from WAAPA. She was the single person I cast without having met - and that meant I had not auditioned for her with my method. So that required each of us to travel a special route and after two weeks or so she got stronger and stronger in every single rehearsal and was well on her way to her own breakthrough. Even when an actor makes a breakthrough with me, it is then still totally up to the actor themselves to honestly realise what they have discovered with me about their own creative potential and most importantly how to negotiate that.

I think the two adult actors (we had four youth actors in our ensemble) that I haven't mentioned yet who played single roles were: Jonathon Dunk (Caesar), and, Paul McNally (Agrippa). They each had a big journey to completely locate their characters, that is, their unique and personal expression of 'Caesar' and of 'Agrippa'.

So that is a bit about the Beginning, the Audition, the Casting.

Natalie Lopes (Charmian and the co-producer with Denby) and I discussed the possibility of working with four of her youth acting students. Natalie is a Drama Teacher in a school and also has a private acting school with about 120 youths. She selected four of her private students and got permission from their parents. I referred to the group of four as "Ms. Lopes' Troupe". The members of the troupe were Miranda, Millie, Brydey, Harry. Their ages were 13-16. They played the messengers, guards, and servants. Their participation brought an exceptional grace to the ensemble. I cut them no slack but respected their youth and managed not to swear too much, too often.

The fact that all the actors had to be 'mindful' as there were youths in the rehearsal room and project, helped to bring about a heightened awareness and generosity. Mind you in the very first moments of rehearsal one of the actors let out a right full ribald exclamation. Well that border was crossed over. The 'kids' were delighted. And that was one of many moments of locking in the ensemble. Tammy (Octavia) was one of two actresses with a child (Bron has two) and due to her house arrangements and philosophical outlook her daughter 5-yr cheeky as could be Pebble came to rehearsal when Tammy did. Ms. Lopes' Troupe automatically looked after the 5-yr old. Erin also was very active to keep Pebble entertained and out of the way. The scoundrel who did not get Pebble out of the way at times was me, Herre Direktor. Amongst my several eccentricities in theatre and rehearsals I actually like it when things go astray a bit. So when Berynn was practicing dying as "Antony", Pebble decided it was a nice time to play skip-to-the-loo-my-darling RATHER close to Berynn a'dying which he was unbelievably tolerant of and I was totally delinquent in delight of the extreme of absurd rehearsal methodology. But there was at least one worse incident with the glory of a delightful freeform 5-yr gallivanting during a tragedy (one I can only refer to at best as a comic-tragedy or an absurdist play). So when "Antony" in Act 3 scene 13 has "Thidias" whipped, our two servants a'whipping were two of the young lasses of Ms Lopes' Troupe and in one rehearsal only one was available so Pebble (ye olde 5-yr olde) knew the cue and the fun action so she helped escort the ragged and whipped "Thidias". This perversity of our sacred theatre is actually the only sacred theatre where all humans are welcome to participate. I have for decades said that "real theatre should be at least three generations if not four". When I started in theatre at college (university) we had a wonderful deeply humane director Trudy Scott and we had a fine eccentric group of zanies as the acting group and this included Bonnie Gilmore who though likely only 21 years old herself, had a 5yr olde we called "Baby Jennifer" who was more often than not in rehearsals. This to me is 'real' theatre where the norms of society don't fit and each ensemble or project can make up their own rules of conduct. Fortunately Berynn and Denby our protagonists and lead actors had the most accommodating demeanours on many levels.

Another organic happening was for some reason Ms Lopes' Troupe took an extreme liking to Tammy (Pebbles' mom) and many a time they were all in a group having found a number of common interests and chatting away. All these little nuances to me were like theatre heaven. Or at least one form of it.

THE HARD STUFF

Peter Brook in a book *Conversations With Peter Brook* (2000) by Margaret Croyden has a chapter of the interview that preceded the premiere of

Brook's Antony & Cleopatra. He said "We've never seen the play.". He meant that at least up until his production, the play had been interpreted so incorrectly that in fact everyone in theatre thinks they know the play but they don't. I think what folks have in mind is Elizabeth Taylor and Richard Burton - so to speak. That was a movie, but, somehow in our consciousness we think we know the play. Most productions of A & C are cut and edited and shortened versions. I have seen the play three times. All pretty horrible. But the one at the Globe in London 2006 had a fantastic Cleopatra - Frances Barber was glorious and as I had long believed and insist - Cleopatra is a form of a clown. A clown not in a ha-ha sense but in the sense of a free though troubled spirit who will do anything at any moment even if it is inappropriate or ludicrous. I also liked that the Clown in Act 5 scene 1 who brings the basket of figs and asps was dressed as a traditional party clown circa 1970s. The rest of the production may have been the Cecil B. DeMille-esque version, but, boring, straight, conservative.

To be sure, A & C is wonderfully complex. The cross themes of war, love, politically plotting, and here I make my claim of infamy, comedy. Comedy? But isn't it a tragedy? Is it? If it is, fine, ok, but why is there a clown at such an auspicious moment? I think that clown's appearance is very suspicious. I think, what I really think, is that there is a LOT of comedy in William Shakespeare's 'tragedy' *Antony & Cleopatra*. I am not saying it is ha-ha-ha-ho-ho-ho raucous knee slapping comedy. Not at all. However, there is plenty of comedy. Where? Actually the interesting point is why do most productions try so hard to stomp out the comedy? That's actually the question because I don't think there is a question about A & C being at least part comedy. I grant the possibility as previously mentioned that the play is a tragi-comedy or an absurdist play. But I am not sure that it is really a tragedy. I think four exchanges between Antony and Cleopatra initiate a comedy. But the stage is set before that in the 'prologue' by "Philo" whose ending is "Take but good note, and you shall see in him the triple pillar of the world transformed into a strumpet's fool. Behold and see." Just after that in rapid fire are several points of contention between Antony and Cleopatra which she taunts and plays with - dare one say - clowns with. That is just scene 1. Scene 2 (Act 1) has even more clear signals of comedy ushered in particularly by "Charmian" and reinforced by the ensemble of and with the Soothsayer who can't get a word in because "Charmian" beats him to the predictions, yet, at the same time clearly (according to the text - the words spoken) frequently she keeps pulling her hand away as the Soothsayer tries to grasp it to read her palm. This scene in fact is broad comedy and borders on, or can easily be portrayed in a slapstick fashion. Though of the Noel Coward witty type supported also by some comic physical repartee.

A & C 2013 - 2nd section

In the previous post Antony & Cleopatra 2013 I dealt with the beginning, how the production came about, the casting, the auditions and the beginning of the hard stuff.
The hard stuff is dealing with the naysayers. Those are particularly the theatre professionals who assume because they have read, studied, or seen the play then they know it. Many scholars note a bit of comedy or absurdity in A & C. I have not made an extensive scholastic survey of the breadth of writings about the play. So there may be a scholar out there who has written more extensively about the comedy within A & C, if you know of one (or some) please forward their name and the name of the written article or book to me at iraseid@gmail.com

Of course besides the theatre practitioners (some) who are naysayers and who insist along with most scholars that A & C is a formal tragedy, there is the dilemma of the theatre critics who may or may not be actual theatre practitioners. Certainly I generally consider reviewers in a positive light in that they provide a service to the industry and can assist and prod things along at times. Of course one can clearly seen a pattern of any single reviewer over time. One can see their leanings, preferences, and whose "pockets they may be pissing into" or who provides them the best premiere/opening status.

I hold scholars (not academics, who may now be closer to bureaucrats than to scholars) in high esteem. It would be virtually impossible to present any production of Shakespeare without extensive notes provided over decades by scholars. The language has changed and evolved since Shakespeare's time and the political and social context of each play is woven in layers of assumed knowledge of the time of the original writing and earliest productions.

I have had the opportunity on several occasions to readdress several 'problem scenes' of Shakespeare. Certain scenes particularly in the longer plays are regularly cut or edited down. Many smaller characters are cut or edited out. So in fact when someone says they have seen a certain play by Shakespeare there is a much higher likelihood that they have not seen the play but have seen a cut, abridged, edited version of the play - especially any of the longer plays. Even *Hamlet* THE play has very rarely been performed in its fuller exposition. There are difficulties in saying what the whole play of Hamlet is since there are at least two versions and they may need to be cobbled together to provide the 'whole' of *Hamlet*.

Our version was the 'whole' play with the most minor exceptions. For example I did not have an actor play Taurus so those few (VERY FEW) lines were left out. In another scene again for the practical needs of not calling on an extra actor nor wanting to call upon any actor to play an extra character - in another scene calling for three characters I had the character who spoke most simply incorporate the lines (VERY FEW) of the third character. The text of that scene was such that this could be done and did not lose the sense. Though naturally as per the writer's concept the more minor character would have added a reinforcing voice. The scene I am referring to is Act 2 scene 1 and we gave Menecrates to the actor playing Menas.

Sunday, June 23, 2013

A & C 2013 section three

Amongst the anomalies in our production that are a reflection of my particular eccentric or eclectic view about the nature of theatre... Artistically I lean towards meta-theatre as a preferred style. Meta-theatre lets practitioners and audiences admit that above all the reality is only that we are presenting or observing a play. That is the only truth. Mark Antony died eons ago and does not stand before us. Who stands before is an actor who is a person who is portraying or specifically pretending in an artistic way to be Mark Antony. I have long sought a way for actors to take back their indigenous nature, their ability to mimic, embody, embrace, pretend, enact, dance any character they choose or are chosen to portray. So here I hint at very big theme - I believe that the Indigenous actors and theatre in Australia have a treasure chest of performance modalities and sensibilities that we, the non-Indigenous artists can learn from. Not to copy their culture but to understand their greater potency as actors even when in some cases they are clearly not trained. As NAISDA happened to have been the fertile ground from where the Page brothers emerged to create Bangarra - I think that there is a more general and broader growth, in part inspired by the Page brothers and Bangarra's many great artists who effect a development in the Indigenous Australian Theatre.

I will return to 'anomalies' and then I will briefly discuss the voices of the actors in A & C 2013.

One of the most blatant oddities was the overall reference to obviously female actors as 'sir', 'he', 'man' etc as was written in the text but certainly was not intended for woman to portray male characters. So clearly I took liberties with the author's intentions. Or did I? As is well known in Shakespeare's time, and company and plays, in their original period all of the female characters were known by the public to be portrayed by Boy Actors. Now some of them may have continued to play female roles past adolescence and past their change of voices, and these actors may have even used falsetto to continue to play female characters. So I simply allowed this to happen in reverse. I have done so when I deemed it appropriate due to the practical choice of what actors were available whether they were male or female. Once when directing *Pericles,* I asked a male actor to play a female character, in a dress, but not to shave. I did that for a very capable actor who I thought simply would benefit by doing a project where he could think out of the box of what is deemed "good theatre". Sometimes you have to be bad to be good. Think Boy George etc.

In one case the actors in a scene decided to change the 'him' and 'he' etc in reference to Enobarbus (played by a woman in our production) - to 'her' and 'she'. It started with one or two actors having made that choice. I said nothing as they were experimenting with their own decision. In this case I chose to not interfere, but, other times in other productions I certainly to interfere with an actors choice if I think there is clearly a better alternative. In this scene then the last and third actor in the scene also changed the him/he-s to her/she-s. This may have likely been for harmony in that particular scene and by verbal agreement between the three actors. That was Act 4, scene 6. However, only a few scenes later a different grouping of three actors kept the him/he even though in this case Enobarbus was actually in the scene and clearly a woman (portraying a scripted male character). I never discussed this matter with the cast. I certainly would not be surprised if the cast discussed this extreme anomaly amongst themselves. In its own way this is one of the more extreme things I have ever allowed/done with a text's expandability. The later was Act 4, scene 9. In this scene the meta-theatre was held purely by the honest, naïve, and well acted if not sincere acting by 3 of Ms Lopes' Troupe. In our small theatre and in my staging when the young actors sidle little more than 1 metre from the ailing/dying Enobarbus. At the same time Brinley who portrayed "Enobarbus" gave a gut wrenching rendition of the inner turmoil with moans that some of you may know happen only in your worst, most private loss of love. This happened in each rehearsal and each performance. In this case I said very little, hesitating to give open and full complements lest I tamper with her deeper work of art and craft in this scene. This was ancient acting, of an indigenous nature, as one may easily image Elenora Duse or Sarah Bernhardt. Yes it was 'melodramtic' but it was unique, personal, and spell binding. Something that the youth actors will likely remember possibly for the rest of their lives. This is 'Hamlet' in the sense of the Player King's enactment of the story of Hecuba. The theatre protocol allows us the indulgence of the Player King because Hamlet then is so moved as to comment on it. Yet, we are so weak and scared of critics (our colleagues as well as those folks employed to write theatre criticism) that we shy away when a young actor still has the courage to make their own deep discoveries. My job in this area is to allow the actor maximum freedom so long as they feel the inner truth of indigenous portrayal and pretending.

As with all of my on-the-floor direction I may come right down on the floor, and did so, at times when the actor is clearly deep in emotion and give a practical direction or two right inches from their face as I whisper the direction. The beauty with Brinley and Berynn who also had such charged emotional scenes was that they not only tolerated my "Ingmar Bergman moments" but were kind and mature enough to use both sides of their brains to incorporate an occasional 'in yer face' direction. Ingmar Bergman would at times have his face intimately close to two lovers while directing as can be seen on some documentary footage of him in action. I have no interest to imitate his mastery; it is more about the allowance for the actor and the director to do what ever seems best and to explore to find what might, possibly, work.

Brinley (Enobarbus) and Paul (Agrippa) had a rich scene - the end of Act 2 scene 2. One day early in rehearsals when it came time to run that scene - they did it more or less non-stop as a fully choreographed tango. What the?!? This was one of the first moments for actors to test and see that with me there is no limit how far they, we, or I, am willing to take things or to support an actor going for an extreme fulfilling interpretation. Mind you I am not for any jackass clown actor just doing what ever they feel like whenever. I only ask that the actor is anchored in their own integrity, their own artistic exploration with a purpose defined by them, and the text, the situation, the drama, the character(s), and the relationship. As I have mentioned elsewhere (Director's Notes) - Shakespeare, above any writer I have so far encountered, can withstand almost any extremity of interpretation, provided the experiment is still anchored in the text or the textures of the images.

When I asked Brinley and Paul how on Earth they accomplished this fantastic exploration and realisation, Brinley replied that they thought about something that I had said. I explained that one of my stream of theories about Shakespeare (i.e. working with the scripts of Shakespeare) is that one should examine each scene as if it were a different style. To explain further here, it is as if each scene were an individual play within itself, or, as if each scene were a short film, or dance. So somehow they hit upon a lark, to try it (T-R-Y) as a tango. I later asked if either of them had ever done tango. Essentially they had not. They looked at videos and took the moves.

That scene 2.2 was a type of crucible for the production. Certainly for most of the audience they could easily comment that it was one of the highlights of the production. I didn't do it. I allowed it and encouraged it. Brinley and Paul accomplished the great task. My next task was how to make their choices work. And by work I don't mean work for some of my professional theatre colleagues who just don't get it, I mean work for our experiment. Certainly numerous theatre professionals LOVED that scene and dance!! So my task and it was a large one, how to make their beautiful efforts work. How to frame. So I asked Yss to play a rhythm that I had the nerve to give him. I then had him play it more fervently. Quite like the horrible acting parable when the director doesn't know what to say and blurts out "Just act better". I told the musician to play stronger. It worked and he got the feel. Of course he did, he's a gifted musician. Then I started to push Brinley about the rhythm, I started to do the other no-no for directors and began to give her the exact way I foresaw that the rhythm of the text in this particular scene would work. So the aesthetics became a beat-box (literally), tango (literally), rap (literally). On top of this the acting of Brinley and Paul was romantic, erotic, passionate, and was most importantly anchored in the text. Not to boring as batshit belief system of 'how the text works'. It was anchored in the actors and the musicians bodies. It was palpable and had the most wonderful cool-down first from Paul "... Whilst you abide here" after he had tossed Enobarbus' sexually soiled and sweat wiped suit jacket and Eno replied in orgasmic exhaustion "Humbly, sir, I thank you".

Note that also in this scene 2.2 Paul as Agrippa also spoke the ten lines of Maecenas.

<u>A & C 2013 - section four Antony and Cleopatra</u>

In this section I will write just a little about our "Antony" portrayed by Berynn Schwerdt and "Cleopatra" portrayed by Denby Weller.

Two important points to start with: 1) Berynn and Denby were arduous in the preparation and development and performance of their roles of which I will write more in a moment, and, 2) they were extraordinarily generous in performance/rehearsal with every single actor with whom they were onstage with. Oh if only every actor were so generous to other actors.

We had about three weeks to rehearse A & C, part-time!! Monday to Thursday 6pm to 10pm. And Saturdays 10am to 4pm. I asked the actors to cooperate by learning their lines prior to the first day of rehearsal. Naturally when we are all freelancers trying to get by and pay the rent etc, it can be very challenging to learn one's lines by oneself. Even more so with Shakespeare, in that there is such an intimacy between the shared text in every scene. So learning a Shakespeare monologue/soliloquy is one thing, learning a scene is a different intellectual challenge. The larger swathes of text belong to Antony, Cleopatra, Enobarbus, Caesar. Some of the actors played three or four characters so in some cases there was a significant amount of text for them.

Berynn and Denby were excellent to work with. My work with them can only be understood in the 'secret ways of theatre'. Amongst the most important things was to understand that I was to support them. It was their project. I shared their project and they were generous to me, very generous in terms of trust and support for my artistic drive(s). I've had the opportunity to teach and work with perhaps 3000 actors. I was one of Berynn's teachers at NIDA. He was OUTSTANDING at 19 years of age (maybe he was 18 or 20??? when I taught him). I worked with him for a few days on a film on which I was the choreographer. We would see each other rarely, occasionally and have a coffee, or a meal. I saw him 'last' in *Titus Andronicus* at ATYP around 2011 when I was directing in Sydney and teaching a short workshop on Shakespeare. I really loved the Titus production. Everyone did a fine job - the actors, the director, the designer. It was the first time I saw Helmut Bakaitis act. He was also the teacher of the director. Berynn was wonderful!!! His "Antony" was HIS! Wonderful. Berynn is very knowledgeable with Shakespeare and many aspects of acting and theatre. For our play reading I deferred any questions of pronunciation to Berynn. He went far with the mercurial, emotional shifts of "Antony". As with any Shakespeare play or character one can see and benefit from cross-referencing other plays by Shakespeare and other of his characters. There were scenes and moments for Berynn/Antony when I thought of Macbeth, others when I saw Richard III, others Falstaff. With other actors in our A & C I would see other such cross-references. For "Lepidus", and I know this is stretching an already stretched tether, but I did say to Branden regarding "Lepidus" that maybe, m-a-y-b-e we could view him as having a bit of "Polonius". Maybe. That was a director's creative suggestion, not a literal one. Likewise I said to Jonathon who portrayed "Caesar" perhaps p-e-r-h-a-p-s he is more like Paul Keating. For Berynn we didn't chit-chat much about his "Antony". It was a giant role and so complex an experience within my conceptualising. So we did things on the floor. At times I played the taboo pesky nuisance crass director with no borders. He was tolerant and playful. He also I hope and trust was able to use his rich knowledge of Shakespeare to help others in the production with their questions. I preferred that. I trust him. He is good and understanding and I am certain he helped folks. On the other hand we had wonderful young actors such as Robert and Jonathon who are also quite savvy with Shakespeare. None the less I think every single actor got a stretch in their beliefs and understanding not only of their roles in A & C but also in the play and in the breadth of possibilities with Shakespeare that rarely get challenged. Really I frame it thus: "I think mostly what is going on in Shakespeare in Australia is a year-ten sophomore in high school mentality. It is like 'the bible tells me so' or 'my father told me so it is must be'. I think many Shakespeare productions are anal retentive. Conservative, boring, much of the same or on the other extreme people being adolescent and doing what they will with it as if that is interesting."

For Berynn, he's 45 now. When I taught him I was 33. He's lived and he should be able to grapple with this giant role and enjoy the 17 relationships with the other actors and myself and our glorious Stage Manager Ruth Horsfall! Berynn, and Denby excelled in their creative and intellectual relationships with each of the other actors and their characters. In many ways it was this work that was 'unique' in our production as compared with the overwhelming majority of productions of Shakespeare that I have ever seen.

Another line in my theories about working with Shakespeare is that repeatedly in Australia and often in the USA and even too often in the UK even with the so-called 'top' companies (ugh!!) so much focus in the directing is about and around the protagonist. I find that approach so extremely limiting and even totally inaccurate to the richness of every single play by Shakespeare. To me, the greatest beauty is not *Antony and Cleopatra* per se but how the actors Berynn and Denby connected - REALLY connected with EVERY single character and every single actor in the play.

Berynn was one of Denby and Brinley's teachers. He may have taught others too at the Actors Centre. Robert also is a graduate of ACA's Journey. So here was a rare three-generation production with me as one of Berynn's teachers and he a teacher of several of the others. Likewise with Natalie and Ms Lopes' Troupe - I was one of her teachers at CSU and she had four of her pupils in this production.

Now a few thoughts about Denby's unique "Cleopatra". It is interesting, sort of, to hear theatre practitioners pontificate about their 'real knowledge' of particulars of plays and theatre practices such as staging, acting, voice, characterisation - as if there weren't a vast, unlimited range of possible interpretations and breadth of aesthetics. Denby has the most beautiful combination of a vastly savvy young person of achievement in several fields (writing, producing, communication, articulation of ideas, mountain climbing, martial arts, and all things current be they politics or cinema or fashion or food), and all that is combined with an open, honest, playful curiosity that borders on innocence and naivety.

Like most actors I deal with, we find ways together to encounter the training they have had before an experience with me. Inevitably I see benefits in any and every acting/theatre training. However, at the same time we discover together (without discussing any of the details) that in fact some aspect of their training may have involved a fallacy. In this case we were dealing with Shakespeare. I have a concept "Shakespeare as a Tool for the Theatre". I am not concerned with the normal sense of 'really do a good or even a great production of a Shakespeare play'. I hear the beat of a different drummer because that other idea of 'good' drummed into us at school, by professional directors, etc is out of tune - as far as I am concerned. In Yiddish we would say it is "drechk".

So with Denby we located a wild and wise, yet vulnerable, yet street wise "Cleopatra". Much more important than having a young Australian actress portray a long dead Egyptian queen is for a young Australian woman to learn to be more herself in all her glory. I have ZERO interest in a 'real good' portrayal of ANY of Shakespeare's incredible, vast, array of characters. I want to see that living breathing actor before me exude their own individual glory as a person and as an artist, an authentic artist of the stage. Through and via this truth the real glory of Shakespeare's wisdom breathes on a stage. Mostly we get very competent, professional actors acting like they are Shakespearean actors acting in a Shakespeare play. Generally it is awful work we see in English productions. We see it over and over not only via the national and regional companies but by their derivatives who imagine they are doing so much better than the national or regional companies. I have recently seen Shakespeare productions from 3 European countries that were utterly and totally phenomenal on every level of acting, theatre, and production.

We, and I say this as an Australian citizen and someone who started touring to Australia in 1981, we still need Australian voiced Shakespeare productions. Rex Cramphorn apparently was ushering in such a voice and no doubt others have. None the less - when I am talking about the Australian voice I am referring to the actors own voice and all of its nuances that get shaved away be 'good voice' techniques. It is pompous malarkey to believe there is a standard for voice training. It is a fallacy. So ironically even though our 'voice' work in A & C was minimal (as was everything else) the actors all, each, had their own totally distinct Australian voices. A few who had 3 or 4 characters chose to put on an accent for some characters. Fine. That is them working as an artist to find, to discover their own ways and means vocally to differentiate their characters. For Denby she had one character with a multitude of voices and moods. She honoured the text and the text honoured her. That is the magic of Shakespeare. He was a bard. A real one and at the time when bards existed. He wrote at during the absolute peak of commedia dell'arte. Supposedly there were two actual

Italian troupes that came to England during the time when Shakespeare would have been able to see them. There is at least one scholar that provides 'evidence' that Shakespeare was very likely in Italy for three years. This is yet to be proved beyond a doubt, yet, there is possible evidence. An unusual number of his plays located outside of England are placed in Italy, and they clearly and obviously have commedia elements. Although *Antony & Cleopatra* has scenes in Rome - I view that A & C has possible elements of commedia incorporated. In commedia the individual lustre of an actor create differences even in the stock characters. Denby showed an intellectual and creative and emotional acting range that any commedia actor should admire. What is important is not formal training and not an 'accurate' portrayal of our cliché image of an Egyptian queen. We can see in the antics of Prince William and Harry - children of Diane and Charles - they have noble and larrikin qualities. They are busy becoming themselves. Likely so was Cleopatra, so is Denby. It was her authentic drive and search for how to execute every single second of this topsy-turvy antics-rich character that made her a queen, it made her glorious in her weaknesses which a second later shone to become a young master of the stage. Still for each actor every performance was a struggle, as in sport, they were all alive and yes, it did help to have a director with courage in their corner coaching them for the next round. So many directors are actually scared of actors, thus they learn how to laud over them in subtle yet no uncertain terms. I enjoy meeting the actor head on in strange and unpredictable ways. Unpredictable even to myself. Denby is both a sweetheart of a person and a person with unlimited veracity in life - as her sports of Taekwondo (past) and mountaineering (current) reveal. There were hundreds of moments of shapeshifting that she mastered in this singular role. There were certain patterns as per the text that reveal an observable character.

But for me, the most important thing was, that a young Australian woman was genuinely allowed, guided, and cajoled to find her totally unique "Cleopatra". Was it Shakespeare's "Cleopatra"? Who gives a flying stuff about that? I don't. What counts is Denby. She and Berynn were the people I made 'the three musketeers' pledge with. She's a young intellectual artist with guts galore who wanted to take a punt - and put her own money and time and energy into. Most actors are remarkably gutless. They've been primed to be useful tools for the industry, for directors, agents, and teachers to pay their own mortgages.

Denby, like each of the actors had resistance training from me. Each had at one point or many a chance to stand up to and with me. Not against me nor I against them. The actor needs a director who can provide resistance not opposition. Why? In the end, at the beginning, I coached the actors to know "you are the artists and I am just here to help facilitate your art work", and, "in the end it is your show, you will be on stage, it is you who have to own the project".

Denby and I worked together hard to resolve several artistically challenging scenes. For example the scene when the messenger can seemingly do no right and "Cleopatra" has to belt the "Messenger" who in this case was a youngster. The others in the scene had to patiently wait as layer after layer revealed itself in an organic mise-en-scene. I definitely directed but via ensemble participation.

One of our early breakthroughs was from my insistence that any sympathetic and romantic portrayal had to be removed before we could discover the romance of passion and conflict and needs. Each section and each scene when the light bulb appeared for Denby was remarkable and suddenly at every step she was leading the other actors. Yes, she was the queen - the leader of her people. Yet, Shakespeare has given us an immensely human portrait of what happens behind closed doors. At times according to the text as I sensed its unfolding - suddenly Charmian, then now Iras would leap ahead and 'manhandle' their mistress. And God does "Cleopatra" need manhandled! As she tells Caesar at one point "Wert thou a man" causing him to take action not towards her but for her. A very Lady Macbeth moment of demanding action from a man.

One of many beautiful experiences in rehearsal was when I asked Denby to please belt one of the young little sweet innocent blonde youngsters full on in the stomach for her insubordination as a guard. I asked young Brydey if that was okay with her. Her pupils dilated an expectant pleasure. Yet at the same time there was a hesitant air in the room generated by everyone's thought 'ok Ira's going too far this time'. So we gave it a go, and, importantly Denby gave it a very gentle go. We three began to work our way thru the mechanics of the punch. I wanted it active enough that Brydey would feel motivated to collapse on the floor. Then we integrated the text and moments leading to and after the punch. When we finished about 5 or 10 minutes later - "whatever it takes" - I asked Brydey if she felt this was okay for her. There was yet another young Aussie gal having a total ball. She jumped up and down a bit and exclaimed that this was now her most favourite scene she was in. Denby found exquisite ways of portraying every second around that, just as she sought every second in her portrait of "Cleopatra" to be fully alive, real, and integrated to each fellow actor's work.

CHAPTER 9

CO-CREATING

I wrote the first scenario below originally late in 1984. That was *A Regular Couple of Guys*. Stephen Champion who had been an early member of Circus Oz wanted to form a duet partnership with me. He set up a one-month workshop for us to teach in physical theatre, clown, acrobatics in 1984 in Canberra at Gorman House. That went well and we decided we would make a duet show sometime soon. I returned to Auckland and wrote the show/scenario and gave it the title of "A Regular Couple of Guys". It took several attempts and years before I finally turned that scenario into a show. The next few pages tell of the path to production.

I wanted to tell the story of two men who had a close working and living situation sharing life together. Later, Stephen suggested that we change the title to *Two Up* which would reference our acrobatics that we would include, and reference also Two-Up that is the iconic Australian gambling game played on Australia Day. We did not get that show up but we did perform as an acrobatic duet at the Sydney Opera House in Sir Robert Helpmann's production of *Romeo et Juliette*. 1985. We also worked together in Canberra and co-created a quartet slapstick and acrobatic theatre show that toured in the A.C.T. Region for a few months. That show was *Building Blocks*, the quartet included the musician/technician. The company that produced it was Jigsaw Theatre. 1986. On the weekends I took a flight to Sydney as I was co-writing a solo piece based on my scenario *Reflextions* which was about an old clown the split second before/of his death. It is said that at such a moment your life flashes before your eyes. Some people who have had 'near death' experiences report such a phenomenon. Stephen helped me by bringing the circular acrobatic mat he had made for *Building Blocks*.

In 1987 I wrote another scenario for a duet *Soldier Boys* which I toured with a Dutch colleague. That was a six months project including one month of rehearsal, several months of touring in schools in New South Wales and Victoria. The same show was performed for school groups from first year to seniors. We also had two theatre seasons one was daytime at Belvoir St Theatre in Sydney and a late night season in Anthill Theatre for the Melbourne Comedy Festival. As part of that six months project I was hoping to rehearse a second show i.e. A Regular Couple of Guys, for a theatre season. Below is the original scenario from 1984 with the opening paragraph related to the 1987 proposal.

When I direct I co-create. I have excelled at writing scenarios for actors who I know. Because I co-create and work collaboratively on the floor the work happens spontaneously. Unless there had been video footage of rehearsal/creation process what happens in the room is subject to the witnesses reports. If two people from each project I created through my collaborative methods would sit with those from any of my other projects then very clear patterns would emerge about how I 'feed' the participants. In particular when it comes to "comic patter" as the old vaudeville clowns knew and which I happen to have a talent for, even if I prefer some olde school schlock vaudeville patter. What I do in the room, for example, and I'm making this up now as I write ... is to tell actor A, for example, to "Say 'Hello you stinkball' to" actor B and I say to actor B "Then you say 'Address me by my honorarium' " then to A "You say 'Huh'? " and to B "You reply 'Mr Stinkball to you' ".

Then either me or the actors write those lines down. Usually all of us write it immediately. Then right after the actors say those 4 lines they often will ad lib another line or two each and we write those down and then I might add 1 more line etc. So it is a co-creation and I am an active part of that. It is like playing creative leap-frog.

Sometimes on a project I will say to a particular actor go and write something for this. For example my play about August Strindberg *Artist i Exile... Requiem for Strindberg* rehearsal was based on my scenario and some text that I had written, some of which was with the assistance of Niclas Abrahamsson. In rehearsal I asked one actor who was to play Soren Kierkegaard to go away for 20 minutes and write a short monologue about Hans Christian Anderson's "ugly duckling". The monologue was for a moment when the trio of protagonists had a existential crisis. When he returned I asked him to read it for us. It was brilliant and touching and neither he nor any of his theatre colleagues knew that he was a gifted writer. I can't remember his name. He was wonderful, extremely quiet and looked like he had come from the times of Anderson and Kierkegaard. He was from the same island where Ingmar Bergman lived which was a protected island of Sweden which had an ancient feel to it. Thordbjorn Laago was that actor (thank you Jenny, Anna, Irina, David for helping to find his name).

Another incident of an actor writing a section was while I directed my scenario based on Ruzzante's scenario from the 1500s *Return from the Wars*. Carlo had given the scenario to Ole and some years later when Ole asked me to direct a commedia show he gave me the Ruzzante piece and asked if maybe I could do something with that. I then wrote a scenario around two professional actors to be two Arlecchinos. Those two actors were a couple who were classically trained actors from Estonia, Haide and Toomas. I also wrote a monologue for Columbina. Pantalone was played by Robert, Columbina was played by Mette, and the two actors who I cast to play The Lovers were Marianne and Loy. Marianne was an experienced actor and writer and came in one day with a script for her main scene with Loy. It was wonderful. The rest of the play was co-created based on my scenario which was inspired by Ruzzante but was a completely different scenario except that I was using one character, Capitano returning from war. Our Capitano claimed he had fought in the Bosnian war of the 1990s, but in fact it turned out he had only been in the UN Security Forces and stayed stationed in the most wealthy German city of Dusseldorf. This play was *Double Arlecchino!! Trouble*! And the two Arlecchinos were played by Haide and Toomas. Linnea was an exceptional Pierrot. She was only about 21 and had a passion and knowledge of Chaplin. I wrote a recommendation for her to get into the Czech film school from which she graduated and started a mime theatre company in Prague. Alma played an old character opposite an another actor.

In 1987 I was the guest Head of Movement filling in for Annie Stainer who wanted to take a semester sabbatical. That was in Perth at WAAPA. It was a great and prolific semester. After 3 weeks the Head of Performing Arts asked me to meet with him. The great Geoff Gibbs. Gibbs had Richard Gill as Head of Music! Aarne Neeme, Lisle Jones, Ross Coli in theatre and acting! Lucette Alder in dance! Pascale was teaching tap and contemporary. Gibbs said "All right Ira. Everybody loves what you're doing. We want to offer you the position as Head of Movement". He offered it to me then, 1987. Also in 88, 89, 90, 91. I always had work and projects. I was always thinking about the offer and opportunity. Late in 1991 it was really that he now needed someone permanent but I had just formalised my contract with Bell Shakespeare Company as "Resident Teacher and Choreographer" and to act in all of the productions, to start rehearsal early January 1992.

After WAAPA's Third Year graduation, one of those graduates contacted me some months later after he had moved to Sydney. That was Fred. We have been friends and colleagues ever since. I will only tell as much as it pertains to this chapter, book, and our artistic collaborations. The meeting point was that even though he was Australian he was being given roles which were mostly, or even only, ethnic Australians. So in our first casual cafe meeting that was central to our discussion and was our meeting point as artists. Like the ethnic background students at the national school NIDA, the ethnic actors apparently saw me in some way as ethnic, as well as American at that time, and as someone non-Australian, and as someone they could confide or talk with. We talked. We also became great friends and went to see some shows, have a meal, have a coffee, and talk about things that really mattered to each of us. But shortly after our early meetings another graduate of WAAPA, a classmate of Fred, Theo Coumbis had just moved back to Sydney where he had grown up. He had similar situation as Fred, i.e. being Australian but being offered only roles as ethnics. Fred and Theo told me that at WAAPA upon graduation each

Acting student had a final meeting with the Acting/Theatre staff. In that meeting the staff and the graduate reviewed their three years together. Both of these men were mature age, excellent students, excellent actors but at the end of the meeting someone on staff warned them that when they now go out into the industry they will be perceived as 'ethnics', even though they were Australian. The three of us met several times and talked. We became friends and colleagues.

I had suggested that they need to make their own material and let the 'industry' that is the directors, producers, agents, casting agents see that they were excellent actors. Before this I had similar conversations with students at NIDA who said 'they needed to talk with me'. Fred and Theo though got it and they decided to start their own company called *Kings Bloody Cross Theatre Company*. They explained to me that "Kings bloody cross" was a saying made famous in the story They're A Weird Mob (first of the books by 'Nino Culotta' aka John O'Grady) about an Italian migrant coming to live in Sydney. Around this time that we three were meeting was also when three ethnic Australians in Melbourne faced the same situation and same decision and made their own show and company *Wogs Out of Work*. After their first two seasons they were still out of work, but, their show was getting more popular, until finally they hit the big time playing to packed out large theatres, eventually having to hire ethnic actors to play unemployed ethnic actors. Eventually they had a TV show Acropolis Now, and more.

I wrote a scenario in front of Fred and Theo. It was on a piece of paper and I wrote this one as a spiral. As usual in the first writing I write as it comes, organically. I said they had to get an ethnic director. Who? I suggested Ross Coli. A day or two later we met again. They had decided that I should direct and they offered me a few thousand dollars. I said I'll take it but I'll give you $10,000 worth.

We decided there needed to be an actress. They were the producers. We set a schedule and a plan. I was going to the USA to visit family for a few weeks. We decided to start the week before I went so they would have material to work on and when I came back there would be a three weeks rehearsal and we would have a short season at The Bondi Pavilion Theatre.

They 'found' an actress. She was an amazing powerhouse. She was half Maori and half Jewish. We worked a few days. Some weeks later when I was soon to come home and spoke with Theo on the phone he informed me that the first actress quit but they 'found' an excellent person to come in. That was Maha Hindi who was a Jordanian born Australian.

What a magical combo: Fred who was we thought by his last name Italian; Theo whose parents were Greek; Maha whose Father was Palestinian and Mother was Kuwaiti, and me. We all just wanted to make theatre. Our theatre. Our way. On our own terms. I had as part of the scenario that each actor would within the play, have a solo monologue that they would write.

I had a very specific seed image for the scenario. I worked with a young Queensland actor in An Imaginary Life. When his father migrated from Italy he had hid one piece of contraband. It was a small branch of a family fig tree. Wrapped in newspaper and hid inside packed clothes. Eventually this father had a tobacco farm and an orchard of fig trees where the son grew up.

I had also heard from various immigrants eclectic stories of their memories of their homeland's flowers, plants, even weeds which often are edible and nutritious. In the scenario's ideas we had to have images around nature. It is no different in Australia as the national anthem puts it "Our land abounds in nature's gifts". I was insistent that some Shakespeare text had to be included.

I explained that Shakespeare was the symbol of the wall that blocked ethnic actors. We weren't allowed to play Shakespeare generally. There is a hidden agenda behind the English language as it was formulated in England in the 1300s by royal decree. It later became the domain of Shakespeare's works to help seal the control the Empire sought. This is related to having ethnic actors, then, at that time, still speak a 'funny' accented English. The actors knew more about Shakespeare than I did, at that time. So they were to find texts for us to incorporate. All three of them knew everything about Australia and Australian plays and literature and sports and entertainment than I did. I had been living in Australia only two years when we first met.

So each of them taught me about Australia. As had other friends before them and friends continue today to assist my ongoing learning about my adopted homeland.

The actors filled in the spaces and themes that my scenario and direction asked for. But, as is my method, I feed the actors in many different ways. In rehearsal one day I gave Theo an insight into something we were creating and rehearsing. He said "Gimme a minute". I did. When he was ready he said about my comment, my direction "That one is going to take me three years to process". It doesn't matter how smart or educated a director or actor is, I am still myself and I have my own secret way of attuning to the co-creation process. The secret I am sharing here is, it doesn't matter how much we know, the intuition and the subconscious is far deeper and greater than all of the information, education, facts one could ever know. One of my secrets is to work with the beauty of the actors intellect and intuition. If the director allows the actors intellect and intuition space there is then a mystery that will unfold. One which no single individual can be in charge of. "Director" is simply a role just as "Hamlet" or "Ophelia" or "Clown" is in a Shakespeare play. By the late 1500s Shakespeare had created one of the greatest metaphors for the cooperative and absurd nature of making theatre. That is not only the players in A Midsummer Night's Dream, but, also the whole play.

We had so many marvellous coincidences happen. Theo and Fred as producers knew already not to tell me anything I didn't need to know. So many directors are control freaks, some are megalomaniacs, some are anal retentive. Maybe they are all good, even very good, but most have issues, a lot of issues. For me as a director I have my own interests some of which I have just disclosed.

Part of the scenario was that the two men were seemingly typical macho Australian men who had to know everything better than everyone especially the waitress at the cafe where the story began. Theo and Fred decided on some text from A Midsummer Night's Dream. Maha wanted at some stage to use King Lear's "Blow winds" speech. The cafe was to be called "Titania's Cafe". We were wondering how to make the sign. We had a section about 'a sign, omens' etc. One day Theo saw some junk on the street. There was a sign "Titania's Cafe". I won't tell more here but the story was intricate. There was no possibility that any theatre person in the world could tell at the beginning where this story was going to go and certainly no chance to foresee it end or final images.

At the first performance in fact after the first act friends of mine said they wanted to see it again and they did.

The show, the play, above all was a celebration of all that is wonderful and complex and rich about living where we are. In this case Australia. But I think every nation and culture needs to have celebratory theatre. Even in Fiddler On The Roof a central song is "L'chaim, to life".

For the first week I was living at Theo's parents and sharing Theo's and his brother's childhood room. I would awake early and call out text across the room to Theo before he woke up. I was playing and clowning as is normal for me first thing in the morning. Of course that was torture for Theo. I found a room in a small flat of Bondi Road.

We did several seasons of this show, which I titled "A Play on Worlds". Several seasons in Sydney. Also seasons in Perth and Melbourne. In Melbourne a young third year actress, Eva Di Caesare, came and saw the show and was very moved by it. When Maha opted out of our 'one more time' season in Sydney Eva was contacted in Melbourne by Fred or Theo. They made a deal. She flew up. Theo got her at the airport and brought her straight to rehearsals at the Crossroads Theatre. When we left rehearsal we saw that Theo's car had been broken into and all of Eva's belongings were gone.

Welcome to the theatre darling. Welcome to Sydney.

Then the theatre, a fab old church got broken into. So a few nights we slept on the stage, armed with golf clubs that Theo brought for us. Then the security was installed.

It was all a great time and we were living theatre lives. We had other things going individually too.

However, Fred and Theo wanted to produce Nicolai Erdman's play *The Suicide*. They wanted to get support this time from the multicultural festival Carnivale. They had both acted in it at WAAPA and loved it. They gave me a copy to read and I read it straight through. Fantastic. My kind of theatre/play. They presented it to the director of Carnivale. He didn't get it. But he told them perhaps we could come up with something 'original'. *The Suicide* is still 'original'. Feh.

We three talked. The two fellows had told me about a phenomenon in Western Australia. At the time in Australia the mail-ordered bride had been happening. Australian men who were unable to secure a relationship with Australian women started to go to Asia and and via this business of 'mail order' they would find a bride and bring her back and in a lot of cases that worked out for those couples. In W.A. one farmer after another got a mail-ordered bride. In one region where there were many such arrangements the farm business was dropping. Eventually the Asian wives got together and via their intellect and verve and computer and ration business abilities they organised and the business all started to have major success.

I knew of another phenomenon of foreigners who came to Australia to see if they could get good work and they had top meetings. When they moved here suddenly the person who said 'no worries' or 'yeah we could really use your experience' ... later upon return to live in Australia the same persons then said 'oh, sorry, no we don't have any room for you'. So the foreigner had already made the move and was stranded and made a go of it. A number of people had told me their story. One though was an Australian who was directing me one day for a commercial. He had a great track record overseas for years and felt he would love to live again at home. He did like the foreigners and came for a short visit with various meetings set up based on his track record. Promises, promises .... but when he moved back everyone reneged their offers. So he was stranded and just had to start again.

Also it was in this period that many immigrants found their way into the business of cleaning offices at night.

These things happen everywhere.

So I wrote a scenario *The Male Adored Bride* using those images. Theo and Fred were to play the scoundrel's who were running a business of promises for foreigners but instead they were locked into being cleaners. The cleaners were to be Aurel Verne and his wife Satchiko who were veteran vaudeville style dancers and entertainers; and my acrobatic teacher Jon Soo who was a Bronze medalist in China's national competition and he had been an acrobatic teacher for the Beijing Opera; and myself. Six people. As Little Britain receptionist says "Computer says 'no'". Mr Carnivale said no money but we could have the use of the venue. Somehow though it seemed that the money was going to come and the publicity had already gone out for our show in the festival program. Theo, Fred, and I were trying to make a go but we couldn't ask the others with no pay. What to do, quickly. Theo decided that's it. He had a contact in L.A. who could get him a simple job. As it turned out, that little job was working at a day care centre. But the children were those of Hollywood's elite including Spielberg's kids. However, Theo got work as an extra in television and films working 4 or 5 days a week and this soon led to better acting roles. He went to the USA about 1990 and has been busy ever since. He is an accomplished acting teacher and coach in Hawaii.

But, I had my scenario of *A Regular Couple of* Guys and if I could stick some acrobatics into the ending .... we could slip it in under the pre-publicity information and keep the name The Male Adored Bride.

One night Aurel Verne, and Satchiko came to see the show and we agreed to meet at the STC bar afterwards. They had a third associate who was also a grand veteran dancer, Peggy Watson! So they brought her to 'have a look at me' even though I only appeared in the finale dream scene. Lo and behold they had an offer that I couldn't refuse. Though I should have. But it was an actual j-o-b with rehearsal pay as well, and working in Japan! A bit hard for a pauper to turn down.

Tim McGarry joined Fred and I and we co-created with the scenario below. After this production Eva Di Caesare joined us in the production of Erdman's play *The Suicide*. Again Fred was the producer. He played the central character. I directed. Eva, TIm, Fred, myself, were part of the 12 actor cast. That was 1993. In October of 1993 I took a semester contract teaching Shakespeare in Copenhagen. I made a King Lear project. This led to 6 years work and development of my method outside of Australia. Fred, Tim, Eva were freelance theatre artists and actors and carried on in their careers. In 1997 Eva, Tim and their friend Sandra Eldridge formed the incredible theatre for young people, Monkey Baa Theatre. Fred formed Moogahlin Performing Arts, Inc with Lily Shearer and Lisa-Mare Syron. They also established The Yellamundie National First Peoples Playwriting Festival.

For brevity, I have not told the complete stories of the projects: *A Play On Worlds*, *The Male Adored Bride*, *The Suicide*, nor of my solo show *The Battler* which also was produced in this period.

This scenario *A Regular Couple of Guys* was written in 1984 by Ira Seidenstein as is with the exception of the introductory paragraph which was for 1987. The 1984 scenario was intended as a duet for Stephen Champion and Ira Seidenstein. The same scenario intended for a duet in 1987 of Ted Keijser and Ira Seidenstein. This scenario with adjustments was performed in 1990 for Carnivale at the STC Wharf Studio as *The Male Adored Bride*. The central duet part was played by Tim McGarry and Fred Copperwaite and four additional actors were part of the finale. Those four were: Cletus Ball, Gina Peluso, Michael Wang, Ira Seidenstein.

A REGULAR COUPLE OF GUYS complete scenario Copyright © 2018 by Ira Hal Seidenstein

Originally written in 1984 by Ira Seidenstein for Ira Seidenstein and Stephen Champion. Retyped in 1986 for Ira Seidenstein and Ted Keijser. Presented for production finally in 1990.

A two handed theatre extravaganza. The story of two men who share a flat and pursue a better balanced household (ie) female energy. The duet of Ira Seidenstein and Ted Keijser promises to be an unforgettable theatre experience. The show is a comedy, using script, slapstick, dance and mime.

1. KITCHEN
2. HOUSE TALK - CLEAN UP
3. WHAT TO DO (ie) TONIGHT
4. DRESS UP FOR DISCO
5. DISCO
6. EMPTY STAGE - VAUDEVILLE ACT. INTERMEZZO
7. SLEEP - DREAM
8. AWAKE - TELLING OF DREAM
9. DRESS UP DRAG
10. ONE MUST GO
11. PACK
12. DEPARTURE - STAY

(FUTON FOR A SET)

1. KITCHEN
Show opens with a stylised freeze or movement. Preparation of meal is in mime with sound effects. (1) Possibly one a vegetarian other a carnivore (2) Preparation of one meal - two chefs (3) Or two meals in small kitchen (4) Or one hyper other slow. Eating of meal. Creative use of mime and partner balances.

2. HOUSE TALK - CLEAN UP
Non-talking about feelings. Everytime a near is touched, gentle freeze and "yeah, I guess so" or "yeah, I know what you mean". Cleaning home the whole time. One is a slob, other neat. Moronic cleaning. One messes up neat piles of other. Or both clean up two piles of clothes at same time. (George Carl idea of pile of boxes).

3. WHAT TO DO (ie) TONIGHT
Discussion of what to do. Boredom. Waiting for Godot. Past chatter of all the coulda and maybes like an auction. Girls. Decide to go dancing. G-U-L-P.

4. DRESS UP FOR DISCO
Need to share and borrow clothes. Put on same jacket (clown jacket gags). Two in one jacket. Little man act. Narcissus. How do I look.

5. DISCO
Arrival. Wow! Gawh! Music. Elbowing to dance. Each asks girls to dance, with a different approach at each attempt, (suave, scared, beg, polite, loud etc). Always rejected. Or girl is never what one expected, (ie) FAT, TALL, SHORT, CLUMSY. Both sit, dejected, "Are You Lonely Tonight" double takes, looks at each other. Dance. Disco. Rock out. Breakdance duet. Happy. About to go then ...

6. EMPTY STAGE - VAUDEVILLE ACT
Spotlight on microphone. Guys spy it. Devilish look. They sneak over (tripping, whooshing, hand slapping, shin kicking a la Laurel and Hardy). Tell stupid jokes. Madness with mic. Fall about laughing, travel home laughing.

7. SLEEP - DREAM
Arrive home, still laughing, go to bed still laughing. Quickly fall asleep. Maybe one is still talking, other nods off, gentle caring look, lights out. ZZZzzz. Sheet pulling off covers. Dream of dancing with a woman. Somehow dream is shared. Back to bed (ie back to sleep).

8. AWAKE - TELLING OF DREAM
One of the characters awakes and excitedly tells dream. The other character is still dozey; until a chord of recognition is struck. Then they both fill in details, with agreement about the imagery, colours, details etc. They shared the same dream. Then they realise the meaning: they need more female energy in the house. They need a woman's energy.

9. DRESS UP DRAG
They decide one of them must dress the part. Special delivery (lighting person /stage manager) brings package which contains dress, high heels, makeup, wig, purse, jewellery. They discuss who should be in drag. The process begins. They argue about appearance, posture, the voice etc.

Husband-Wife bickering until they finally realise, they each need to live seperately and with a woman.

10. ONE MUST GO
They decide one should leave the flat and the other should stay. Gentlemen's dis-agreement as to who should do what (as in picking up the bill at a restaurant).
Decision is delayed, undecided ...

11. PACK
Both decide to take action. They begin to pack ... one bag. Talking the whole time. The bag is packed. They both click one latch and grab (the) one handle ... oops.
They sag in relaxation.

12. DEPARTURE - STAY
It's decided now who will go and who will stay. Gentle worlds of encouragement exchanged.
One goes. One stays.

END OF *A REGULAR COUPLE OF GUYS* SCENARIO.

SOLDIER BOYS Copyright © 2018 by Ira Hal Seidenstein

SOLDIER BOYS is a slapstick comedy which examines dissatisfaction with academic study and naivety about the military. It is the story of two boys newly arrived at young manhood. They are bored with school and want some manly adventure. Running mates that they are, a mutual decision to enlist in the military (army) is taken. The initial joy soon becomes hard work as they battle through basic training. One emerges a General, the other a Private. As an abrupt change of circumstance they are throwing into a cataclysmic war. They are only as unprepared for this war a is the rest of the world. Somehow they escape alive. They search for a new function in life. A new partnership is decided on. They want to open a horticulture and landscaping business to beautify the war torn areas. They make a three year plan. One will pursue the scientific and business aspects, the other will pursue the practical skills and alternate methods.

When this show goes into performance the 1987 Year of Peace will be over. The need to educate will be the same as in 87 as in 86 or 88. As the dollar hits an all time low people will be seeking security. The military's security package becomes very enticing at these times.

The medium of the play is slapstick, comedy and mime.

One of the great clown sketches is "The Sergeant and the Recruit". IN 1980, Ted performed this sketch in Le Cirque Du Paris. Traditionally clowns have always tried to "take the micky" out of the military. It is the opposite occupation of a clown. One hints at chaos and joy, the other order and death.

From 1969-1973 Ira was in the U.S.Navy (not as a clown). He has in the seven years created three shows which partially dealt with the military and security. This show is meant not to just throw red noses and laughter at the military. It will portray the decision making process of youth and people at a time of impending change. It will, through the discipline of theatre, portray the need and benefits for personal discipline and purposeful goals.

In 1985 Ira represented the Pacific Peace Vigil in the USSR and the USA. The Peace Vigil was held in Wellington, New Zealand (August 1985 to portray and examine the role of the artist as a Peace Worker.

ARTHUR BOYD RETROSPECTIVE PERFORMANCE - WAGGA REGIONAL ART GALLERY - 2000

Arthur Boyd, AC, OBE Passed away April 24, 1999. Elsewhere in this book I tell some of the story of our performance project in the year 2000. From the program:
Some very brief comments from Arthur Boyd himself, concerning works on display:
"The burning book represents Aboriginal wisdom which has also suffered from the encroachment of white civilisation. If the white settlers had taken a page out of the Aboriginal 'book' they might not have ruined the landscape. The aeroplane is a reminder of the harshness of the land - they were used that year to rescue people when the Shoalhaven flooded. They actually

used helicopters but I felt a bi-plane had close connections - grasshoppers and dragonflies for instance"
A few brief comments about Boyd.
".... Boyd displays his endearing habit of eclectic borrowing."
Another comment:
"... not of course, that there is any attempt in Boyd's Aborigines at anything approaching conventional realism .... one becomes aware of their minds and spirits. Although the trees, the scrub and, particularly, the birds which so frequently recur in Boyd's work are all redolent of Australia, it is the Aborigines, ... which constitute the most strongly Australian element in his oeuvre."
One last comment:
"Boyd frequently portrayed Biblical reality juxtaposed into the Australian landscape."

Performance Poetry © 2018 by Ira Hal Seidenstein
Created for the National Touring Exhibition of Arthur Boyd's
The Exile of Imagination
Wagga Regional Art Gallery, March 2000

EXILE OF IMAGINATION

The Exile of Imagination is the name fo this whole exhibit.
Imagine exile from the place you wannabee
To hoppin' around like a wallabee.
Imagine being taken back
Or imagine being taken in the first place.
The first ones were exiled from Mama.
Mr. Boyd was exiled from his Earthly roots.
A puerile exile compared to some.
An exile no less
Lest we forget
Forget what you know
And forgive real quick
Let's get on with the burning of the right holy wick
The candle which lightens our load
Hop to it like a thousand cane toads.

BYE BYE BOY-D

Go on get outa here we don't need your kind
Piss off mate we don't want your ilk
Take your ink and paint
And poof, wacko disappear
You must be queer not to work

The whole world needs to work
What do you do wilt away ya lily pod.

It's stupid it's senseless whatever ya do.
Nah I don't understand it
What's to understand?
Beauty? Wouldn't give you a two bob for it.
Yeah I got plenty of beauty in my life mate at any rate.

Beauty is when me horse comes in first and I put me whole wad on the bastard.
Yeah, and with the winnings I get a right royal piss-up 'til I spew me guts out.

Don't talk to me about the millennium that's yonk's off.
We will all be dead by the time it comes around.
Besides Australia will still be the same mate, true blue.

Youse arty types haven't got a chance in the real world nobody would pay money for your crap.
My dog could paint that crap by wigglin' its arse in paint.
Me? I don't need no art. Besides if I wanted to see any of that crap I'd piss off to England or per of them places. Get my fill and forget it.
Who needs it?! Nobody! Kids? Har, bullshit mate. They just need a swift kick in the behind.

'course I could paint if I wanted to. I had me chance. In school you know. Some pretty art teacher

Lady did the rounds in those days. She came to our school one day. I couldn't put nothing down. Every time I went to lift my brush onto the paper all I could see was terrible things, destruction mate real destruction. So I'd close my eyes and all I could see was glory. You know what I meant? Yeah I think you do. So I tried then to paint that and tears started to well up in me. Then, I was frozen-like. All me school chums started to take the micky outa me. I never got over it. I guess painting gets things out of your system. Maybe that's what all the fuss is about. Blokes like yourself can do something that others can't. So they pay you rather than suffer themselves.

Yeah, I guess you could call it fear to face that blank paper or cloth and paint what's inside you or paint your own truth.

Then have one of us wankers or a mob of us run you into the ground.
I'll give you this you must be a tough lot 'cause nothing stops you.
You always pop back up and do more if I understand right?
'Course that's just my opinion. I guess you'd know all about it, it's your whole lot in life.
No turning back. You're doomed with your gift.

I just wish I knew what my gift was. Wish that art lady could'a stayed another day.
She would've protected me from the mob. Sometimes I dream about what I could've put on that paper. The good book says you always get a second chance in life.
Maybe you're here to remind me.
Bye bye Boy-D

WHAT'S THE DIFFERENCE

What's the difference 'tween a ruff, a rabbit, a ruuf from a dog
A rippling, ribald riotous ripple coming from Herre Boyd rollicking larfing c/ripple?

Who's in touch with the feted feral black dogged canine,
Crouching mounting any figure bending painting running

Does it mean wherever the artist roams
From Rome to Nome to Home
That black dog of fate will feline its feathers to cover his endeavours?

Does it mean the airplane will crash when there is no chance of
Does it mean the refrain of cash when we divorce out of love?

A bush tree bends
The plane that goes up must come down
The lover that is nude is bound to be rude.
The windmill that's silent is but wasting away
The artist that's idle is praying to play.
A sketch is a retch from the inner glow angst.

The gold coins rattle my chain
A lucrative lust makes me feel 'bout to bust.
Rust is the colour of life
Blue is the colour of death
White is the colour of abandon
Black is the colour of things yet to come.
Azure assures a fluid flow with no final.
The sun dawns upon me at the musk of dusk I drop to my knee.
Glory is inner, outer, around.
The ruff on my figure is a clown in a gown
I lavish the oil that froths from nature
I lover the loverly in her bush phrases.
We gain in the sand what we couldn't remand
Colours and colours and sketches delight
Leave it to me I'll paint while I'm free.

WHISP WHISPER WHISPERING WILLOW

Stogy heat
Whispering willow, stogy heat.
Suffolk hasn't got any stogy heat
Beat feel the beat
Thus it feels like stogy heat

… without the stogy heat of a swatherin' swagman's sweaty rags
…. hags are beautiful too you know
I dug me hoe to see what'd grow
… nothing whilst one to and fros

'tis a long cool night
with no need to be af right
'tis a slight breeze
along me knees
as the painter paints
a feint ghost is about to roast
in the slithering seat of ol' Suffolk Green
makes me spleen want to spew
from an exotic loon

I feel like a goon out of tune
… with nature
I'll mature I'll paint I'll study
I'll I'll I'll
Down the aisle without a bleeding bride
A side matter to my reality
Painting is
Painting is
Painting is
Listen Liz just go have a wiz in the bush
That's all one needs
To feel the depth of a breeze
Along me knees
Then who gives a hoot for ol' Socrates
Don't need the mug
When I've got the Murrum-budge
Sludge you say
Forsooth say I
Beauty is in the spry of the older
The older has wisdom beyond our days
I want to go home

This place feels like Nome
I vant to go 'ome, piss off l'Somme
You call this summer
I'm starting to know you are really dumber

Been across the channel and over and back. It was great
It was grand, but I prefer red sand.
I'm going bush
Goina sit on my tush
See a goanna spring for a fling.

Uncle Bill calls the Big Book the Guiding Light
That bit o' wisdom comes from traveling light.

I'll roll up the results of my 16 days
Now that I'm returning my exile is over
Now that I'm
Now that
... I'm learning
thru my painting patience
I've established my way of passing thru the human zoo
The Big Book that guides me is
The one you see and the one you don't
Matter anti-matter
Now you see it
But soon you won't
The ghost appears in his underwear
Was it Asher about to flee?
I can't see
I'll simply gaze and paint a-ways
Sure enough
The ghost appears and the book lies open for those who pass through
Our own bush grass
I'm on my knees to ol' Mother Murrumbidgee
I start to gather the image
Of my past as the canvas unrolls to a colourful future

CO-CREATING

The colours arrive with the passing globe called the break of day
The dawn the dusk and the midday musk a s the moon is my loon
I take a spoon of the span in my gaze
The mixed paint becomes a glaze
In the heat of the days
The sight, the smell, the sense of a hell
I'm trapped in the artists exile it matters not why
Stop asking why
It is simply this way
That is all that I'll say
That is all all to say
Exile if fine
So long as I ponder, and patiently paint images feint or images bold
I'll not be told to do it your way
I'll not be sold down the river to Hay
I'll stand by my guns
My stick with a brush
A lush green,
A glorious blue
A hue so thick it passes for stew
A billie boil
Is a thrill I had since I've became a mature nature lad
A cad you say. Oh go away
Leave me to dither
Go slither away
Go find a will and a way

Come here my love
My true myrtle dove
My loon
With the lush grass
Sit down in the bush
A lie with a lover
Let the ghost always hover
As we flutter away
Let me take your image / to canvas again

Let the golden cons flow I don't give a dam
I'll paint 'til I bust
Or kick the can
It's time to go and here's just the sight
That makes you remember my spirit tonight.

END OF PERFORMANCE POEMS FOR ARTHUR BOYD

CHAPTER 10

FRIENDS AND COLLEAGUES

This is a prelude to my planned second book.
As Polonius said, I shall be brief. He wasn't. Nor have I been.

First I am relating only some of my friends in particular related to my work or for lack of a better word my career. Careen is more accurate than career. As in reality I seemed to bounce, careen, from situation to situation. My friend Jane Birmingham after observing my life for a few years said "If you fell into a bucket of shit you'd come out smelling roses". Like most of my close friends when I first lived in Australia and they heard about the circumstances of my arrival and survival here Jane would call me a battler and some even paid the highest compliment of calling me "a little Aussie Battler", at other times they'd call me a larrikin.

So to those who first welcomed me and were part of those early phases in Australia I will only quickly mention a few. I have already mentioned meeting with the original Circus Oz mob in Holland 1980 and one of those, Stephen Champion pursued me to form a duet circus/clown duet which was shortly lived but certainly got me started. Thank you. On my second tour along with my partner we were in the Festival of Sydney 1984. We had two shows: one was as guest artists in Limbs Dance Company season at the Footbridge Theatre. We did two of our own mime/clown drama 'dance' pieces. We were an extreme hit with the audience! Yet, the national dance critic chose not to even mention that there were guest artists who were a part of the Limbs program!!! My partner, being a dancer, was very hurt and angry at such an intentional oversight. I said it was just obvious whoever that critic was, she had no sense of humour. As I came to know this critic's work over the years she showed herself to be nationalistic to a fault. As a critic she also had numerous other weaknesses! After that partner and I understood and admitted that our relationship was impossible we split up and retrieved our deep friendship. About two years after the split we decided to do a collaborative show which at first I rejected until we realised we could to two solo shows in one program. We did not say anything about what we would do except we would each do about a 45 minute solo. As it happened, we each chose to do a show about the split second when death occurs, when the soul leaves the body. That same dance critic nearly faced her own split second before death. My solo was first, then we had a short interval, and I could watch my colleague's solo. I stood behind the audience. The Performance Space had been a small warehouse. They had several platforms to raise the seating levels. The seats were old metal chairs placed individually before the days of "Health & Safety" regulations for small companies. Interval over, the critic entered. She's a large lady. Very large. She took her seat. At the outside edge of the second row. But in sitting down the back leg of the chair shifted and the chair leg fell into a crack. The critic took a tumble out of the chair and over the platform edge and onto the floor. There went the review which was primarily about how much she hated the Performance Space. She did mention us this time. It was a night when many NIDA (national acting school) of my students came. They did not know the dance critic but told me that during interval they heard her complaining about the venue.

The show was called *Eclectic Eccentrics*. For my piece as it had some acrobatics, Stephen was kind enough to loan me the circular mat he had made for our acrobatic clown show *Building Blocks* which was for a three months season as Jigsaw Theatre in Canberra. Stephen's then partner, Antoinette made the poster for *Eclectic Eccentrics*. As noted elsewhere in this book Antoinette and Stephen were my hosts when I landed with hopes gone awry. It was on the first day that I was told the work we were to have was non-existent. After that first project which I had written the scenario for (included at the back of this book as *A Regular Couple of Guys* which became *The Male Adored Bride*, the next day after I landed in Sydney we were told that the following project we were to be a part of did not get funding. That was for Meryl Tankard's intended first show after she had been dancing in Pina Bausch's company! So I was "up the creek without a paddle", except for the great kindness of my hosts and other friends who were soon to appear.

Antoinette's poster was certainly wonderful, like a mini masterpiece. However, people loved the poster/artwork and stole it wherever we posted it up. We two were used to issues with postering! In Auckland we had a 'spiritual art group' regularly put their A-4 posters on top of ours, covering ours in public spaces. We would remount them so both posters could be seen. One time I had just put up a poster in a dance studio's notice board. It was at the university and I was about to teach the first of a series of evening mime classes. My poster was the only one on this studio's notice board. I then went to lay on the floor to relax and think about what I would teach. While I was laying down a woman came in with her own A-4 handbill. She looked at my poster, stood and read it, then as usual with this group she was connected with (a 'spiritual' performing arts group) .... she covered over my poster so only hers could be seen. As usual I simply moved it so both could be seen. The final straw happened in Auckland's main dance studio, Limbs, when we arrived for morning Ballet class our poster was missing. Oh, it's just covered up again by the same group ('spiritual' performing arts). My partner wanted to rip up the 'spiritual' group's poster. Instead I moved their poster next to ours as usual. Only this time I wrote on their poster asking why they keep covering our posters. They stopped doing so.

On our Festival of Sydney season we also had our own duet clown/circus show *Lilla Cirkus*. That was the last year the central part of the festival was in Hyde Park. There was an exceptional locally made outdoor venue we performed in. It had two huge overlapping white sails. One over the stage and one over the tiered seating. On another stage one day I saw THE most astounding comedy acrobatic duet - "Price & McCoy". Terry Price and Tim Freeman. They were doing tricks I had only seen in a book. A particular book that I used to teach myself what I could. Price & McCoy were taught by the man that knew every trick in that book! His name is

Cletus Ball who was the original master teacher of the Flying Fruit Flies. So at the end of their show I met Terry and Tim and then they came and saw our show that was in the same genre but the exact opposite end in terms of aesthetics. Our acrobatics was basic but we excelled in mime, choreography and acting. We also had a wonderful choreographed juggling act. Terry was the base and Tim was the flyer. Terry could throw Tim every single way possible. Tim could saulto no matter which way he was thrown or based. To this day I've never seen a duet act with that many saultos. Plus they had the comedy of Australian Knockabout. A year later when I moved to Sydney so too had Terry. So had Cletus. So Terry took me to meet him.

Terry was already contracted for Jupiter's which I tell about in two other places in this book. By this time Terry was able to start with another of Clete's few students. This flyer was Peter Dagger. He was just as incredible as the great acrobat Tim, but Peter flew and tumbled in a completely different way. I think Peter had a dance background. Tim was like a nugget and flew like a rocket. Peter was like a gazelle and flew like a hawk. They went to Jupiter's together but Peter was less inclined to practice as much as Terry. Terry had the classic show business dreams and wanted to tour the world. Lo and behold, the next angel flyer was contracted into Jupiters as a chorus dancer/acrobat. This is the equally inimitable flyer Henning Pederson from Brisbane. He wanted to learn all that Terry could teach him. A few years ago I got to meet Henning's original performance teacher Barry. Barry had been a hand balancer who went into clowning. Henning by the time he was 12 could dance, do tumbling acrobatics, play music, and ..... At 12 years old Henning went to Barry and said he wanted to learn to be a clown. Barry thought what on Earth does this kid think? So Barry asked can you do anything. Could he what! That immediately began a six years apprenticeship. As a flyer Henning was like a star. He was like Australia's Donald O'Connor and he loved to practice and learn. He also shared the dream with Terry and the rest is history. They had a very full 25 years partnership and they have both been living in France for that long, and past their duet time they both have families and Terry has remarkably reinvented his work threefold! He has been performing for several years with two young acrobats whom he taught. He has a circus and acro youth program. He has for several years also developed a program for

FRIENDS AND COLLEAGUES

using show business performing arts of dance, singing, acrobatics, clown to teach local children to speak English. Terry is the person I have long called "My Guardian Angel of Australia" as when I was stranded he provided the single audition that changed my luck. Plus he took me to one of my greatest teachers Clete.

There was Clete, a living legend in Australian acrobatics, at about 55 years old in 1985 and teaching in this small old sports hall in the afternoon. He just taught a few ragtag wayward youths other than Terry and Peter. I had my own methods and was able to find 'a way in' and two of those fireball youths just needed a few clear pointers which I provided. Suddenly a few basic tricks which were vital to an acrobat were rectified with my method. Then Clete could teach them much more of course and those two excelled and a few years later joined Tim in his fab knockabout clown troupe Leapin' Loonies. Clete also had a cleaning business. His clients were a few apartment buildings in Bondi near where I lived. So occasionally when he finished cleaning at 6am or 7am he would a few minutes later be knocking on my door on days when he had an idea or wanted to talk. Eventually we did a few clown/acro gigs together. Then I was able to have him in the Regular Couple of Guys/The Male Adored Bride show at the Sydney Theatre Company's Wharf Theatre. With me and him and two others coming in for the final dream sequence of the duet which was the main scripted part of the play. The actors and co-creators were Fred Copperwaite and Tim McGarry. The others in the finale dream sequence which included Clete, Tim, Fred, myself were Gina Peluso who had then recently been national champion in Rhythmic Gymnastics and Michael Wang who was from China's great Wang circus family. Michael was like my Chinese doppleganger. He was a great clown and had been a unicycle master and of course also an acrobat. He did not speak English then but understood a lot. He worked as a cleaner. His brother Peter worked as a head cook at the University of NSW student union. Peter had been a strongman in the circus breaking rocks and bending steel. He also coached one of their sisters on tight wire and - I think - she won once at the circus competition in Monte Carlo. Michael and Peter were in the wave of people coming to learn English and to have more freedom pre-Tiananmen tragedy which resulted in the Chinese 'students' here getting Citizenship.

This chapter has looked at a few early friends in Australia. There are more. My friend Kerry Dwyer taught a theatre class at One Extra where I started to teach evening acrobatics. We had a great adventure of conversations and seeing shows. We had a small collection of friends who I would call in the positive sense 'seekers' that including Angela Toohey the Queensland actress and singer who was in the original production of *Away*, and the percussionist Greg Sheehan with whom I started to do a variety of duo gigs. Along there I met the wonderful actress and director Aku Kadogo. Kerry and Aku helped me in an embryonic stage of developing the third act of my show *The Battler*. Both were tough as old boots as directors. Fab!!! Ritchie Singer came to my earlier show, my first show as a resident in Sydney *Absurd Moods* and introduced himself after and we too have been friends since that same period 1985. I haven't mentioned Roberto, nor Ellen (except as she was in Henry V and The Suicide) and Tom, and a long list of folks who looked after me. Next book.

Next chapter, the last, is related to much more recently established friends and colleagues and closure points about CLOWN SECRET.

CHAPTER 11

LAST BUT NOT LEAST

I have plans and structures for two followup books. One of which is to address projects that I have left out or have simply given a brief description about to serve the point being made in a particular section of this book CLOWN SECRET.

Let's start alphabetically. That will work as a way to start but a few letters will be enough.

A is for Amanda-Lyn, Associates, Auckland...
Auckland came first. 1981-85 Auckland was 'home' and the last place I lived was on Home Street in Arch Hill the hill end of Ponsonby. In my earliest classes of Ballet besides having a great teacher Dorthea Ashbridge, the classes were Company Classes and almost all of the participants were members of Limbs Dance Company at its peak which included Doug, Adrian, Kilda, Alfred, Felicity, Bruce, company director Mary Jane, and others.

In one period class also included Katrina Todd and Isabelle Koch who are still two of my dearest longest friends in the world. In the first week of Company Class something happened in my brain, in my mind, suddenly I saw right through this mystery called 'choreography'. It was the mental shock of the combination of live pianist, counts, posture, instructions from the ballet master Dorthea, and the presence and concentration of these fine and unique dancers. Within two years my partner and I would be guest artists in Limbs for the Festival of Sydney 1984. Isabelle became the third member for our clown and contemporary work. Auckland included friends Scarlett (aka Debbie) Wallingford and Jonathon Acorn both extraordinary clowns. There too I got to know the greatest New Zealand clown Russell "Byko" Middlebrook.

Amanda-Lyn Pearson is an extraordinary clown! When she was 18 she started choreographing her own hip-hop dance troupe Atomika. At 22 she started in clown as "Blade" her wiz-bang clown character on roller blades and with non-stop comic patter. She connected totally in a unique way with each person. Although I had seen her dance troupe before I knew her, we met after I saw her solo theatre show. After that I saw her perform "Blade". I began to coach her one to one and began to mentor her. Like many others, she would suddenly cry while we were working. This was mainly women. Some of them discussed why this occurred unusually frequently in my classes or coaching. I was told they cry because they can, because there is no stigma. With my dear friend Jane we named this occurrence of spontaneous crying "playing Teardrop the Clown". The Maoris say it is an honour for a man to cry.

Near this time Amanda-Lyn became part of the expanded six-person Polytoxic which has a prolific legacy. Polytoxic was nuclear that went ballistic. It was three outstanding performers for several years Lisa Fa'alafi who went on to create the ensemble Hot Brown Honey, her cousin Fez who co-created the ensemble Briefs, and Leah who I worked with for several years in Frank Theatre. Polytoxic's six person included briefly Kristy Seymour but then Mark who is a great clown and burlesque-circus artist and co-creator of Briefs, and Natano who is brother of Fez and cousin of Lisa and he is creator of Cassus ensemble, and Amanda-Lyn. Natano made one of the finest solo circus acts I have ever seen. It began with a short documentary of his patriarchal initiation ritual Samoan tattooing supported by his brother Fez. As the film ended Natano appeared on stage with in a pair of acrobatic shorts which were short enough to reveal the legendary Samoan leg tattoos. He then did the most extraordinary corde lise (Spanish web, rope) act - non-stop choreography to traditional Samoan drumming.

LAST BUT NOT LEAST

Amanda-Lyn went on to create the unique The Crackup Sisters who for ten years now have entertained in the rural areas of Queensland, the outback, the royal agricultural shows of Queensland, Western Australia, Victoria. I have mentored her since the conception of the The Crackup Sisters and then with her first partner who was Australian national whip-cracking champion; then her fire ball parter Katie with whom she built *The Homestead Show*, and then for the most recent years with the wonderful zany partner Alyssa Venning with whom they can now develop further their work with youths in the Outback . They've also been hosting some of the biggest and most unusual Outback festivals including The Birdsville Races! Before The Crackup Sisters, Amanda-Lyn was in our quintet show *Chaplin's Eye* for our Adelaide season.

Associates. I.S.A.A.C. - International School for Acting And Creativity's Associates. Two dozen are listed on my website's Associate page with their own testimonials and their own websites, others are Patrons and are listed with their letters of support and company sites found on the I.S.A.A.C. page of www.iraseid.com
Some of those Associates and Patrons I have written about within this book. I will write more, particularly about the Associates in the book which will be a followup to CLOWN SECRET.

B is for Brisbane and Belfast.
Each a huge topic in my work and life.
Brisbane. My first contract was in 1987 as a solo performer portrayed as Marcel Marceau's clown "Bip" for a commercial for Today Homes of Queensland. I was about to drive with my friend Dina for a picnic. The phone rang. It was one of Sydney's main casting agents. They asked if I could pop in for an audition this morning. I said no as I had plans and was about to leave. The casting agent said they thought I'd really like to do this one. I had made enough commercials. But I asked "Why is that"? They said "Marcel Marceau is going to direct this". I asked if they were kidding. No. So I said yes and went over there immediately. Marceau was on tour with his show in Perth so he was only taking videoed auditions. It was open to me to do whatever I wanted for up to 3 minutes. I did one take. I was asked if I wanted to do another. No. Do I want to look at it

to check. No. Marceau selected me to play him as "Bip". When I arrived in Brisbane I was informed that the actors union refused permission for Marceau to direct a commercial because that was not what he was on tour with. So a wonderful TV director Ron Wey directed. Ron was Chinese-Australian and had directed many episodes of television dramas. The next contract to Brisbane was 1988 when I played The Sky Wizard in Kim Carpenter's modern pantomime *The Sky Wizard*. With the exception of the acrobatic dance I did with Roz Hervey, I choreographed all of the mime and slapstick which was most of the show. That was all done in the workshop period. When we started rehearsals Krissie Koltai was brought in as 'official' choreographer. She was fab to work with! And left my work alone, she gave us a great movement class each morning as a warmup and also choreographed the said 'dance' number. Roz was a dancer and I'm not. In 1991 I was in Brisbane to direct a show to tour Queensland. It was Tony Kishawi who hired me. We first met when he was a 3rd year theatre student at the VCA in 1981. I gave a premiere performance of a silent solo "Security". I wanted to make a piece about the pathetic phenomenon that had begun in the USA of having security guards who pistols in a holster posted at fast food places, and bars etc. My guard had to guard a small bag by getting up from his chair periodically and doing a security march around the imaginary perimeter surrounding the small bag. Gradually the marching became playful walks. Each round being more eccentric until finally he stepped inside and opened the bag and played with what was inside. Concluding was a straight normal march around the perimeter. After the performance I taught short workshop for the 3rd year actors.

The scenario was created by Tony, Annie Lee, John Haag who were to tour as a trio. Some parts of the show were decided before and I worked with all of that and the actors and developed everything further. One of the pieces I wrote was a hilarious sketch that I would gladly remount today! John and Tony were meant to be co-workers in a factory. Basic down to earth blokes. John's character was to have won the lottery and Tony's character was constantly trying to 'suck up to him' i.e. trying to convince John of all the great things they could as two friends enjoy together. As John took more status Tony's character became ever more desperate. They were brilliant! Hilarious. However, as I understand on tour John who is a great improviser, liked to do things 'differently' rather than stick to a script. Fine. Except that Tony, bless him, has likely a level of dyslexia which in his case makes learning a script challenging. In his case if it is a set script he is perfect as he was in rehearsal. In fact art imitates life and the reality was that the character I had surmised for this sketch had a truth about them in relation to one another. EVERY actor has their weaknesses!!!! Any actor that says they have no weaknesses, no vulnerabilities as actors .... well that hubris is their weakness and usually everybody knows this except for themselves. Annie is one of Australia's great clowns along with Amanda-Lyn. During that rehearsal period Tony had me housed at his friend's Therese Nolan Brown and her family. The following year 1992 I was hired to help establish the national touring company, BSC, our first season of three plays in repertory had its premiere season in Brisbane in the Lyric Theatre where I had also been the Sky Wizard ('88) and in *Slava's Snowshow* (2013). For BSC I had about 40 minor roles including two fantastic clown roles. The plays were: *Richard III*; *Hamlet*; *The Merchant of Venice*.

I was overseas from 1993 to 1999. I had a rich creative period in 2000 and 2001 in Wagga Wagga, Sydney, San Diego (directed by Joan Schirle for the San Diego Repertory Theater). In 2002 I was to be in a themed variety show sent from Sydney to perform in Taiwan for several weeks. I got a call that there was a financial issue and the whole project was postponed. I had no other work ahead. Not good. I got a call the next morning from a friend, a former student at WAAPA, Sarah Grenfell. She and another WAAPA graduate Cesca Lejeune thought my approach could bring a new direction to the local youth circus Flipside. I was offered a small part-time contract for the exact dates I would have been in Taiwan! It was during that contract that I decided to take an official sabbatical by enrolling in the Doctorate of Education program at the University of Queensland. In between the circus contract and starting at U.Q. I had a contract which Sarah had hired me for. That was acting in an hilarious play by Nicky Silver *Fit To Be Tied*. I got to play opposite a great comic and classical actress Emily Weare! And we were directed by former ballet dancer Stephen Colleye! Heaven! The next morning I moved to Queensland. Hosted by Therese's friends, Igneous directors Suzon Fuks and James Cunningham.

Since 2002 I've been based and even one might say settled in Brisbane. It has been wonderful. I did live in Brisbane in about 55 places from 2002 until 2014 and since then I've lived in an independent small flat within an informal communal environment.

I certainly won't be going through the alphabet nor too many more letters, but, B is also for Belfast.

Belfast. Wow! Leonie McDonagh! Wow! Thank you many times over! This happened directly via my Brisbane friend Maryke Del Castillo! A fantastic clown!! She and I first met at Woodford Folk Festival after I saw her duet show *Ski-Boom* under her company banner Tutti-Fruitti. Her partner was Charmaine Childs now famous for her beautiful strong lady act performed mainly in European festivals. We met in 2003 and I loved their show and we had a coffee and spoke for several hours. By 2008 Maryke was temporarily residing in Belfast and working with her new partners Penny Lowther and Hugh Brown. There was a collective of circus and clown performers. They worked at and from the Belfast Community Circus which for several years by then had been managed by Will Chamberlain - May He Rest In Peace. Like Sarah and Cesca in Brisbane, Maryke felt that I had something to offer to the circus/clown collective in Belfast. Like anywhere and everywhere of course everybody else always had something to give to me. I taught a nine days workshop. I was doing the same things as them but we were approaching things from very different angles. None the less by the end Will at BCC had heard good reports and suggested he and I meet. He wanted to bring me back as soon as possible for one month. So a few months later I was teaching inside the BCC building this time and all day and an intro curriculum I had set up which included Acrobatics (*Irabatics* to be specific), The Four Articulations, clown. 3 days towards the end was on Choreography & Creativity and in those days I saw a big shift in the Swedish artist Tina Segner. She and her partner Ken Fanning had a fantastic aerial street act - Tumble Circus! Their duet was like a whole new genre that I called "Standup Circus". They had two conflicting characters like a modern day George Burns and Gracie Allen or Lucille Ball and Desi Arnaz. They were Irish humour and male in a cultural clash with Swedish deadpan humour and female. Plus they were super athletic on the aerial rig.

Ken's parenting partner was Leonie. When I taught the first workshop arranged by Maryke, on the last day, the last session, the last exercise ... Leonie arrived sans baby i.e. infant and wanted 'it' whatever 'it' was that she had heard I was dishing out. She's a fireball. An automatic God created clown. She's magic incarnate. But, that was the last session. However, when I came back for the month she and Ken would take turns with their still toddler son. Each afternoon I would also coach the participants who wanted to develop their acts with me. That included a duet act of Flora Herberich and Hillas Smith; and, Anita Woods and Kelsey Harrington, and working with the brilliant comic juggling team Migilligans! As well as solo clown and circus performer Hugh and some work with him and Maryke. Anita and Kelsey had a very professional approach to work and were excellent to work with.

There were others and there's no doubt the folks at BCC had talent and skill in abundance. During this time I also worked with someone who was not in the month-long workshop. This was by special request from Will. His brief was 'this guy's got a lot of talent but needs some focus and you'. The one the only Paul Currie! Wow! I asked what do you do and what do you want to do. One of his skills was as a puppeteer in addition to being funny and absurd. What he wanted to do, as he told me then and there on the spot - that one day he'd like to do his own show in the Edinburgh Fringe. Next I asked can you show me anything that you do or that you want to work on. So we started and worked a few hours. The rest is history as they say. Paul's history, so far. Paul worked viciously hard for several years doing every possible gig in the smallest venues as well as organising comedy events. Each difficult step was him taking command of the wind. More of those steps were showing signs of victory. He did several seasons in the Edinburgh Fringe but in between each he was blossoming. This year his shows were mainly full houses. Great reviews continue to come for him. He was on the streets handing out leaflets for his shows several hours a day. All indicators are that he is a great clown and artist. Will knew that. I saw that in the embryonic state. But it took Paul's own bionic efforts repeatedly over and over, year after year. As Ted "Guboo" Thomas would always tell us "The best is yet to come". And one of the best was Leonie. On the last day of my month workshop we all said goodbye. A few minutes later

Leonie rushed in huffing "Hey Ira I'm applying for a grant can I put you in it and bring you back to work with me and my dancers"? Sure. Great! And gone she was.

Another 'secret' is that the key to success which can happen in a thousand different colours, is based not on who you trained with but on who you are. Although schools for performers are cocoons for butterflies, most graduates will not fly. Most graduates of performing arts schools and trainings will not even start. They have the drive to want and desire but they don't have the drive to as I say in class to "suffer for your art". I don't make anyone suffer. I explain to help them not avoid the maelstrom of their fear but to simply, and gently embrace their fear. To make a 2 minute good clown act is not so easy. I try to get people to make 6 or 7 or 8 small acts to stretch the parameters of their own creativity.

In addition or as the base for their free creative exploration are the exercises which come first to build up the participant's concentration now, in the present moment. Exercise after exercise the same principle is in operation. There are clear very simple instructions which the practitioner needs to have in the back of their mind. The first exercises The Three Loosenings start this practice of concentration while in action. As the English saying goes "do the math' which means 'figure it out'. The counts count. In The Three Loosenings the basic count as explained in Chapter 2 is 3-3-2-2-1-1-1-1. 3 on one side at a time is easier then 1 every other time changing the side of your body that is working. Then comes the ten minute miracle "Core Mechanics" with hundreds of counts which builds the performer's concentration for ten minutes non-stop.

After the month training Leonie's application enabled her to bring me back (south of Belfast) to work three weeks just with Leonie and her Ponydance company. The company was her, Paula, Oona, Neil, Carl. Later Duane and Deirdre and a few others joined Ponydance. We worked hard. They worked the hardest. They were very young. Five completely different dance backgrounds.

As usual, dancers, generally speaking work harder than anyone. The discipline is work and repeat and hone, and again, endlessly. A life of classes and corrections. Never good enough. Always more. And the shortest career lifespan. Most dancers finish their main dancing by the time they are 30. Those are only the 1% who got into a company who got to start a career. So we worked. Like most dancers they will do anything you ask. With some actors, some, s-o-m-e, if you ask them to do something twice they give you a look as if to say 'What are you kidding? You want me to THAT .... AGAIN?' With a dancer you can say 'one more time' one hundred times. Dancers also have an advantage in that dance technique can be a stabile base for any other performing art. However, dancers can and must put on a mask. A work mask for rehearsal and even for performance. They are busy concentrating and working. I said you do anything I ask but you don't feel anything. Sure we do. Yes but I can not see anything that you feel.

So I invented an exercise on the spot so we could meet halfway. That is "The Ponydance Circle". It is the 7th of "The Seven Solos" in Chapter 2 - The Four Articulations for Performance. It worked for Ponydance. It is a remarkable exercise that combines several of my key principles. Most importantly the performer has to transform what they feel or imagine into form and rhythm that is palpable to the performer and visible to a viewer, or a partner, or a director. It is not just clever movement. It is movement that utilises ones feeling and imagination on the spot - now.

I almost never discussed anything about 'clown'. Leonie wanted the final week to be in Dublin so that arts funding people could visit or at least would come to the casual workshop showing. On that Friday there was plenty of material and structure. The dancers were clowns. They were eclectic dancers who were genuinely funny people. We sat at the end as is normal in a showing to take questions from the viewers. As usual people address most questions to the director or choreographer or the teacher, in this case to either Leonie or myself. Most questions I got I diverted to the others. The workshop was for them. I respected each of them enormously. The showing was for them. Leonie too is extremely supportive of people who work with her. She's an automatic 'mama' and mentor. Several visitors who attended were said to be clowns. They were shocked that dancers could be so funny. They asked what did we do in terms of clown training. The dancers were perplexed. They said we didn't discuss anything about clown or being funny. That is my method. Do the mechanics and the hard stuff will happen organically. In my work your own humour comes before being funny for others. If you can do both at once on day one the simplicity of the exercises will allow things which were hidden from yourself and your previous teachers and directors. That is how this method's use of universal principles works - for anyone, veteran performer or novice.

Leonie and Ponies went on to make a fabulous piece of comic dance theatre which I saw in Adelaide. They were exciting. Extremely athletic in their dance. Totally present in their acting and comedy. I gave them very good tools which are all in Chapter 2. The rest, like Paul Currie, is totally up to them. Things started to happen for Ponydance and Leonie was growing obviously. Other choreographers in Ireland started to hire the dancers more and more. The dancers with Leonie's mentoring and support and with a firm use of my method and/or principles, each began to become an artist in their own right. Other dancers came in to Ponydance. Leonie started to stretch her instincts and drive for theatre and comedy. It is still early days, but, the seeds are planted and growing. I have a deep love for each of them. The last and most recent workshop Leonie set up for me to teach was a few years ago in Belfast. That included several people I had never met who were not dancers. Good folks each! One was Alice McCoullough, Keith Singleton, David Quinn, Suzie Ferguson. All excellent professionals. Alice is an extraordinary poet. The real deal. Some of her performance poetry is on youtube. Suzie is based in Glasgow and has long been a clown doctor. David is a wonderful physical actor. Keith is a great classical actor with an exceptional sense of humour and timing.

One of the Ponydance team Oona Doherty got a gig with a tough, anarchic dance theatre company T.r.a.s.h. dance/performance group - based in Tilburg, Holland which was for 20 years directed by Kristel van Issum with her collaborators Arthur van der Kulp, and Paul van Weert. Like a number of medium size companies a few years ago the government stopped funding many. Oona had said to the director/choreographer that she should hire me, add in my method and create something with me. Oona worked with T.r.a.s.h. through a four year period. In 2014 I co-created with T.r.a.s.h. a quartet dance piece "Swamp". Severe physical theatre. The company was run by the three people from Tilburg; the choreographer/director the composer, the production manager/designer. The aesthetic was to mix dance, physical theatre, live classical instruments, and passionate love relationships. The dancers were: Lucie Petrusova, Blazej Jasinski, Georgia Puchalski, Jason Gwen; and musicians Jacqueline Hamelink and Walter de Kok.

Recently, 2018, I saw Oona in a solo performance in Paris and in some ways it was an example of how far someone can use and stretch themselves using my method. The work of art and performance is all hers. The years of dance training. Her own unique artistic expression which also involves her work as a visual artist in collage, social activism, and exceptional video dance art. My method and ideas are tools for her own development and discretion.

This chapter is a lead into my next book. Part of that book deals with a few projects in more depth. Also that book will have a few dialogues with ISAAC Associates.

ISAAC first began in 2005 and the *Chaplin's Eye* show was an artistic expression of my related methods and principles. ISAAC is a school in the sense of a 'school of thought, experimentation, art' and not a building nor a set curriculum. ISAAC is also all of my workshops, and, ISAAC network of associates and patrons.

In 2011 with the support and encouragement of Jai Luke Hastrich there was a 13-weeks full time course. There were two full time participants and others who attended part time. I mentioned within this book the outstanding joy of working with the two full time participants Jai, and, John Latham. A few years later ISAAC had support from Deb Wiks and Kate Malone of Cluster Arts and ISAAC had two full time participants who came for 2016 January to October. Emily Burton from the USA and Park Sanghyun from South Korea. Emily was a graduate of USC in Acting and after graduation stayed in L.A. working for a casting agent. Sang had been in the theatre and film course in Incheon. They were outstanding to work with - every day. The long course was 9am to 1pm but the actors could come in at 8am and stay an extra hour until 2pm. I arrived every morning at 850-855am. Sang arrived at 8am and Emily shortly after. Each day when I arrived they were either rehearsing, or training, or they had something new to tell me. I taught a workshop in Sydney for Horizon Theatre and public. One person who came was originally from Russia and had just attended my visiting colleague Caspar's workshop in Sydney. So he, Nikita attended my 2 day workshop and the next two days was focused on Shakespeare and I asked if he was going to be in that. He said he had no experience in Shakespeare. I suggested a short monologue and he did the extra 2 days. He had spoken with Emily and Sang and told them he wanted to run away and join us in the long course. He had a good I.T. job and it took him several months to settle up his living and work situation and to make arrangements to move to Brisbane for ISAAC. With the exception of some improvisation classes he had no experience in theatre or acting. As I was extremely challenging as a theatre student so too was dear Nikita. He was not only challenging for myself, Emily, Sang to work with, but, one could say that even to himself he was likely hidden behind many layers. After a few months finally during our commedia Dell'arte sketch (from Barry Grantham) he asked one day "Could I try something". It was that moment that showed his breakthrough. We had only a few weeks left at that point during which he began to 'open up'. Although all through his preliminary 3 months I was meticulous to find something each day that he could progress with in the physical exercises and in the physical creative exercises. My end of year break as usual was for my European teaching tour. In January 2010 to 2018 started again in January with a three-weeks intensive in Brisbane. Nikita rejoined in January 2017 through to about August.

Part of my recommendation to anyone who wants to study with me is to get a weekly class (once or twice per week) in either Ballet, martial art, or Iyengar Yoga. All three have an anatomical and scientific base, all have clear chronological progression, all three have ongoing re-qualification processes for their teachers. Emily found a yoga centre and Sang found a twice a week evening acrobatic class. It was Ballet that Nikita settled on and that reinforced the my method that the body comes first if you are interested in acting, theatre, clown, or performance (even in improvisation). Each person has a completely different trajectory and engagement with their own process.

During this period I also had a part-time participant who was a retired scientist who took to performing arts study as a mature age person not long before retirement. Jim Pickles. We first met in a burlesque course I taught. Nikita and I found our way through the complexity of one on one training, with humour, tolerance, patience. He called me "The Oracle" and I called him "The Living Miracle". He's a wonderful fellow and has been pursuing improvisation, acting, clown and time will tell how it pans out. It will pan out in its own way in due course of course. Jim recommended that I write out my exercises in a procedural way which became most of Chapter 2. The 'final' participant most recently was Flavien Renaud from Switzerland. He studied full time January 2018 to May 2018 as the hall I used had been sold. In 2017 his last year of completing his PhD in Anthropology was in Paris and he decided to try improvisation classes with the Improfessionals. His teachers were ISAAC Associates Caspar Schjelbred and Florian Bartsch. In January in one small assignment to imitate one minute of film available via youtube or dvd of a notable clown such as Chaplin, Lucy, Tati, Toto, etc, Flavien chose a minute or so of Stan Laurel. The detail was impressive. That was the first indicator that Flavien had a natural gift for mime and comic mime which became obvious more so each week in the five months. That assignment is to assist participants to look again at the greatest clowns available in film and to be able to actually see the mechanics of their body and movement. To attempt to get inside their craft mastery.

With the full time participants Jai, John, Emily, Sang, Nikita, Flavien I coached them to create about 7 or more clown or comic mime pieces as well as text pieces. None of these people were used to this process per se of 'creating a short clown act'. Emily and Sang and I transformed 7 of their pieces into a show *The Book of Clown*. They did that show in Brisbane, Sydney, the Blue Mountains, Melbourne, Adelaide, London, Paris. They gave themselves the chance to experience touring a small show and facing all of the problems which naturally occur. In my next book I will write about *The Book of Clown* which was certainly one of my favourite projects and processes ever. With Jai and John we created a drastically different show but from the same method. That was *Just Clowning*. Small shows like this need to be performed "100 times" before the artist actually fully understands what they have created. During that process they become more creative. But also importantly they find out if they should stick with this duet or solo and as my teacher Carlo explained it "You have to face your own ghosts".

This is exactly what virtually every excellent clown of my generation did, naturally. We all understood we need to create 'an act'. It was irrelevant how short or long the acts were. But everyone did this!!!! Not only my generation Slava, Jango, Bill Irwin, David Shiner, ... everyone of our generation. How else were you going to start?

Chaplin did it Keaton did.... but .... it is perhaps 'the hardest thing'. To create two good minutes of material. Like a painter who first learned to sketch or used sketching as a way of daily warmup for the eye and hand. So for each of the full time people I had to push not only in the beginning but also in the editing over weeks of developing several short pieces. The exception was Flavien. From the daily Solo exercise The Nothing Exercise he was able to create spontaneous mimes that lasted 3 to 7 minutes, every day a new one. Some of those he wanted to pursue so we did. If I see an interesting moment in an actor's exercise or improvisation I will point out such moments and guide the actor to see the range of possibilities in virtually any moment. Nikita had a very hard time for whatever reason to get into the studio before it was time to start. But he came in. As the saying goes "In life sometimes the hardest thing is to just show up". To show up at the gym, to show up at the dance or yoga or martial art or painting class. To show up for your morning walk.

So every day when a person comes into the studio their life is unfolding. Flavien told me as a PhD student he was free to work his own hours so he was not inclined to get up before 11am. I said I understand, but, class starts at 9am. Very soon he turned himself around and he would 'show up' no matter what about 8am. When I arrived at 850 or 855am he was always working and showed signs that he had been working quite a while.

If I am honest, the work is self-transformation. It is as all spiritual and even pseudo-spiritual ideologies propose, as the legendary fitness coach Jack Lalanne said "Life is one big battle, you against you". That is from one of the most disciplined people imaginable.

It is my job, as I see it, to assist whoever shows up in my class in any way that might assist them on any particular day. There are of course times when I just sit and listen to whatever the person is getting off their chest. In Yiddish the wonderful word for personal angst is *tsuris* and the word for telling your *tsuris* to another person is to kvetch. In class I talk the most, by far. I also continually several times a class simply ask "What do you notice". It is a much deeper process than some people who studied with me understood. If in a group I notice that somebody is reluctant to share or comment or add or speak up then soon I will ask them by name what do you notice? This is a deep process for the participant to become an artist. It is a horrible mistake to 'give over to your teacher' especially in clowning. You are the artist not your teacher. What do you notice when you do an exercise? I explain that for an actor anything they notice in their process is good. If they notice something negative such as they stopped using their legs and got stuck on the spot, it is positive that they noticed. If they notice the same thing several times they will start to invent a way to move through the problem by working with it. First they have to note what do they notice.

Sometimes I hear, see, and feel that someone needs to talk so I listen. What they tell me is private. It is in a way none of my business. It is very very very dangerous to mix therapy or psychology with theatre. The making of art is in itself therapeutic by its very nature. Teachers, especially those who have tricks up their sleeves from therapy and psychology or spiritual books or theories can easily become manipulative. They first appear very 'nice' or they appear very 'helpful'. Beware. It is my job to only listen to the point where the participant is then suddenly ready to get up on their feet and try again and again. Keep it simple. Keep it clean. Focus on the art work.

If a participant has a hard time so do I. With Flavien we had one three week period when we would spend about one hour a day on a very simple exercise. After some days of this intense hour I said "How many times do you practice going up in a handstand each day"? We understood it was perhaps 20 to 30 times. I suggested then perhaps it is just that you need to keep trying this exercise. However, after the three weeks he could do that creative exercise (structured improvisation) better than anyone I have seen. Every time he did it - after three weeks of 'failing' - he was magical and doing great clowning. Every time. That was "The Clown Knows Exercise". It is so simple.

Here is one of the last secrets in this book. Every secret follows after the main one which is that your grace, your talent, your genius, your humour happen when you do two things at once which are to take conscious control of what you are actually doing physically in space and time, and, while doing that you allow your subconscious to open and guide you. The secret I will tell you now is that almost every one of my exercises is mechanically very simple and has only a few clear steps. For sure, the only complicated exercise I have is purely physical (and mental) and that is The Twist Choreography. That is #6 movement in the Core Mechanics series described step by step in Chapter 2 of this book.

Because those exercises are so simple, that is why so much gets revealed so quickly. Even though there is a quick revelation, it may take days or weeks or years to integrate what is revealed.

"There is no conclusion. There is only discussion. Let the discourse begin".

CLOWN SECRET 2018
IRA SEIDENSTEIN

Printed in Poland
by Amazon Fulfillment
Poland Sp. z o.o., Wrocław